Revision WorkBook

Family Law

EDITED BY
R. Hughes LLB, CQSW
AND
S. Migdal Barrister

THIRD EDITION

HLT Publications

HLT PUBLICATIONS
200 Greyhound Road, London W14 9RY

First Edition 1990
Reprinted 1991
Second Edition 1992
Reprinted 1992
Third Edition 1994

ISBN 0 7510 0449 9

British Library Cataloguing-in-Publication.

A CIP Catalogue record for this book is available from the British Library.

Printed and bound in Great Britain.

CONTENTS

ACKNOWLEDGEMENT

Some questions used are taken or adapted from past University of London LLB (External) Degree examination papers and our thanks are extended to the University of London for their kind permission to use and publish the questions.

Caveat

The LLB answers given are not approved or sanctioned by the University of London and are entirely our responsibility.

They are not intended as 'Model Answers', but rather as Suggested Solutions.

The answers have two fundamental purposes, namely:

a) To provide a detailed example of a suggested solution to an examination question, and

b) To assist students with their research into the subject and to further their understanding and appreciation of the subject of Law.

INTRODUCTION

This Revision WorkBook is aimed to be of help to those studying family law. Its coverage is not restricted to any one syllabus but embraces all the core topics which can be found in university and polytechnic examinations.

Students will hopefully find it useful not only at examination time but also as a helpful summary of and introduction to the subject when studying it for the first time.

The WorkBook has been designed specifically to address common problems suffered by students when studying any legal subject. All examination based courses consist of four main processes, all of which may cause problems for some students. The WorkBook can be of help with each of these processes.

a) *Acquisition of knowledge*

This is achieved by individual work - attending lectures and reading the relevant textbooks and source materials such as cases and articles. The WorkBook is not intended to be a textbook and is in no way a substitute for one. However, the 'key points' and 'recent cases and statutes' sections will help students to direct their study to the important areas within each topic.

b) *Understanding*

Whilst difficulties in understanding a topic or particular point are best solved by a teacher's explanation, the WorkBook offers a summary of the essential points together with cases. This is the key to understanding for many students.

c) *Learning*

The process of learning is also a highly individual one. As a rule, however, students find it much easier to learn within a clear structure. The WorkBook will be an aid to those who find learning a problem.

d) *Applying the knowledge to the question*

This is, perhaps, the most common problem of all. The WorkBook includes examination questions and answers covering possible question variations within each topic. All such suggested solutions are of a length which a student could reasonably be expected to produce under the time restraints of an examination.

In this revised 1994 edition the final chapter contains the complete June 1993 University of London LLB (External) Family Law question paper, followed by suggested solutions to each question. Thus the student will have the opportunity to review a recent examination paper in its entirety, and can, if desired, use this chapter as a mock examination - referring to the suggested solutions only after first having attempted the questions.

HOW TO STUDY FAMILY LAW

The importance of statute

While family law is a heavy case law subject all the major areas are covered by legislation; eg the Matrimonial Causes Act 1973 covers the whole of the basic law on divorce, nullity and ancillary relief, three major examination areas. Accordingly students must be able to paraphrase (examiners would not expect precise repetition) the major provisions of the statutes as highlighted in this book.

The use of cases

The doctrine of precedent is not applicable to family law - per Ormrod LJ in *Sharpe* v *Sharpe* (1981) 11 Fam Law 121. While, therefore, you will come across a large number of cases these should be used to illustrate how the judiciary approach Family Law matters and how, by analogy, the problem in any particular question can be resolved both in practice and in the resolution of academic problems. When writing an answer to a problem question, it is seldom necessary to refer to large numbers of cases nor to refer to the facts of cases in any depth. The cases should be used to show principles upon which the particular problem will be resolved.

Approach to the examination

It is artificial in family law to advise a wife, for example, that she can divorce and not then go on to consider the implications of the divorce as regards maintenance, property adjustment and children. It is increasingly common for examiners to require the student to demonstrate a wide general knowledge of family law. The University of London LLB (external) examiners do this by asking questions which include up to three discrete areas whereas other examiners sometimes set a compulsory question that can include almost any of the areas studied. In short, it is dangerous to question spot in the sense of choosing to revise a limited number of topics. Whilst minor topics eg domicile or custodianship may be superficially dealt with you must know in depth the major overlap areas ie the law relating to the termination of marriage, ancillary relief, matrimonial injunctions and children.

Dealing with essay questions

Examiners favour problem questions. Consequently there will rarely be more than three essay questions on an examination paper.

No essay question will be asking you to write everything you know about a particular topic even though that tends to be the common approach of students to such questions. The examiner will be seeking to see whether you are able to adapt your general knowledge of the area in question to a particular slant. The skill, therefore, is to identify the particular slant of the question and ensure that each paragraph you write is relevant to that slant. If you do this you will achieve high marks whereas if you simply write everything you know, you will achieve no more than a bare pass.

Because family law is a topical subject it is quite likely that essay questions will require comment on current proposals for reform or current issues eg the debate surrounding surrogacy.

Dealing with problem questions

Problem questions are often lengthy. Whatever the length, it is important to read the issues you are being asked to advise on at the end of the question before reading the facts. In this way you are more likely to identify the relevance of the facts. Be clear who you are asked to advise, be concise and relevant, support your answer with evidence and if you are asked to advise X be sure that you do.

REVISION AND EXAMINATION TECHNIQUE

(A) REVISION TECHNIQUE

Planning a revision timetable

In planning your revision timetable make sure you don't finish the syllabus too early. You should avoid leaving revision so late that you have to 'cram' - but constant revision of the same topic leads to stagnation.

Plan ahead, however, and try to make your plans increasingly detailed as you approach the examination date.

Allocate enough time for each topic to be studied. But note that it is better to devise a realistic timetable, to which you have a reasonable chance of keeping, rather than a wildly optimistic schedule which you will probably abandon at the first opportunity!

The syllabus and its topics

One of your first tasks when you began your course was to ensure that you thoroughly understood your **syllabus**. Check now to see if you can write down the **topics** it comprises from memory. You will see that the chapters of this WorkBook are each devoted to a topic. This will help you decide which are the key chapters relative to your revision programme. Though you should allow some time for glancing through the other chapters.

The topic and its key points

Again working from memory, analyse what you consider to be the key points of any topic that you have selected for particular revision. Seeing what you can recall, unaided, will help you to understand and firmly memorise the concepts involved.

Using the WorkBook

Relevant questions are provided for each topic in this book. Naturally, as typical examples of examination questions, they do not normally relate to one topic only. But the questions in each chapter *will* relate to the subject matter of the chapter to a degree. You can choose your method of consulting the questions and solutions, but here are some suggestions (strategies 1-3). Each of them pre-supposes that you have read through the notes on key points and question analysis, and any other preliminary matter, at the beginning of the chapter. Once again, you now need to practise working from *memory*, for that is the challenge you are preparing yourself for. As a rule of procedure constantly test yourself once revision starts, both orally and in writing.

Strategy 1

Strategy 1 is planned for the purpose of *quick revision*. First read your chosen question carefully and then jot down in abbreviated notes what you consider to be the main points at issue. Similarly, note the cases and statutes that occur to you as being relevant for citation purposes. Allow yourself sufficient time to cover what you feel to be relevant. Then study the *skeleton solution* and skim-read the *suggested solution* to see how they compare with your notes. When comparing consider carefully what the author has included (and concluded) and see whether that agrees with what you have written. Consider the points of variation also. Have you recognised the key issues? How relevant have you been? It is possible, of course, that you have referred to a recent case that *is* relevant, but which had not been reported when the WorkBook was prepared.

Strategy 2

Strategy 2 requires a nucleus of *three hours* in which to practise writing a set of examination answers in a limited time-span.

Select a number of questions (as many as are normally set in the examination you are studying for), each from a different chapter in the WorkBook, without consulting the solutions. Find a place to write where you will not be disturbed and try to arrange not to be interrupted for three hours. Write your solutions in the time allowed, noting any time needed to make up if you *are* interrupted.

After a rest, compare your answers with the *suggested solutions* in the WorkBook. There will be considerable variation in style, of course, but the bare facts should not be too dissimilar. Evaluate your answer critically. Be 'searching', but develop a positive approach to deciding how you would tackle each question on another occasion.

Strategy 3

You are unlikely to be able to do more than one three hour examination, but occasionally set yourself a single question. Vary the 'time allowed' by imagining it to be one of the questions that you must answer in three hours and allow yourself a limited preparation and writing time. Try one question that you feel to be difficult and an easier question on another occasion, for example.

Mis-use of suggested solutions

Don't try to learn by rote. In particular, don't try to reproduce the *suggested solutions* by heart. Learn to express the basic concepts in your own words.

Keeping up-to-date

Keep up-to-date. While examiners do not require familiarity with changes in the law during the three months prior to the examination, it obviously creates a good impression if you can show you are acquainted with any recent changes. Make a habit of looking through one of the leading journals - *Modern Law Review, Law Quarterly Review* or the *New Law Journal*, for example - and cumulative indices to law reports, such as the *All England Law Reports* or *Weekly Law Reports*, or indeed the daily law reports in *The Times.* Specialist journal(s) for the subject, eg *Family Law,* are also helpful sources.

(B)   EXAMINATION SKILLS

Examiners are human too!

The process of answering an examination question involves a *communication* between you and the person who set it. If you were speaking face to face with the person, you would choose your verbal points and arguments carefully in your reply. When writing, it is all too easy to forget *the human being who is awaiting the reply* and simply write out what one knows in the area of the subject! Bear in mind it is a person whose question you are responding to, throughout your essay. This will help you to avoid being irrelevant or long-winded.

The essay question

Candidates are sometimes tempted to choose to answer essay questions because they 'seem' easier. But the examiner is looking for thoughtful work and will not give good marks for superficial answers.

The essay-type of question may be either purely factual, in asking you to *explain the meaning* of a certain doctrine or principle, or it may ask you to *discuss* a certain proposition, usually derived from a quotation. In either case, the approach to the answer is the same. A clear programme must be devised to give the examiner the meaning or significance of the doctrine, principle or proposition and its origin in common law, equity or statute, and cases which illustrate its application to the branch of law concerned.

The problem question

The problem-type question requires a different approach. You may well be asked to advise a client or merely discuss the problems raised in the question. In either case, the most important factor is to take great care in reading the question. By its nature, the question will be longer than the essay-type question and you will have a number of facts to digest. Time spent in analysing the question may well save time later, when you are endeavouring to impress on the examiner the considerable extent of your basic legal knowledge. The quantity of knowledge is itself a trap and you must always keep within the boundaries of the question in hand. It is very tempting to show the examiner the extent of your knowledge of your subject, but if this is outside the question, it is time lost and no marks earned. It is inevitable that some areas which you have studied and revised will not be the subject of questions, but under no circumstances attempt to adapt a question to a stronger area of knowledge at the expense of relevance.

When you are satisfied that you have grasped the full significance of the problem-type question, set out the fundamental principles involved. You may well be asked to advise one party, but there is no reason why you should not introduce your answer by:

'I would advise A on the following matters ...'

and then continue the answer in a normal impersonal form. This is a much better technique than answering the question as an imaginary conversation.

You will then go on to identify the fundamental problem, or problems posed by the question. This should be followed by a consideration of the law which is relevant to the problem. The source of the law, together with the cases which will be of assistance in solving the problem, must then be considered in detail.

Very good problem questions are quite likely to have alternative answers, and in advising A you should be aware that alternative arguments may be available. Each stage of your answer, in this case, will be based on the argument or arguments considered in the previous stage, forming a conditional sequence.

If, however, you only identify one fundamental problem, do not waste time worrying that you cannot think of an alternative - there may very well be only that one answer.

The examiner will then wish to see how you use your legal knowledge to formulate a case and how you apply that formula to the problem which is the subject of the question. It is this positive approach which can make answering a problem question a high mark earner for the student who has fully understood the question and clearly argued his case on the established law.

Examination checklist

1 Read the instructions at the head of the examination carefully. While last-minute changes are unlikely - such as the introduction of a *compulsory question* or *an increase in the number of questions asked* - it has been known to happen.

2 Read the questions carefully. Analyse problem questions - work out what the examiner wants.

3 Plan your answer *before* you start to write. You can divide your time as follows:

    (a)   working out the question (5 per cent of time)

    (b)   working out how to answer the question (5 to 10 per cent of time)

    (c)   writing your answer

Do not overlook (a) and (b)

4 Check that you understand the rubric *before* you start to write. Do not 'discuss', for example, if you are specifically asked to 'compare and contrast'.

5 Answer the correct number of questions. If you fail to answer one out of four questions set you lose 25 per cent of your marks!

Style and structure

Try to be clear and concise. Basically this amounts to using paragraphs to denote the sections of your essay, and writing simple, straightforward sentences as much as possible. The sentence you have just read has 22 words - when a sentence reaches 50 words it becomes difficult for a reader to follow.

Do not be inhibited by the word 'structure' (traditionally defined as giving an essay a beginning, a middle and an end). A good structure will be the natural consequence of setting out your arguments and the supporting evidence in a logical order. Set the scene briefly in your opening paragraph. Provide a clear conclusion in your final paragraph.

TABLE OF CASES

TABLE OF STATUTES

1 FAMILY LAW AND SOCIETY

As society changes so too the law must change to reflect prevailing social norms, and this is particularly the case in the study of the law that relates to the social group defined as the family. The history of family law reflects changes that have occurred in society's attitude towards divorce, to the significant changes that have occurred in the status of women, to the recognition of the separate status of children and to the acknowledgement that the state has a role to play in protecting members of a family who are 'at risk', in the sense that they are the victims of sexual abuse or violent attack.

Since the mid-1850s social reform in both public and private law which has had an impact on the regulation of family life has gained momentum. In private law, the establishment of a coherent secular divorce law, together with the development of the separate legal status of the wife within marriage, has now reached a point where a divorce petition is based on the 'irretrievable breakdown' of the marriage and husbands and wives enjoy equal rights and obligations within marriage. In public law, legislation which started by regulating child employment and introduced compulsory education has now reached a point at which the state can remove children from a family if it is established that they are 'at risk' through physical and sexual abuse.

Social change has been significant during the last 25 years. The changing role of women, a massive increase in reported child abuse, the very rapid increase in the divorce rate, the problem of 'wife abuse and the large numbers of couples who choose to cohabit rather than marry are social phenomena which have posed and continue to pose problems for family law. Accordingly, there have been a number of reforms during that period - for example reforms which seek to give protection to the battered wife, and others which seek to remove the stigma associated with illegitimacy. The Children Act 1989 is a comprehensive measure which has introduced radical changes in both public and private law.

Laws which relate to the family include welfare, housing, taxation and education, to name but some. Family law, however, focuses on the more traditional question of status and the rights and obligations that arise from that status.

1

2   NULLITY OF MARRIAGE

2.1   Introduction

A marriage may be terminated in two ways: either a petition for divorce or a petition for nullity. Insofar as there are some 160,000 divorce petitions but less than 500 nullity petitions presented each year the practical importance of the law relating to nullity of marriage is put into its proper perspective. A person would only seek a decree of nullity if, for some reason eg religious objection, he or she was not willing to petition for divorce. However, despite its relative lack of practical importance it remains a popular examination area.

2.2   Key points

a) *The difference between a void and voidable marriage*

Section 11 of the Matrimonial Causes Act 1973 lists grounds of nullity which make the marriage void; s12 those that make the marriage voidable only. The s11 grounds result in such a fundamentally flawed marriage that the law considers there to have been no marriage at all - technically a party to a void marriage can go ahead and contract another marriage without having the first marriage declared void by a court.

The s12 grounds are of less fundamental effect and the law recognises a marriage which is affected by one of the s12 grounds as valid until such time as one party petitions the court that it should be deemed void. However, a party to such a potentially void marriage cannot delay too long. Section 13 of the Matrimonial Causes Act generally bars an application to make a voidable marriage void unless the application is brought within three years of the date that the applicant knew that he/she could rely on one of the s12 grounds. It should be emphasised that s13 does not apply to s11 at all, nor does it apply to s12(a) or 12(b) - the non-consummation grounds.

b) *The s11 grounds*

    i) Failure to comply with Marriages Acts 1949-70

- within prohibited degrees of relationship

- either party under 16

  This only applies to a marriage (wherever in the world it is contracted) if at least one of the parties is domiciled in England at the time of the marriage.

  Compare *Pugh* v *Pugh* [1951] 2 All ER 680 with *Mohamed* v *Knott* [1968] 2 All ER 563.

- failure to comply with the formalities of marriage

  The purpose behind reading the banns is that publicity is given as to who is getting married, therefore the banns must be published in the name one is commonly known by even if that is not one's real name: *Dancer* v *Dancer* [1948] 2 All ER 731.

    ii) That at the time of marriage either party was already married - ie bigamous marriages

    iii) That the parties are not respectively male and female

English law only recognises marriages between parties of the opposite sex: *Hyde* v *Hyde* (1866) LR 1 P & D 130. In *Rees* v *UK* [1993] 2 FCR 49 the ECHR refused to depart from this principle in the case of homosexual marriage.

But what of the person who changes his or her sex? In *Corbett* v *Corbett* [1970] 2 All ER 33 it was held that a person has the sex he/she was born with and cannot change it. Accordingly English law would not recognise a marriage between homosexuals. Furthermore this principle is of general application so that a man who has lived his working life as a woman would not be permitted to claim a state pension if he retired at 60.

In certain of the United States of America if a person anatomically changes his/her sex then that person is treated as being of the changed sex. That was the position in *Corbett* v *Corbett*.

The decision in *Corbett*, insofar as it denies the right of an anatomically sex-changed person to contract a valid marriage, has been followed by the European Court of Human Rights in the cases of *C* v *UK* [1993] FCR 97 and *B* v *France* [1993] FCR 145.

    iv) Actual or potentially polygamous marriages

This ground only applies where:

- the marriage was contracted abroad; and

3

- at least one of the parties was domiciled in England at the time of the marriage; and

- in the case of a potentially polygamous marriage, it could on the facts become actually polygamous.

A marriage between an English domiciled woman and a Pakistan domiciled man in Pakistan would be void under this ground because by the law governing the husband (Pakistan law) he could marry another during the currency of this marriage. However a marriage between an English domiciled man and a Pakistan domiciled woman in Pakistan would not be void under this ground because by the law governing the husband (English law) he could not marry another whilst he remained married to his first wife: *Hussain* v *Hussain* [1982] 3 All ER 369.

c) *The s12 grounds*

   i) Non-consummation through incapacity - s12(a)

   Note:

   The degree of consummation necessary: *W* v *W* [1967] 3 All ER 178.

   A petitioner can rely on his own impotency: *Pettit* v *Pettit* [1962] 3 All ER 37.

   Refusal to undergo a simple operation without danger to health which would cure the physical incapacity may amount to wilful refusal under s12(b): *D* v *D* [1979] 3 All ER 337.

   ii) Non-consummation through wilful refusal - s12(b)

   Note:

   The definition of wilful refusal - must be more than a temporary unwillingness due to shyness but rather a fixed and steadfast refusal come to without just excuse: *Horton* v *Horton* [1947] 2 All ER 871.

   Therefore there will not be wilful refusal where:

- The marriage was between elderly persons 'for companionship only': *Morgan* v *Morgan* [1959] 1 All ER 539; but probably not companionship marriage between those of child bearing age: see *Brodie* v *Brodie* [1917] P 271.

- The validity of the marriage was dependent as far as the parties were concerned on a religious ceremony which has not taken place: *Jodla* v *Jodla* [1960] 1 All ER 625; *Kaur* v *Singh* [1972] 1 All ER 292; *A* v *J (nullity)* [1989] Fam Law 63.

   iii) Lack of consent through duress, mistake, unsoundness of mind or otherwise - s12(c)

- Duress

This is a very popular examination area - look for a scenario where one party is coerced into marrying another.

A useful framework for an answer is provided by the three requirements suggested by Scarman J in *Buckland* v *Buckland* [1967] 2 All ER 300, namely:

a sufficient degree of fear to vitiate consent;

that the fear be reasonably entertained;

that the fear arose from some external factor which the petitioner had not brought upon himself.

'Sufficient degree of fear'

This was usefully defined in *Szechter* v *Szechter* [1970] 3 All ER 905 as requiring a threat to 'life limb or liberty'.

More recently in *Hirani* v *Hirani* (1983) 4 FLR 232 Ormrod LJ adopted the phrase 'such a coercion of the will so as to vitiate consent' to indicate the degree of pressure required.

Examples of such pressure are found in both *Szechter* v *Szechter* and *Buckland* v *Buckland* [1967] 2 All ER 300 namely consenting to marriage to escape unjust imprisonment.

'Fear to be reasonably entertained'

The debate here has been whether the test should be subjective or objective ie is it sufficient that the petitioner was frightened or must it be shown that a reasonable person in her position would have been frightened as well.

Initially the test was purely subjective: *Scott* v *Sebright* (1886) 12 PD 21. However, cases such as *Buckland* v *Buckland* and *Szechter* v *Szechter* strongly favoured an objective approach.

The question of whether the test should be objective or subjective is of great importance in the area of arranged marriages where someone marries out of respect for his/her parents' wishes. If an objective test applies, then such marriages cannot be annulled due to duress. This was so in the case of *Singh* v *Singh* [1971] 2 All ER 828 which followed an objective approach. However, in *Hirani* v *Hirani* the Court of Appeal reverted to the subjective approach and allowed a decree in such an arranged marriage.

After *Hirani* it is generally accepted that the test is now purely subjective: was the petitioner in fact sufficiently frightened so as to give his/her consent to marriage?

'Not brought on himself'

For example if, in *Buckland* v *Buckland*, the petitioner had in fact had sexual relations with the Maltese girl he would not have succeeded.

• Mistake

It must be a mistake as to the nature of the ceremony not as to its effect.

Compare *Mehta* v *Mehta* [1945] 2 All ER 690 with *Way* v *Way* [1949] 2 All ER 959 and *Vervaeke* v *Smith* [1982] 2 All ER 144. In *Militante* v *Ojunwomaju* [1993] FCR 355 the distinction made seems difficult to justify.

• Unsoundness of mind

One does not have to be very sane to understand the nature and effect of marriage: *In the Estate of Park* [1953] 2 All ER 1411.

• Or otherwise

There have been no cases on this - it probably covers the situation where someone consents to marriage while under the influence of alcohol or drugs.

iv) Mental disorder within meaning of Mental Health Act 1983 - s12(d)

Virtually any mental illness is covered by Act. If you do not understand the nature and effect of marriage you can annul it under s12(c); if you do understand the nature and effect but are incapable of carrying out the normal marital duties because of a mental illness then the marriage may be annulled under s12(d): *Bennett* v *Bennett* [1969] 1 All ER 539

v) Suffering from venereal disease - s12(e)

vi) Pregnancy by another - s12(f)

Section 12(e) and s12(f) only apply if the petitioner was ignorant of the facts at the time of marriage.

The s13 requirement to petition within three years of marriage only applies to s12(c) to s12(f).

d) *The s13 Bar*

Remember this section can only bar s12 petitions; it does not apply to s11 grounds.

One needs to show:

i) Conduct by the petitioner (after he/she became aware that a petition for nullity was available to them) which leads the respondent to believe the marriage will not be annulled eg adopting children: *D* v *D* [1979] 3 All ER 337; and

ii)   That it would be unjust to grant the decree.

Note that where the marriage is an empty shell it would seldom be just not to grant the decree: *D* v *D* [1979] 3 All ER 337.

As regards the three year time limit remember this only applies to the grounds in s12(c) to s12(f) and while time generally runs from the date of the marriage this is not so when, during that period, the petitioner has suffered from a mental illness within the meaning of the Mental Health Act 1983.

2.3   Recent cases

C v *UK* [1993] FCR 97

B v *France* [1993] FCR 145

Militante v *Ojunwomaju* [1993] FCR 355

A v *J (nullity)* [1989] Fam Law 63

2.4   Analysis of questions

Problem questions normally concentrate on the voidable grounds contained in s12 of the Matrimonial Causes Act in particular s12(a) and s12(b) - the non-consummation grounds - and/or s12(c) lack of consent due to duress. An answer to a problem question involving the s12 grounds is never complete without the candidate going on to consider whether the action may be barred by reason of the matters in s13. It should also be noted that it is sometimes the case that a nullity problem question is combined with another aspect of family law eg financial/property provision or matrimonial injunctions.

Essay questions fall into two types; either requiring a critical discussion of a particular ground (the most common being s11(c) and the effect thereon of the decision in *Corbett* v *Corbett* [1970] 2 All ER 33 and s12(c) the law relating to lack of consent due to duress) or a more general question requiring the candidate to consider whether or not there is a continuing need for a law of nullity in its existing form ie can it be abolished altogether or should it be modified so that only s11 - the void grounds - are retained?

2.5   Questions

Question 1

'It is sometimes suggested that, although the concept of the void marriage must clearly be preserved, that of the voidable marriage might be abolished.' (Cretney). Do you agree?

University of London LLB Examination
(for External Students) Family Law June 1987 Q1

General comment

This is an unusual question on nullity in that it is in essay form rather than in problem form. However the topic raised in the quotation is discussed in some detail by

7

Professor Cretney in his textbook *Principles of Family Law* and a student who has read the relevant chapter and who has a thorough knowledge of the grounds for a nullity decree under s12 Matrimonial Causes Act 1973 should experience no difficulty in adequately answering the question.

Skeleton solution

• Discuss the legal consequences of divorce and a decree of nullity under s12 MCA 1973.

• Discuss the arguments for and against a retention of the concept of voidable marriages put forward by the Law Commission and Professor Cretney respectively.

Suggested solution

This proposition is based on the fact that in modern times the importance of the law of nullity has diminished as the law of divorce has been extended and simplified. Further, many of the legal consequences of a marriage have been attached to both void and voidable marriages, for example a party may claim all the ancillary reliefs available to a spouse under ss22-24 Matrimonial Causes Act 1973 whether the marriage is void, voidable or is dissolved by a decree of divorce. In the case of a voidable marriage, it is deemed to be a valid and subsisting marriage until it is dissolved by decree (s16 Matrimonial Causes Act 1973) and so legally the parties are man and wife in the same way as parties to a valid marriage, until a decree has been obtained. The difference between a decree of divorce and a decree of nullity under s12 Matrimonial Causes Act 1973 is therefore one of form only and it has been argued before the Law Commission that in the case of the nullity decree the decree misleadingly states that the marriage never existed when in fact it has been treated as a valid marriage until that moment. It is argued that it would be more logical therefore to terminate the marriage by divorce rather than by nullity under s12 Matrimonial Causes Act 1973 as this would more accurately record the reality of the situation.

The Law Commission rejected these arguments on the grounds that although the consequences of the two decrees were essentially the same, the concepts giving rise to them were quite different for whereas the decree of divorce is based on a cause for the breakdown of the marriage which arose after the celebration of the marriage, in the case of a nullity decree under s12 Matrimonial Causes Act 1973 recognition is given to the existence of an impediment which prevents the marriage from becoming effective from the outset.

The Law Commission also considered the views of the Church of England on this matter. Essentially the grounds under s12 Matrimonial Causes Act 1973 are based on the absence of consent on the part of at least one of the parties. Consent to marriage includes consent to sexual relations between the parties and so the Church takes the view that impotence, or the inability to consummate the marriage in effect vitiates consent. The church considers that all the other grounds set out in s12 (with the exception of wilful refusal to consummate the marriage which the church considers should be a ground for divorce rather than nullity because it relates to a problem which arises after the ceremony) also fall under the head of conditional consent and certainly they all include conditions which must be satisfied at the time of the marriage ceremony. Even under the ground in s12(d) which is based on a party's mental disorder, which is often evidenced by a deterioration in the party's condition after the ceremony, so as to render them unfit to be married, even though they were mentally capable of giving a valid consent to the marriage at the time of the ceremony, it must be shown that the party's mental condition was in existence at the time of the ceremony.

The Law Commission also objected to the abolition of the distinction between voidable marriages and divorce because it would offend a substantial minority of the population and could not be recommended unless a worthwhile advantage in abolishing the distinction could be shown. Finally the Commission felt that so long as there remained a three year bar to presenting a divorce petition, the assimilation of voidable marriages and marriages which could be dissolved by divorce would be incomplete. This latter objection has now been removed by s1 Matrimonial and Family Proceedings Act 1984 which has amended s3 Matrimonial Causes Act 1973 by reducing the period during which a petition for divorce may not be presented from three years to one year and it is argued that adequate remedies exist to protect the legal rights of the parties during that year.

Professor Cretney rejects the other arguments put forward by the Law Commission which he finds to be unconvincing. He does not accept that there is a fundamental conceptual distinction between voidable marriages and those which can be dissolved by divorce. He points out that the courts have increasingly taken into account supervening events when considering a nullity petition under s12 and he cites as an example the ground of wilful refusal to consummate the marriage which formed the basis of two thirds of all nullity petitions under s12 in 1982. Further, with regard to the ground of mental disorder Professor Cretney points out that one of the reasons given for allowing a petitioner to rely on the other party's mental disorder even where the petitioner knew of that party's mental illness at the time of the marriage ceremony, was that the mental disorder might worsen after the marriage, and so a supervening factor is given consideration in this ground also.

Professor Cretney rejects the Church of England's objections as being a valid reason for preserving the distinction between nullity and divorce in this area for he argues that family law no longer relies on religious doctrine and any persons who did attach importance to the church's views could seek the church's approval for the termination of their marriage under modern canon law.

Finally he argues that there would be substantial benefits to be gained by replacing these nullity proceedings with divorce proceedings. By reason of the nature in the grounds to be relied upon, nullity proceedings can involve the parties in considerable distress and humiliation. Professor Cretney argues that in divorce proceedings such effects could be avoided particularly as most of the grounds could be included under s1(2)(b) Matrimonial Causes Act 1973, that is, be based on the fact of the respondent's behaviour and the court's finding of intolerability. Further, parties could be encouraged to avoid a detailed investigation into their personal problems altogether by agreeing to a divorce under s1(2)(d) Matrimonial Causes Act 1973, that is on the basis of the separation of the parties for two years, and the respondent's consent to the decree.

Question 2

Adrian and Betty, aged 19 and 16 respectively, met and fell in love in January 1989. They wanted to get married but their parents objected. In defiance of the wishes of their families they lived together in Adrian's flat. Over the past three years Adrian has been suffering from schizophrenic episodes during which he becomes angry and confused. Unaware of the nature of Adrian's illness, Betty thinks that she can make him better.

In July 1989, Betty had a brief sexual encounter with Cedric, a local plumber. Adrian knows nothing of this incident.

In August 1989, Betty discovered that she was pregnant. She told Adrian that they had to get married before either of their parents learned the truth. They got married that week.

Because of her condition, Betty declined to consummate the marriage until after the baby arrived. Adrian reluctantly agreed to this. Believing the child to be his and excited at the prospect of fatherhood, he bought a cot and some toys. Betty gave birth to Deidre in April 1990. Adrian is surprised that Deidre has black hair (both he and Betty have blonde hair) and he leaves home immediately, accusing Betty of infidelity.

a)   Can Adrian have his marriage to Betty terminated?

b) Would your answer to (a) be different if the marriage had taken place in August 1986, Deidre had been born in April 1987, and Adrian has suspected nothing until Betty confessed in April 1990 that he might not be the father of her child?

Adapted from University of London LLB Examination
(for External Students) Family Law June 1986 Q1

General comment

A typical if rather all embracing question covering a number of the nullity grounds.

Skeleton solution

a)   • Distinguish between void and voidable marriages for nullity purposes - discount void grounds on these facts - age of parties, parental consent - consider voidable grounds - s12(b), wilful refusal to consummate - but note s13(1).

   • Also consider s12(c) and (d), and the more likely option of s12(f).

   • Discount divorce in view of s3 MCA 1973.

b)   • Void marriage - due to Betty's age (13) in 1986.

   • Discount s12(b) on the new facts.

- Section 12(c), (d) and (f) may still be relevant subject to the reservations expressed above, but now discuss s13(2) - time bar; and amendment made to it by the Matrimonial and Family Proceedings Act 1984.

- Consider divorce in detail - s1(2)(a) and s1(2)(b) MCA 1973.

Suggested solution

a) As advice is sought on the termination of the marriage, consideration must be given to whether the marriage can be annulled under ss11 or 12 Matrimonial Causes Act 1973 (hereinafter referred to as MCA 1973), or dissolved by a decree of divorce under s1 MCA 1973.

For a marriage celebrated after the 31st July 1971 to be annulled, the grounds set out in ss11 and 12, which deal with void and voidable marriages respectively, must be considered. If the marriage is void it is deemed never to have existed and any decree is merely declaratory. If the marriage is voidable it is in all respects valid until a decree of nullity is pronounced.

On the facts of this question, it appears that the marriage is not void under s11. Both parties are over 16 at the date of the marriage and so fulfil the age requirements of this country. Although Betty, being under 18, requires her parents' consent to her marriage to comply with the formalities of the marriage ceremony, this defect will not invalidate a marriage by common licence or Superintendent Registrar's Certificate (s48(1)(b) Marriage Act 1949) and therefore s11(a) MCA 1973 will not apply in this case.

The marriage may be voidable under s12(b) MCA 1973 on the ground that the marriage has not been consummated owing to Betty's wilful refusal to consummate it. A marriage is consummated as soon as the parties have had sexual intercourse that is 'ordinary and complete and not partial and imperfect' (*D* v *A* (1845)) after the marriage, and any intercourse which takes place before the marriage is irrelevant. We are told that because of her pregnancy Betty declined to have sexual intercourse until after the baby was born. It seems that the marriage never was consummated because Adrian left Betty immediately after the baby's birth, believing the child not to be his. If there has been no consummation Adrian would have to show wilful refusal to consummate on Betty's part as there is no evidence of an incapacity. Wilful refusal is defined as a settled and definite decision come to without just excuse: *Horton* v *Horton* (1947). Although it could be argued that Adrian may be wilfully refusing to consummate the marriage after Deidre's birth by leaving Betty, it could be said that he has a just excuse in believing Deidre not to be his child and in any event advice is sought on whether Adrian can terminate the marriage, and a party cannot rely on his or her own refusal. The success of his petition under s12(b) against Betty will depend on the court's view of her excuse, namely her pregnancy. There appears to be no physical or medical reason for intercourse not to take place during the pregnancy, certainly in its early stages, and therefore it may be that prima facie the ground is made out. We are told however that Adrian agrees, albeit reluctantly, to the arrangement and this may give rise to a bar to the petition under s13(1) MCA 1973 which provides that the court will refuse to grant a decree if satisfied by the respondent (Betty) that Adrian, with knowledge that it was open to him to have the marriage avoided, so conducted himself in relation to Betty as to lead her reasonably to believe that he would not do so, and that it would be unjust to her to grant the decree.

If Betty decided to raise this bar she would have to prove that Adrian knew he could have the marriage annulled by reason of her refusal to consummate the marriage, and any conduct which is to be relied upon as evidence of leading her to believe that the marriage would not be avoided must be performed with this knowledge. It is not clear whether Adrian was aware of his legal position when he agreed with Betty's refusal. If he did, then he could be barred from relying on her refusal if it can also be shown that it would be unjust to Betty to grant the decree. If he had no such knowledge the bar will not apply: *Slater* v *Slater* (1953).

If Deidre is not Adrian's child, he could rely on s12(f) MCA 1973, namely that at the time of the marriage the respondent (Betty) was pregnant by another man (Cedric). On these facts no bar under s13 would apply as Adrian had no knowledge of Betty's affair with Cedric, and so, although he knew she was pregnant at the time of the ceremony, he thought the child was his. Therefore s13(3) will not apply, nor will s13(1) as on discovering the truth he left Betty and could not be said to have conducted himself in such a way as reasonably to lead her to believe he would not annul the marriage. His conduct in buying articles for the baby and remaining with Betty occurred before the birth and his discovery that the child is not his, and therefore it will be ignored.

Consideration should also be given to Adrian's schizophrenia as this could give rise to grounds for annulling the marriage under either s12(c) or s12(d) MCA 1973. Under s12(c) the marriage may be annulled if it can be shown that either party did not validly consent to it, whether in consequence of duress, mistake, unsoundness of mind, or otherwise. On these facts only unsoundness of mind could apply as there is no evidence that Adrian was forced into the marriage by threats or persuasion such as to wipe out the reality of his consent (*Szechter* v *Szechter* (1970); *Hirani* v *Hirani* (1983)); and for mistake to operate, it must relate to the nature of the ceremony or the identity of the other party. Other frauds such as a deception as to paternity would not suffice: *Moss* v *Moss (orse Archer)* (1897); but note that a deception re staying in the country might: see *Militante* v *Ojunwomaju* (1993).

For unsoundness of mind to be made out, the question is whether the party could understand the nature of the ceremony. It was stated in *In the Estate of Park* (1954) that the test is whether the party was capable of understanding the nature of the contract into which he or she was entering, that is, capable of appreciating that it involved the duties and responsibilities of marriage. There is a presumption that each party validly consented to the marriage, and as marriage is a simple contract with no high degree of ceremony (*Durham* v *Durham* (1885)), it would be difficult on these facts to show the ground, particularly as, although Adrian became confused in his schizophrenic episodes, there is no evidence that he suffered such an episode at the time of the marriage, or, in any event, that the confusion would be such as to render him incapable of understanding the contract into which he was entering.

It may be easier to rely on s12(d) which provides that at the time of the marriage either party, though capable of giving a valid consent, was suffering (whether continuously or intermittently) from such mental disorder within the meaning of the Mental Health Act 1959, of such a kind or to such an extent as to be unfitted for marriage. In this case Adrian's schizophrenia would fall within the Act. However it is questionable whether it renders him unfit for marriage, that is, incapable of carrying on a normal married life (*Bennett* v *Bennett* (1969)) as all we are told is that during his episodes he becomes angry and confused. If his condition is likely to worsen so that he would be unable to cope with the responsibilities of married life the ground may apply.

Adrian cannot divorce Betty at this time as they have not been married as yet for a year and s3 MCA 1973 as substituted by s1 Matrimonial and Family Proceedings Act 1984 (hereinafter referred to as MFPA 1984) provides an absolute bar to the presentation of a divorce petition within one year of marriage. Even if Adrian does decide to wait until August to divorce Betty he may be in difficulty in establishing the requisite irretrievable breakdown of marriage since the only relevant facts ie s1(2)(a) and s1(2)(b) may not be appropriate as will be explained in part (ii) herein.

b) Assuming that Betty's age remains at 16 in 1989 the answer would be different in one fundamental respect if the marriage took place in August 1986 because at that time Betty would be only 13 years old and under s11(a) MCA 1973 a marriage will be void if either party is under the age of 16 years: *Pugh* v *Pugh* (1951). So Adrian could have the marriage annulled on this basis and there are no bars to a petition under s11 MCA 1973. Thus on the basis of the new information, a new ground for annulling the marriage arises.

With regard to the other nullity grounds referred to in part (i), the advice given regarding pregnancy per alium under s12(f) would remain the same, subject to the bar under s13(2) MCA 1973 which will be considered in below.

In view of the new information, from which we can gather that Betty and Adrian lived together for 3 years following Deidre's birth, it seems that s12(b) may no longer apply, for although it may have been some time before the marriage was consummated, as soon as sexual intercourse took place after the marriage, consummation is effected.

With regard to Adrian's schizophrenia, the advice given in (i) above concerning s12(c) and s12(d) remains the same subject to the bar under s13(2) MCA 1973.

It is in fact in relation to the bars to nullity proceedings that the new circumstances make further differences to the answer given in part (i). Dealing with the s12(f) ground first, as in part (i), s13(1) and s13(3) will not apply as Adrian was not aware until Betty's confession that Deidre may not be his own child, whereupon it seems he left her. However s12(f) and s12(c) or s12(d) if applicable would be affected by s13(2) MCA 1973 as substituted by s2(2) MFPA 1984 which provides that nullity proceedings must be commenced within 3 years of the marriage unless leave is given under s13(4) to institute them after that period on satisfying the judge that the petitioner has at some time during that period suffered from mental disorder within the meaning of the Mental Health Act 1983, and he considers that in the circumstances of the case it would be just to grant leave to institute the proceedings.

Question 3

In 1985, Gerda left her home in Ruritania in order to visit England. She met Herbert and married him soon afterwards in a London Register Office. Because Gerda experienced pain when Herbert attempted having sexual intercourse with her, the marriage remained unconsummated.

In 1989, Gerda returned to Ruritania to visit her mother. During her visit, there was a military coup in Ruritania. Gerda's first cousin, Ian, was unpopular with the new regime and, since the laws of Ruritania permitted polyandry, he suggested to Gerda that she marry him to enable him to leave Ruritania for England, as her husband. Gerda only agreed to his plan because Ian threatened to tell Herbert that, at the age of 14, Gerda had had an operation giving her an artificial vagina. After their marriage in Ruritania, Gerda and Ian came to England and immediately parted, Gerda returning home to Herbert. Herbert has recently left Gerda and wishes to marry Janet, while Ian wishes to marry Kate.

Advise Herbert and Ian on the validity of their marriages to Gerda.

Adapted from University of London LLB Examination
(for External Students) Family Law June 1983 Q2

General comment

A long question involving consideration of nullity alone. The student is expected to be able to differentiate between void and voidable marriages, and to discuss in some detail the validity of the marriages in question in the light of the rules regarding domicile, polygamy, the sex of the parties, lack of consent due to duress, and non-consummation. This is a question that the well-prepared student would have no difficulty in answering, but it requires a lot of thought to unravel the rather complex facts, and careful planning in the answer to avoid confusion.

Skeleton solution

- Is either marriage void under s12?

    - respectively male and female: s11(c)

    - potentially polygamous: s11(d)

    - already married: s11(b)

- Is either marriage voidable under s12?

    - non-consummation through incapacity: s12(a)

- non-consummation through wilful refusal: s12(b)
- duress: s12(c)

Suggested solution

The marriage between Gerda and Herbert appears to be void, although the evidence suggests that a discussion of the grounds on which a marriage may be deemed to be voidable is also required.

Sections 11 and 12 Matrimonial Causes Act 1973 set out the grounds upon which a marriage celebrated after the 31 July 1971 shall be deemed void and voidable respectively. If one of the grounds in s11 is made out then the marriage is void, that is, it is deemed never to have existed and any decree is purely declaratory. If the marriage is voidable however, it is in all respects a valid marriage until a decree absolute of nullity is pronounced.

Under s11 MCA 1973 a marriage shall be void if, inter alia, the parties are not respectively male and female: s11(c). If both parties are female, or as apparently in this case, male, then the parties lack capacity to marry according to English law. A party's capacity to marry is governed by the law of their country of domicile and Gerda's domicile is uncertain in this case as there is no clear evidence to show that her domicile of origin (Ruritania) was changed when she came to England merely to visit. To assume a domicile of choice one must assume residence in the country of choice and must have the present intention of remaining there permanently. Whether Gerda does intend to remain here permanently is unclear; the fact that she marries an Englishman does not necessarily prove that she has acquired a domicile of choice here. Hence her capacity may be governed by Ruritanian law. If it is, we are not told whether Ruritanian law differs from English law in its requirements that to have capacity to marry the parties must be male and female. However even if it does differ it seems that Herbert is domiciled in England and Wales in any event and therefore he would lack capacity to marry Gerda if she is not female, and consequently the marriage would be void.

We are told that Gerda had an operation when she was 14, giving her an artificial vagina. This suggests that what in fact happened was that Gerda underwent a sex change operation and, if this is the case, in the eyes of the English courts, she will be considered to be male. In *Corbett* v *Corbett* (1971) the respondent had undergone an operation for the removal of 'her' male genital organs and the construction of an artificial vagina. Ormrod J concluded that a person's biological sex is fixed at birth at the latest and cannot be subsequently changed by artificial means. That being the case, the respondent who was male at birth, was not a woman and therefore the marriage was void. The basis for the decision in Corbett was followed by the European Court of Human Rights in *Cossey* v *UK* (1990). If as seems to be the case, the same circumstances apply to Gerda, then she will be deemed to be male and the marriage to Herbert will be void. If so, Herbert is free to marry Janet immediately as he is deemed never to have married Gerda.

Even if this is not the case the marriage may be voidable if it has not been consummated owing to the incapacity of either party to consummate it (s12(a)); or owing to the wilful refusal of the respondent to consummate it (s12(b)). Non-consummation as such does not make the marriage voidable, but one of the grounds referred to in s12(a) or (b) must be proved. A party may rely on his or her own capacity, but cannot rely on his or her own wilful refusal. There is no time limit for proceedings under s12(a) or (b).

There seems to be no question of any wilful refusal in this case, but it may be that the difficulties experienced by Gerda amount to incapacity on her part. Therefore either Herbert or Gerda could petition for a decree of nullity on this ground.

A marriage is consummated as soon as the parties have sexual intercourse after the marriage. The intercourse must be 'ordinary and complete and not partial and imperfect': *D* v *A* (1845). If inability to consummate is to be relied on, it has been said at common law that it would apply only if the impotence is incurable. The term 'incurable' has been given an extended meaning however, and any impotence will be deemed incurable not only if it is wholly incapable of any remedy, but also if it can only be cured by an operation attended by danger or, if it is improbable that the operation will be successful, or the party refuses to undergo it: *S* v *S (orse C)* (1956). It seems that Gerda's situation might on these facts amount to incurable. Further, at common law, the impotence had to be in existence at the time of the marriage, and there had to be no practical possibility of the marriage being consummated at the date of the hearing: *Napier* v *Napier* (1915). The MCA 1973 makes no reference to incapacity at the date of the marriage, and it may be that if the incapacity arose after the marriage it could still be relied upon to annul the marriage. In this case however it appears that if Gerda's difficulties are deemed to amount to an incapacity, they will also be found to be in existence at the time of the marriage in any event.

In conclusion therefore it seems that Gerda's marriage to Herbert is void. However even if the ground under s11(c) cannot be made out, it may be voidable under s12(a). If it is void it will be viewed as if it never existed and Herbert will be free to marry Janet at this time. If it is merely voidable however, Herbert must obtain a decree absolute of nullity before he will be able to marry Janet.

Turning now to her marriage in 1989 to Ian, it is noted that this ceremony took place in Ruritania, whose laws allow polyandry, that is the plurality of husbands. As stated earlier, it is not clear whether Gerda has acquired a domicile of choice in England and Wales. If she has, her capacity to marry is governed by the laws of England and Wales. Therefore if her marriage to Herbert is deemed void, as is likely, then it is as if it never occurred and technically she is free to marry again without the necessity of obtaining a decree of nullity. However if Gerda is indeed male, then any marriage to another man (that is Ian here) will be void.

In any event if Gerda is domiciled in England the marriage to Ian may be void for another reason, namely that the marriage is a polygamous one entered into outside England and Wales (s11(d)), and for the purposes of this section a marriage may be polygamous although at its inception neither party has any spouse additional to the other. Polygamous marriages celebrated abroad, between persons whose country of domicile gives then capacity to enter into such unions, are recognised as valid in this country: *Radwan* v *Radwan (No 2)* (1972). Thus if Gerda is still domiciled in Ruritania, as Ian seems to be, the marriage will prima facie be valid here as long as both have capacity to marry according to Ruritanian law (that is as cousins, a relationship that is allowed in this country, Marriage (Enabling) Act 1960), and if they have complied with the formalities required by Ruritanian law. However if Gerda is domiciled in this country at the time of the marriage it may be deemed void on the basis that she lacks capacity to enter into such a union.

It must be noted however that the marriage must be actually polygamous or potentially polygamous. In *Hussain* v *Hussain* (1982) a husband domiciled in England married in Pakistan a wife domiciled in Pakistan. Under that form of marriage the husband was permitted to take a second wife during the subsistence of the marriage but the wife was not permitted to marry a second husband. It was held by the Court of Appeal that a marriage contracted abroad in a country which allowed polygamy was only potentially polygamous and thus void if at least one of the spouses had capacity to marry a second spouse during the subsistence of the marriage. As the husband could not, according to the law of his domicile, contract a valid marriage when he was already lawfully married, and the wife by Pakistan law could not marry during the subsistence of the marriage, the marriage could never become polygamous and it was therefore not void under s11(d) MCA 1973. So if Gerda is domiciled in England and Wales at the time of her marriage to Ian then she lacks capacity to take a second spouse during the subsistence of a first marriage. However the laws of Ruritania only allow polyandry which suggests that only a wife can take further husbands during the subsistence of a marriage and it seems that a husband cannot take further wives. Therefore, applying the principle in *Hussain* v *Hussain* to these facts, it seems that if Gerda does have an English domicile, the marriage will not be actually or potentially polygamous, because Gerda will lack capacity to take further spouses during the subsistence of any existing marriage according to English law, which governs her capacity to marry, and Ian, who appears to have a domicile in Ruritania and is therefore governed by Ruritanian law in this respect, does not appear to have the capacity either to take further spouses during the subsistence of any existing marriage. It seems therefore that the marriage will not be void under s11(d).

If Gerda's marriage to Herbert is not void, because her operation at 14 was not a sex change operation, but is at the most voidable, and if it has not been voided at the time of her marriage to Ian, then if she has an English domicile her second marriage, to Ian, will be bigamous under s11(b) and will be void. If her domicile is Ruritanian, technically both parties would have capacity to enter into this union. However it is suggested by Professor Bromley that English law will recognise several polygamous unions so long as they are all of that character. However, if, as here, there is a monogamous union, it would be incongruous to recognise that marriage and its monogamous character which means that the marriage is between a man and a woman, to the exclusion of all others, and yet accept a subsequent marriage as valid during the subsistence of the monogamous union, even though by the law of the parties' domicile

17

it is valid. Therefore, having recognised the first marriage as valid, the second will be deemed void in English jurisdiction, and in these circumstances the laws of a party's domicile will not necessarily govern their capacity to marry.

It may be however that the marriage is voidable under s12(c) MCA 1973, namely that either party to the marriage did not validly consent to it, in consequence of duress, mistake, unsoundness of mind or otherwise. In this case there appears to be evidence that Gerda did not validly consent to the marriage due to duress arising from Ian's threats to her, such threats being due to the threat to him from the new regime in Ruritania.

In *Szechter* v *Szechter* (1971) it was stated by Sir Jocylin Simon P when giving the test for lack of consent due to duress, that 'it must ... be proved that the will of one of the parties thereto has been overborne by genuine and reasonably held fear caused by threat of immediate danger (for which the party himself is not responsible) to life, limb or liberty, so that the constraint destroys the reality of consent'. In that case the petitioner, who was a Polish national, was arrested and after 14 months interrogation and detention in appalling conditions was sentenced to three years imprisonment. Her health deteriorated rapidly and she felt it unlikely that she would survive in prison, or that if she did, she would be re-arrested immediately after her release. The respondent was to be allowed to emigrate from Poland and, in order to effect the petitioner's release, he divorced his wife and married the petitioner. All the parties reached England, where the petitioner brought proceedings for nullity to enable the respondent and his wife to remarry. It was held that the marriage was voidable applying the test referred to above. Whether there is a sufficient degree of fear to vitiate the party's consent is a question of fact in each case. If a party is more susceptible to pressure brought to bear on him or her than another person might be, the marriage might still be annulled even though a person of ordinary courage and resilience would not have yielded to it: *Scott* v *Sebright* (1886). It seems that the court will not necessarily apply the test of a threat to life, limb or liberty too literally. In *Hirani* v *Hirani* (1983) Ormrod LJ thought that when giving the *Szechter* test Sir Jocylin Simon P was merely contrasting a disagreeable situation with one that constituted a real threat and he went on to say, 'the crucial question in these cases ... is whether the threats, pressure or whatever it is, is such as to destroy the reality of consent and overbears the will of the individual.' In that case it was held that a girl who was wholly dependant on her parents and who was forced into a marriage with a man neither she nor her parents had ever seen, on threat that she would be turned out of the home if she did not go through with the marriage, had not validly consented to the marriage due to duress. It seems therefore that although there may not literally be a threat to Gerda's life, limb or liberty as a result of the pressure put on her by Ian, if it does overbear her will, it could be deemed to be duress applying the *Hirani* test. Similarly Ian may be deemed to be suffering duress as well in view of his unpopularity with the regime in Ruritania and the dangers that may imply so far as his personal safety and liberty are concerned.

It was stated in *Buckland* v *Buckland* (1967), however, that the fear must arise from some external circumstances for which the party is not himself responsible, and whether this would affect Gerda's position particularly in view of the nature of Ian's threats, is doubtful. Professor Bromley suggests that the rule is incorrectly expressed and he refers to *Griffith* v *Griffith* (1944) which stated that the fear must be unjustly imposed. Therefore it could not be justly imposed if the party was not responsible for the events which gave rise to the threat, but it does not follow that it will be justly imposed if he was responsible.

It seems therefore that either Ian or Gerda could petition for a decree of nullity under s12(c), but it must be done within three years of the marriage (s13(2) MCA 1973). However it should be noted that Ian could not rely on his own threats to Gerda to petition on the basis of her lack of consent as he will probably fall under the provisions of s13(1) MCA 1973, namely that with knowledge that it was open to him to have the marriage voided (that is he must know it is a ground for nullity), he so conducted himself in relation to the respondent (Gerda) as to lead her reasonably to believe that he would not seek to do so (such an inference could arise from his marriage to her), and that it would be unjust to her to grant the decree.

If the marriage between Gerda and Ian is merely voidable, Ian must obtain a decree of nullity before he will be free to marry Kate.

If the marriage between Gerda and Herbert was voidable, and as there appears to have been no proceedings by either of them to annul the marriage prior to her second marriage in 1981, the question arises as to whether that second marriage could be void for another reason, namely that it is bigamous.

Under s11(b) MCA 1973 a marriage will be void if at the time of that marriage either party was already lawfully married to someone else. If Gerda was domiciled in England and Wales at the time of her marriage to Ian, then it is void because even though it is conducted abroad, she lacks capacity according to lex domicili as she is already married to Herbert: *Baindall* v *Baindall* (1946). The situation is less clear if Gerda was domiciled in Ruritania at the time of her marriage to Ian. Her marriage to Herbert will be deemed to be monogamous as the character of the union is determined by lex loci celebrationis and any marriage celebrated in England must be monogamous at its inception. It seems that English law will recognise the validity of a second marriage during the subsistence of the first but only if both marriages are polygamous. Thus as her first marriage to Herbert is monogamous according to English law she is unable to contract the second marriage during the subsistence of the first despite the fact that that second marriage is conducted in Ruritania and that she is domiciled in that country. So, for Ian's purposes, he will be free to marry Kate at this time if Gerda's marriage to Herbert was voidable as her subsequent marriage to him would fall under s11(b) MCA 1973. To conclude therefore, Ian's marriage to Gerda may be void on the grounds that if her previous marriage to Herbert was not void, then her marriage to Ian would fall under s11(b). If Gerda's previous marriage to Herbert was void then technically she is free to marry Ian, subject to the problem created by the doubt as to her sex. In any event the marriage may be voidable under s12(c) and if so a decree of nullity will have to be obtained before Ian will be free to marry Kate.

Finally it should be stressed that in the absence of fear or duress, if an intention can be shown by the parties to contract a marriage even though it is only for a limited purpose, such as in this case to enable Ian to leave Ruritania and to enter this country, the marriage will be unimpeachable and will be deemed to be valid: *Silver* v *Silver* (1958).

Question 4

Anthea and Bob, aged 16 and 19 respectively, went through a ceremony of marriage at the head office of the 'Peace and Purity Church'. No formalities were required by the church, which is located on the thirtieth floor of an office block in Manchester. Anthea had not told her parents that she was getting married.

After the ceremony, the couple spent a weekend in a hotel. There were repeated attempts to consummate the marriage, but Bob was nervous because the bed creaked and the hotel walls were thin and he failed to penetrate Anthea for more than two seconds. His confidence was damaged and he has refused to attempt to consummate again until he receives counselling.

Clarissa, Bob's counsellor, advised him to undergo a course of sex therapy with her, during which they fell in love and began a sexual relationship. Anthea, who became suspicious and believed Bob was cured, asked Bob to attempt to consummate the marriage. Bob found he was unable to have intercourse with her and asked her to wait until he has further therapy.

Anthea, who is still in love with Bob, but depressed, wants to know whether the marriage can be annulled.

University of London LLB Examination
(for External Students) Family Law June 1991 Q1

General comment

This is an unusual question in that it concerns nullity alone and it was thought that this type of question, testing one area of the syllabus only, was a thing of the past. The question raises an issue on formalities with regard to the void grounds of nullity which has not been examined in recent years. However, the remainder of the question relates to non-consummation, a tried and tested examination topic, and so should hold no surprises for the well prepared student.

Skeleton solution

- Consider void marriages - s11(a) MCA 1973 - failure to comply with formalities. Query whether the civil preliminaries have been complied with; thereafter discuss whether the place of celebration is a 'registered building'.

- Anthea's age must be discussed and following on from that the question of whether her parents' lack of consent would also make the marriage void.

- Deal with the voidable grounds - s12(a) and (b) MCA 1973. Consider if the marriage has been consummated.

- On the basis that it has not, consider incapacity - define and discuss psychological defects. Also consider if the incapacity must be in existence at the time of the celebration of the marriage.

- Next consider wilful refusal to consummate - define and consider whether Bob is in fact refusing to consummate - refer to the attempts to consummate during the honeymoon and subsequently. Query his motives for asking Anthea to delay any further attempt to consummate until he received further therapy.

Suggested solution

For a marriage celebrated after 31 July 1971 to be annulled, one of the grounds set out in s11 or s12 Matrimonial Causes Act 1973 (hereinafter MCA 1973), which deal with void and voidable marriages respectively, must be made out. A void marriage is deemed never to have existed and any decree is merely declaratory. A voidable marriage is in all respects a valid marriage until a decree of nullity is pronounced.

Under s11(a) MCA 1973 a marriage will be void if the parties have failed to comply with the requirements as to the formation of the marriage. All marriages, other than those conducted in the Church of England, must be preceded by preliminary formalities which are designed to give notice of the intended marriage and therefore to allow objections to be made. The usual procedure, which includes giving notice to the Superintendent Registrar of the registration district(s) where the parties have resided for the previous seven days, and thereafter the notice of the intended marriage being displayed in the Superintendent Registrar's office for 21 days, leads to the issue of the Superintendent Registrar's certificate, which authorises the solemnisation of the marriage within three months from the day when notice was entered in the marriage notice book.

We are told that the church required no formalities to be fulfilled prior to the marriage ceremony. If this means that Anthea and Bob did not fulfil the civil preliminaries required under the Marriage Acts 1949-1986 and therefore that they did not obtain a Superintendent Registrar's certificate or other licence, then the marriage will be void for lack of formality.

There are two other problems with regard to formalities to be discussed on these facts. The certificate, if obtained, will state where the marriage is to take place. Normally this must be a registered building in the district where one of the parties resides. A registered building must be a 'separate building' which is a 'place of meeting for religious worship' (s41(1) Marriage Act 1949). In *R v Registrar-General, ex parte Segerdal* (1970) Lord Denning stated that religious worship involved reverence or veneration of God or a supreme being and that the 'place of meeting' meant a place where people came as a congregation to do reverence to a deity.

Anthea and Bob marry at the church's head office which is sited in an office block. It may be therefore that it is not to be construed as a place of meeting for religious worship and it may not be a registered building under the Marriage Acts. Although it is possible for a marriage to be authorised outside a register office, Anglican church or registered place of worship under a Registrar General's licence, such a licence is only available where there is evidence that one of the persons to be married is seriously ill and is not expected to recover and that he/she cannot be moved to a place where the marriage could be solemnised under the Marriage Act 1949.

This exemption will not apply to Anthea and Bob and therefore if the church's head office is not a registered building under the Marriage Act 1949 the marriage will be void for want of formality on this basis also.

The second problem referred to relates to Anthea's age and the obvious lack of parental consent to her marriage. Being 16 Anthea is of the legal age to get married. However, between the ages of 16 and 18 a party to the marriage requires the consent of his/her parents to the marriage. This defect will not render the marriage void if it was conducted pursuant to a common licence or a Superintendent Registrar's certificate (s48(1) Marriage Act 1949). So if the other problems referred to above do not apply, the lack of parental consent is unlikely to render the marriage void on its own. It seems however that Anthea and Bob's marriage is void for lack of formality in that the civil preliminaries were not complied with, the ceremony took place in a place which is not a designated registered building, and the required parental consent is absent.

Consideration must also be given to whether the marriage is voidable under s12(a) or (b) MCA 1973 on the basis that it has not been consummated, due to either the incapacity of either party to consummate it (s12(a)), or the wilful refusal of the respondent (s12(b)). A marriage is consummated as soon as the parties have sexual intercourse that is 'ordinary and complete and not partial and imperfect' (D v A (1845)) after the marriage. We are told that Bob was unable to penetrate Anthea for more than two seconds on the occasions that sexual intercourse was attempted on the honeymoon, since which time it has been attempted, unsuccessfully only once it seems. To fulfil the requirements of consummation there must be an erection and penetration for a reasonable length of time (R v R (1952)), although it is not necessary for either party to have an orgasm. It is submitted therefore that the attempted sexual intercourse on the honeymoon will not amount to consummation.

The next question to consider is whether the non-consummation is due to incapacity on the part of Bob, or his wilful refusal. To satisfy the requirements of the incapacity, it must be shown that Bob's problem is permanent and incurable which has been held to mean not only that it is incapable of remedy, but also that it can be cured only by an operation which is dangerous, or which has little likelihood of success or where the respondent refuses to undergo the treatment (S v S (1956)). The incapacity does not have to relate to a physical defect; a psychological impotence may also suffice. Further, incapacity can be made out in a situation where the party suffering from the incapacity is capable of having intercourse with other partners but not with his or her spouse (G v M (1885)); (G v G (1924)).

It is not clear whether Bob's problem can be classified as permanent and incurable and Anthea would be advised that the courts have shown a willingness to await the outcome of treatment to decide whether the defect complained of should be so viewed (S v S (1963)).

A further consideration with regard to incapacity relates to the point whether the incapacity must be in existence at the time of the marriage, or whether a supervening incapacity as appears to apply in Bob's case where the problem seemingly arose during the honeymoon, will suffice. It was a requirement of the common law, on which the current law of nullity is based, that the incapacity exist at the time of the celebration of the marriage. The codification of the law was not intended to effect any change. However the wording of the statute makes no reference to the fact that the incapacity must be in existence at the time of the marriage. It may be therefore that a supervening incapacity will suffice, but the point is unclear.

Turning now to wilful refusal to consummate the marriage, this is defined as 'a settled and definite decision ... without just excuse' (*Horton* v *Horton* (1947)), not to consummate. It is submitted that this ground cannot be made out on these facts because Bob has attempted to have sexual intercourse with Anthea on several occasions. Although the last occasion occurred after he had been able to have sexual relations with Clarissa, there is no evidence that when Bob attempted to have intercourse with Anthea he deliberately failed in the attempt. He has asked her to wait until he has further therapy before they attempt to consummate the marriage. Certainly if this is a genuine request on his part then the ground under s12(b) will fail because essentially Bob is prepared to consummate the marriage when his problem is resolved. If however, his request to wait is a ploy to allow him to continue his relationship with Clarissa then it is possible that this ground will now apply as it may be evidence that he has no intention to pursue a married life after all (*Ford* v *Ford* (1987)).

In conclusion it seems that the marriage is void under s11 MCA 1973 for lack of formality in relation to an apparent failure to comply with civil preliminaries and the question whether the church's head office is a registered building where marriages can take place within the law. The lack of consent on the part of Anthea's parents is unlikely to render the marriage void on its own although if the civil preliminaries have not been complied with, this also will be a problem.

With regard to voidable grounds the application of s12(a) and (b) MCA 1973 is questionable on these facts.

Question 5

Hector, aged 22, and Andromache, aged 27, who are both members of a small religious community, the Trojans, resident in southern England, were married in December 1989. Although they had had a casual sexual relationship prior to their marriage, they did not really wish to marry each other, but did so because it is customary for Trojans to marry and because the community elders threatened to ostracise them socially and financially if they did not marry.

The wedding took place in the customary place of worship of the community and was celebrated by a Trojan prelate. Andromache, however, refuses to have sexual relations with Hector because he has still not arranged the wedding breakfast that all Trojan grooms must provide before the community will consider the wedding ceremony to be complete.

Advise Andromache who would like to bring her marriage to an end, but who has told you that Trojans disapprove of divorce.

University of London LLB Examination
(for External Students) Family Law June 1992 Q4

General comment

The question requires consideration of the rules relating to termination of marriage by nullity and not by divorce because we are told that Trojans do not approve of divorce.

Skeleton solution

• Deal with s11 MCA 1973.

• Consider s12(a) and disregard s12(b).

• Next consider s12(c) - lack of consent.

• Bars under s13 MCA 1973.

Suggested solution

Andromache says that Trojans, the religious community of which she is a part, do not approve of divorce, so we will not advise her on ending her marriage by divorcing Hector. Instead we must decide whether the marriage between Andromache and Hector can be annulled.

For a marriage celebrated after 31 July 1971, annulment can only occur if a ground under s11 or s12 of the Matrimonial Causes Act (MCA) 1973 can be made out. Section 11 deals with void marriages and s12 with voidable marriages.

Under s11(a)(iii) MCA 1973 the marriage may be void on the ground that the parties have intermarried in disregard of the formal requirements.

Because the marriage was not a Church of England marriage, it will not be void on the grounds of non-publication of banns etc but instead it must comply with the requirements laid down by the Marriage Act 1949 for celebration of non-Anglican marriages. It must have been celebrated pursuant to a superintendent registrar's certificate with a licence and in a registered building.

The marriage took place in the customary place of worship of the community and was celebrated by a Trojan prelate. The Marriage Act 1949 states that the marriage must take place at a building registered by the Registrar General as a place of meeting for religious worship and be conducted by a minister of religion concerned, namely a person authorised to carry out marriages, in public and in the presence of two or more witnesses. Therefore, provided that the above requirements have been complied with, the marriage will not be void. And in any event the Marriage Act 1949 specifically enacts that a marriage shall not be rendered void if the registered building in which the parties were married had not been certified as a place of worship.

Next consideration should be given to s12 MCA 1973 which sets out the grounds upon which a marriage may be deemed voidable. Under s12(a) the marriage may be voidable on the ground 'that the marriage has not been consummated owing to the incapacity of either party to consummate it'. Under s12(b) a marriage may be voidable owing to the wilful refusal of the respondent to consummate it. A marriage is consummated as soon as the parties have sexual intercourse that is ordinary and complete (*D* v *A* (1845)) after the marriage.

Andromache and Hector had sexual relations before the marriage but this does not amount to consummation; there must be intercourse after the marriage: *Dredge* v *Dredge* (1947).

Section 12(a) does not appear to be relevant here because it is not due to the incapacity of either party that the marriage has not been consummated but instead due to Andromache's wilful refusal to consummate.

A person may not, however, petition on his/her own refusal to consummate, therefore in this instance Andromache may not rely on this ground in respect of her own refusal to consummate the marriage. However she may be able to argue that Hector has wilfully refused to consummate the marriage.

Wilful refusal connotes 'a settled and definite decision come to without just cause' and the whole history of the marriage may be looked at (per Lord Jowitt LC in *Horton* v *Horton* (1947)).

Following the decision in *Kaur* v *Singh* (1972) Hector's refusal without just excuse to make arrangements for the wedding breakfast could amount to wilful refusal to consummate the marriage.

Alternatively, it may be possible for Andromache to argue that she had not given proper consent to the marriage and it is provided that if either party to the marriage did not validly consent to it in consequence of duress, mistake, unsoundness of mind or otherwise, the marriage will be voidable: s12(c).

In this case there is evidence that both Andromache and Hector did not validly consent due to duress arising out of the fact that the community elders threatened to ostracise them socially and financially if they did not marry.

To decide whether the threats amounted to duress the following points should be considered. In the case of *Szechter* v *Szechter* (1970) Sir Jocelyn Simon P stated that 'It must ... be proved that the will of one of the parties thereto has been overborne by genuine and reasonably held fear caused by threat of immediate danger (for which the party himself is not responsible) to life, limb or liberty so that the constraint destroyed the reality of consent'.

Whether there is a sufficient degree of fear to vitiate consent is a question of fact in each case and if a party is more susceptible to pressure brought to bear on him than another person might be, the marriage may still be voidable: *Scott* v *Sebright* (1886). The court will not necessarily apply the test of threat to life, limb or liberty too literally as stated in *Hirani* v *Hirani* (1982) Ormrod J thought that in his test Sir Jocelyn Simon P was merely contrasting a disagreeable situation with one that constituted a real threat and he stated that 'the crucial question in these cases is whether the threats, pressure or whatever, is such as to destroy the reality of consent and overbears the will of the individual. In Hirani v Hirani a threat to turn a girl who was wholly dependent on her parents out of her home unless she married the man of her choice was sufficient to vitiate her consent and the marriage, making it voidable.

In this case there is no literal threat to life, limb or liberty, but it may be argued that the threat to ostracise them socially and financially was enough to override their true will because the threat of financial and social ruin may work as strongly as the threat of physical violence in some minds.

In these circumstances this seems to be satisfied and the marriage could be annulled.

Next we must consider whether Andromache can be barred from relying on this. Section 13(2) MCA 1973 states that proceedings for nullity under s12(c), (d), (e) or (f) must be instituted within three years of the marriage. Andromache and Hector were married in December 1989 and it is now June 1992 therefore Andromache must petition for nullity before December 1992 as there does not appear to be a ground on these facts to warrant an application for leave to institute proceedings after the three year period.

3 DIVORCE

3.1   Introduction

The first modern law relating to divorce dates from 1937. The grounds for divorce were fault based eg adultery, cruelty and desertion and had to be proved beyond reasonable doubt - the criminal standard of proof. The term 'matrimonial offence' characterised divorce grounds as being quasi-criminal in nature. By the late sixties the need for reform had become apparent. It was argued that the divorce laws did not accord with social reality and the quasi-criminal nature of the proceedings resulting in unnecessary bitterness between the divorcing couple. Two reports published at this time, *Putting Asunder* (presented by a group appointed by the Archbishop of Canterbury) and *Reform of the Grounds of Divorce The Field of Choice* (Law Commission Report No 6 (1966), Cmnd 3123), paved the way for reform. The objectives of the reforms were twofold:

a) To buttress rather than to undermine the stability of marriage;

b) To enable the empty shell of marriage to be destroyed with the minimum of bitterness, distress and humiliation.

The Divorce Reform Act of 1969 made irretrievable breakdown of marriage the sole ground for divorce. The breakdown had to be established by one of five 'facts' which included two years living apart with consent and five years living apart without consent. These are the no fault grounds. However adultery, desertion and behaviour were retained as evidence of irretrievable breakdown alongside the no fault grounds and it remains possible to obtain a divorce on proof of, for example, behaviour which the petitioner cannot reasonably be expected to tolerate. The law is now contained in the Matrimonial Causes Act of 1973.

In 1977 procedural changes were introduced. Undefended divorces are now dealt with by the District Judge. The District Judge examines the petition and a supporting affidavit and, if satisfied that the contents are proved, will issue and file a certificate to that effect. The decree nisi is then issued in open court at a later date. The result has been that the 'ability of the court to carry out its statutory duty to enquire into the facts alleged is greatly circumscribed' (see the Booth Report - Report of the Matrimonial Causes Procedure Committee 1985) and District Judges do little more than rubber stamp petitions. In some respects this is tantamount to divorce on demand. Alongside these procedural changes, parties are increasingly encouraged to resolve disputes over the custody of children and over maintenance and property themselves. This process, referred to as conciliation, has as its objective the establishment of a settlement which involves both parties and which will therefore result in less future hostility between them.

The present law is again considered to be out of tune with the realities of practice. The Law Commission have published both a discussion paper on the ground for divorce in which they undertake a comprehensive review of the law and final recommendations (see chapter 4: *Divorce law reform*).

3.2 Key points

a) *One year ban*

Under the Matrimonial Causes Act (MCA) 1973 a petition could not be presented within three years of the marriage unless the petitioner suffered 'exceptional hardship' or where the respondent was 'exceptionally depraved'. Section 1 Matrimonial and Family Proceedings Act 1984 replaced s3 of the MCA 1973, putting an absolute bar on the presentation of a petition within one year of the celebration of marriage.

b) *The ground for divorce*

A petition for divorce may be presented by either party to a marriage on the ground that the marriage has broken down irretrievably - s1(1) MCA 1973. The petitioner must satisfy the court of one of five facts set out in s1(2). It is important to emphasise that there is no causal connection between s1(1) and s1(2). In other words the petitioner has to prove two things: firstly that the marriage has irretrievably broken down and secondly that one of the facts in s1(2) is satisfied. The petitioner does not have to prove that the marriage has broken down because of one of the facts in s1(2). (See *Buffery* v *Buffery* [1988] 2 FLR 365.) Note that the ability of the court to inquire into the facts alleged is very limited in undefended cases. This is especially so as regards a petition based upon the respondent's adultery. Since October 1991 the petitioner does not have to cite the co-respondent (the person with whom it is alleged the respondent has committed adultery) even if she knows the identity of the co-respondent. It suffices for the petitioner to state that the identity of the person with whom the respondent is known to the petitioner but the petitioner prefers not to cite that person as co-respondent.

c) *The 'five facts' - s1(2) Matrimonial Causes Act 1973*

i) Section 1(2)(a): That the respondent has committed adultery and the petitioner finds it intolerable to live with the respondent.

• The adultery must be voluntary. This clearly excludes rape.

- Sexual intercourse is the penetration by the male of the female genitalia: *Dennis* v *Dennis* [1955] 2 All ER 51.

- The definition of adultery presupposes a sexual relationship with a person of the opposite sex. The respondent's homosexuality may be sufficient for a petition based on s1(2)(b).

- The standard of proof is high: *Serio* v *Serio* (1983) 4 FLR 756. This will by and large only be an issue in defended cases.

- The Act is not clear on whether the intolerability must arise from the act of adultery or whether it can be independent of it. The Court of Appeal took the latter view in *Cleary* v *Cleary* [1974] 1 WLR 73 and although some doubts were cast on this interpretation in *Carr* v *Carr* [1974] 1 WLR 1534 this is now the established position.

- The petitioner will not be permitted to rely on this ground where the parties have lived together for a period or periods exceeding six months following disclosure to the petitioner of the adultery. The disregard of a shorter period is intended to allow the parties to attempt reconciliation: s2 MCA 1973; *Biggs* v *Biggs* [1977] 1 All ER 20.

ii) Section 1(2)(b): That the respondent has behaved in such a way that the petitioner cannot reasonably be expected to live with the respondent.

- The test is whether a right thinking person would come to the conclusion that this husband has behaved in such a way that this wife cannot reasonably be expected to live with him taking account the whole of the circumstances and the characters and personalities of the parties.

  There exists therefore both a subjective and objective element: *Livingstone-Stallard* v *Livingstone-Stallard* [1974] 2 All ER 776; *Buffery* v *Buffery* [1988] 2 FLR 365.

- A wide range of behaviour is included

  Financial responsibility: *Carter-Fea* v *Carter-Fea* [1987] Fam Law 131.

  Physical violence: *Bergin* v *Bergin* [1983] 1 All ER 905.

  Alcoholism coupled with violence: *Ash* v *Ash* [1972] 1 All ER 582.

  Acts which trivial in themselves were 'a constant atmosphere of criticism, disapproval and boorish behaviour': *Livingstone-Stallard* v *Livingstone-Stallard* (above); *O'Neill* v *O'Neill* [1975] 3 All ER 289.

- Some forms of behaviour will fail. It must depend on all the circumstances: *Birch* v *Birch* [1992] Fam Law 290.

  Mere lack of affection: *Pheasant* v *Pheasant* [1972] 1 All ER 587.

  Extreme moodiness: *Richards* v *Richards* [1972] 3 All ER 695.

Unsatisfactory sexual performance: *Dowden* v *Dowden* (1977) 8 Fam Law 106.

• Involuntary behaviour. It is not necessary to prove intention and the fact that the respondent is suffering from some illness is not necessarily a bar to a decree.

Manic depressive illness: *Katz* v *Katz* [1972] 3 All ER 219.

Epilepsy: *Thurlow* v *Thurlow* [1976] Fam 32.

It is a question of fact and degree in each case: *Richards* v *Richards* [1972] 3 All ER 695.

• Any period of less than six months cohabitation after the last incident relied upon in the petition shall be disregarded for establishing the reasonableness of continued cohabitation: s2(3) MCA 1973.

A longer period will be disregarded if the petition had no alternative but to remain with the respondent.

iii) Section 1(2)(c): That the respondent has deserted the petitioner for a period of at least two years immediately preceding the presentation of the petition.

• It is only necessary to rely on this ground where the respondent will not consent to a petition based on two years separation, there are no other grounds for divorce and the petitioner does not want to wait for the expiry of the five year period under s1(2)(e).

• The fact of separation. There must be a complete withdrawal from cohabitation.

Desertion is a withdrawal from a state of affairs rather than a place: *Milligan* v *Milligan* [1941] 2 All ER 62.

Separation can be complete under the same roof: *Naylor* v *Naylor* [1961] 2 All ER 129; *Hopes* v *Hopes* [1948] 2 All ER 920.

• Intention to desert. Usually inferred from the fact of departure. An involuntary desertion can constitute desertion once the intention is formed and communicated: *Beeken* v *Beeken* [1948] P 302; *Nutley* v *Nutley* [1970] 1 All ER 410.

Desertion will continue through involuntary separation if the intention had been formed beforehand.

Where the respondent suffers from mental illness the question is whether he is capable of forming the necessary intention to desert.

• Petitioner does not consent.

Consent can be expressed - a separation agreement - or implied, but relief at departure is not consent: *Harriman* v *Harriman* [1909] P 123.

Consent after the de facto separation can bring desertion to an end: *Pizey* v *Pizey* [1961] P 101.

Consent to separation can be for a limited period in which case desertion will begin at the end of the period: *Shaw* v *Shaw* [1939] P 269.

The refusal of a reasonable offer of reconciliation can result in desertion beginning: *Gallagher* v *Gallagher* [1965] 2 All ER 967.

- No just cause to leave.

  There are few recent authorities on this point but it is logical to assume that it must be lined to behaviour in s1(2)(b).

  Where the petitioner's conduct is relied upon it must be 'grave and weighty' and not merely the wear and tear of married life: *Quoraishi* v *Quoraishi* [1985] FLR 780.

- No period of six months cohabitation shall break the continuity of separation for the two year period but any period of cohabitation shall not count towards that two year period.

- The termination of desertion. Factors include an agreement to live apart, a decree of judicial separation, the resumption of cohabitation for a prolonged period and by the deserting spouse making a genuine offer to resume cohabitation.

- Constructive desertion. This is conduct by one spouse which has the effect of driving the other spouse out. Such behaviour would almost always give rise to a petition based on s1(2)(b).

iv) Section 1(2)(d): That the parties to the marriage have lived apart for a continuous period of at least two years immediately preceding the presentation of the petition and the respondent consents to a decree being granted.

- Living apart. Section 1(6) states that the parties will not be living apart if they are living in the same household. The term household is not defined.

  There must be recognition by at least one of the parties that the marriage is at an end but oddly this need not be communicated to the other: *Santos* v *Santos* [1972] 2 All ER 246.

  The parties can live apart in the same household: *Mouncer* v *Mouncer* [1972] 1 All ER 289; *Fuller* v *Fuller* [1973] 2 All ER 650.

- Consent. Consent must be freely given and may be withdrawn at any time up to the decree nisi. There must be capacity to give consent.

- No account will be taken of any period or periods not exceeding six months during which the parties resumed living together.

- The day of separation is excluded for the purpose of calculating the two year period.

v) Section 1(2)(e): That the parties to the marriage have lived apart for a continuous period of at least five years immediately preceding the presentation of the petition.

- Interpretations of living apart are the same as considered above.

vi) Financial protection to petitions based on s1(2)(d) and s1(2)(e).

- Under s10 the courts have powers to consider on application the respondent's financial position on divorce and to delay the decree absolute unless satisfied that the financial provision is fair and reasonable or the best that can be made in the circumstances.

- Section 10(3) directs the court to consider all the circumstances including the age, health, conduct, earning capacity, financial resources and financial obligations of each of the parties and includes regard to the financial position of the respondent after the death of the petitioner: *Lombardi* v *Lombardi* [1973] 3 All ER 625.

- The sole purpose is to delay the decree absolute until a financial settlement is reached. The court can refuse the application if there are circumstances which make the granting of the decree desirable and has obtained an undertaking that satisfactory provision will be made: *Grigson* v *Grigson* [1974] 1 All ER 478.

vii) Refusal of a decree after five years separation.

- Under s5 of the Act the respondent can oppose the grant of the petition on the grounds that dissolution of the marriage would result in grave financial or other hardship and that it would be wrong in all the circumstances to dissolve the marriage.

- Cases on financial hardship have focused almost exclusively on the loss of pension rights particularly where the parties are approaching retirement and the marriage has lasted many years: *Le Marchant* v *Le Marchant* [1977] 1 WLR 559.

- Other forms of hardship alleged have relied on the social stigma attached to divorce within certain cultures. None have been successful: *Banik* v *Banik* [1973] 3 All ER 45; *Parghi* v *Parghi* (1973) 117 SJ 582.

- Grave in this context has its ordinary meaning. Accordingly young petitioners will find it hard to establish grave financial hardship. *Mathias* v *Mathias* [1972] 3 WLR 201.

- The likely refusal of the petition can result in an improved offer of a financial settlement to offset any loss: *Le Marchant* v *Le Marchant* [1977] 1 WLR 559.

The compensation must however offset the loss: *Julian* v *Julian* (1972) 116 SJ 763.

- The court will consider the conduct of the parties, the interests of the parties and any children or other persons concerned in deciding whether it would be wrong to dissolve the marriage.

d) *When do English courts have jurisdiction to grant divorces?*

A party can petition for divorce in an English court provided he or she brings herself within the requirements of s5 of the Domicile and Matrimonial Proceedings Act 1973. This section gives the court jurisdiction in two situations: firstly, if either party is 'domiciled' in England or Wales immediately prior to the presentation of the petition or, alternatively, if either party has been 'habitually resident' in England or Wales for a continuous period of 12 months immediately preceding the presentation of the petition.

Note:

i) Only one of the parties has to be domiciled or habitually resident.

ii) 'Habitual residence' is akin to semi-permanent residence; it is something more than being a mere visitor but rather less than permanent residence. If a wife accompanied her United States diplomat husband on, say, a three year posting to London she would be deemed 'habitually resident'.

In *Kapur* v *Kapur* [1985] Fam Law 22 it was held that habitual residence had the same meaning as 'ordinary residence' ie voluntary residence with a degree of settled purpose. In *Kapur* the petitioner was only in England while he was studying for his Bar examinations but was, on this test, held to be 'habitually resident' and entitled to petition for divorce in the English courts.

iii) 'Domicile' is of two types. Firstly, one acquires a domicile of origin at birth, namely the domicile of one's father. However one can change one's domicile of origin and obtain a domicile of choice. A domicile of choice is a state of mind. If one comes from a foreign country but intends to stay in England or Wales 'until the end of his days unless and until something happens to change one's mind', per Buckley LJ in *IRC* v *Bullock* [1976] 1 WLR 1178 at 1185, then one second after landing at Heathrow Airport one would be deemed to be 'domiciled' and eligible, therefore, to present a divorce petition in the English courts.

In assessing this intention a court would look at all the circumstances eg has a house been bought here, does s/he pay UK taxes, does s/he have a UK passport, has s/he married an English person, but no one factor is conclusive. It is a case of looking at all the evidence and deciding whether the petitioner has the requisite intention.

For example in *Cramer* v *Cramer* [1987] 1 FLR 116 a French woman met an English lecturer when he was on holiday in France. She returned to England with him and immediately tried to petition for divorce from her French

33

husband in the English courts. It was held that she could not establish sufficient intention to prove English domicile. She had left property in France and was still employed by her French employer. The court refused to accept that she had abandoned her domicile of origin in France and acquired a domicile of choice in England.

iv) It should be emphasised that even if one is not 'domiciled' one need only wait 12 months to satisfy the habitual residence qualification.

v) Finally, note that an English court has jurisdiction to hear an application for ancillary relief even if the divorce was obtained abroad: see Part III of the Matrimonial and Family Proceedings Act 1984.

3.3   Recent cases

The scarcity of any recent case law is indicative of the ease with which divorce is obtained and emphasises the point that divorce is now largely an administrative process. But see *Buffery* v *Buffery* [1982] 2 FLR 365 and *Birch* v *Birch* [1992] Fam Law 290.

3.4   Analysis of questions

Problem questions are fairly standard, requiring students to analyse a given situation and advise on the applicability of the 'five facts' to establish irretrievable breakdown. Care should be taken to apply the law on divorce relevantly and avoiding the temptation to simply provide the examiner with a simple summary of the five facts. Questions invariably require a detailed analysis of one or two of the facts in support of irretrievable breakdown.

Students will often be expected to advise not only on the divorce implications but also on maintenance, either during marriage or on divorce.

Occasionally examiners may ask a fairly straightforward essay question which requires students to review the law on divorce and comment critically on whether it has achieved its original objective.

3.5   Questions

Question 1

Arthur and Betty married in 1978 and have two children. Early in 1982 Arthur developed a mental illness, as a result of which he erroneously believed that his wife was having an affair with their bank manager. After many heated arguments, which caused distress to the children as well as to Betty, Betty announced that she was leaving home, taking the children with her, and that she was not going to return. Arthur replied that he was glad she was leaving, as he had never wanted to live with an adulteress, but that he was sorry to see the children go and that he would pay Betty £40 a week for their upkeep. Betty left home a few days later and went to stay with her mother.

Arthur was admitted to a mental hospital a few months later but continued to pay Betty £40 a week out of capital he possessed. Betty visited him occasionally both out of a genuine concern for his health and because she was anxious that he should keep up the payments.

In April 1987 Arthur met Celia, a new nurse at the mental hospital, whom he wishes to marry. Betty does not want a divorce because she thinks Arthur will stop paying her the money if he marries Celia.

Advise Arthur whether he can obtain a divorce from Betty.

Adapted from University of London LLB Examination
(for External Students) Family Law June 1987 Q2

General comment

This is a fairly standard question in that the topic is regularly examined. The second part of the original question, dealing with financial provision during marriage, is covered in chapter 5: *Rights and obligations during marriage.*

Skeleton solution

- Discuss the one ground for divorce under s1 MCA 1973 and thereafter discount, in outline detail, the facts under s1(2)(a), (b) and (d) MCA 1973.

- Section 1(2)(c) MCA 1973 will have to be discounted in a little more detail.

- Discuss in detail s1(2)(e) MCA 1973 - that is the physical and mental elements of separation; also discuss Betty's possible defence under s5 MCA 1973.

Suggested solution

There is only one ground for divorce, namely that the marriage has broken down irretrievably (s1(1) Matrimonial Causes Act 1973 (hereinafter MCA 1973)), and this must be evidenced by proof of one or more of the facts set out in s1(2)(a)-(e) MCA 1973: *Richards* v *Richards* (1972).

As it is made clear in the facts of the question that Betty has never had an affair with the bank manager or with anyone else, Arthur cannot rely on s1(2)(a) MCA 1973, namely that Betty has committed adultery and he finds it intolerable to live with her. Nor is there any evidence of behaviour on Betty's part which would lead the court to take the view that it is unreasonable to expect Arthur to live with her, and so make out a petition under s1(2)(b) MCA 1973. Further, even if Betty were in desertion which is unlikely on these facts, simple desertion cannot be evidence of behaviour under s1(2)(b): *Stringfellow* v *Stringfellow* (1976). It seems that it is Arthur's behaviour brought on by his mental illness, which is the cause of the breakdown of the marriage. However a petitioner cannot rely on his or her own behaviour under s1(2)(b).

Arthur may be able to base a petition for divorce on the fact that the parties appear to have been living separate and apart for a period of time, although the exact length of the separation is unclear. Arthur developed his mental illness early in 1982 and from that time on the marriage began to deteriorate and eventually Betty left the matrimonial home.

Under s1(2)(c) MCA 1973 a petition can be presented on the basis that the respondent has deserted the petitioner for a period exceeding two years immediately preceding the presentation of the petition. In this case it seems likely that the parties have lived apart for the relevant two years, but it is unlikely that all the other constituents of desertion can be made out against Betty. It must be shown that she intended to desert, that is to withdraw permanently from the marriage, that she had no just cause for doing so, and that she left without Arthur's consent. The fact that Arthur declared that he was glad Betty was leaving does not necessarily mean that he gave his consent to her departure, as such a reaction may be construed merely as an acceptance of a situation which he has no power to alter. When Betty left she may have intended to withdraw permanently from the marriage, and this intention may be continuing at this time. However it is unlikely that the court would find that she had no just cause for leaving Arthur in view of his groundless allegations of adultery which gave rise to arguments which distressed both Betty and the children: *Marsden* v *Marsden* (1968).

It seems therefore that Arthur would not be able to rely on s1(2)(c) MCA 1973 to divorce Betty and indeed he may be in constructive desertion, that is he may be deemed to have driven Betty away by his own behaviour, but even if this can be established, which is doubtful as Arthur may not have had the mental capacity to form the intention to desert, as with petitions under s1(2)(a) and (b) a petitioner cannot rely on his or her own misdeeds.

The only remaining facts which Arthur may seek to rely on are based on separation from Betty for specified periods. Section 1(2)(d) MCA 1973 provides that a petition may be presented on the basis that the parties have lived separate and apart for at least two years immediately preceding the presentation of the petition and the respondent (Betty) consents to the decree being granted. Clearly this fact cannot apply as Betty does not want a divorce and therefore will not give her consent to the decree. Without such consent the petition cannot be granted despite the fact that there may be a clear evidence that the marriage has irretrievably broken down and that the parties have lived separately for the relevant period: *Mason* v *Mason* (1972).

Therefore the only remaining fact is s1(2)(e) MCA 1973, namely that the parties have lived separate and apart for a continuous period of five years immediately preceding the presentation of the petition, in which case Betty's consent to the decree is not required.

Arthur must show that the parties have in fact been living apart for the preceding five years. This involves living apart in a physical and a mental sense. To establish the mental element it must be shown that at least one of the parties was treating the marriage as at an end for the five year period although it is not necessary for that party to communicate this fact to the other party: *Santos* v *Santos* (1972). From the facts of this case it seems that both parties regarded the marriage as dead from the time that Betty left, and so it seems that the mental element is satisfied.

Arthur must also show that the parties have lived apart in the physical sense for the relevant period. To establish physical separation it must be shown that the parties have lived in separate households for the five year period; in other words there must be a rejection of all the obligations of marriage, a cessation of cohabitation, and the test to be applied is whether there has been any sharing of a domestic life and whether one spouse has been providing matrimonial services for the other: *Mouncer* v *Mouncer* (1972); *Fuller* v *Fuller* (1973).

In this case Betty and Arthur have been living in separate houses since Betty left. Further it can be argued that there has been a complete cessation of a shared domestic life as Arthur's provision of maintenance will not be seen as a continuance of their domestic life in the required sense and Betty's occasional visits to the hospital, made out of concern for his health, and a desire to ensure the continuation of the maintenance payments cannot be said to represent a continuing common life or the performance of matrimonial services. The parties have lived completely separate lives since Betty left the home. They have not had sexual intercourse since that date and neither has performed the usual matrimonial services for the other. There has been no sharing of a common life in any form and therefore so long as this arrangement has been continuing for five years, that is that Betty left Arthur before June 1982, Arthur may present a petition for divorce under s1(2)(e) MCA 1973.

Betty could seek to oppose the petition by relying on the defence in s5 MCA 1973 which provides that a respondent may oppose the grant of a decree nisi under s1(2)(e) even though the fact relied upon has been proved satisfactorily, on the ground that the dissolution of the marriage will result in grave financial or other hardship to the respondent, and it would be wrong to dissolve the marriage in all the circumstances of the case. Both elements of the defence would have to be proved by Betty.

Section 5(2)MCA 1973 provides that in considering such an application, the court will have regard to all the circumstances of the case including the conduct of the parties and the interests of those parties and of any children and other persons concerned (for example Celia). Section 5(3) provides that for the purpose of this section, hardship shall include the loss of the chance of acquiring any benefit which the respondent might acquire if the marriage is not dissolved.

Betty will seek to show financial hardship in this case, but she would be advised that such hardship must arise from the *dissolution* of the marriage and not merely its breakdown. The hardship must be grave and this will be considered objectively in relation to the particular marriage and the circumstances in which the parties lived while it subsisted (*Talbot* v *Talbot* (1971)), and what matters is not whether Betty considers that she will suffer grave hardship, but whether ordinary people knowing all the facts of the case would think so.

The usual sort of financial loss relied upon in this defence is the loss of a pension entitlement. However there is no evidence relating to such a loss in this case. It seems that Betty's only fear is that Arthur will stop paying maintenance if he marries Celia. This is not a loss which properly can be said to arise out of the divorce itself and in any event Betty will be able to obtain financial orders under ss23 and 24 MCA 1973 for the provision of herself and the children in the divorce proceedings, and to enforce the same through the court process should Arthur default. Further there is no evidence to suggest that Arthur has been, or will be unreliable in respect of the maintenance payments. It seems therefore that a defence under s5 MCA 1973 will fail.

If Betty has genuine concern about her financial provision or divorce she can apply under s10 MCA 1973 for her financial situation to be considered before the decree nisi is made absolute.

Question 2

Eric and Fiona married in 1976. In 1979 Eric was severely injured in a car accident as a result of which he was paralysed from the waist down. He was in hospital for a year, during which time Fiona regularly visited him. He was then moved back to the matrimonial home, occupying a room which had been specially adapted for his needs. Fiona, who is a qualified nurse, cared for Eric while continuing to pursue her nursing career on a part-time basis at the local hospital. She considered that the marriage was effectively at an end but nevertheless she looked after him faithfully, dressing him and cooking for him. From June 1981 she occasionally slept with George, who was a surgeon at the hospital where she worked, but she repeatedly told him that she would not leave Eric for as long as he needed her help.

In January 1986 Fiona changed her mind and decided that it was hopeless to continue to look after Eric, and she now wants to divorce him in order to marry George. Eric does not want a divorce. He considers that he cannot do without Fiona's continued care and attention. Moreover, if there is a divorce, he argues that he will lose the benefit of the widower's occupational pension to which he would be entitled, should he survive Fiona.

a) Can Fiona obtain a divorce from Eric?

b) If Fiona obtains a divorce, can Eric obtain financial provision from Fiona? If he can, what sort of award, if any, might a court make?

University of London LLB Examination
(for External Students) Family Law June 1986 Q2

General comment

This is a relatively straightforward question on divorce and financial provision thereon. Part (a) is rather long and requires candidates to consider virtually all the facts in s1(2) MCA 1973, although not all in detail. Particular emphasis will be placed on s1(2)(b) and s1(2)(e) MCA 1973. Part (b) is a fairly typical question on financial provision on divorce and candidates are expected to refer to s25 MCA 1973 and apply the relevant factors therein to this case. A conclusion as to the probable order is difficult in view of the lack of information in the question. Financial provison following divorce is dealt with in chapter 7. Note that questions which require an examination of both divorce and financial provision in relation to the same facts are not uncommon.

Skeleton solution

a)   •   One ground for divorce under s1(1) MCA 1973, evidenced by one or more of the facts set out in s1(2) MCA 1973.

      •   Discount s1(2)(a), discuss s1(2)(b) with particular reference to behaviour arising out of illness, but note that there is no evidence of behaviour as such, so this fact is unreliable.

- Discount desertion under s1(2)(c), and separation for two years with consent from the respondent to the divorce under s1(2)(d) - as Eric will not consent.

- Discuss s1(2)(e) in detail - separation physical and mental elements - problems with both here, particularly physical separation.

- Also discuss defence under s5 MCA 1973 to s1(2)(e) divorce petition.

b) • Consider the orders that can be made - s23 and s24 MCA 1973.

- Discuss s25 MCA 1973 and apply to the facts of this case.

Suggested solution

a) There is only one ground for divorce, namely that the marriage has broken down irretrievably (s1(1) Matrimonial Causes Act 1973) (hereinafter MCA 1973) and this is evidenced by proof of one or more of the facts set out in s1(2)(a)-(e) MCA 1973: *Richards* v *Richards* (1972).

Although it is clear that Fiona has committed adultery with George, this fact will be inappropriate in this case, as Eric will not institute proceedings against her and a party cannot rely on their own adultery.

Under s1(2)(b) MCA 1973 a petition may be presented on the basis that the respondent has behaved in such a way that it is unreasonable to expect the petitioner to continue to live with the respondent. It is not the respondent's behaviour which must be shown to be unreasonable, but the prospect of continued cohabitation.

The test to be applied is both subjective and objective. It is objective in that it is for the court to decide whether Fiona can reasonably be expected to live with Eric, but in doing so, the court will take into account all the circumstances of the case including the history of the marriage, and the character and personality of the parties as well as their faults and attributes good and bad: *Livingstone-Stallard* v *Livingstone-Stallard* (1974); *Ash* v *Ash* (1972).

The whole history of the marriage will be considered by the court. It will not be necessary for Fiona to show that Eric is morally culpable for his behaviour, but the question is whether the facts are such that after making allowances for his disabilities and the temperaments of both parties the character and gravity of his behaviour is such that Fiona cannot reasonably be expected to live with him *Katz* v *Katz* (1972). The behaviour may be positive or negative and may: comprise a course of conduct (*Pheasant* v *Pheasant* (1972)) and in *Thurlow* v *Thurlow* (1975) the court indicated that a decree may be granted where there is no evidence of cruelty as such. The court must take into account the obligations of married life including the duty to accept and share the burdens of a spouse's illness, and it must consider the length of time the petitioner has had to bear these burdens, (in this case seven years) and the effect it has had on her health, and her capacity to bear the stresses imposed.

Fiona may be able to argue that she is no longer able to endure the strain of looking after Eric. However it must be noted that the MCA 1973 requires that Eric should have 'behaved' in such a way that Fiona can no longer be expected to live with him and in *Katz* the court held that behaviour amounted to '... acts or conduct by one which affects the other...'. We are given no information as to any behaviour on Eric's part which may satisfy the requirements of s1(2)(b), and so without further evidence this fact may be unreliable in these circumstances.

The only other fact that Fiona could perhaps rely on would be based on her allegation that the parties have been living separately for the last few years. Section 1(2)(c) MCA 1973, namely that the respondent has deserted the petitioner for a period exceeding two years immediately preceding the presentation of the petition cannot apply here even if separation for the relevant period can be made out, as it would seem that only Fiona could be said to be in desertion (unless there is behaviour on Eric's part which could amount to constructive desertion), and Fiona cannot rely on her own desertion. Section 1(2)(d) MCA 1973, namely that the parties have lived separate and apart for at least two years immediately preceding the petition, and the respondent (Eric) consents to a decree being granted, clearly will not apply here as Eric opposes the divorce and a s1(2)(d) petition cannot proceed without his consent given freely and with full understanding of what it entails: *Mason* v *Mason* (1972).

Therefore the only remaining fact is s1(2)(e) MCA 1973, namely that the parties have lived separate and apart for five years immediately preceding the presentation of the petition, in which case no consent of Eric is required. However there are two problems to be faced by Fiona in respect of such a petition.

Firstly, Fiona must show that the parties have in fact been living apart for the preceding five years. This involves living apart in a physical and a mental sense. To establish the mental element, it must be shown that at least one of the parties regards the marriage as at an end for the length of the relevant period, although it is not necessary for that party to communicate this fact to the other: *Santos* v *Santos* (1972). We are told that since 1979 Fiona has considered the marriage effectively to be at an end, although her statements to George and her conduct to Eric unless this can be explained as being in the character of a nurse towards her patient, may contradict her view. However even if the court is satisfied that Fiona has treated the marriage as at an end for the five year period, she may have difficulty in establishing physical separation for that period.

To establish physical separation, it must be proved that the parties have lived in separate households for the relevant period, although not necessarily in different houses. In other words there must be a rejection of all the obligations of marriage, a cessation of cohabitation, and the test to be applied is whether there has been any sharing of domestic life and whether one spouse has been providing matrimonial services for the other: *Mouncer* v *Mouncer* (1972); *Fuller* v *Fuller* (1973).

In *Mouncer* it was held that the parties were not living apart where they shared meals and living accommodation even though they slept in separate bedrooms, no longer had sexual intercourse and largely led their own lives. In *Hopes* v *Hopes* (1949) the wife did no mending or washing for her husband and never cooked separate meals for him, but he had most meals with the family, and when he was not in his bedroom, he shared the rest of the house with the family. There was held to be no cessation of cohabitation in that case. However in *Fuller* the parties were treated as living apart where the wife, having left her husband to go to live with another man, subsequently took the husband in as a lodger because he had nowhere else to go. The nature of the relationship between the parties had changed and it could not be said that the wife was performing matrimonial services for the husband whom she treated as a lodger and who paid for the services.

Therefore it will be a question of fact and degree whether Fiona and Eric have been living apart for a continuous period of five years. We are told that Eric occupies a room specially adapted to his needs, but whether that means that he uses no other part of the house is uncertain. What is perhaps most damaging to Fiona's case is the fact that she has continued to look after him, dressing him and cooking for him. Therefore, although they may no longer share some aspects of marital life such as sexual intercourse, there may not be the complete cessation of cohabitation as is required to satisfy this fact as in *Mouncer*. So unless Fiona can show that her care of Eric is merely in her capacity as a nurse and that their relationship is no longer that of husband and wife, but has been that of nurse and patient since 1979 and so falls within the principles of *Fuller*, she will be unable to proceed with a petition under s1(2)(e).

Even if she can prove separation, she faces a potential second problem in that Eric could oppose the petition under s5 MCA 1973 which provides that a respondent may oppose the grant of a decree nisi under s1(2)(e) even though the fact relied upon has been proved satisfactorily, on the ground that the dissolution of the marriage will result in grave financial or other hardship to the respondent, and it would be wrong to dissolve the marriage in all the circumstances of the case. Both elements must be proved by Eric.

Section 5(2) MCA provides that, in considering such an application, the court will have regard to all the circumstances of the case including the conduct of the parties and the interests of those parties and of any children and other persons concerned. Section 5(3) provides that for the purpose of this section, hardship shall include the loss of the chance of acquiring any benefit which the respondent might acquire if the marriage is not dissolved.

In this case, as in the majority of cases, the hardship relied upon will be financial, and Eric must be advised that it must result from the dissolution of the marriage and not its breakdown. The hardship must be grave and this will be considered objectively in relation to the particular marriage and the circumstances in which the parties lived while it subsisted (*Talbot* v *Talbot* (1971)), but what matters is not whether Eric considers that he will suffer grave hardship, but whether ordinary people knowing all the facts would think so.

We are told that Eric will lose the pension entitlement payable to a widower if he survives his wife, a loss that will arise by reason of the dissolution of the marriage. In *Parker* v *Parker* (1972) it was held that the loss to a 47 year old wife of a contingent claim under her husband's pension scheme was a grave hardship when considered in the light of her probable financial position on attaining 60 when she would expect to receive the pension. The court will have to make a reasonable assessment of Eric's loss and it will be impossible to claim grave hardship if it is too remote a contingency as it may be in this case depending on the parties' ages, but particularly in view of the fact that a husband is not usually expected to survive his wife of the same age, and the fact in this case that Eric's life expectancy may have been shortened by the accident in any event.

Whether Eric is likely to be adversely affected by the loss of the pension entitlement must also be considered. He may have received compensation for his injuries in which case the pension entitlement may not be so important to him when looking at his overall financial position. However further comment on this point is impossible on the evidence available.

Even if grave hardship can be shown, if it can be offset, for example, by the purchase of an annuity, or if Fiona secures payments of premiums on an insurance policy of equal value to the expectation the court deems Eric to have lost, then the decree will be granted: *Parker* v *Parker* (1972); *Julian* v *Julian* (1972).

If grave hardship can be shown, the court must consider whether it would be wrong to grant the decree taking into account the conduct of Fiona and Eric (*Brickell* v *Brickell* (1974)) and the contribution of either to the breakdown of the marriage. The interests of the parties and other persons, for example George in this case, also will have to considered.

It is difficult to say whether Eric could defend successfully Fiona's petition under s5 as more information on his financial circumstances and those of Fiona would be required, although it may be that his claim to the pension entitlement may be considered too remote in any event. For Fiona's part she may have difficulty in making out the fact under s1(2)(e) as there is some doubt as to whether they have been living separately since 1979; and for s1(2)(b) purposes, the evidence of behaviour is missing.

b) In the event of a divorce the court has power to make various orders for financial provision under s22 and s23 MCA 1973, namely maintenance pending suit (s22), and periodical payments and/or a lump sum order for the applicant (s23). The court may also make a property adjustment order (s24 MCA 1973) and may order the sale of property under s24A.

Therefore Eric may apply for financial provision from Fiona in the event of a divorce. Both parties come before the court on an equal basis, so a husband is as entitled to receive maintenance from his wife, as she is from him, subject to need and ability to pay.

The guidelines set out in s25 MCA 1973 as substituted by s3 Matrimonial and Family Proceedings Act 1984 (hereinafter MFPA 1984) will have to be considered by the court in deciding what order, if any, to make in Eric's favour. In this case therefore the court will take into account the income, earning capacity, property and other financial resources which each party has or is likely to have in the future, including in the case of earning capacity, any increase which a party can reasonably be expected to obtain: s25(2)(a). In this case it appears that Eric has no income from employment any longer although Fiona has income from her part time job. Clearly Eric cannot be expected to work, but Fiona can, and indeed her income could be increased by her taking on full time work which would not be an unreasonable expectation at this time. Further we are told that she intends to marry George who is a surgeon. If so this will mean that the court will have to recognise that as George will be sharing the financial burdens of the home with her, more of her own income will be available to support Eric if necessary.

Although Eric has no apparent financial resources he may have received damages as a result of the motor accident for loss of earnings, pain and suffering and loss of other amenity. If so, this compensation will form part of his resources for the purposes of the MCA 1973 (*Daubney* v *Daubney* (1976)) although it will be recognised that such compensation will have to provide for Eric's future needs, and may in any event need supplementing by Fiona.

The financial needs, obligations and responsibilities which each party has or is likely to have in the future will also be relevant here: s25(2)(b). Eric's needs will be greater because of his incapacity, and will include the need for suitable, adapted accommodation. His physical disabilities, (s25(2)(e)) may give rise to other needs such as professional care which may involve additional expenses.

The court will also consider the standard of living enjoyed by the parties before the breakdown of the marriage (s25(2)(c)); the age of the parties and the duration of the marriage (s25(2)(d)), and linked to this, the contribution made by each of the parties to the welfare of the family, including any contribution made by looking after the home or caring for the family (s25(2)(f)).

The parties are still probably relatively young so that Fiona could be expected to continue to work at this time. The marriage seems to have lasted for ten years and both parties have contributed to the family during that time. Eric had done so in material terms probably from 1976-79 but Fiona's contribution has been greater it is submitted in view of her care of him since 1980.

The conduct of each party must be considered if it is such that in the opinion of the court it would be inequitable to disregard it (s25(2)(g)), that is if it is 'obvious and gross': *Wachtel* v *Wachtel* (1973); *Robinson* v *Robinson* (1983). As indicated in part i), it is difficult to decide if conduct will play a role in these proceedings, and if a s1(2)(e) petition applies then it is likely that conduct will be ignored.

Finally the court will consider the value to each party of any benefit which by reason of the dissolution of the marriage that party will lose the chance of acquiring. Here the loss to Eric of the widower's pension entitlement would be considered in support of Eric's claim, so long as it is not too remote.

In the absence of any fuller information as to the parties' financial status, it is difficult to advise on the most appropriate order in these circumstances. It is not known whether Eric in fact needs periodical payments from Fiona as he may have sufficient funds to provide for his everyday needs from any compensation received. Further it must be noted that Fiona may have to cease employment in the future, or at least go back to part time work if she and George have a family. In the immediate future however it is reasonable to expect Fiona to undertake full time work and therefore a periodical payments order in Eric's favour may be appropriate if he needs such support. A lump sum order may not be feasible unless Fiona has funds to provide for the same or there is property which could be sold for this purpose. The court may be more interested in ensuring that Eric's accommodation requirements are adequately provided for as in *Calderbank* v *Calderbank* (1975) where a lump sum was provided by the wife for the husband to purchase accommodation for himself. Eric needs specially adapted accommodation. Depending on the equity in the property and the shares which the court decides each party has in it, it may be appropriate to transfer the house to Eric, as it appears to satisfy his needs. If the property is too large for his sole occupation, or if on considering the equitable shares this would be unfair to Fiona, the court could order that the house be sold and the net proceeds of sale divided between Eric and Fiona in shares ordered by the court. In this way the court could work towards providing sufficient funds for Eric to acquire suitable accommodation, and the court could in fact order that a larger share of the proceeds of sale be provided for him to secure this objective.

Question 3

Has divorce law, as it is now interpreted by the courts, satisfied the Law Commission's objectives of 'buttressing the stability of marriage, while enabling marriages which have broken down to be destroyed with the minimum of bitterness, distress and humiliation'?

University of London LLB Examination
(for External Students) Family Law June 1988 Q2

General comment

This is a relatively straightforward essay question on current divorce law and requires candidates to consider whether the present law enables divorces to be conducted without bitterness, distress and humiliation, whilst at the same time safeguarding the stability of marriage. A review of the current law involving a detailed examination of s1(1) and s1(2) MCA 1973 as well as s3 MCA 1973 is required. Further, candidates must be aware of the findings of various Commissions on the subject and therefore it is a question to be tackled only by those candidates who have done some wider reading on divorce law.

Skeleton solution

- Review the underlying policy of divorce law and the reports of the Morton Commission, the Archbishop of Canterbury's group and the Law Commission.

- Consider the current law by reference to s1(1) and (2) MCA 1973 with particular reference to the 'conduct' facts. Consider also recent developments in the law in respect of s3 MCA 1973.

Suggested solution

The underlying policy expressed in the development of divorce law since the nineteenth century could be said to encompass the beliefs inter alia, that no law should be so lax as to lessen the regard for the sanctity of marriage, and therefore there should be restrictions on the availability of divorce; no law should outrage a popular sense of justice and therefore the law should not assist anyone to gain advantage from his own wrong doing, particularly if it should cause injury to an innocent party; and the law should facilitate reconciliation between spouses and should be based on understandable and respected principles.

It has been argued that if divorce is made too easy it creates 'a habit of mind in the people' and therefore weakens the security of marriage in that the parties would not make the necessary effort to preserve the marriage when there are problems in it and would opt for the easier solution, that is a dissolution. This view, that easier divorce means less security and happiness, was appealed to the Morton Commission which reported in 1956 and which believed the root of the problem to be 'a tendency to take the duties and responsibilities of marriage less seriously than formerly . . . there is less disposition to overcome difficulties and to put up with the rubs of daily life and in consequence, there is an increasing disposition to regard divorce not as the last resort, but an obvious way out when things begin to go wrong.'

The majority of the members of the Commission recommended the retention of the matrimonial offence as the basis of the divorce law, although some members were in favour of introducing the breakdown of the marriage as evidenced by separation for a period of seven years as a new ground for divorce. In 1956 only grounds based on matrimonial misconduct applied to divorce, and it was asserted that the proper function of the law was to give relief where a wrong had been done, not to provide a dignified and honourable means of release from a broken marriage.

This latter view however gained more favour as time passed and in 1966 in its report *Putting Asunder*, the Archbishop of Canterbury's group favoured the substitution of 'breakdown' for the matrimonial offence as the basis of divorce law, taking the view that a divorce decree should be seen as a judicial recognition of a state of affairs with a consequent redefinition of status. The committee did favour the view that the divorce court should carry out a detailed inquest into the alleged facts and causes of the breakdown of the marriage relationship in each case to avoid possible abuse of the law. However the Law Commission which was appointed to investigate the reform of the divorce law following the publication of *Putting Asunder* did not agree that there should be such a detailed inquest arguing that such a course would be impracticable.

The Commission recommended that the grounds that existed already for divorce should be retained but that an additional ground as evidenced by a period of separation which would be shorter if the respondent consented than if he or she did not should be introduced. The Commission's aims were to preserve the stability of marriage but it recognised also the social function of divorce, that is to allow parties to enter into new legal unions if they so wished while giving any necessary protection to the children of the family and dealing with financial and property adjustment as required. Further, it believed that a machinery to allow for reconciliation should be provided if there was any possibility that a marriage could be preserved.

The resulting Divorce Reform Act 1969 which forms the basis of the modern divorce law was a compromise between the two basic principles expounded by the Archbishop of Canterbury's committee and the Law Commission. Irretrievable breakdown of the marriage became the sole ground for divorce. However it could only be inferred by proof of one or more specified facts which were akin to the old matrimonial offences, although they do include two new facts based on separation.

This legislation has been described as an uneasy compromise between two inconsistent views of divorce policy. One view is that divorce should be available to either party to the marriage where it has irretrievably broken down and that the old matrimonial offences are mere symptoms of that breakdown. Another view however, is that it would be fundamentally unjust to allow a party to petition for divorce on the basis of irretrievable breakdown alone as that could allow a party to rely on his or her own wrongdoing and to obtain a divorce even against the will of an innocent spouse.

The current law allows a divorce where there is evidence of irretrievable breakdown of the marriage, but such breakdown can be shown only by relying on one of the 'facts' and a divorce must be refused even where it is clear that the marriage has broken down if one of the facts cannot be made out: see *Richards* v *Richards* (1972). The requirement to establish one of the 'facts' is to ensure that the 'innocent' spouse cannot be divorced against his or her will at least until the five year separation fact can be made out. However, even in the case of a petition based on five year separation the respondent can prevent the divorce by showing that he or she would suffer grave financial or other hardship as a result of the divorce and that it would be unjust to grant a decree.

This defence could be used as a form of blackmail by a respondent who is anxious to obtain a more favourable financial order from his or her spouse than the court would order in the usual ancillary proceedings, and therefore, possibly hinders a civilised and speedy conclusion to matrimonial difficulties caused by the breakdown.

The present law has been criticised because it has not been totally successful in eradicating the 'bitterness, distress and humiliation' from divorce proceedings. One area where this was particularly the case, prior to 1984, was in applications to present a petition within three years of the marriage, for until the enactment of the Matrimonial and Family Proceedings Act 1984 no petition could be presented within the first three years of the marriage unless the case was one of exceptional hardship suffered by the petitioner or exceptional depravity on the respondent's part. Evidence suggested that far from relieving humiliation, bitterness and distress, the requirement to prove one of these grounds to dissolve the marriage at an early date actually caused the parties these feelings. It is clear that some people were prevented from making the application because of the embarrassment of airing their serious marital problems in public, whereas other parties may have exaggerated their allegations to ensure a successful conclusion to the application. However in its report *Time Restrictions on Presentation of Divorce and Nullity Petitions*, the Law Commission, while accepting the problems attendant upon the then current law, felt that a time restriction on presenting a divorce petition was useful to '... safeguard against irresponsible or trial marriages during the difficult first years'. The Commission sought to impose a compromise between causing unnecessary hardship to a spouse by preserving an obviously dead marriage and making divorce so quickly available that marriage is viewed merely as a transient state which can be repudiated at whim. They decided to impose an absolute bar against presenting petitions for divorce within the first year of marriage and this was implemented by the Matrimonial and Family Proceedings Act 1984. An absolute bar has the advantages of certainty and consistency and avoids the embarrassment associated with proving reasons for presenting a divorce petition early on in the marriage. The Commission recognised that any period would be arbitrary but felt that the one year period would not cause undue hardship to a potential petitioner even where the marriage breaks down in the first months. Further, it must be remembered that reliance can be placed on any of the facts which commence during that first year.

So recently the law has been amended to facilitate an easier and more humane severance on the marital breakdown in one respect. However, the necessity to rely on one of the 'facts' still causes problems when considering the Law Commission's original aim to avoid bitterness, distress and humiliation.

The offence based facts allow a divorce without a lengthy period of living apart, and have remained popular in petitions for this reason. Statistics for the year 1985 show that over 70 per cent of all petitions were based on the facts of adultery or behaviour, or both. However, there is evidence that even in the case of an undefended 'behaviour' petition, hostility is encouraged between the parties, or at the very least, there is a lack of cooperation between them, encouraged by the fact relied upon in the petition. The 'behaviour' fact preserves the concept of breach of marital obligation with its corollary of guilt and innocence. One advantage of adopting irretrievable breakdown of the marriage as the sole ground for divorce is that the decree would recite a state of affairs without attributing blame and thereby avoid bitterness between the parties. In truth, in many cases, the conduct of both parties has contributed to the breakdown of the marriage.

It is also argued that the existence of two facts based on separation and depending on whether the respondent agrees to the divorce or not, is reminiscent of the matrimonial offence because a spouse who wishes to divorce an 'innocent' respondent against his or her wish is penalised in that the petitioner has to wait five years before a petition can be presented rather than the two years required where the respondent agrees to the divorce. It is argued that if two years is a long enough period to evidence marital breakdown where the respondent consents to the divorce, it should also be a sufficient period where the respondent does not consent. The existing law allows a respondent spouse to delay, perhaps unnecessarily, the divorce which after five years is inevitable, unless the grave hardship defence referred to earlier can be relied upon.

A hope has been expressed by MPs led by Leo Abse, that 'the end of the contested divorce and the emphasis on guilt and innocence would mean that the courts, released from their task of making painstaking judgments on the morality or conduct of the parties, would be able to turn their attention to what is now described ... as the ancillary matters, above all, the children.'

It has been suggested therefore, that the law should be reformed further in a way that will recognise the requirements of a modern society, and will be rid of existing pretences, and a procedure which admits that divorce has become an administrative rather than a judicial function. The use of the Special Procedure makes it impossible for the courts to carry out the investigation required by the present law in any event, and therefore it has been said that all judges do is rubberstamp agreements or arrangements made by the parties, at public expense. However the Law Commission thought that a divorce law based on separation alone could be impracticable because there would be cases of perhaps gross conduct where relief should be available quickly. Further, if one party, or both have established stable unions with other partners there would be little point served in keeping the marriage alive until the statutory period has expired.

The requirements of a divorce law in modern society relate in the main to the ancillary matters, that is the financial and custodial applications, and it is suggested that the courts should be free to consider these matters without having to consider reasons for the breakdown of the marriage first. This suggestion may well become reality in the light of the final recommendations of the Law Commission: Report No 192 entitled *The Ground for Divorce* (1990).

Question 4

Colin and Deidre married in 1980. They have one child, Edward, now aged six. Deidre was aware at the time of the marriage that Colin suffered from acute depression but she believed she could cure him. In April 1984 Colin, who wrongly believed that Deidre was having an affair with the postman, refused to speak to her. He communicated only by writing notes to her. They ate meals together in silence and assumed joint responsibility for looking after their child, Edward, who was becoming increasingly upset by his father's silence towards his mother.

By 1987 Deidre had decided that she could no longer stand occupying the same house as Colin, and that his behaviour was having an adverse effect on Edward's health. She informed Colin that she was never going to live with him again, and that she and Edward were going to live with her sister, Freda. Colin has refused to pay any maintenance for Deidre or Edward because he considers that she is still having an affair with the postman.

a) Can either Colin or Deidre obtain a divorce?

b) What avenues of financial support, if any, are open to Deidre prior to applying for a divorce?

University of London LLB Examination
(for External Students) Family Law June 1989 Q2

Skeleton solution

This is a straightforward question that simply requires the application of the law on divorce to the facts and a consideration of the financial relief available to parties during marriage.

a) Consider the facts in relation first of all to Colin's position and then Deidre. The question invites an analysis of all five 'facts' to prove irretrievable breakdown and it is necessary to demonstrate the relevance of each to the situation of the parties.

b) Financial support in these circumstances requires the application of provisions under the Domestic Proceedings and Magistrates' Court Act 1978, s27 Matrimonial Causes Act 1973 (as amended) and s9 of the Guardianship of Minors Act (as amended by the Family Law Reform Act 1987).

Suggested solution

a) The Matrimonial Causes Act 1973 (hereinafter MCA 1973) provides only one ground for obtaining a divorce - the irretrievable breakdown of the marriage: s1(1). This can only be established by showing the applicability of one of the facts set out in s1(2): see *Buffery* v *Buffery* (1988) where it was held that ss1 and 2 of the Act are separate requirements to be shown independently of each other. In the instant case, it has to be seen if any of those facts can found a petition for divorce for either of the parties involved and whether irretrievable breakdown can be shown.

Colin's divorce

Section 1(2)(a) MCA 1973 is the first subsection which may enable Colin to get a divorce - this is based on the respondent having committed adultery and the petitioner finding it intolerable to live with the respondent (the two limbs of subs(a) are disjunctive: see *Cleary* v *Cleary* (1974) which was followed by the court in *Carr* v *Carr* (1974) albeit reluctantly). However, it is submitted that Colin is unlikely to be able to prove adultery - it is only his belief that it has taken place, and this should therefore be discounted as a possible cause of action.

Colin could possibly obtain a divorce under ss1(2)(c), 1(2)(d) and 1(2)(e).

Section 1(2)(e)

Under s2(6) of the Act, the parties to a marriage are to be treated as living apart unless they are living in the same household. The meaning of the phrase 'living in the same household' has to be determined and is a question of fact to be decided by the court. However, any sharing of a common life will mean that separation is not made out: *Mouncer* v *Mouncer* (1972). In the instant case, Colin and Deidre ate their meals together and assumed joint responsibility for looking after their child and accordingly, it cannot be said that they were living apart. For this reason, the

49

possibility of Colin assuming a divorce on the basis of s1(2)(e) should be ruled out since he cannot show a period of five years' separation from his wife despite the lack of communication between the parties.

Section 1(2)(d)

Colin will be able to obtain a divorce using this subsection. Deidre moved out of the matrimonial home in 1987 so that the requirements that the parties live apart for a continuous period of two years prior to the presentation of the petition will be satisfied either immediately or in the near future depending upon the exact date on which Deidre moved out. Unless Deidre refuses to consent to the divorce for some reason, a petition based on s1(2)(d) will be successful.

Section 1(2)(c)

Finally, Colin may be able to rely on s1(2)(c) - a section which is rarely used. To do this, he will have to establish four things:

- i) the de facto separation of the spouses;
- ii) the intention on Deidre's part to remain separated;
- iii) the absence of his consent;
- iv) the absence of any reasonable cause for his wife's departure.

The first factor should cause no problem since Deidre has left the matrimonial home. The same should be true of the second requirement since Deidre told Colin that she was never going to live with him again.

The issue of consent is a question of fact. It may be expressly given but it may also be implied from the conduct of the deserted spouse. It may be the case that Colin has impliedly consented to his wife leaving by his conduct, ie his unswerving belief in her adultery and his refusal to communicate other than by writing notes may suffice to demonstrate his consent to the parties living apart. If this were so, he could not assert that his wife was in desertion. However, it is clear that there must be an agreement to live apart - it is not enough that one party is simply glad to see the other go - and it is submitted that, on the facts, there is not enough evidence to prove the requisite consent on Colin's part such that he could still rely on s1(2)(c).

Finally, it must be shown that there was no reasonable cause for his wife to leave, otherwise there will be no unjustifiable separation and thus no desertion on her part. The petitioner's behaviour is obviously relevant here for it may be such that the respondent was justified in leaving. It has been said that the conduct must amount to 'such a grave and weighty matter as renders the continuance of the matrimonial cohabitation virtually impossible': *Young* v *Young* (1964). Looking at the facts of this case, it may be that, provided Deidre left because of Colin's behaviour, she cannot be held to be in desertion.

Deidre's divorce

The same factors relating to s1(2)(d) and (e) are relevant here. However, with regard to Deidre, the most important issue is whether she can obtain a divorce based on s1(2)(b) - ie by showing that the respondent has behaved in such a way that the petitioner cannot reasonably be expected to live with him. The test to be applied is an objective one but the court must have regard to the people actually before it: *Livingstone-Stallard* v *Livingstone-Stallard* (1974); *Ash* v *Ash* (1972); *Buffery* v *Buffery* (1988). Since defended petitions are rare, examples of behaviour which will satisfy s1(2)(b) are not plentiful. However, in *O'Neill* v *O'Neill* (1975), allegations by the husband that the children of the family were not his were sufficient to satisfy the section. By analogy, it is possible that repeated accusations of an adulterous relationship which are untrue may well suffice. As a result of *Thurlow* v *Thurlow* (1976), the court has to take into consideration all the obligations relating to marriage, including that of caring for a spouse who is unwell. The fact that Deidre knew of Colin's mental illness when she married him may operate against her establishing his behaviour. However, regard should be had to the principle in *Katz* v *Katz* (1972) where it was held that while a spouse may reasonably be required to care for a partner who is unwell and to tolerate a certain degree of abnormal behaviour, there may come a time when that partner's condition becomes such that the spouse can no longer reasonably be expected to continue living with the other party. This is of particular relevance here where Edward, the couple's son, was also becoming upset by his father's behaviour. Negative behaviour can also be taken into consideration but it should be intentional behaviour which Colin's does appear to be.

Deidre could also seek to rely on s1(2)(c) to show that Colin was in constructive desertion of her. The court will have to determine whether the four criteria referred to in relation to Colin's divorce are satisfied in this situation. In particular, it will have regard to Colin's conduct to determine whether he made living together for any further period of time impossible. It may well find that he behaved in such a way as to drive his wife away, eg by persisting in the unsubstantiated belief that Deidre was committing adultery and refusing to communicate with her other than by note. In addition, his conduct was having an adverse effect on his son's health.

With regard to the other criteria, Deidre can obviously prove that she and her husband are separated. She can also show that there was no reasonable cause for Colin's desertion since she was not, in fact, committing adultery. A reasonable but mistaken belief in her adultery would have justified his desertion but not Colin's persistent and unreasonable belief. Since he continues to insist that she is having an affair, he remains in desertion - and this fact would seem to evince an intention on his part to remain separated permanently from his wife.

b) *Financial provision*

Firstly, Deidre could apply under s2 of the Domestic Proceedings and Magistrates' Courts Act (hereinafter DPMCA) 1978 for financial support. All of the grounds specified in s1 may be relevant to any application which she may make, that is failure to provide for her and Edward, Colin's behaviour being such that she can no longer reasonably be expected to live with him and his desertion of her. With regard to the last two of these grounds, the wording of them corresponds to ss1(2)(b) and (c) of the MCA 1973 and according to *Bergin* v *Bergin* (1983), the interpretation of the DPMCA 1978 provisions must be the same. However, the problem with regard to s1(c) is that an application for financial relief must be brought within six months of the occurrence of the behaviour alleged. In Deidre's case, she moved out of the home some two years ago and so any claim made under this subsection will fail by reason of being outside the relevant time limit: see s127(1) Magistrates' Courts Act 1980.

When deciding whether to make an order and, if so, what the terms of it should be, the magistrates are directed to have regard to 'all the circumstances of the case, first consideration being given to the welfare while a minor of any child of the family who has not attained the age of eighteen' and to the criteria to be found in s3 of the 1978 Act (as amended by s9 Matrimonial and Family Proceedings Act (MFPA) 1984). In respect of Deidre's application for support for herself, the court will consider s3(1) looking, in particular, at Colin's conduct as directed by s3(1)(g). It is submitted that his conduct since 1984 has been so bad that it should constitute a relevant issue in the court's determination of the matter. In relation to provision for Edward, the court has to consider s3(3) - this section directs its attention specifically to his resources and requirements.

The orders which could be made under the provisions of this Act are:

i)   that unsecured periodical payments be made to Deidre;

ii)   that a lump sum not exceeding £500 be paid to her;

iii) that unsecured periodical payments be made to or for the benefit of Edward;

iv)   that a lump sum not exceeding the aforementioned amount in b) be paid for him.

Secondly, Deidre could apply under s27 MCA 1973 (as amended by s4 MFPA 1984) for financial relief to be provided during the marriage. In practice, very few applications are made under this section; people prefer to use the options available in the magistrates' courts. The advantages of this section are that it empowers the court to order that secured periodical payment be made to the applicant or for any child in respect of whom an application is made and that there is no upper limit applicable to any lump sum orders made. However, when compared to applications before magistrates, the s27 proceedings are more expensive and more prolonged.

The relevant grounds for an application are that the respondent has failed to provide reasonable maintenance for the applicant and/or for any child of the family. In addition, the court has to take the same factors into account as under the DPMCA 1978 except that first consideration need only be given to the welfare of a child of the family under eighteen years of age if an order has been sought in respect of that child: see s25.

Finally, Deidre could seek an order for financial provision in respect of Edward alone under the Children Act 1989 s15 and Schedule 1. This is only available where the child is the biological or adoptive child of the parents. This appears to be so from the facts given. As a result of the Children Act 1989, it is no longer necessary that the question of custody be put into issue as between the parents. This will work to Deirdre's favour since it does not appear that this matter has been considered as yet and this new provision obviates the need for it to be determined, at least for the time being. In this case, there is no need to prove a separate ground either to justify the action unlike the MCA 1973 and the DPMCA 1978. The relevant factors for consideration are to be found in Schedule 1 of the Children Act 1989 and are the same as under the DPMCA 1978 apart from the fact that there is no provision requiring the court to take the standard of living enjoyed by the family into account or to consider the issue of the child's education. It should be emphasised that the welfare of the child is the first consideration under the Children Act 1989.

Question 5

Mary and John, who have two children aged 6 and 7, were married in 1980. Since the beginning of the marriage, John has been an active human rights campaigner. In 1985, John's activities began to take up a considerable amount of time and Mary complained that if he did not devote more attention to the family, she would consider leaving him. John promised that he would spend more time with the family, but he did not really do so. At the end of 1986, Mary therefore decided to move into the spare room.

In January 1988, John went to Burma to study the human rights situation there. Unfortunately, he was taken hostage by a terrorist group, and while it is clear that he is still alive, he has not yet returned to England. Advise Mary, who would like to divorce John.

University of London LLB Examination
(for External Students) Family Law June 1991 Q3

General comment

This is an awkward question on divorce which requires detailed consideration of the facts in s1(2)(b), (c) and (e) Matrimonial Causes Act 1973. Whereas the separation for five years fact is relatively straightforward, the question of whether behaviour or desertion applies is more complex and care must be taken to point to the difficulties arising on the facts of the problem.

Skeleton solution

• Consider the one ground for divorce - s1(1) MCA 1973. Discount adultery.

• Discuss a behaviour petition - s1(2)(b). Identify possible behaviour. Discuss subjective and objective elements of the test and s2(3) MCA 1973. Is such a petition appropriate on these facts?

- Desertion - s1(2)(c) - discuss when separation begins. Does John have an intention to desert? Does Mary consent?

- Separation - discount s1(2)(d) - lack of consent to decree

- Consider s1(2)(e) - have the parties been separated for the required period? *Santos* point to be considered.

Suggested solution

There is one ground for divorce, namely that the marriage has broken down irretrievably (s1(1) Matrimonial Causes Act 1973, hereinafter MCA 1973) and Mary must prove this by relying on one or more of the facts set out in s1(2) MCA 1973. In the absence of proof of one of these facts no divorce will be granted even if it is clear that the marriage has broken down irretrievably (*Richards* v *Richards* (1972); *Buffery* v *Buffery* (1988)).

There is no evidence of adultery in this case so a petition under s1(2)(a) MCA 1973 is not appropriate. Similarly a petition under s1(2)(b) MCA 1973 may be inappropriate on these facts. Under s1(2)(b) a petition is available where the respondent has behaved in such a way that the petitioner cannot reasonably be expected to live with the respondent. This involves establishing behaviour against John and whereas it might be alleged on the basis of his lack of attention to the family in the past, it would seem inappropriate to rely on it at this time. Certainly simple desertion, if his leaving the home to visit Burma in 1988 can be construed as such, will not be accepted as evidence of behaviour (*Stringfellow* v *Stringfellow* (1976)).

If John's failure to give proper attention to the family can be regarded as behaviour, it is for the court to decide if Mary can reasonably be expected to live with him taking into account the behaviour of both parties, their characters and personalities, their faults and other attributes good and bad, and the whole history of the marriage (*Ash* v *Ash* (1972); *Pheasant* v *Pheasant* (1972); *Livingstone-Stallard* v *Livingstone-Stallard* (1974)).

A factor which may work against Mary relates to the reconciliation provisions in s2 MCA 1973. By virtue of s2(3) MCA 1973, the court must disregard any period of cohabitation after the last act of behaviour complained of, if it is less than six months, when deciding if it is reasonable to expect the petitioner to continue living with the respondent. If, as discussed below, it is deemed that when Mary moved into the spare room this did not terminate cohabitation, then the parties continued to live together. It could be argued that John's behaviour continued throughout the cohabitation up to and including his decision to go to Burma since which time the parties have of course been living separately. If so the parties have not lived together for more than six months since the last act complained of and therefore this will not be a factor to be considered when deciding if Mary can be expected to continue to live with John. However, the fact that Mary continued to cohabit with John and the fact that the alleged behaviour took place so long ago may indicate that a s1(2)(b) petition is not appropriate at this time.

To establish a petition under s1(2)(c) MCA 1973 it must be proved that the respondent has deserted the petitioner for a continuous period of at least two years. 'Desertion is not a withdrawal from a place, but from a state of things' (*Pulford* v *Pulford* (1923)) so it is necessary to establish that John has withdrawn from the marriage. Further it must be shown that he has the intention 'to bring the matrimonial union permanently to an end' (*Lang* v *Lang* (1955)). As a matter of fact we know that John and Mary have been separated since, at the latest, January 1988 and the fact that John has been captured by terrorists and has been unable to return home since then would not necessarily interfere with a desertion petition if his intention to desert before his capture could be established. However, unless it could be argued that his continued attention to the human rights campaigns, despite Mary's warnings should he fail to give attention to the family, could be construed as evidence of an intention to bring the marriage to an end, it is unlikely that an intention to desert can be made out against him.

There may be another problem in proving desertion in that it is necessary to establish that the petitioner does not give consent to the separation. In view of Mary's behaviour in moving into the spare room it may be difficult to establish such lack of consent on her part although it is doubtful anyway whether such action establishes separation in its own right. It could be argued that John's behaviour drove Mary to separate herself from him and so constructive desertion may arise. However, as indicated above, the intention to desert on John's part may be difficult to establish.

This leaves the separation facts under s1(2)(d) and (e) MCA 1973. Under s1(2)(d) it has to be established that the parties have lived apart for a continuous period of at least two years immediately preceding the petition and that the respondent consents to the decree being granted. However, although the fact of separation for the required period can be established together with the mental element required, Mary will be unable to obtain John's consent to the decree and without this a petition under s1(2)(d) will fail. Mary would have to provide positive evidence that John freely gave his consent to the decree with full understanding of the nature and consequences of what he was doing (*Mason* v *Mason* (1972)). Clearly, as it seems that Mary has had no contact with John since he was taken hostage, no such consent will be forthcoming at this time.

To establish a petition under s1(2)(e) MCA 1973 Mary must prove that the parties have lived apart for a continuous period of five years immediately preceding the presentation of the petition. If such separation can be made out together with the required mental element, there is nothing further to be proved by Mary and the divorce would be granted.

Living apart involves living apart in a physical and a mental sense. To establish physical separation Mary must prove that the parties have lived in separate households for the relevant period although this does not necessarily involve living in separate houses. In other words there must be a rejection of all the obligations of marriage, a cessation of cohabitation. The test to be applied is whether there has been any sharing of a domestic life and whether one spouse has been providing matrimonial services for the other (*Mouncer* v *Mouncer* (1972); *Fuller* v *Fuller* (1973)). In *Mouncer* the parties were held to be living together where they shared their meals and living accommodation even though they slept in separate bedrooms, no longer had sexual relations and largely led separate lives. Similarly in *Hopes* v *Hopes* (1949) the wife did no mending or washing for her husband and never cooked separate meals for him although he had most meals with the rest of the family and when he was not in his bedroom he shared the rest of the house with the family. There was deemed to be no living apart in that case. Conversely in *Fuller* there was deemed to be a separation where the wife, having left her husband to live with another man, subsequently took the husband in as a lodger because he had nowhere else to live. The nature of the relationship between the parties had changed and it could not be said that the wife was performing matrimonial services for the husband whom she treated as a lodger and who paid for the services provided.

Therefore it will be a question of fact and degree whether Mary and John have been living apart for a continuous period of five years. Certainly when John left in January 1988 physical separation can be established from that time. However it is questionable whether separation can be established earlier than that date. We are told that at the end of 1986 Mary moved into the spare room suggesting that she no longer shared a bedroom with John and that there was no further sexual relationship between them. However we are given no information as to the other household arrangements, that is whether Mary cooked meals for John or did cleaning for him or whether he shared the house with the rest of the family etc. It seems that he probably did share the house with the family and probably ate his meals with them when he was at home. If so, the mere fact that some part of the matrimonial life has come to an end, (in this case the sexual relationship) does not mean that the parties are living separate and apart. It seems therefore that separation cannot be established in 1986, but that it started only in January 1988 when John left for Burma. If this is the case no petition under s1(2)(e) can be presented until January 1993.

Once physical separation is established the mental element must also be shown. In *Santos* v *Santos* (1972) it was held that the parties would not be treated as living apart unless consortium had come to an end and so long as both spouses intend to share a matrimonial home when circumstances permit, consortium is regarded as continuing. Therefore to establish living apart it is also necessary to show that one party at least regards the marriage as at an end for the whole of the relevant period, although it is not necessary for that party to communicate this fact to the other. In this case it could be argued that Mary treated the marriage as at an end from the end of 1986 when she moved into the separate room. If so, the mental element of the fact is established and when the physical separation can be made out for the relevant period she will be able to obtain a divorce under s1(2)(e).

Question 6

John and Susan married in 1984. They have twin boys, Damien and Derrick, who are now aged six. At the time she married John, Susan was aware that he suffered intermittently from depression, but she believed she could cure him. In late 1987 John, who concluded without foundation that Susan was having an affair, moved into the spare room and refused to speak to her. He communicated with her by leaving messages on his personal computer. They continued to eat meals together in silence and both looked after the twins, who started to exhibit signs that they were upset by their father's behaviour to their mother.

In June 1990 Susan decided that she could no longer go on living with John, particularly in view of the fact that his behaviour was affecting the twins. Accordingly, after leaving a message on the computer indicating that she believed the marriage was over, she left, with the twins, to live with her parents.

Can either John or Susan obtain a divorce? In the event that either wishes to resist the other's petition, what avenues are available to them?

University of London LLB Examination
(for External Students) Family Law June 1992 Q5

General comment

A general question regarding divorce.

Skeleton solution

MCA s1(1) - and consideration of the facts to show application of s1(1) - discounting those that are irrelevant.

Suggested solution

Under the Matrimonial Causes Act (MCA) 1973, there is only one ground for divorce, namely that the marriage has broken down irretrievably s1(1). This can be shown by establishing one of the five facts in s1(2).

a) *Whether John can obtain a divorce*

John may try to rely on s12(9) - 'That the respondent has committed adultery and the petitioner finds it intolerable to live with the respondent'. However, there is no evidence of adultery at all, in fact we are told that John's belief is without foundation, therefore John will not be able to rely on this fact.

Next we will consider if John may obtain a divorce by establishing any of the other facts.

Firstly, s1(2)(e): 'That the parties have lived apart for a continuous period of at least five years immediately preceding the presentation of the petition'.

'Living apart' - under s2(6) of the MCA 1973 the parties to the marriage are to be treated as living apart unless they are living in the same household. The meaning of the phrase 'living in the same household' has to be determined and is a question of fact to be decided by the court. In this case John and Susan ate their meals together and assumed joint responsibility for looking after their children and following the decision in *Mouncer* v *Mouncer* (1972) it probably cannot be said they were living apart. A rejection of the normal relationship between husband and wife coupled with the absence of normal affection was not sufficient to constitute living apart. So John will not be able to rely on s1(2)(e), as he cannot show a

57

period of five years separation from his wife despite the lack of communication between them.

Secondly, consider s1(2)(d):

'That the parties have lived apart for a continuous period of at least two years immediately preceding the presentation of the petition and the respondent consents to a decree being granted.'

Living apart means more than the physical separation of the parties. There must be a recognition by at least one of the parties that the marriage is at an end.

Susan moved out of the house in June 1990 and it is now June 1992, so that the requirement that the parties live apart for a continuous period of two years prior to the presentation of the petition will be satisfied either immediately or in the near future depending upon the exact date on which Susan moved out. To satisfy the requirement that there must be recognition by at least one of the parties that the marriage is at an end, the computer message left by Susan may be referred to. Therefore unless Susan refuses consent to the divorce for some reason, a petition based on s1(2)(d) will be successful.

Finally, John may be able to rely on s1(2)(c) 'That the respondent had deserted the petitioner for a continuous period of at least two years immediately preceding the presentation of the petition' - this section is not used very often.

To rely on it he will have to establish four things:

1. the de facto separation of the spouses;
2. the intention on Susan's part to remain separated;
3. the absence of his consent;
4. the absence of any reasonable cause for his wife's departure.

The first factor should cause no problems since Susan has left the matrimonial home. The same should be true of the second requirement, since Susan, by way of the computer, told John she believed the marriage was over. The third requirement of consent is a question of fact. It may be expressly given but it may also be implied from the conduct of the deserted spouse. It may be the case that John has implied consent to his wife leaving by his conduct, ie his unswerving belief in her adultery and his refusal to communicate other than by leaving messages on his personal computer may suffice to demonstrate his consent to the parties living apart. If this were so, he could not assert that his wife was in desertion. However, it is clear that there must be an agreement to live apart - it is not enough that one party is simply glad to see the other go - and it is submitted that, on the facts, there is not enough evidence to prove the requisite consent on John's part such that he could still rely on s1(2)(c).

Lastly, it must be shown that there was no reasonable cause for his wife to leave otherwise there will be no unjustifiable separation and thus no desertion on her part. John's behaviour is obviously relevant here, for it may be such that Susan was justified in leaving. It has been said that the conduct of the petition must amount to 'such a grave and weighty matter as renders the continuance of the matrimonial cohabitation virtually impossible': *Young* v *Young* (1984).

Looking at the facts of this case, John refused to speak to Susan, ate his meals in silence and only communicated by leaving messages on his personal computer. It may be that, provided Susan left because of John's behaviour, she cannot be held to be in desertion.

b) *Whether Susan can obtain a divorce*

The same factors relating to s1(2)(d) and (e) above are relevant here, but Susan will probably rely on s1(2)(b) - 'That the respondent has behaved in such a way that the petitioner cannot reasonably be expected to live with him'.

The test to be applied is an objective one but the court must have regard to the people actually before it: *Livingstone-Stallard* v *Livingstone-Stallard* (1974); *Ash* v *Ash* (1972); *Buffery* v *Buffery* (1988).

It is not really clear what sort of behaviour will satisfy s1(2)(b). However, in *O'Neill* v *O'Neill* (1975) allegations by the husband that the children of the family were not his were sufficient to satisfy the section. By analogy, it is possible that repeated accusations of an adulterous relationship which are untrue may well suffice. As a result of *Thurlow* v *Thurlow* (1976), the court has to take into consideration all the obligations relating to marriage, including that of caring for a spouse who is unwell. The fact that Susan knew of John's mental illness when she married him may operate against her establishing his behaviour. However, regard should be had to the principle in *Katz* v *Katz* (1972) where it was held that while a spouse may reasonably be required to care for a partner who is unwell and to tolerate a certain degree of abnormal behaviour, there may come a time when that partner's condition becomes such that the spouse can no longer reasonably be expected to continue living with the other party. This is particularly relevant here, where the children, Damien and Derrick were also becoming upset by their father's behaviour. Negative behaviour can also be taken into consideration but it should be intentional behaviour which John's does appear to be.

Susan could also seek to rely on s1(2)(c) to show that John was in constructive desertion of her. The court will have to determine whether the four criteria referred to in relation to John's divorce (above) are satisfied in this situation. In particular, it will have regard to John's conduct to determine whether he made living together for any further period of time impossible. It may well find that he behaved in such a way as to drive his wife away, for example by persisting in the unsubstantiated belief that Susan was committing adultery and refusing to communicate with her other than by leaving messages on his computer. Also his conduct was having an adverse effect on his children's health.

With regard to the other criteria, Susan can obviously prove that she and her husband are separated. She can also show that there was no reasonable cause for John's desertion since she was not in fact committing adultery. A reasonable but mistaken belief in her adultery would have justified his desertion but not John's persistent and unreasonable belief. Since he continues to insist that she is having an affair, he remains in desertion, and this fact would seem to show in intention on his part to remain separated permanently from his wife. Therefore Susan can probably have a divorce on this ground.

4   DIVORCE LAW REFORM

4.1   Introduction

4.2   Key points

4.3   Recent statutes

4.4   Analysis of questions

4.5   Questions

4.1   Introduction

Examiners in all law subjects like to ensure that students are aware of current developments and will often set an essay question on proposals for reform. Family Law is a subject in which Parliament and the courts are forever attempting to keep up with and reflect current social policy. Accordingly it is one of the most topical subjects and one, therefore, in which an examination question requiring knowledge of that year's proposal for change can confidently be expected.

Both the private and public law relating to children has been dramatically changed by the Children Act 1989 which came into force in October 1991. This is therefore both an important and topical area, which is covered in chapters 8 to 13.

All the major political parties have committed themselves to reform of the law relating to divorce. This follows publication of the Law Commission Reports No 170 entitled *Facing The Future - A Discussion Paper On The Ground For Divorce* (1988) and No 192 entitled *The Ground for Divorce* (1990). No legislation has yet been formulated and it is unlikely that any change will occur, therefore, before 1995. However, since the law relating to divorce is certain to be changed in line with one of the proposals for reform in the Law Commission report, examination questions requiring knowledge of the suggested reforms and the reasons for them are likely over the next few years.

4.2   Key points

a) *The existing law - Matrimonial Causes Act 1973*

    i)   The sole ground - irretrievable breakdown: s1(1).

    ii) The only ways to prove it - the five facts: s1(2)(a)-(e).

        It is possible for a marriage to have irretrievably broken down but for no divorce to be possible yet because no fact has been proved - does that make the law an ass?!

iii) Observations on the existing law:

- Three 'facts' are still fault based.

- No 'incompatibility' basis for divorce.

- Adultery and behaviour amount for over 70% of divorces.

Therefore, there is still much bitterness associated with divorce which does nothing to assist continuing relationships between divorced parents and their children.

iv) Some statistics

- High divorce rate - 160,000 per annum. One in three marriages end in divorce.

- High monetary cost.

- High social cost - assuming an average household of four (husband, wife and two children) then 600,000 people a year are affected by divorce.

b) *The existing procedure*

When assessing both the existing divorce law and proposals for reform it is not sufficient to simply refer to the law. Some mention must be made also of the procedure ie the fact that over 95 per cent of divorces are undefended and are, therefore, dealt with by way of the 'special procedure' trial - a speedy 'paper' procedure requiring no court attendances save to consider the proposed arrangements for the children should the divorce be granted. This procedure is relevant when considering, for example, the objective that empty shells of marriages should be ended with the maximum speed and with the minimum of bitterness (see section (c) below).

c) *The objectives for an ideal divorce law*

Both the Law Commission report leading to the introduction of the existing law (*Reform of the Grounds of Divorce - The Field of Choice* Law Commission Report No 6 (1966) Cmnd 3123) and the current report *Facing the Future* agree on the following objectives for an ideal divorce law:

i) It should buttress rather than undermine the stability of marriage; and

ii) When, regrettably, a marriage has irretrievably broken down it should enable the empty legal shell to be destroyed with the maximum fairness, and the minimum bitterness, distress and humiliation.

In addition both Law Commission reports recognised the following as further considerations to be borne in mind when assessing the quality of a divorce law:

iii) Does the law avoid injustice to an economically weak spouse, usually the wife?

iv) Does the law adequately protect the interests of the children of failed marriages?

v) Is the law understandable and respected?

These objectives give a useful framework for the answer to any question requiring discussion of the proposals for reform. Students should be prepared to test both the existing law and the proposals for reform against the objectives stated above.

One common comment is that the two major objectives (to buttress marriages but to let empty shells of marriages be ended speedily) are incompatible; to achieve the latter you make divorce 'easier' whereas to achieve the former you make divorce 'harder'.

d) *'Facing the Future' - what are the recommendations?*

Students must know the four proposals for reform that were considered and the Commission's view of each, namely:

i) Immediate unilateral demand

Rejected:

- Unacceptable to public opinion.
- It does nothing to buttress marriage.
- It provides no time for parties to adjust to the financial consequences of divorce.

ii) Divorce by mutual consent

Rejected:

- How could court be sure that consent was freely given?
- Would allow one party the power of veto - this could be used as a bartering tactic to force the other spouse to 'buy his divorce' thereby increasing bitterness.

iii) Separation (for 12 or, perhaps, six months)

Considered a possibility but:

- What about people who cannot afford to separate?
- How long should the period of separation be? Twelve months is the normal period adopted by other countries. However, if that were adopted here that would make it more difficult (in terms of time) to obtain a divorce than is currently the case. Should, therefore, the period be six months?
- Separation does not provide any indication as to whether or why the marriage has broken down.

iv) Divorce after a period of transition in which the parties are given time and encouragement to reflect and make the necessary arrangements for the future.

- Once one party has come to the view that the marriage has irretrievably broken down a process of 'uncoupling' should begin to take place.

- Over a period of 'transition' that party would reflect on the desirability of divorce and deal with the effects of it on the children and with the financial consequences.

- The period of transition would be short - no more than 12 months.

- If, having dealt with the consequences of divorce during the transitional period, the party still wants a divorce he/she gets it automatically.

- The procedure simply requires letters of intent at both the beginning and end of the transitional period.

Supported:

This is the most radical option but it is the one that is clearly preferred by the Law Commission and, indeed, the one that is currently being supported by the present government albeit in a modified form.

Advantages:

- Divorce would take a much shorter time than at present considering that not only the divorce but the financial consequences would also be sorted out within the transitional period.

- As there would be no need for either party to leave the other this avoids the problems that arise with the separation ground.

- It does provide divorce on a unilateral request but not until children and finances are sorted out therefore making it more publicly acceptable.

- No party has the power of veto.

Disadvantage:

It does nothing to meet the first objective ie to buttress marriage.

e) *The final recommendation*

On 31 October 1990 the Law Commission published its final recommendation for reform (Law Commission 192 - *The Ground for Divorce* (1990)). As anticipated it plumped for the most radical proposal in its working paper, divorce by process of time. The intention is to allow a period of time for consideration and reflection by the parties - to see whether a divorce is really the answer to the marital problem. This report contains a draft Bill (The Divorce and Separation Bill) which all major political parties in Great Britain have pledged to introduce into English law.

The ground of divorce will remain irretrievable breakdown of marriage but it will be proved in only one way, namely the passing of a period of one year from the date one or both of the parties to the marriage registered their wish to get divorced by filing with the court a statement that the maker or makers believe that their marital relationship has broken down. The statement will be sworn before a Commissioner for Oaths or a court official.

The court will thereupon provide both parties with an information pack explaining what procedures will be adopted to finalise the divorce. The District Judge will lay down a strict timetable by which matters relating to financial and property provision and children will be dealt with within the 11 month period from the filing of the divorce statement. During this period counselling, mediation and conciliation services will be made available to the spouses. There is power to extend the period if matters relating, say, to the future residence of the children have not been resolved.

If ancillary matters as to finance and children have been resolved and the applicant(s) still want a divorce after the 11 months have elapsed then at that time a decree nisi will be pronounced and at the end of 12 months the decree absolute will be pronounced and the parties will be divorced.

The Report also makes recommendations for changes in terminology in order to ameliorate the present adversarial nature of divorce:

i) the parties to the divorce will be known as 'husband' and 'wife' as opposed to 'petitioner' and 'respondent';

ii) the action will no longer be entitled '*X* v *X*' as now but rather '*in the matter of the marriage of X*';

iii) the marriage will be dissolved by 'order' rather than as now be 'decree'.

f) *Observations on the final recommendation*

The question to be asked is to what extend does the final recommendation meet the accepted objectives of a good divorce law: namely to save those marriages that can be saved but to allow empty shells of marriages to end as speedily as possible and with the minimum amount of bitterness.

Does a divorce after a year's period of consideration and reflection do anything to buttress a marriage that is capable of being saved? Arguably the period of reflection may operate as a buttress insofar as all the consequences of the divorce will be known to the applicant before a final decision has to be made. On the other hand the proposal requires the parties to make decisions as to property finance and children at the time that they may feel most bitter towards each other. The parties may feel that they are so far along the conveyor belt to divorce that it is too late to jump off.

Most divorces today (some 80%) are based on the fault facts of adultery and behaviour. It is not known whether this is because the innocent party needs to be able to cast blame and have public condemnation of their partner's wrongdoing or whether it is simply a matter of expediency - these facts provide immediate divorce; the others require two or five years' separation. If it is the former, and casting blame has some therapeutic value, then it is difficult to see how the proposal for reform will gain public acceptability. There is no blame to be cast and, furthermore, a spouse does not even have to leave the matrimonial home once he/she has registered his/her wish for a divorce!

4.3 Recent cases and statutes

Candidates would be advised to obtain a copy of the Law Commission Report No 192 *The Ground for Divorce* (1990). It is available from Her Majesty's Stationery Office, and is concisely written with excellent footnotes.

At the time of going to press (November 1993) the Lord Chancellor has indicated that a Bill will be shortly introduced.

4.4 Analysis of questions

Examination questions on current developments will always be of the essay type requiring the candidate to show knowledge of the existing law and to critically assess the proposals for reform. Now that there is a final and firm recommendation candidates can expect questions requiring constructive criticism of 'the proposals for reform contained in the Divorce and Separation Bill 1990'. In answering such a question some mention ought to be made of the other possibilities for reform contained in the working party report in 1988 but rejected in the final report. When looking at the existing law the candidate should draw on aspects that were unsatisfactory and then discuss the extent to which the proposed reforms will improve the existing/previous law. Most examiners will want rather more than a mere repetition of the proposals for reform - the best marks will be reserved for those candidates who go further and put forward some of their own thoughts and ideas on the proposed reforms.

4.5 Questions

Question 1

Critically assess both the existing divorce law and the proposals for reform.

Written by the Editors

Skeleton solution

- A brief review of the existing law emphasising the extent to which the law fails to achieve its original stated objective.

- An examination of the Law Commission proposals for reform together with some consideration of the merits and demerits of each of the suggested alternatives.

- Conclusion arguing the case for one of the proposals.

General comment

A very general question which requires that the student be concise. The salient points of the existing divorce law should be discussed but avoid a lot of detail - time does not permit. Note that alternative questions could be asked which could require the student

4 DIVORCE LAW REFORM

to examine existing divorce law in more detail - for example, unreasonable behaviour. Essentially most questions will be of a 'compare and contrast' nature.

Suggested solution

The existing law of divorce, which is contained in s1 of the Matrimonial Causes Act 1973, was introduced following the Law Commission Report in 1966 entitled 'The Field of Choice'. That report advocated that the objectives of a good divorce law were primarily twofold: to buttress marriages that were capable of being saved but to allow empty shells of marriages to be ended with the minimum of acrimony and as speedily as possible. The current proposals for reform are contained in another Law Commission Report published in 1988 and entitled 'Facing the Future'. This report retains the same two primary objectives. Indeed it is difficult to see how any one could argue against such common sense goals. Accordingly this question will be answered by reference to the extent to which either the existing law or the proposals for reform meet these objectives.

When the existing law was introduced, the bar on bringing divorce proceedings within the first three years was retained. This bar could certainly be seen as a buttress to marriage. However, in 1984 the three year period was reduced to one - a move that made divorce easier and, thereby, weakened the buttress. The argument was, of course, that three years was far too long for someone to have to wait to be released from an unhappy marriage. The reduction assists the second objective, namely to end empty shells of marriages as speedily as possible, but at the same time works against the first objective; an example of the two objectives being incompatible which is, sadly, often the case. The other buttress in the existing law is found in the six month reconciliation provision contained in s2. These provisions allow the innocent party to continue living with his/her spouse for up to six months after he/she became aware of the particular act complained about without losing the right to rely on that act in any subsequent divorce proceedings. These provisions are important because they recognise that a marriage may be able to survive the occasional crisis. It is not clear as yet whether either of these buttressing measures will be retained in any reform of the law.

A major criticism of the existing law centres on the fact that three of the 'facts' upon which irretrievable breakdown may be founded are fault based, namely adultery, unreasonable behaviour and desertion. Indeed the first two of these account for over 75 per cent of all divorces. Making accusations against one's spouse does nothing to assist the objective of ending marriages with the minimum of bitterness. And, of course, the bitterness engendered in the divorce is often carried over to the ancillary matters of property, finance and children.

As we shall soon see, a major aspect of the proposals for reform is the abolition of all the existing 'facts'. Whilst the abolition of fault based grounds is generally to be welcomed there is an argument in favour of retaining fault. This argument proceeds along the lines that being able to accuse your ex-spouse of adultery, behaviour etc does have a degree of therapeutic value for the spouse who feels that there has been a complete breach of faith committed by the other spouse.

Turning to the proposals for reform, the Law Commission has put forward the following four proposals:

a) Mutual consent

b) Unilateral demand

c) Separation

d) Transitional process

The Law Commission rejected the first two proposals. Divorce by mutual consent was deemed to be impractical because the need for consent allowed one party the power of veto which could be used to obtain better financial terms on divorce. Alternatively, a weak spouse may be forced into giving her consent. Unilateral demand was also rejected. It was felt that it would not have public support and, in any event, would do nothing to encourage reconciliation or, indeed, the conciliation of the consequences of divorce ie what was to happen to the children or the matrimonial home.

This left separation and divorce over a period of time as the two most practical bases for divorce. Separation has been the favoured basis for divorce in other jurisdictions. The Law Commission did not conclude on the period of separation. In other jurisdictions 12 months separation is required. If this were adopted then, in theory, it would take longer to get divorced in future than is the case at present. However if parties have separated without reason for twelve months this is excellent evidence of irretrievable breakdown of marriage. Furthermore it does give the parties time to think again and is sufficiently lengthy to be regarded as a buttress to marriage. The Law Commission fears that in many families it is not possible to separate but, of course, at present the law allows separation in the form of withdrawal from a state of affairs rather than from a place. Therefore this concern could be met by a recognition that withdrawal from the normal marital relationship would be sufficient 'separation' for these purposes.

The Law Commission by elimination appears to favour the 'divorce over a period of time' proposal sometimes referred to as 'transitional process'. With this, no basis for divorce has to be shown other than the registration by one party of their desire to end the marriage. Following such registration there will then follow a fairly short transitional period (expected to be about nine months) during which the courts will sort out all the consequences of divorce, namely custody of children, maintenance and property adjustment. Thereafter if the party still wants a divorce he becomes automatically entitled to a decree nisi followed by a decree absolute.

The criticisms one would make of this proposal are as follows. Firstly, it appears to allow divorce against one party's wishes and it must be questioned whether this is publicly acceptable without some safeguards for the spouse who does not want a divorce. Secondly, it requires matters such as custody to be sorted out when the parties may be at their most bitter towards each other. Thirdly, whilst there is much to be said of the proposal as regards the criterion of ending empty shells of marriages as speedily as possible it appears to do little to buttress marriages.

I would advocate 12 months' separation as the basis for reform provided, of course, that there was a very liberal test for deciding separation where the parties were, for economic reasons, obliged to remain in the same house after the breakdown of their marriage. Such separation is excellent objective proof of irretrievable breakdown of marriage and provides a sufficiently lengthy period to satisfy the 'buttress' requirement without being so long as to offend the 'buttress' requirement without being so long as to offend the 'speed' objective. It would be important that child custody is sorted out within the first 12 months of separation but matters of finance and property could properly be left to be dealt with, say, within six to nine months of the decree absolute.

Question 2

'The current law of divorce is confusing and misleading, discriminatory and unjust, provokes unnecessary hostility and bitterness and does nothing to save the marriage.' Discuss. What reforms, if any, to the law of divorce do you consider appropriate?

University of London LLB Examination
(for External Students) Family Law June 1991 Q2

General comment

This question requires a consideration of the proposals for reform of divorce laws set out in the Law Commission's report *The Ground for Divorce* (1990). Candidates should review the existing law and consider whether its aims have been met, and thereafter consider to what extent the Law Commission's proposed reforms will fulfil these aims.

Skeleton solution

- Discuss differing views relating to object of divorce law expressed by Archbishop of Canterbury's group in *Putting Asunder* and Law Commission.

- Outline current divorce law.

- Consider criticism of current law made by Law Commission in its report *The Ground for Divorce* (1990).

- Does reliance on fault facts add to the distress, bitterness and humiliation?

- Can divorce law save marriages?

- Is the current law confusing and misleading? Is it unjust and discriminatory?

- Consider the Law Commission's main proposals for reform - one ground, but divorce to be granted only after a transitional period to allow for reflection and the making of arrangements for children and property.

Suggested solution

The Divorce Reform Act 1969 which forms the basis of the current law on divorce was a compromise between two basic principles expounded by the Archbishop of Canterbury's Committee in its report *Putting Asunder* published in 1966, and the Law Commission.

The Archbishop of Canterbury's group favoured the substitution of 'breakdown' for the matrimonial offence as the basis of divorce law, taking the view that a divorce decree should be seen as a judicial recognition of a state of affairs with a consequent redefinition of status. The committee favoured the view that the divorce court should carry out a detailed inquest into the alleged facts and causes of the breakdown of the marriage relationship in each case to avoid possible abuse of the law.

However, the Law Commission, which was appointed to investigate the reform of divorce law following the publication of *Putting Asunder*, did not agree that there should be such a detailed inquest, arguing that such a course would be impracticable. The Commission recommended that the grounds that existed already for divorce should be retained but that an additional ground as evidenced by a period of separation, which would be shorter if the respondent consented than if he or she did not, should be introduced. The Commission's aims were to preserve the stability of marriage but it recognised also the social function of divorce, that is to allow parties to enter new legal relationships if they so wished while giving any necessary protection to the children of the family and dealing with financial and property adjustment as required. Further, it believed that a machinery to allow for reconciliation should be provided if there was any possibility that a marriage could be preserved.

Under the Divorce Reform Act 1969 irretrievable breakdown of the marriage became the sole ground for divorce. However, it could only be inferred by proof of one or more of the specified facts which are akin to the old matrimonial offences, although they included two new facts based on separation.

This legislation has been described as an uneasy compromise between two inconsistent views on divorce policy. One view is that divorce should be available to either party to the marriage where it has irretrievably broken down and that the old matrimonial offences are mere symptoms of that breakdown. Another view, however, is that it would be fundamentally unjust to allow a party to petition for divorce on the basis of irretrievable breakdown alone as that could allow a party to rely on his or her own wrongdoing and to obtain a divorce even against the will of the innocent spouse.

Under the current law a divorce is obtainable only where there is evidence of irretrievable breakdown as evidenced by one of the 'facts' set out in s1(2) Matrimonial Causes Act 1973 and a divorce cannot be granted in the absence of one of these facts even where it is clear that the marriage has broken down irretrievably (*Richards* v *Richards* (1972)). This requirement of proof of one of the facts is to ensure that the innocent spouse cannot be divorced against his or her will, at least until five year separation is established and even then the respondent can prevent the divorce if grave financial or other hardship can be established along with injustice in granting the decree.

It is recognised that this reformed law has made it possible for virtually all broken marriages to be dissolved, even though in some cases it may only be after a period of delay. However, it is also recognised that the most commonly used 'facts' on which irretrievable breakdown is evidenced are the fault based ones and in particular adultery and behaviour. One of the objectives of the reformed law was to bury decently a dead marriage and enable the 'empty legal shell' of marriage to be destroyed with the maximum fairness and the minimum bitterness, distress and humiliation. It could be argued that reliance on the fault based facts would only add to the contention between the parties and this view was expressed by the Law Commission in its report *The Ground for Divorce* (1990) Law Com No 192. This would be particularly the case where serious allegations of behaviour were made. However, many practitioners also recognise that the fault facts are frequently used by their clients merely as a device on which to hang the decree nisi, and that any bitterness and hostility arise not really because of the divorce petition, but as a result of the consequences which flow from divorce, namely loneliness, a reduced standard of living and in some cases loss of close contact with one's children. It is argued that even if the basis for divorce was changed to allow a more civilised process, these consequences would still arise and the resultant bitterness would still be present (see Mears [1991] Fam Law 231).

The present law is also criticised by the Law Commission for failing to do anything to save marriage. However, it could be argued that because a petitioner is unable to obtain a divorce (except where the spouses have been separated for five years) without showing one of the fault facts is established or without the consent of the respondent, the law does go some way to saving marriages. In any event it is difficult to see how divorce law can save marriages except by making a divorce more difficult to obtain, and that may have the effect of adding to the tension and acrimony felt by the parties. It is recognised that it is pointless to try to keep any obviously dead marriage alive and by the time spouses seek legal advice on how to dissolve their marriage they have decided their marriage is dead. Therefore any counselling or mediation aimed at saving the marriage is futile at that stage. Divorce does not make a marriage break down. It is merely the mechanism by which the marriage is legally dissolved. The process should be as constructive as possible and the Law Commission stated in its report *The Ground for Divorce* that the aim of the law must be to promote the amicable resolution of practical problems in relation to finance and property and children, to minimise the harm suffered by children and to promote shared parental responsibility.

The Law Commission argues that the current law is confusing and misleading in that, for example, the facts relied upon to obtain a divorce may not really be the true reason for the marriage breakdown. This may be a valid point, for many spouses will seek to rely on a fact which will provide a speedy divorce and this may mean that the facts are used as a convenience rather than as a true reflection of the problems in the marriage. Some writers would question whether anyone is really confused or misled by the law, however, and argue that if the law worked well in practice, this would not be an important criticism.

The Law Commission also argues that the present law is unjust and discriminatory in that inter alia it is unfair that divorce is not readily available at the behest of one party and that the other party may use the requirement of his or her consent (where a petition under s1(2)(d) MCA 1973 only is relevant) as a basis for bargaining on other ancillary matters. However, given that the divorce may cause other adverse consequences such as a reduced standard of living or loss of home, it is questionable whether it is unfair to a petitioner that the respondent should seek to exact a price for his or her consent.

71

Under the present law the 'innocent' spouse cannot be divorced without his or her consent (except where the parties have been separated for five years, subject to the s5 MCA 1973 defence). The Law Commission considers this to be unfair and favours the principle of divorce on demand (albeit after a period of reflection). But the divorce procedures cannot be looked at without also considering their consequences in relation to money, property and children, and given that these are the most important concerns of the parties it should be asked why an innocent spouse should have those consequences unilaterally imposed upon him or her.

The Law Commission's main proposals for reform of the divorce law are based on the principle that divorce should be available after a period of transition in which the parties are given the time to reflect on this step and to make necessary arrangements with regard to money, property and children.

The Commission recommends that there would be one ground for divorce, namely the irretrievable breakdown of the marriage. This would be established by a sworn statement by either or both parties. Statements giving details of any minor children of the family and the arrangements made for them, and where financial relief and property adjustment is sought, giving information relating to the financial positions of the parties, would also be filed in court.

The parties would be given information regarding the effects of divorce and counselling and conciliation services. These services could provide the forum in which the parties can air their grievances and resolve disputes with each other, a process which is recognised as essential to reduce future conflict and encourage co-operation between the parties.

On the expiration of twelve months either party will be entitled to a divorce decree, save in exceptional circumstances. In their discussion paper *Facing the Future* (1988) Law Com. No 170, the Law Commission suggested that a decree could be postponed where the issues in relation to the children had not been resolved or where proper financial or property arrangements had not yet been made. In *Principles of Family Law* (fifth edition) S M Cretney and J M Masson argue that if such postponements were allowed this would encourage hostile litigation to resolve these disputes. The objects of the 'cooling off' period of twelve months must include the opportunity to allow the parties to address the feelings of bitterness and hostility attendant on the marital breakup in an unpressured environment. These potential postponements could operate to exert further pressure on the parties.

It is argued (see Walker [1991] Fam Law 234) that the Law Commission's proposals have much to recommend them if they mean that the aims of the divorce process will be to provide support for families, particularly children, and to avoid conflict if possible. Any divorce process will involve pain and upheaval for the parties concerned and perhaps the most that can be expected of a divorce law is that it does not add to these problems. It must be remembered however that the real areas of conflict, namely financial and property matters and children, remain.

5 RIGHTS AND OBLIGATIONS DURING MARRIAGE

5.1 Introduction

5.2 Key points

5.3 Recent cases

5.4 Analysis of questions

5.5 Questions

5.1 Introduction

The common law has long recognised that there are a number of mutual rights and obligations that are owed by the spouses to each other (although very often in practice these are obligations owed by the bread-winning husband to the non-earning wife) during marriage. These are sometimes referred to as 'consortium rights'. In this chapter we look at the two most important of such rights, namely the right to occupy the matrimonial home and the right to maintenance.

5.2 Key points

a) *Rights to maintenance during marriage*

    i) It must be emphasised that we are only concerned here with powers of the court to award maintenance during marriage, not on or after a decree of divorce. After decree absolute the courts have wide powers to grant maintenance and so forth under ss23-25 of the Matrimonial Causes Act (MCA) 1967 (see chapter 6: *The financial consequences of divorce*). Such applications are known as ancillary relief applications simply because they are ancillary to, and dependent upon, a divorce decree.

       Here we are dealing with the pre-divorce stage. The powers of the Magistrates' Court to grant maintenance during marriage are contained in ss1-7 of the Domestic Proceedings Magistrates' Court Act 1978 (DPMCA).

    ii) Before looking at the powers under the DPMCA it should be noted that very often concerns about maintenance only arise because the marriage is on the rocks ie the likelihood is that divorce proceedings are going to be commenced in the foreseeable future. Accordingly the wife's concern is for maintenance to cover the period between the breakdown of marriage and the divorce decree. Although a maintenance application can be made under the DPMCA to cover this period such an application takes some time to be finally concluded. The wife's need is for immediate monies and, consequently, she will often take advantage of the immediate availability of welfare benefits from the State (ie income support or family credit). In practice she will be content with such State benefits until such time as a maintenance application is dealt with post divorce under ss23-35 MCA 1973.

iii) The scheme of the DPMCA is as follows:

- The application must be made to the Magistrates' Court.

- The applicant (known as the Complainant) must prove one of the grounds of complaint listed in s1:

  - failure to provide reasonable maintenance for the Complainant;

  - failure to provide reasonable maintenance for a child of the family;

  - that the Respondent has behaved in such a way that the Complainant cannot reasonably be expected to live with the Respondent (ie unreasonable behaviour);

  - that the Respondent has deserted the Complainant.

  Note:

  Intention in relation to failing to provide maintenance is irrelevant; the only question for the court is whether as a matter of fact reasonable maintenance has not been paid.

  The law relating to unreasonable behaviour is exactly the same as for divorce. There is no separate ground for complaint based on adultery therefore this must come under 'behaviour'.

  The law relating to desertion is the same as for divorce except that there is no minimum period of desertion required. One day's desertion would be sufficient.

- Once a complaint is proved under s1 the court can make one or more of the awards in s2 ie: maintenance and/or a lump sum for the complainant; maintenance and/or a lump sum for a child of the family.

  In deciding the quantum of maintenance for the complainant wife the same rules apply as on divorce (one-third rule, net effect etc).

  In deciding the quantum of maintenance for children again the same rules apply as on divorce (the DSS income support and the NFCA (National Foster Care Association) figures are used as guidelines).

  There is no power to make property adjustment orders and the power to award a lump sum is limited to a maximum of £1,000 per applicant ie an application on behalf of a wife and two children would, in theory, allow the Magistrates' Court to grant a lump sum of up to £3,000.

- In deciding what order to make, if any, the court has a list of guidelines laid down in s3 of the Act which are almost identical to those found in s25 of the Matrimonial Causes Act 1973 and the applicable law is, for practical purposes, the same.

- The Magistrates' Court is given power by s6 to make an order that is agreed by the parties - this is roughly the equivalent to a consent order made after divorce. The majority of applications to the Magistrates' Court under the DPMCA end up being agreed orders under s6.

b) *Rights of occupation of the matrimonial home*

   i) We are looking here only at rights of occupation, not ownership. Ownership of the matrimonial home can be declared by the courts on application under the Married Women's Property Act 1882 although in practice most wives do not make such applications. The question of ownership only normally arises on divorce and, as seen in chapter 6: *The financial consequences of divorce*, the courts have wide powers to transfer property from one spouse to the other regardless of their strict existing ownership rights.

   ii) As regards occupation of the matrimonial home there are two persons who may threaten the spouse's (normally the wife's) occupation:

   - the other spouse (the husband); or

   - a third party purchaser or mortgagee to whom the husband has sold or mortgaged the property without the wife's knowledge.

   As we shall see, a spouse can protect herself against both by exercising her statutory rights under the Matrimonial Homes Act (MHA) 1983. In paragraphs iii)-v) below, however, we shall start by looking at the position other than under the MHA.

   There are three possible situations:

   iii) If the home is in joint names:

   Neither party can exclude the other and both have rights of occupation. Furthermore, a third party cannot obtain good legal title to that property (in the absence of fraud) because both parties have to sign the documents of transfer.

   Note the particular problem when a house is charged to the mortgagee to secure a loan to the husband's business. In *Barclay's Bank* v *O'Brien* (1993) The Times 2 October. A mortgagee loaned money to a business in which the husband *but not* the wife had an interest and the loan was secured by a charge on joint matrimonial property. The House of Lords held that such a charge may be unenforceable as against the wife unless the mortgagee has taken steps to ensure that the wife knew exactly the nature and effect of the charge that she was being asked to sign. Two conditions have to be satisfied:

75

- the transaction was not on its face to the financial advantage of the wife; and

- there was a substantial risk that the husband would put pressure on the wife in procuring her to act as surety.

In this case the husband had said the charge was limited to £60,000 for three weeks, whereas in fact it was unlimited in time and duration and had reached £154,000 when the bank sought to enforce. Where these two conditions apply the charge would only be binding on the wife if the mortgagee had seen the wife in private and in the absence of the husband and explained to her the risk she was running by agreeing to the charge and the advisability of taking independent legal advice.

However, where the two conditions do not apply and it appears to the mortgagee that this is a loan to husband and wife for joint purposes then the *O'Brien* requirements do not apply: *CIBC Mortgages* v *Pitt* (1993) The Times 22 October.

iv) If the home is in one spouse's name (we shall assume the husband's) alone:

If the wife has a beneficial interest (by way of substantial contributions within the meaning of s37 of the Matrimonial Proceedings and Property Act 1970 and/or contributions, direct or indirect, giving rise to an implied or constructive trust - see, for the legal principles, chapter 13: *The law's response to the unmarried family*) then once again she has a right to occupy as against her husband.

As against third party purchasers or mortgagees she may be protected particularly if resident in the home at the time of the transaction but only if the husband has not, when attempting to sell or mortgage the property, appointed two trustees to receive the purchase/mortgage monies.

Compare: *Williams & Glyn's Bank* v *Boland* [1981] AC 487; *Kingsnorth Finance Co Ltd* v *Tizard* [1986] 2 All ER 54; *City of London Building Society* v *Flegg* [1988] AC 54.

v) If the house is in one spouse's name alone and the other spouse has not contributed so as to have acquired a beneficial interest:

- The husband has no duty to allow her to stay in the matrimonial home itself. His duty is only to provide a roof over her head - it does not have to be the roof of the home. Although, of course, if a husband tried to exclude his wife and/or children from the matrimonial home he would soon be faced with applications for injunctions under the domestic violence legislation (see chapter 7: *Domestic violence*).

- If the husband sold to a third party purchaser/mortgagee then such third party purchaser or mortgagee would be entitled to possession as against the wife.

vi) The protection given by the Matrimonial Homes Act 1983

- By s1 the non-owning spouse has an automatic right as against the other spouse not to be evicted from the matrimonial home without the leave of the court. This right against her husband exists whether or not the wife has registered her right of occupation.

- By s2 she has similar rights against third party purchasers or mortgagees but only if her right of occupation has been registered prior to the third party purchase or mortgage.

  The right of occupation is registered as a Class F land charge in unregistered land and a Notice in registered land.

- Anyone who purchases or grants a mortgage on a property after the right of occupation has been registered takes subject to that right. Effectively, therefore, no-one would buy or grant a mortgage where a right of occupation is registered.

- If the owning spouse wishes to remove the right of occupation he must apply to the court under s1(2) of the MHA. In deciding what order to make on such an application the court must have regard to the guidelines set out in s1(3) ie:

  - the financial resources of the parties;
  - their conduct;
  - the interests of the children;
  - all the circumstances of the case.

  You will remember that these criteria are of great importance when deciding whether to grant an ouster injunction on the grounds of domestic violence and similar principles apply to those developed in domestic violence cases (see chapter 7: *Domestic violence*).

- Very often the following situation occurs. The mortgage is taken out before the house is acquired (therefore the MHA protection cannot operate) and the mortgage is in the husband's sole name. He leaves his wife and she some time later discovers that he has not been paying the mortgage and the Building Society wishes to repossess the property. The MHA gives the wife in these circumstances a certain degree of protection. Firstly, by virtue of s1(5) she is entitled to take over the mortgage. Secondly, by virtue of s8, as long as she has registered her right of occupation she is entitled to be notified of, and to become a party to, any repossession proceedings that the Building Society intends to commence. This in practice will allow the wife to attend the repossession proceedings and normally persuade the court to suspend any repossession on condition that she clears the arrears over a period of time (usually not longer than two years).

5.3 Recent cases

One of the important consortium rights that a husband hitherto has had is the right to demand sexual intercourse of his wife. The effect of this right (said by Hale in his 'Pleas of the Crown' - written in the 17th century - to be a right that the wife consents to by reason of the marriage contract and confirmed by Parliament by virtue of the Sexual Offences Act 1956) was that a husband who forced his wife to have intercourse against her will could not be convicted of the crime of rape or indeed of any sexual assault. The only crime that could be charged was assault. This exemption from prosecution for the crime of rape when the victim is the wife of the offender has now been removed by the House of Lords in *R* v *R* [1991] 4 All ER 481.

CIBC Mortgages v *Pitt* (1993) The Times 22 October

Barclays Bank v *O'Brien* (1993) The Times 2 October

5.4 Analysis of questions

It is most unlikely that an examination question will be set dealing only with consortium rights. However it is often the case that part of an examination problem does require you to, for example, reassure a wife whose husband has left her and has not paid any housekeeping and/or who is threatening to sell the matrimonial home over her head. In other words, the question is asking about rights of maintenance and occupation.

5.5 Questions

Question 1

Arthur and Betty married in 1978 and have two children. Early in 1982 Arthur developed a mental illness, as a result of which he erroneously believed that his wife was having an affair with their bank manager. After many heated arguments, which caused distress to the children as well as to Betty, Betty announced that she was leaving home, taking the children with her, and that she was not going to return. Arthur replied that he was glad she was leaving, as he had never wanted to live with an adulteress, but that he was sorry to see the children go and that he would pay Betty £40 a week for their upkeep. Betty left home a few days later and went to stay with her mother.

Arthur was admitted to a mental hospital a few months later but continued to pay Betty £40 a week out of capital he possessed. Betty visited him occasionally both out of a genuine concern for his health and because she was anxious that he should keep up the payments.

In April 1987 Arthur met Celia, a new nurse at the mental hospital, whom he wishes to marry. Betty does not want a divorce because she thinks Arthur will stop paying her the money if he marries Celia.

Assuming that Arthur does not obtain a divorce, how, if at all, can Betty ensure that Arthur makes financial provision for herself and the children?

Adapted from University of London LLB Examination
(for External Students) Family Law June 1987 Q2

General comment

Financial provision during marriage is regularly examined; in its original form this question also dealt with whether Arthur could divorce Betty - see chapter 3: *Divorce* for this. In answering the question candidates must remember to discuss, in relation to the Magistrates' Court proceedings, orders under s7 as well as s2 DPMCA 1978.

Skeleton solution

- Discuss the two major jurisdictions available to a spouse to obtain financial relief during a marriage, namely s27 MCA 1973 and s1 DPMCA 1978.

- Explain the grounds to be relied upon, and the orders available under s27 MCA 1973 and ss2 and 7 DPMCA 1978 and the factors to be considered by the court applying the guidelines in s25 MCA 1973 and s3 DPMCA 1978.

Suggested solution

On the assumption that Arthur does not obtain a divorce at this time there are two procedures available to Betty to ensure that he makes financial provision for herself and the children.

Betty could apply to the High Court or County Court under s27 MCA 1973 for financial provision for herself and the children on the ground that Arthur has failed to provide reasonable maintenance for herself and/or the children, and even though Arthur has been paying maintenance regularly, the sum of £40 for the family's support may not be deemed reasonable. However this will depend on Betty's resources as well as Arthur's and it may be that the provision he has been making is reasonable in all the circumstances.

Alternatively she could apply to the Magistrates' Court for an order under s2 Domestic Proceedings and Magistrates' Courts Act 1978 (hereinafter DPMCA 1978) on one of the grounds set out in s1, namely that Arthur has failed to provide reasonable maintenance for Betty and/or the children (which ground is similar to that set out in s27 MCA 1973 and therefore the reservations mentioned above must be applied to it); or on the ground of Arthur's unreasonable behaviour (which has the same meaning as under s1(2)(b) MCA 1973); or on the ground that Arthur has deserted her (and desertion in the Magistrates' Court has the same meaning as under s1(2)(c) MCA 1973 although there is no minimum period of desertion so long as it is continuing at the date of the hearing, and will include constructive desertion).

Betty could rely on Arthur's behaviour, ie his false accusations of adultery, which gave rise to arguments between the parties, and even though such behaviour is attributable to his mental illness the court will take it into account having made allowances for the illness and the performance of marital obligations: *Katz* v *Katz* (1972). Alternatively she could rely on s7 DPMCA 1978 which provides that where the spouses have been separated for a continuous period exceeding three months, neither party being in desertion (which may be the case here particularly in view of Arthur's mental illness which may have prevented him from forming the intention to desert), and one spouse has been making periodical payments for the benefit of the other party and for a child of the family, that other party may apply to the magistrates for an order, specifying in the application the aggregate amount received during the three months preceding the application. On hearing such an application the court may order the respondent to make such periodical payments to the applicant, or for the benefit of a child of the family, but the amount ordered must not exceed the aggregate amount stated in the application. However, if as a result of this limitation the magistrates feel that reasonable maintenance cannot be awarded, they may refuse to make an order on this ground and treat the application as one for financial provision under s1 and make a suitable order under s2.

So Betty has a choice of applications before her. If the maintenance paid by Arthur is not reasonable she can rely on s27 MCA 1973 or s1(a) DPMCA 1978. Alternatively, she could rely on s1(b) DPMCA 1978, namely on Arthur's behaviour. If she is satisfied with the maintenance paid by Arthur voluntarily, then a s7 DPMCA 1978 application would seem appropriate.

The orders that can be made under s27 MCA 1973 and s2 DPMCA 1978 are similar and include a periodical payments order in favour of the applicant and/or any child of the family, but which in the County Court can be secured although this cannot be done in the Magistrates' Court. Further, in both jurisdictions the court may make a lump sum order. However, whereas in the County Court there is no limit on the amount of the lump sum, in the Magistrates' Court it is subject to a limit of £500, although on application for variation further lump sum awards can be made. It is unlikely that Betty will require a lump sum in excess of £500 in any event. It should be noted that under s7 DPMCA 1978 the magistrates have no power to make lump sum provision so if Betty requires a lump sum, say to pay off existing debts, then a s7 application would be inappropriate.

Under s27 MCA 1973 the court will take into account all the circumstances of the case first consideration being given to the welfare of any minor child of the family, including the matters set out in s25(2) MCA 1973 as substituted by s3 Matrimonial and Family Proceedings Act 1984 (hereinafter MFPA 1984), insofar as they apply to an application which does not affect the status of the marriage. Similarly in the Magistrates' Court, s3 DPMCA 1978 as substituted by s9 MFPA 1984 which sets out the guidelines to be considered when deciding what if any order to make, follows the provisions of s25 MCA. Therefore in this case the relevant factors will include the income, earning capacity, including any increase in that capacity which the court considers it reasonable to expect a party to take steps to acquire, property and other financial resources of the parties (as well as the income and resources of the children, if any); the financial needs, obligations and responsibilities of the parties (and the children) both immediately and in the foreseeable future; the standard of living enjoyed by the family before the breakdown; the age of the parties and the duration of the

In deciding what order to make the court is directed (Schedule 1 para 4(1)) to have regard to all the circumstances of the case including the following matters:

a) the income, earning capacity, property and other financial resources which [any parent, the applicant and any other person in whose favour the court proposes to make the order] has or is likely to have in the foreseeable future;

b) the financial needs, obligations and responsibilities which [as in (a)] has or is likely to have in the foreseeable future;

c) financial needs of the child;

d) the income earning capacity, property and other financial resources of the child;

e) any physical or mental disability of the child;

f) the manner in which the child was being or was expected to be educated or trained.

Clarissa needs to have financial support to go to university. We are not told what, if anything, Benjamin or Anthea do for a living. If they are both working they would both be required to make financial contributions towards her support. If only one is employed it would be him/her and not the other - unless the latter has the means/resources anyway.

Therefore on the present facts Clarissa is likely to obtain an order for periodical payments and perhaps even a lump sum order too.

ii) Firstly, Edward lives with Anthea and Dominic. But we are told that Anthea told Benjamin that Dominic was his child - even though she had been having an affair with Edward for the past two years. Therefore the first point to be addressed is the paternity of Dominic; this may be established by means of blood tests and/or DNA testing. If Edward is the natural father of Dominic he, as an unmarried father, will have no parental responsibility for Dominic. Section 2(1) and (2) Children Act 1989 provides that where parents are not married at the time of the child's birth, only the mother shall have parental responsibility and the father shall not have any unless he acquires it in accordance with the provisions of s4 of this Act. Section 4 provides that an unmarried father may acquire parental responsibility by means of a formal agreement with the mother, in the prescribed form or by obtaining an order that he shall have parental responsibility jointly with the mother; or alternatively by applying for a residence order under s8 of the CA 1989. An unmarried father may apply for this order if the court grants him a residence order. This does not of itself give Edward parental rights but s12(1) provides that the court must grant him a parental responsibility order when it grants him a residence order.

It should be noted that once the father has acquired parental responsibility he is in the same position with regard to his legal rights in respect of the child as if he were married to the child's mother. Where two people have parental responsibility each may act alone.

83

In deciding whether it should make a residence order the court will have regard to factors set out in s1(3) CA 1989, such as the ascertainable wishes and feelings of the child, the child's physical, emotional and educational needs, child's age, sex, background, how capable each of the parents are of meeting the child's needs and other s1(3) factors. It should be noted that the welfare of the child is the paramount consideration for the court in determining any question relevant to the child's upbringing: s1(1) CA 1989.

In this case as Edward is living with the mother anyway, the court may extend parental responsibility to him. Anthea may even agree to it.

An important point to note is that any s8 order may:

a) contain directions as to how it is to be implemented;

b) impose conditions which must be complied with by specified persons;

such as where there is a real fear that a parent may not consent to medical treatment, eg where a parent is a Jehovah's Witness as in this case.

If Edward is not Dominic's natural father, he may still apply to the court for a residence order under s11(3): 'any person who is not entitled to apply for a s8 order may apply to the court for leave to do so'. The court will consider:

1) his connection to the child - here Edward lives with Dominic and his mother and therefore can be seen to be the father figure in Dominic's life;

2) the effect on the child;

3) the parents' feelings.

Anthea would be asked how she feels. If she feels her relationship with Edward is long term and permanent she may be willing for him to have parental responsibility.

If the court grants Edward leave to apply for a residence order the points stated above will be relevant.

Edward can be reassured that should Anthea not agree to medical treatment for the child he, as a person with parental responsibility, may do so.

iii) The question does not state whether Anthea and Benjamin are getting divorced. If they are getting a divorce then Anthea will be able to make an application under s23 of the Matrimonial Causes Act 1973 for periodical payments and/or a lump sum order or s24 MCA 1973 for a property adjustment order. On the basis that they are not getting divorced the options available to Anthea for obtaining financial relief for herself and her children are as follows:

1) An application to the county court under s27 MCA 1973; or

2) An application to the magistrate's court under s2 of the Domestic Proceedings and Magistrates' Courts Act 1978, one of the grounds set out in s1 DPMCA 1978.

directed (Schedule 1 para 4(1)) to have regard to all the circumstances of the case including guidelines that are the same as discussed above in the DPMCA 1978 save that the court is not specifically enjoined to have regard to the family's standard of living and no weighting of the child's welfare is specified.

On this basis, it would probably be the case that Edward would be ordered to make financial provision for Dominic.

6 THE FINANCIAL CONSEQUENCES OF DIVORCE

6.1   Introduction

6.2   Key points

6.3   Recent cases and statutes

6.4   Analysis of questions

6.5   Questions

6.1   Introduction

This is an important topic both in practice and as far as the examination is concerned. The issue here is how the matrimonial finances are distributed on or after a decree of divorce, nullity or judicial separation. The court's powers are contained in ss23 and 24 of the Matrimonial Causes Act 1973 (as amended by the Matrimonial and Family Proceedings Act 1984). By s23 the court is empowered to award money in the form of a lump sum and/or periodical payments to either the spouse and/or the children of the family. By s24 the court may transfer or settle 'property' (which in most marriages means the former matrimonial home) for the benefit of either spouse and/or the children of the family. Section 25 gives guidelines to the court as to how to exercise its powers under ss23 and 24. It is knowledge and understanding of how these powers are likely to be exercised that will be tested in any examination question. A thorough understanding of the major principles as established in case law is, therefore, required.

6.2   Key points

a) *Maintenance for the spouse*

Structure of answer:

With any question about maintenance the answer must begin by considering the clean break principles laid down by s25A(1)-(3). In other words first consider whether there will be any maintenance awarded at all (ie will there be an immediate clean break - s25A(3), and, if so, whether such maintenance may be of limited duration (ie the postponed clean break - s25A(2)). Only after this is it then proper to proceed and consider on what principles the quantum of such maintenance will be assessed.

Accordingly the following matters should be understood:

i) What is the practical importance of s25A?

The possibility of imposing an immediate or postponed clean break must be explored in every case: s25A(1).

However, as long as it has been considered, the appeal court will not interfere with the way the court below exercised its discretion unless its decision is 'plainly wrong': *Whiting* v *Whiting* [1988] 1 WLR 565; [1988] 2 FLR 189.

In particular there is no presumption in favour of a clean break - the court's duty is only to consider it: *Barrett* v *Barrett* [1988] 2 FLR 516.

ii) When will there be an immediate clean break?

- The short childless marriage where neither party has been financially disadvantaged as a result of the marriage: *Fisher* v *Fisher* [1989] Fam Law 269.

- As compensation for a spouse who loses all his interest in the matrimonial home: *Hanlon* v *Hanlon* [1978] 2 All ER 889. A problem has arisen with this basis for having a clean break order because of the coming into force in October 1990 of s15 of the Social Security Act 1990. This section amends s24 of the Social Security Act 1986 (now re-enacted in ss106-108 of the Social Security Adjudication and Administration Act 1992) so as to allow the Department of Social Security to recoup from a divorced spouse any monies by way of income support and/or family credit which have been paid to that spouse's ex-wife and/or children under 16. Hitherto this power to recoup had only applied whilst the parties were still married.

  Accordingly where an ex-wife is likely to have to rely on State benefits after a divorce a court cannot any longer justify an absolute transfer of a house to a wife on the basis that the husband is being compensated because he does not have to pay any maintenance. The DSS may well require to pay maintenance at some time in the future by reason of these statutory powers!

- Where the payer is on a low income and the recipient is in receipt of state benefits so that it would be a genuine struggle for the payer to make any payments and any such payments would still leave the recipient dependent on state support: *Ashley* v *Blackman* [1988] Fam 85; [1988] 1 WLR 222. Note that *Ashley* v *Blackman* and also *Delaney* v *Delaney* [1990] 2 FLR 457 should now be looked at in the light of ss106-108 of the Social Security Adjudication and Administration Act 1992.

- Where the recipient is cohabiting: *Suter* v *Suter and Jones* [1987] 2 All ER 336.

But not if is she is cohabiting with a poor man: *Duxbury* v *Duxbury* [1987] 1 FLR 7; *Atkinson* v *Atkinson* [1987] 3 All ER 849.

- In wealthy families where a lump sum may be ordered in lieu of maintenance.

But how is that lump sum to be assessed?

Duxbury v *Duxbury* [1987] 1 FLR 7 - a computer programme was applied which assessed the lump sum that would be needed to provide sufficient for the wife's annual reasonable needs but would also be used up during the course of her life's expectancy. Its use in this case gave rise to the expression the '*Duxbury* calculation'.

Note, however, that the *Duxbury* calculation is no more than a useful tool, a means to an end; it should not be used as an end in itself so that courts simply award the Duxbury figure without reference to the s25 guidelines.

The *Duxbury* calculation may be of most use where there has been a long marriage and the wife has not worked but has contributed over a long period of time to both looking after the household and bringing up the children of the family.

In particular it will not be appropriate where the wife has not only looked after the family but also contributed to the success of the husband's business so that she has 'earned a share' in his current assets.

For example in *Gojkovic* v *Gojkovic* [1990] FLR 140 the parties were Yugoslav refugees who had come to England in the 1940s. They had bought a hotel and the wife had acted as maid, cook, porter etc. The hotel was successful and provided funds to allow the husband to become a property developer in the 1970s. He was now worth £4.5 million. The *Duxbury* calculation would have given the wife £532,000. The court however awarded her £1,000,000.

iii) When will there be a postponed clean break?

There will only be a postponed clean break where, on the facts before it on the day the order is made, the court can foresee a time when the recipient spouse would be able to adjust without undue hardship to the termination of maintenance: *Morris* v *Morris* [1985] FLR 1176; *Fisher* v *Fisher* [1989] Fam Law 269.

An example of such a situation would be where the wife has such qualifications (eg she is a teacher) that the court can be reasonably confident that once the children are at school full time (or have left school) she would be able to return to work and earn sufficient to maintain herself.

Generally there is a judicial reluctance, however, to crystal ball-gaze. There is no particular need to limit the duration of a periodical payments order because if circumstances change either party can return to court and seek an end of the order at that time: *M* v *M* [1987] 2 FLR 1.

Note that where the court is minded to make a postponed clean break order it has a choice:

- It may award maintenance for 'x years or further order'. In such circumstances the recipient is permitted to return to the court before the expiry of those 'x years' for an extension of the term; or

- Alternatively it may award maintenance for 'x years; it being further directed that the recipient shall not be entitled to apply under s31 for an extension of that term': s28(1)(a). In this case no matter what the financial circumstances of the recipient are at the expiry of those 'x years' she will not be able to ask for the maintenance to be continued.

  This latter type of order has been described as 'draconian' (ie 'cruel', 'harsh') by the Court of Appeal in *Waterman* v *Waterman* [1989] 1 FLR 380 and, accordingly, should only be made in the rarest of cases.

iv) How is the amount (quantum) of maintenance assessed?

- Is there a one third starting point?

  The court has absolute discretion as to whether to use such a starting point: *Foley* v *Foley* [1981] 2 All ER 857.

  In any event, its application is not popular today. If it is to be used it would normally only be used in an attempt to assess maintenance; it should not be used to assess the share of the capital assets: *Potter* v *Potter* [1982] 3 All ER 321.

  However, if a sum equal to one third of the capital assets can be raised by the payer without the need to sell such assets then the one third rule may be applied to capital assets: *Bullock* v *Bullock* [1986] 1 FLR 372; *Dew* v *Dew* [1986] 2 FLR 341.

- If the one third rule isn't applied, what alternatives are there?

  Simply apply the guidelines in s25(1) and s25(2): *Sharpe* v *Sharpe* (1981) 11 Fam Law 121 CA.

  In particular note s25(2)(a) and s25(2)(b) which require the court to contrast each party's income and expenditure positions and then balance one party's reasonable needs against the other's ability to pay: *Lombardi* v *Lombardi* [1973] 3 All ER 625.

- Is the court able to give more than is necessary to provide for the wife's reasonable needs - ie provide a 'cushion' against future uncertainties? In *Re Besterman* [1984] 2 All ER 656 the court held it could; in *O'Neill* v *O'Neill* [1993] FCR 297 and *H* v *H* [1993] FCR 308 the opposite view was taken.

v) The use of the s25 guidelines

Whether a court uses a starting point or not, it must go through the s25 factors and assess a proper award accordingly.

When answering a question, it is important to realise that the examiner will give very little credit for a repetition of the whole of s25. Instead simply mention that the court will have regard to the s25 guidelines but only deal in depth with those guidelines that are relevant to the particular problem being answered.

vi) The net effect approach

It is crucial when considering the amount of maintenance to emphasise that whatever approach the court takes to arrive at a figure it must have regard to the net effect of such an award on both parties before making an order. How does it leave the parties at the end of the day?; are their standards of living going to be, as far as possible, roughly comparable?: *Stockford* v *Stockford* (1982) 3 FLR 58; *Furniss* v *Furniss* (1982) 3 FLR 46.

b) *Property adjustment orders*

What happens to the matrimonial home?

The court's prime concern is to ensure that, as far as possible, both parties have adequate accommodation after the divorce. If there is enough equity to permit the matrimonial home to be sold and the proceeds divided in such proportion as to enable both parties with the aid of a mortgage to purchase elsewhere, such an order will be made.

If there is not sufficient equity then the court's prime concern is to provide a home for the person who has custody of the children: *Browne* v *Pritchard* [1975] 3 All ER 721.

How may the home be preserved for occupation by the custodial spouse?

i) By ordering a sale and giving the custodial spouse such of the proceeds as are necessary to buy suitable alternative accommodation.

ii) By an outright transfer with or without compensation (ie reduced or no maintenance) to the husband: *Hanlon* v *Hanlon* [1978] 2 All ER 889. Note the potential difficulties with this type of order in the light of ss106-108 Social Security Adjudication and Administration Act 1992.

iii) By settling the property on both parties but giving the custodial parent sole occupation until one or more of a number of 'triggering' events (occurrences which trigger the sale) happen eg:

• the youngest child reaching 18: *Mesher* v *Mesher* [1980] 1 All ER 126

and/or (whichever shall last occur)

- the wife's death, remarriage or cohabitation for more than six/twelve months: *Martin* v *Martin* [1977] 3 All ER 762.

Both *Mesher* and *Martin* type orders have fallen into disfavour in recent years for the following reasons. Firstly a *Mesher* order delays the day when the wife would have to move out of her home and purchase elsewhere to a date when she will be much older and, therefore, perhaps less able to obtain paid employment and accordingly less able to secure or finance the mortgage necessary to purchase elsewhere. Secondly a *Martin* order which ties the parties together until death offended the philosophy behind the clean break policy. Accordingly these two orders were seldom made in recent years.

However such orders were a way of allowing the non-custodial spouse to retain something from the family's main, if not only, valuable asset namely the matrimonial home. Accordingly District Judges may become more willing to grant such orders in the light of the recent Court of Appeal decision in *Clutton* v *Clutton* [1991] FLR 242.

In this case (in which the equity in the former matrimonial home was worth £50,000) the Court of Appeal whilst emphasising the exceptional nature of such orders nevertheless did indicate that such orders could be made in the following circumstances: if there was sufficient equity in the former matrimonial home at the time of divorce to allow both parties to be able to purchase elsewhere (with the aid of some of the sale proceeds and a mortgage) BUT if it was not in the interests of the children for the house to be sold at that time then the court should consider a *Mesher* order. If, however, there was doubt about the wife's ability to be able to raise the additional money to purchase elsewhere when the youngest child reached 18 then the court should make a *Martin* order.

iv) By an immediate transfer of the property into the custodial parent's name with a charge in favour of the non-custodial parent equal to a particular percentage of the equity but such charge not to be realised until one or more of the above mentioned triggering events: *Browne* v *Pritchard* [1975] 3 All ER 721.

c) *Particular points concerning the s25 guidelines*

i) What is the practical importance of conduct?

It is generally irrelevant; in most marriages both parties are to a greater or lesser extent to blame for the breakdown of the marriage and so one's conduct is cancelled out by the other's: *Leadbeater* v *Leadbeater* [1985] FLR 789; *Anthony* v *Anthony* [1986] 2 FLR 353.

Conduct will operate so as to reduce the award that would otherwise be made in two situations:

- Where one party is substantially blameworthy and the other substantially blameless: *Robinson* v *Robinson* [1983] 1 All ER 391; *West* v *West* [1977] 2 All ER 705.

- Where both parties are to blame but there is an such an imbalance of conduct that it would be inequitable to disregard it: *Kyte* v *Kyte* [1987] 3 All ER 1041; *K* v *K* [1990] Fam Law 19 - see 7.3 Recent cases and statutes.

Note that even where conduct is taken into account it will only reduce an award, it will seldom extinguish it: *Kyte* v *Kyte* [1987] 3 All ER 1041; *Bateman* v *Bateman* [1979] 2 WLR 377.

ii) What is the relevance of a short marriage?

It will normally reduce an award: *Browne* v *Pritchard* [1975] 3 All ER 721; *Khan* v *Khan* [1980] 1 All ER 499; *Cumbers* v *Cumbers* [1975] 1 All ER 1.

But what of pre-marital cohabitation?

The court has a discretion whether to take into account pre-martial cohabitation: *Campbell* v *Campbell* [1977] 1 All ER 1; *Kokosinski* v *Kokosinski* [1980] 1 All ER 1106.

But the courts are likely to do so where there are children: *H* v *H* (1981) 2 FLR 392.

iii) The importance of potential earning capacity

As indicated above, the court is most concerned with the parties' income and expenditure positions. But it is not simply their present actual incomes that should be taken into account but rather their potential incomes. If the court considers that it is reasonable to expect either party to earn more in the future then it should deem a greater income to that party than they actually have: *Hardy* v *Hardy* (1981) 11 Fam Law 153; *McEwan* v *McEwan* [1972] 2 All ER 708.

d) *Maintenance for children*

As from 1 April 1993 (the date that the Child Support Act 1991 came into force) *new* applications for maintenance for children are dealt with by the Child Support Agency and *not* the courts. It is anticipated that by 1996 all *existing* maintenance orders will have been taken over and re-assessed by the Child Support Agency. The Agency will assess the amount of child support payable for the children of the family as a whole by reference to fixed formulae - there is *no* discretion to increase or reduce the assessed sum to take into account the particular circumstances of the payer. This has already been the subject of criticism by fathers, Members of Parliament and judges. The assessments made by the Agency are much higher than the maintenance orders traditionally made by the courts. A father on state benefit will pay the minimum of £2.20 per week, whereas the maximum amount is £380 per week.

It has been objected that it is not always in the child's interest to have the parent pay high sums by way of child support if that so impoverishes the parent as to adversely affect his/her relationship with that child.

6.3   Recent cases and statutes

K v K [1990] Fam Law 19

The husband had not worked since 1980 and had a serious drink problem; he was now living on income support of £50 per week. The wife had been industrious, her income was £24,600 per annum, she had a flat worth £85,000 and other assets worth £20,000. The matrimonial home had been sold and the £101,000 sale proceeds had been paid into court. The husband sought half of the equity plus a lump sum and maintenance. There was held to be such an imbalance of conduct so as to be taken into account under s25(2)(g). The husband received £60,000 to purchase alternative accommodation but because of his 'conduct' received no additional lump sum nor periodical payments.

Gojkovic v Gojkovic [1990] FLR 140

This case establishes that there is no such thing as a ceiling to a lump sum award in wealthy families based on the so-called 'Duxbury calculation'. In this case the wife had not only looked after the family during the course of a lengthy marriage but also by her efforts in relation to the husband's business had earned a share in the value of his business assets. She was held to be entitled to a lump sum of £1,000,000, almost twice the figure arrived at by use of the Duxbury calculation.

Waterman v Waterman [1989] 1 FLR 380

The judge awarded the wife a lump sum of £2,000 together with periodical payments of £37.50 per week for five years. He also applied s28(1)(a) and directed that she could not apply to extend that term. The Court of Appeal referred to s28(1)(a) as a 'draconian' provision, indicating its dislike generally of a 'five year and no more' type order. It substituted an order of 'five years or further order' thus indicating that if a court is minded to impose a postponed clean break that it should adopt this type of wording when doing so. If circumstances do dramatically change so that the recipient is not going to be financially independent at the end of the term indicated then she has the option of returning to the court to extend the term.

Delaney v Delaney [1990] 2 FLR 457

This is an important case dealing with the court's approach to awarding maintenance to a wife who is in receipt of State benefits. In such a case every pound that the wife gets by way of maintenance from her husband reduces pro rata the money she receives from the State; accordingly she is practically no better off. However, the traditional view has been that a husband should not be allowed to pass his liability to maintain on to the State by arguing that he should not pay maintenance to an ex-wife who is in receipt of social security payments because it would make no difference to her.

Delaney suggests a different approach to be applied where an order against the liable husband would financially cripple him. In this case the wife and three children were in receipt of £98 per week including family credit. The husband and his cohabitee received £212. However the husband had little to spare because he had taken out a mortgage to provide him with alternative accommodation. In such circumstances the Court of Appeal held that it must give recognition to the fact that there is life after divorce; that having a mortgage to buy alternative accommodation was a reasonable step to take after divorce. Accordingly the Court of Appeal approved nominal orders (ie 5p per annum) for both the wife and the children holding that the court could take into account the availability of State benefits to a wife so as to be able to 'avoid making orders which would be financially crippling to the husband'.

Delaney follows similar reasoning to that applied in *Ashley* v *Blackman* but it should be noted that in *Delaney* the court preferred nominal orders rather than a clean break, thereby allowing the wife and children to apply for a later upwards variation.

Clutton v Clutton [1991] 1 FLR 242

In this case the Court of Appeal has indicated that in exceptional cases a *Mesher/Martin* order may be appropriate in relation to the former matrimonial home. The equity involved here was £50,000 and this would have enabled both parties with the aid of additional monies to purchase suitable alternative accommodation. However to order a sale at the time of the divorce was not in the interests of the children. In these circumstances the Appeal Court stated that a *Mesher* order might be appropriate requiring a sale and division of the proceeds when the youngest child reached the age of 18. If there was doubt about the wife's ability to purchase alternative accommodation at that time then a *Martin* order postponing sale until her death or remarriage would be appropriate.

The Child Support Act 1991.

6.4 Analysis of questions

There will always be at least one question on this area in every examination. It may be an essay question requiring either a critique of the way the courts have interpreted the s25 guidelines generally or a more particular analysis of one aspect of s25 (the 'clean break' or the relevance of conduct being the most likely topics).

Since, however, the examiner usually wants to test candidates' understanding of how the principles are applied in a particular case, it is more likely that a problem solving question would be set. This would usually be a free-standing question but some examination boards (notably University of London LLB External) have been known to link this area to a question involving other aspects of family law eg nullity or divorce. A free-standing question usually requires knowledge of the principles relating to both maintenance and property adjustment.

A question linked to another area usually requires knowledge of either maintenance or property adjustment, but seldom both. It is important, therefore, when attempting a question in this area to first sort out whether the examiner is asking about maintenance or property adjustment or both!

6.5   Questions

Question 1

Desmond and Esmerelda, who are both solicitors, married in 1975. The matrimonial home, Rose Cottage, was a wedding present from Esmerelda's parents and is registered in her name. Esmerelda enjoyed greater professional success, and when their first child, Freddie, was born in 1978 they agreed that Desmond should give up his job to look after the child. They had another child, Gertie, born in 1985. Desmond has never resumed legal practice. Freddie was sent away to a boarding school when he was eight, and Esmerelda pays the school fees.

In 1987 Esmerelda began an affair with Hugo, the senior partner of her firm. Desmond became acutely depressed when he found out about this affair. He began drinking heavily and neglecting Gertie.

Esmerelda has just obtained a divorce on the ground of Desmond's behaviour. They have agreed that Desmond should have custody and care and control of the children, with Esmerelda being entitled to reasonable access. Esmerelda and Hugo live together but do not plan to marry.

a) Can Desmond obtain financial provision from Esmerelda for himself and the children? If he is awarded financial provision, what factors do you think will be especially important in assessing the amount of the provision?

b) Desmond would like Rose Cottage transferred to him as a home for himself and the children. Esmerelda considers that it should be sold and that she should be entitled to the proceeds of the sale. How do you think that a court will resolve this dispute?

University of London LLB Examination
(for External Students) Family Law June 1988 Q3

General comment

This is a standard question on financial and property adjustment on divorce. It is divided into two parts, separating the maintenance award from the property adjustment order. Advice in each part will overlap to the extent that candidates are expected to explain and apply s25 MCA 1973 in some detail in each part, although candidates must avoid repetition in this area. Part (a) is straightforward enough, but part (b) should be tackled only after giving careful thought to the proposed answer.

Skeleton solution

a)   • Explain the orders available under ss22 and 23 MCA 1973 in respect of a spouse and/or child of the family.

• Discuss s25 MCA in detail with particular reference to s25(1) MCA and s25(2) (a), (b), (c), (d), (f), (g) and (h), discussing each solution in the light of the facts given in the question.

• Discuss also s25A MCA 1973.

b) • Explain the orders available under ss24 and 24A MCA 1973.

   • Again apply s25 MCA insofar as it is relevant to the property issues.

   • Discuss alternative forms of orders, eg immediate sale and division of proceeds; outright transfer to husband; transfer to husband with deferred charge in wife's favour; *Mesher* order and its problems (*Carson* v *Carson*), alternatives as illustrated by *Harvey* and *Brown* cases.

Suggested solution

a) In divorce proceedings the court has wide powers to make orders for financial provision, that is maintenance pending suit for a spouse under s22 Matrimonial Causes Act 1973 (hereinafter referred to as MCA 1973), and periodical payments and/or lump sum orders for a spouse and/or any children of the family under s23 MCA 1973.

Although at this present time it is still relatively unusual for a husband to claim financial relief from his former wife, it must be noted that neither of the provisions referred to above prevent him from making such a claim, indeed both parties come before the court on an equal basis (*Calderbank* v *Calderbank* (1976)) and generally the court's main criteria for making such orders will be balancing the claimant's need against the payor's ability to pay. Desmond with therefore be entitled to claim financial provision from Esmerelda for himself under ss22 and 23 MCA 1973. He will also be able to claim maintenance for the two children as they are children of the family within s52 MCA 1973 in that they are the children of both parties.

The matters set out in s25 MCA 1973 as substituted by s3 Matrimonial and Family Proceedings Act 1984 will have to be considered by the court when deciding what, if any, orders should be made in favour of Desmond and the children. Therefore the court is under a duty to have regard to all the circumstances of the case, first consideration being given to promoting the welfare while a minor of any child of the family under the age of eighteen. This does not mean that the children's interests will be viewed as paramount, to prevail over other considerations, but they will be an important factor: *Suter* v *Suter & Jones* (1987).

In addition to this factor the court will have to consider, in this case, the income, earning capacity, property and other financial resources which each of the parties has or is likely to have in the foreseeable future, including in the case of earning capacity, any increase in that capacity which it would in the opinion of the court, be reasonable to expect a party to the marriage to take steps to acquire: s25(2)(a) MCA 1973.

The court must also consider the financial needs, obligations and responsibilities that each of the parties have or is likely to have in the foreseeable future (s25(2)(b)); the standard of living enjoyed by the family before the breakdown of the marriage (s25(2)(c)); the age of the parties and the duration of the marriage (s25(2)(d)); the contributions made by each of the parties to the welfare of the family, including any contribution made by looking after the home or caring for the family (s25(2)(f)); conduct of the parties if it would be inequitable to ignore it (s25(2)(g)); and the value of any benefit which by reason of the divorce either party will lose the chance of acquiring (s25(2)(h)). Finally the court must consider the clean break provisions set out in s25A MCA 1973.

In the circumstances of this case Esmerelda's financial status is greater than Desmond's. She has continued to work throughout the marriage, and it can be assumed that as a successful solicitor she is earning a good salary and will continue to do so, and of course will increase it in the future. We are told that Esmerelda is living with Hugo although they do not intend to marry. If it is established that Esmerelda and Hugo's relationship is a stable, long term one, then this may affect the court's view of Esmerelda's financial status, in the same way as it would if she had remarried. A second spouse's means are relevant to the extent that they diminish the needs of the spouse (here Esmerelda) thereby leaving more of her own resources available for her first family. However, whether the court will take into account Hugo's means is debatable and will depend on the nature of his relationship with Esmerelda. If it is a stable, long term relationship then the court will take the view that Esmerelda's own needs are diminished to a certain extent and that more of her resources can be taken in account when calculating what is available for Desmond and the children: see *Wynne* v *Wynne & Jeffers* (1980).

With regard to Desmond's financial position, he has not worked for ten years, that is since Freddie was born. Instead he has remained at home to care for the two children. He is a qualified solicitor and therefore does have a good, secure profession to fall back on. However, the court must take into account the fact that he has been out of the profession for ten years, and therefore may have difficulty in re-establishing a career quickly and therefore being able to support himself. Further, it must also be considered whether he can be expected to return to work immediately in any event. As Freddie is now at boarding school, Desmond's presence at home all day is not required for him, although thought must be given to arrangements that will have to be made during his school holidays. He is ten years old, and clearly cannot be left on his own all day.

Gertie is only three years old and will not yet be attending school. She will require more daily care therefore and it can be assumed that it would be in her interests to be looked after by her father with whom she is familiar as he has looked after her all her life, rather than by a stranger, an arrangement that would have to be made if Desmond was expected to return to work immediately. The court will wish to ensure that Desmond becomes financially independent of Esmerelda as soon as is practicable and its aim will be to secure a smooth transition from the status of marriage to the status of independence (see s25A MCA 1973). Therefore, whereas Esmerelda will be expected to contribute to the maintenance of the children throughout their minority at least, her responsibility to Desmond may be more limited. The position with regard to Desmond is likely to be therefore that he will be expected to take steps to become more financially independent of Esmerelda in due course because he has a good profession which should be able to provide for his own support and he cannot expect to rely on Esmerelda for the rest of his life. However, the court must take into account, when considering when he could reasonably be expected to become independent, the fact that he has not worked for ten years and therefore may have difficulty in finding suitable employment easily. Further, one can expect that his salary will be a lot lower than Esmerelda's for a considerable time. In addition to these points it is unlikely that the court will expect Desmond to go out to work while Gertie is at home and requires care. Desmond's career is not one that may easily fit into part-time employment arrangements, and therefore even when Gertie starts school it may be that his presence at home will be required when she returns from school for a few years.

These points are made on the basis that there is no other person who is available or suitable to care for Gertie (and Freddie during the holidays). However, suitable alternative arrangements may be made, especially when Gertie starts school, and if so Desmond will be expected, at that stage, to seek employment and work towards financial independence.

Therefore it seems that Esmerelda will have to provide for Desmond's reasonable needs (*Leadbeater* v *Leadbeater* (1985)) as well as for the children for a period of time. Desmond's needs will include the common everyday needs such as food, clothing, accommodation etc. These needs, and those of the children must be balanced against those of Esmerelda, but as stated earlier these may be deemed somewhat reduced in view of her relationship with Hugo.

The standard of living enjoyed by the family before the breakdown will be relevant insofar as the court will be anxious, if practicable, to ensure that the parties, particularly the children, do not suffer any undue hardship by reason of the divorce and so will try to maintain, as far as possible, the standard of living enjoyed during the marriage: *Calderbank* v *Calderbank* (1976). However, neither party's standard of living should be raised to a level above that which it would have been had the marriage continued, and so Desmond cannot expect a more generous settlement, that is one beyond that whichhe would have enjoyed had be remained married to Esmerelda, merely because, for example, she is living with Hugo. It must also be noted that the requirement to seek to put the parties in the position they would have been in had the marriage not broken down which applied before 1984 no longer applies.

The age of the parties will be particularly relevant when looking at career prospects, and in this case Desmond's age and the effect it will have on his ability to take up his career again must be considered. The length of the marriage must be considered in conjunction with the contribution made by each party to the welfare of the family during that time. Looking after the home and caring for the family will be the sort of contribution considered under this head as will a financial contribution. So both Desmond and Esmerelda will be deemed to have contributed towards the family's welfare during this fairly lengthy marriage. The court must also consider the contributions each party is likely to make in the future and therefore the fact that Desmond will continue to look after the children will be important and this, as indicated earlier, is likely to counter any argument that he should return to work immediately to facilitate a 'clean break' order.

Conduct is relevant only if it would be inequitable to disregard it, that is, it is 'obvious and gross': *Wachtel* v *Wachtel* (1973); *Robinson* v *Robinson* (1983). Now that conduct is specifically mentioned as a factor to be considered under s25(2) MCA 1973 it is felt that the courts may have to pay greater regard to it in that an enquiry into the parties' conduct will have to be made before a decision as to whether it is inequitable to disregard it or not can be made. However it is suggested that in practice there has been no change in the court's attitude towards the relevance of conduct since 1984. On these facts allegations of conduct can be made against both parties for although Esmerelda obtained a divorce based on Desmond's behaviour, presumably arising out of his depression and drinking, she too is guilty of misconduct in her affair with Hugo. Therefore it is likely that conduct will not be relevant in this case in dealing with the financial claims as each party's conduct will cancel the other's out as in *Leadbeater* v *Leadbeater* (1985).

Finally, on the facts of this case there is no evidence to suggest any financial losses such as pension entitlements which should be taken into particular account under s25(2)(h) MCA 1973. Assuming that the parties married in their twenties, they are now in their mid to late thirties or early forties and in Desmond's case, assuming that he will be expected to return to work in due course he will be able to provide for his own pension entitlements.

Similar considerations apply when deciding what, if any, order should be made for the children: s25(3) MCA 1973. In this case the children do not appear to have any financial resources of their own so the court will have regard to their everyday needs and also to the manner in which they were being and in which the parties expected them to be educated. Therefore, it will be assumed that Freddie will remain at boarding school and therefore Esmerelda will have to continue to pay the school expenses although in due course when Desmond returns to work he may be able to contribute to the same. Gertie is only three and so will not yet be attending school. However, if it was intended that she also be privately educated then the court will seek to implement this plan and again Esmerelda will have to bear the brunt of the expenses until Desmond is in a position to make a contribution.

When assessing the amount of the order for Desmond the court may be minded to take into account the one third principle as a guideline particularly if we are dealing here with a middle income family: *Wachtel* v *Wachtel* (1973); *Slater* v *Slater* (1982). However this guideline must be regarded as merely a starting point in assessing the financial award and must be considered in conjunction with the matters referred to in s25(2) MCA 1973.

b) Rose Cottage, the matrimonial home, was registered in Esmerelda's sole name and so prima facie belongs to her. However, it was a wedding present, presumably to both herself and Desmond, and intended to be used as the matrimonial home, and perhaps therefore it cannot be argued that there is evidence that it was intended as a gift solely to Esmerelda: *Kelner* v *Kelner* (1939). The fact that the property was the matrimonial home suggests that the gift was intended to benefit both parties.

In any event, on divorce the court has wide powers under s24 MCA 1973 to adjust property interests and it can, inter alia, order a party to transfer such property as may be specified and to which he or she is entitled in possession or reversion, to the other party or to a child of the family, or to order the settlement of such property for the benefit of the other party and/or any child of the family.

So the fact that the property is registered in Esmerelda's sole name, and may have been intended as a gift to her alone, will not prevent the court from making an order in respect of it in the divorce proceedings and therefore Desmond will be able to make a claim to the property under s24 MCA 1973.

In deciding what order to make under s24 MCA 1973 the court must consider the matters set out in s25 MCA 1973 referred to in part (i) above and may create an interest in the property on Desmond's behalf taking into account, in particular, his own needs and those of the two children for accommodation. It seems that at the present time Desmond has no resources of his own to secure his own and the children's accommodation. Esmerelda on the other hand appears to have the resources to provide for their accommodation and as a spouse and parent she is under an obligation to provide for her family if practicable and necessary. Another factor under s25 MCA 1973 which will be particularly relevant in this case will be the contribution made by Desmond to the welfare of the family, as this is often the factor which contributes in a major way to establishing an interest for that spouse in the matrimonial property: *Wachtel* v *Wachtel* (1973). Desmond will continue to look after the children and this future commitment will be taken into account also. The standard of living enjoyed by the family before the breakdown of the marriage will be relevant particularly as the court will wish to ensure that the children are properly provided for as far as accommodation is concerned and do not suffer any undue detriment in this respect by reason of the divorce. In *Calderbank* v *Calderbank* (1975) a wealthy wife was ordered to provide a lump sum for her husband who had no capital in order that he could purchase a home of an equivalent standard to that occupied during the marriage so that he could provide suitable accommodation for his children when they visited him.

In determining what kind of order to make under s24 MCA 1973 the court has considerable flexibility and its decision will rest ultimately on practical considerations such as the size of Rose Cottage, and its value, the availability of other assets, or sums to provide alternative accommodation for Desmond and the children and the shares in the property which the court assess each party has.

Applying the principles of s25 MCA 1973 it is clear that Desmond will be deemed to have some interest in the property, and particularly if Esmerelda's parents were deemed to have intended to make a gift to both spouses, his interest may be up to a half. The court may also take into account other matrimonial assets if any and compensate Desmond for their loss, if applicable, by giving him a further share in Rose Cottage.

On the facts of this case it is impossible to say with certainty what share Desmond will have in Rose Cottage. However it is clear that Esmerelda will not be solely entitled to it and cannot insist that it be sold and the proceeds of sale given entirely to her.

Assuming that Rose Cottage provides no more than adequately for the accommodation needs of Desmond and the children, that is that it is not too large for them, the court could consider various options for dealing with it. It could consider ordering the immediate sale of the property and the division of the proceeds of sale in shares assessed by the court: s24A MCA 1973. Such an order has the advantage of certainty and finality, but the court would not consider it unless assured that the sums available to Desmond would be sufficient to purchase alternative accommodation for himself and the children. In the view of his lack of resources this may not be feasible at this time even if Esmerelda were to give him assistance with any mortgage. However the practicality of such an order depends to a large extent on the value of the property. Presumably there is no mortgage on the cottage so the equity may be large enough to provide sufficient funds for the purchase of alternative accommodation at this time.

The court could order the property to be transferred into Desmond's sole name, on the basis for example that he be responsible for the discharge of the outgoings on the same and perhaps even that he foregoes any maintenance claim for himself: *Hanlon* v *Hanlon* (1978). Again certainty is an advantage of such an order but its feasibility is doubtful as it seems that Desmond cannot support himself at this time and will have to rely on Esmerelda. Further Esmerelda will not have to support him indefinitely and it may be unduly generous to Desmond and unfair to Esmerelda to give Desmond her share of the property. Obviously the greater the value of the property the more unreasonable such an order may appear.

As an alternative the court could transfer the cottage to Desmond with a deferred cash payment being made to Esmerelda. An immediate payment would not be feasible because of Desmond's lack of resources, but a deferred payment may be a practical solution, that is the payment of cash to represent Esmerelda's interest be deferred until the property is sold. Esmerelda would, accordingly, take a charge over the property: *Hector* v *Hector* (1973). However, such an order could involve Esmerelda in an unduly long wait for the payment unless the court specified that the property be sold by a certain date.

Another possible order would be the deferred trust as in *Mesher* v *Mesher* (1973) reported in 1980 which usually involves the property being held in the joint names of the parties upon trust until for example, the youngest child reaches school leaving age or the party in occupation remarries, whereupon the property will be sold and the net proceeds divided between the parties in the shares decided by the court. The *Mesher* order has been criticised in recent years (eg *Carson* v *Carson* (1983)) because it fails to recognise that the party remaining in the home with the children is often at a disadvantage when the house has to be sold as he or she may have limited resources even after the sale and may have difficulty in rehousing himself or herself. Alternative orders were made in such cases as *Martin* v *Martin* (1978); *Harvey* v *Harvey* (1982) and *Brown* v *Brown* (1982), allowing the spouse to remain in occupation of the home even after say the children had completed their education. However these alternatives would not be necessary on these facts as Desmond is likely to be in a position to acquire suitable alternative accommodation when Rose Cottage is sold as by then he will have returned to work and in addition to his share in the proceeds of sale will have his own resources from his career.

The *Mesher* order may be unfavourable to Esmerelda in that she could have to wait for 14-15 years, that is until Gertie reaches school leaving age, but if it is the only means by which adequate accommodation can be provided for the children it will be adopted.

In conclusion an immediate sale of the property and division of the proceeds of sale may be appropriate and fair to both parties if the equity in the property is sufficiently large to provide adequate sums for the purchase of alternative accommodation for Desmond and the children. Alternatively, an order in the terms of *Mesher* may be possible or, depending on when Desmond is likely to resume his career and what resources he may be able to acquire thereby, a deferred charge as in *Hector* v *Hector*.

Question 2

Cedric, a successful barrister, married Deidre in 1966. They have two children, Norah, now aged 19, and Laura, aged 12. Deidre is an accountant who has worked throughout her marriage except when taking her maternity leave. Cedric purchased the family home, Lovenest, and paid all the mortgage instalments. Norah left home last year and rented a flat shortly before starting her degree studies at London University. Laura is being educated at a private school. Cedric has always paid the school fees.

In 1985 Cedric discovered that Deidre had been having an affair for the previous three years with Rufus, a partner in Deidre's firm. Cedric left home and went to live with his elderly mother. Deidre and Rufus plan to get married in 1988. Cedric has just met, and started living with Tina, a nightclub owner, whose business assets exceed £2,000,000. He has just obtained a divorce from Deidre on the ground of her adultery.

a) What principles will the court apply in assessing financial provision for Deidre?

b) What principles will the court apply in assessing financial provision for Norah and Laura?

c) To what extent, if at all, will the court take into account Tina's resources when assessing financial provision for Deidre and the children?

University of London LLB Examination
(for External Students) Family Law June 1987 Q3

General comment

This is a somewhat unusual question on financial provision on divorce. It requires a very detailed discussion on the guidelines contained in s25 MCA 1973 with particular reference to the effect of remarriages and a second spouse's income, and a careful application of those guidelines to the facts of the problem. Further, the division of the question into three parts makes planning the answer a little awkward as obviously there will be considerations to be applied in all parts and candidates must be careful to avoid repetition. It can perhaps be assumed from the way the question is drafted, that not all parts will carry equal marks. On the whole this is a straightforward enough question.

Skeleton solution

a) Discuss the financial orders available to a spouse on divorce - ss22-24 MCA 1973 and thereafter apply the principles of s25 MCA 1973 and s25A MCA 1973 in detail with particular reference to the effect of a spouse's remarriage - s28 MCA 1973 in relation to maintenance awards; and on property adjustment orders.

b) • Discuss and apply s25(1) and (3) MCA 1973.

   • In relation to Norah consider s29 MCA 1973.

   • Consider the effect of their parents' remarriages on orders for the children.

c) Discuss the effect of a second spouse's income in assessing financial and property orders on divorce, with particular reference to ss25(2)(a) and (b) MCA 1973.

Suggested solution

a) In divorce proceedings the court has power to make various orders for financial provision for a party to the marriage and/or any children of the family under ss22 and 23 Matrimonial Causes Act 1973 (hereinafter MCA 1973), namely maintenance pending suit for Deidre (s22) and periodical payments and/or lump sum orders for Deidre and/or the children of the family (s23). Further, under s24 MCA 1973 the court may make a property adjustment order, that is, it can, inter alia, order a party to transfer such property as may be specified to the other party, or to order the settlement of such property for the benefit of the other party and/or a child of the family. It can also order the sale of property (s24A MCA 1973).

When deciding what orders if any to make in Deidre's favour the court will consider the matters set out in s25 MCA 1973 as substituted by s3 Matrimonial and Family Proceedings Act 1984 (hereinafter MFPA 1984). Under s25 the court is under a duty to have regard to all the circumstances of the case, first consideration being given to the welfare of any minor child of the family under the age of 18 years. Therefore consideration of Laura's welfare may affect Deidre's claims. In addition the court will consider the matters set out in s25(2) MCA 1973 insofar as they are relevant to the case, and on these facts the matters to which the court will have regard will be the income, earning capacity, property and other financial resources which each of the parties has or is likely to have in the foreseeable future including, in the case of earning capacity, any increase in that capacity which it would, in the opinion of the court, be reasonable to expect a party to take steps to acquire (s25(2)(a)); the financial needs, obligations and responsibilities that each of the parties have or is likely to have in the foreseeable future (s25(2)(b)); the standard of living enjoyed by the parties before the breakdown of the marriage (s25(2)(c)); the age of the parties and the duration of the marriage (s25(2)(d)); the contributions made by each party, or likely to be made in the foreseeable future to the welfare of the family (s25(2)(f)); the conduct of the parties if it would be inequitable to disregard it (s25(2)(g)); and the value of any benefits which by reason of the dissolution of the marriage a party will lose the chance of acquiring (s25(2))(h)).

We are told that Cedric is a successful barrister and therefore we may assume that he has a good income from his bar practice. However we have no information as to any other resources he may have save that the matrimonial home is probably in his name as he purchased it and paid the mortgage instalments. Further, as will be explained in part (iii) Tina's income will not be aggregated with Cedric's to increase his own, but will be deemed to release more of Cedric's own resources to expend on his first family as necessary. Further his needs will be reduced in that it can be expected that the expenses of their home will be shared between himself and Tina.

Deidre also has a professional career as an accountant, and it can be assumed that she too has a good income of her own. Certainly she does not seem to have interrupted her career to any great extent by having a family and perhaps therefore we can assume that she has reached a relatively senior position in her profession. Further, as there are definite plans for her marriage to Rufus, we must take this fact into account for any maintenance commitment to her on Cedric's part will therefore be short-term.

The court will have regard to any increase in earning capacity which it is reasonable to expect both Cedric and Deidre to take steps to acquire in the future.

The resources of the parties must be balanced against their financial needs and obligations. As already indicated in Cedric's case the fact that he is living with Tina will have an effect on his deemed resources and needs. One obvious obligation he has is Laura's school fees which he has been paying and will continue to pay. It will be considered as an obligation to be taken into account on his behalf: *Sibley* v *Sibley* (1979).

On consideration of these two factors, and particularly in the light of Deidre's own career it seems unlikely that the court will consider it necessary to make a periodical payments order in her favour as it is likely that her own resources provide adequately for her needs. Of course consideration of other factors such as Deidre's contribution to this lengthy marriage and the standard of living enjoyed by the family before the breakdown of the marriage may give rise to the view that a maintenance award would be necessary to maintain, so far as is reasonable, the standard of living enjoyed by the family, and Deidre's own resources may not be sufficient to enable her to do this. However two factors operate against such a view being taken in this case. Firstly Deidre's adulterous conduct may affect her maintenance claim for the court may consider it inequitable to ignore it as it appears to be the sole reason for the breakdown of the marriage. In *Robinson* v *Robinson* (1983) a wife's maintenance award was substantially reduced as her unilateral decision to leave her blameless husband, which was the sole reason for the marital breakdown, was deemed to be obvious and gross conduct: *Wachtel* v *Wachtel* (1973).

Secondly it must be noted that when Deidre remarries in 1988 any periodical payments order will end automatically (s28 MCA 1973).

Taking these two factors into account, as well as the fact that Deidre is in a position to support herself as she has a good career, it is unlikely that the court will deem a maintenance order as necessary. In any event this seems to be a case where the court would be minded to dismiss any such claim in the light of other adjustments that can be made between the parties, for example with regard to the matrimonial home (s25A(3) MCA 1973).

It is likely that the court would consider making some capital provision for Deidre in the circumstances of this case and in this respect the effect of Deidre's proposed remarriage must be considered along with other factors set out in s25 MCA 1973. The court must consider the effect of the remarriage on Deidre's financial position: *H v H* (1975). In this case it seems that there will be little difference in her position on marrying Rufus who as a partner in an accountancy firm can be assumed to be making a good living. However, Deidre will not lose out in respect of her claims to the matrimonial assets merely because she is likely to be as well off with Rufus as with Cedric. The attitude of the courts when considering the proposed remarriage of an applicant in these matters has been shown to be that the applicant has earned a share in the family assets by virtue of his or her contribution to the welfare of the family and the assessment of this share would generally be unaffected by the future plans of the applicant: *Wachtel* v *Wachtel* (1973); *Trippas* v *Trippas* (1973); *Cumbers* v *Cumbers* (1974). Therefore once a share has been established as having been earned, it should be reduced only if on consideration of all the circumstances of the case it is right to do so. In *H v H* (1975) a wife who had remarried a wealthy man had her share in the matrimonial home reduced to one twelfth, as in the circumstances of the case any larger share would have put her in a better financial position than if the marriage had continued. Her former husband had remarried a woman with no income or assets, and he was responsible for the education expenses of the four children of the family.

In this case the parties seem to be financially very secure in their own right as well as with their new partners. In fact Cedric's situation has improved in that Tina's resources exceed those of Deidre. The only asset that we have any details of and which will be the subject of these proceedings is the matrimonial home, Lovenest, which was purchased by Cedric. Despite the fact that he paid the mortgage instalments on the house there is no doubt that in view of Deidre's contribution to the marriage over a nineteen year period, both in financial terms (for we can assume that her income was used for the family's benefit) as well as in terms of caring for the home and family, she would be deemed to have a considerable interest in the house, an interest which is unlikely to be reduced to any great extent, if at all, by her subsequent conduct: *Wachtel* v *Wachtel* (1973). Usually the home would be deemed to be jointly owned in circumstances such as these.

The question now to be considered is what should be done with the house. Cedric may object to Deidre remaining there, particularly in view of her proposed remarriage to Rufus and the consequent prospect of her new husband being accommodated at his expense. However Cedric has a responsibility to ensure that his family are adequately accommodated and a particularly important concern in the court's view will be Laura's welfare and the need to provide her with a suitable home. As we are given no information as to the value of the house, or the equity in it, it is difficult to give precise advice as to the course of action to take. If the equity in the property is such that on sale of the same and division of the proceeds of sale in the shares decided by the court, there would be sufficient funds available to enable Deidre to purchase an alternative house, suitable for their needs, taking into account the standard of living enjoyed by the family during the marriage which, it is suggested, can be maintained in this case, then it seems that an order for the immediate sale of the property and a division of the proceeds of sale would be appropriate, thereby effecting a clean break as between the parties themselves: *Suter v Suter and Jones* (1987). Deidre's share in the proceeds of sale could of course be increased if necessary to enable her to purchase a suitable home, and/or to take into account her interest if any, in other matrimonial assets. Of course, if on her remarriage to Rufus it is planned that she and Laura should live with him in his house, then an immediate sale of Lovenest and division of the proceeds of sale would be appropriate. It should be noted however that Rufus is not under an obligation to provide suitable accommodation for Laura, that is a responsibility which continues to rest with Cedric.

b) As indicated in part (a) the court has powers to make financial provision orders under s23 MCA 1973, and property adjustment orders under s24 MCA 1973 in favour of children of the family as well as spouses.

As regards Laura an assessment will be made by the Child Support Agency according to fixed formulae. Such assessment *cannot* include school fees as to which a court application will have to be made. As regards Norah the CSA cannot make assessments on behalf of children undertaking further education. Again a court application would have to be made.

c) Tina's resources will be taken into account to a limited extent when assessing the financial provision to be made by Cedric for Deidre and the children, as she is cohabiting with Cedric on a stable basis and it can be assumed therefore that their financial arrangements will be adapted accordingly. No order will be made however that effectively has to be paid out of Tina's income or capital, but the fact that Tina has her own resources will be deemed to mean that the availability of them will release Cedric's personal resources that is his income from his bar practice, making more of them available for the maintenance of his first family: *Slater v Slater* (1982). What happens in effect is that Cedric would be prevented from saying that he needs all or most of his own resources to provide for the needs of himself and any new family because those needs are being met not only from his resources but also from his partner's, and therefore he has more of his own resources available to discharge his obligations to Deidre and the children.

The effect of this approach will be that in some cases a man will be ordered to pay more maintenance for his first family if his new partner has financial resources of her own, than if she had none. However in its Discussion Paper 'The Financial Consequences of Divorce: The Basic Policy', the Law Commission took the view that it was logical and just that if the order in favour of the wife and children was appropriate, the husband should not be allowed to avoid that obligation by suggesting that he needed all his income to provide for his second family when that obviously was not the case. The Law Commission felt that if this approach were to be abandoned then in some cases it would mean that the burden of the first family's maintenance would be cast onto the state, a development which it would find to be unacceptable.

The Law Commission emphasised the fact that the question remained essentially one of fixing an appropriate level of maintenance for the first family and in deciding what the appropriate level will be the court must be guided by the principles and factors set out in s25(1) and s25(2) MCA 1973.

Question 3

'If the old law of financial provision was based upon defective principles, the new law enacted by the Matrimonial and Family Proceedings Act 1984 is based upon no clear principles at all.'

Is this a fair criticism of the new law of financial provision? To what extent, if at all, do cases decided under the new law substantiate this criticism?

University of London LLB Examination
(for External Students) Family Law June 1989 Q3

General comment

A typical essay question requiring the candidate to critically discuss the amendments to this area of law made by the MFPA 1984.

Skeleton solution

- Major change: introduction of clean break - case law interpretation of new principles.

- Other changes: - removal of status quo directive.

    - introduction of welfare of child as first consideration.

    - introduction of 'conduct' as a specific factor.

    - case law interpretation of above changes.

Suggested solution

The law relating to financial provision on the breakdown of a marriage evolved over a long period of time in a somewhat piecemeal and haphazard manner. As a result inconsistencies arose which required modification. After the Divorce Reform Act 1969, the law was, to a large extent, developed and clarified in the Matrimonial Causes Act 1973 (this replaced the Matrimonial Proceedings and Property Act 1970).

However, with the emergence of a changing attitude to the provisions relating to divorce, it was felt that a reappraisal of the mode of determining what financial relief should be available was now necessary. The results are to be found in the Law Commission's recommendations - 'The Financial Consequences of Divorce' which are enacted in the Matrimonial and Family Proceedings Act 1984. The Act extends the options open to the court on divorce and it also alters some of the principles which guide the exercise of the court's powers. The Law Commission said that the modifications recommended were designed to be 'evolutionary rather than revolutionary' and it is submitted that, contrary to the view expressed in the statement quoted, they represent a carefully considered response to the underlying policy issues.

Changing attitudes to divorce are reflected in the greater emphasis which the Act places on self-sufficiency. The provisions relating to this concept are controversial but they have also attracted a great deal of support. Critics of the self-sufficiency principle point to the undesirability of a spouse being denied financial assistance but it is submitted that this is a fallacious argument since the Act merely requires the court to consider the advisability of a 'clean break' and not to impose one automatically: see *Barrett* v *Barrett* (1988) which clearly states that there is only a duty imposed under s25A(2) to consider the appropriateness of a clean break being imposed after a few years. The same is true of s25A(1). The objective of these sections is to promote economic independence where appropriate either immediately or after a defined number of years. This is a sensible aim and the Act is sufficiently flexible to allow for financial relief where necessary: see *Day* v *Day* (1988) where there was not enough evidence to satisfy the court that a clean break should be ordered. Policy statements about s25A express the view that a clean break would mostly be appropriate where the marriage involved was a short, childless marriage (although in *Soni* v *Soni* (1984) such an order was not granted because the spouse could not find employment) and judicial dicta hold that the modern practice is to 'favour the clean break whenever possible' (per Balcombe LJ in *Harman* v *Glencross* (1986)). In *Suter* v *Suter and Jones* (1987), it was, however, held that the existence and welfare of children does not rule out the possibility of a clean break. hence it is submitted that this is a clear policy decision on the part of Parliament which is of substantial merit and which has been applied as such by the courts.

In addition, the requirement in s25 MCA 1973 that the parties be placed 'in the financial position in which they would have been if the marriage had not broken down' (this is the status quo ideal) has been removed. This provision guaranteed a continuing right to support for a spouse from the other even after divorce. Given the fact that the only ground for a divorce is that of irretrievable breakdown and that women are becoming increasingly able to support themselves, it was time that this provision was removed. It is also nearly always impossible for one spouse to maintain two homes on one income. Again the clear theme of the amendments contained in the Act can be discerned - that is the establishment of one spouse (normally the wife) as an economically independent person after the divorce. It is not as yet totally clear how the removal of this provision will affect the courts' decisions but it seems very unlikely that cases such as *Potter* v *Potter* (1982) would still be decided in the same way. Here the wife received a lump sum payment on divorce after six years of marriage. She had worked during the marriage and there were no children.

Section 3 of the 1984 Act amends s25(1) MCA 1973 so that an obligation is placed upon the court to give first consideration to the welfare of any child of the family who is under 18 years of age. The preservation of the well-being of the children of the family is an important characteristic of English law and this is a direct recommendation of the Law Commission aimed at ensuring this. It was, however, stated in *Suter* v *Suter and Jones* (above) that this is an important consideration and not the paramount one. It relates only to the care of the child during his or her minority and thus reflects the desire of the legislature that economic independence should be established as soon as reasonably practicable unless there are special circumstances justifying continued support. Again, it is as yet unclear how the courts intend precisely to apply the provision. The actual criteria to be considered have not changed but the emphasis is now placed on the priority of the children. Their financial needs will have to be determined ahead of those of the parent. It is conceded that some critics take the view that the introduction of this provision does little to alter existing practice but it is argued that this new emphasis on the children of the family is much more an important manifestation of the principle that their welfare should be protected. This concern for the children is also clearly evident in the Law Commission discussion paper on the reform of the grounds for divorce.

Section 25(2)(g) is perhaps the one area where the courts have not perceived any very clear principle that they can follow. This subsection requires the court to consider the conduct of the parties when making an award where 'it would in the opinion of the court be inequitable to disregard it. However cases on the issue seem to consider that the conduct of the spouses will rarely be a relevant issue: see *Anthony* v *Anthony* (1986) and *Leadbeater* v *Leadbeater* (1985). The problem with this element is that it requires the court to consider the conduct before it can decide whether it is relevant or not.

On the whole the principles to be found in the 1984 Act governing the provision of financial relief on divorce can be said to be meritorious. They seek to enable both parties to establish separate lives again and to protect any children of the family. To call them unclear is not an accurate assessment of their value.

Question 4

Edward, a wealthy company director, began living with his secretary, Fiona, in 1977. They married in 1981 and the matrimonial home, Rose Cottage, was purchased by Edward in his name. In 1982 Edward met Gertrude and, deciding that she was the love of his life, he left Fiona in order to live with her.

Three months later, however, regretting what he had done, Edward returned to Fiona. They had a child, Henry, who was born in 1984.

In January 1985 Edward was injured in a car accident as a result of which he became incurably impotent. Fiona looked after him for several months but, unable to endure the strain, she left Rose Cottage, taking Henry with her and went to live with her parents. Since her parents occupy a one-bedroom council flat, she has been forced to sleep on the lounge sofa.

a) What financial provision, if any, is Fiona likely to be awarded for herself and Henry? What factors will be taken into account in assessing financial provision?

b) Fiona considers that she needs Rose Cottage as a home for herself and Henry. Will the court order the home to be transferred to her and, if so, what conditions, if any, might be imposed on the transfer?

Adapted from University of London LLB Examination
(for External Students) Family Law June 1985 Q2

General comment

The candidate must remember to comment in some detail on the factors set out in s25 Matrimonial Causes Act 1973 (as amended) and the type of property adjustment order relevant on these facts. A definite conclusion cannot be reached in view of the lack of adequate detail and to some extent this adds to an already long answer. (It should be noted that this question originally contained an additional part dealing with the law relating to adultery and behaviour.)

Skeleton solution

a) Section 23 MCA 1973 - advise on financial orders on divorce with reference to s25 MCA as substituted by s3 Matrimonial and Family Proceedings Act 1984.

b) Section 24 MCA 1973 - general advice on property adjustment orders, and an assessment of the order best suited to the circumstances of this case which will require reference to be made once again to s25.

Suggested solution

a) In the event of a divorce the court has power to make various orders for financial provision for Fiona and Henry under ss22, 23 Matrimonial Causes Act 1973, namely maintenance pending suit for Fiona (s22), periodical payments and/or lump sum orders for Fiona and/or Henry who is a child of the family, being a child of Edward and Fiona (s53 Matrimonial Causes Act 1973) including if necessary an interim maintenance order for Henry (s23).

The guidelines set out in s25 Matrimonial Causes Act 1973 as substituted by s3 Matrimonial and Family Proceedings Act 1984 will have to be considered by the court when deciding what orders, if any, should be made in favour of Fiona and Henry. Under s25 as amended, the court is under a duty to have regard to all the circumstances of the case, first consideration being given to promoting the welfare while a minor of any of the family who has not attained the age of 18. In addition, in this case, the court will consider the income, earning capacity, property and other financial resources which each of the parties has or is likely to have in the foreseeable future, including in the case of earning capacity, any increase in that capacity which it would in the opinion of the court be reasonable to expect a party to the marriage to take steps to acquire (s25(2)(a)); the financial needs, obligations and responsibilities that each of the parties have or is likely to have in the foreseeable future (s25(2)(b)); the standard of living enjoyed by the parties before the breakdown of the marriage (s25(2)(c)); the age of the parties and the duration of the marriage (s25(2)(d); any physical or mental disability of either of the parties (s25(2)(e)); the contributions made by each party, or likely to be made in the foreseeable future, to the welfare of the family (s25(2)(f)); the conduct of the parties if it would be inequitable to disregard it (s25(2)(g)); and the value of any benefits which by reason of the dissolution of the marriage a party will lose a chance of acquiring (s25(2)(h)).

Maintenance for Henry will be assessed by the Child Support Agency.

We are told that Edward is wealthy, but his present and future earning capacity is uncertain on the facts and therefore it is impossible to comment fully on his income, resources and earning capacity, or his needs, particularly in the future. Suffice it to say that if he will be unable to work because of his injuries, which is probably unlikely, then this would affect his capacity to maintain Fiona and Henry. As far as Fiona is concerned the court will wish to ensure that if possible she becomes financially independent of her husband and their aim will be to secure a smooth transition from the status of marriage to the status of independence. Therefore, whereas Edward will be expected to contribute to the support of Henry throughout his minority, his responsibility to Fiona will be limited, assuming as seems likely on these facts, that she can be expected to work to support herself, although if she would not have worked had the marriage not broken down, the onus will be upon Edward to show that it is reasonable to expect her to work in the future. Therefore the position will probably be that Fiona will be expected to have an income of her own, if not immediately, then in the future, when she can resume her secretarial career. As Henry is only approximately one year old it would be unreasonable to expect her to go out to work immediately, and indeed it would be in Henry's best interests that she remain at home to look after him at this time. However, when he reaches school age there will no longer be a necessity for Fiona to be at home and she could resume work, albeit perhaps on a part-time basis initially. This will be particularly so as it seems that she is young and is therefore capable of picking up her career quite easily in three to four years' time.

The marriage is a relatively short one, being from 1981 to 1985, although the parties did live together for four years prior to 1981. The question will be whether the court will consider the period of cohabitation during which Fiona would seek to establish a contribution to the welfare of the family in addition to that made during the period of the marriage itself. In *Campbell* v *Campbell* (1976) the court held that 3 1/2 years of pre-marital cohabitation was not to be taken into account under s25 although later in *Kokosinski* v *Kokosinkski* (1980) where the parties had cohabited for 25 years before their marriage which lasted only one year, it was held that the conduct of the parties was relevant not only to reduce claims for financial provision, but also to increase them, and in the circumstances to that case it could only do justice to the parties to take into account the wife's conduct during the period of cohabitation before the marriage. In that case the courts did not feel bound by the words 'duration of the marriage' to have regard to the wife's contributions to the welfare of the family during the few months that the marriage lasted. However, the correct view is probably as stated in *Foley* v *Foley* (1981) where it was held that only the period of marriage applied in s25(2)(d) but that the cohabitation was one of the other circumstances of the case, and the weight to be attached to it was a matter for the court's discretion. Therefore, although the period from 1977-1981 will not be considered as part of the marriage, it will most likely be considered as a relevant circumstance to which weight should be attached, and therefore both parties' contributions during that period would be taken into account.

Conduct will be considered only if it would be inequitable to disregard it, which probably means that as in *Wachtel* v *Wachtel* (1973), as followed in *Robinson* v *Robinson* (1983) it will be considered relevant if it is 'obvious and gross'. In this case the initial conduct arising out of Edward's accident is vague, although there is evidence of conduct in his adultery. However, in view of the parties cohabitation after that adultery including the birth of their child, the court is likely to consider it irrelevant to the financial matters.

It is clear that a periodical payments order will be required at this time for both Fiona and Henry, the figures depending on their needs and Edward's ability to pay. Whether any lump sum orders are feasible here is uncertain. Usually such an order will be relevant if Fiona was to be compensated for losses arising out of the divorce, for example pension rights, or as a method of adjusting matrimonial property between the parties. We are given no details of the matrimonial property generally and therefore further comment on the feasibility of the lump sum order is impossible, save to say that as the family was wealthy there may be other property to be distributed between the parties taking into account particularly their contribution to the family, which may be appropriately dealt with through a lump sum order or a transfer property order under s24 Matrimonial Causes Act.

b) The cottage which is the matrimonial home was purchased in Edward's name and therefore prima facie belongs to him. However, on divorce the court has power under s24 Matrimonial Causes Act to adjust property interests and it can, inter alia, order a party to transfer such property as may be specified and to which he or she is entitled in possession or reversion, to the other party or to a child of the family, or to order the settlement of such property for the benefit of the other party and/or the child of the family.

In deciding what, if any, order to make under s24 the court will consider the matters set out in s25 Matrimonial Causes Act 1973 referred to in part (a) above, and may create an interest in the property on Fiona's behalf, taking into account her own future needs and those of Henry particularly with regard to the provision of accommodation, the ability of Edward to provide for those needs, and the contributions already made by Fiona to the welfare of the family, including her care of Edward and Henry and further her future contributions in her continuing care of Henry and her assumption of responsibility for his upbringing. Edward does have a responsibility to provide accommodation for his family so far as that is feasible.

114

We are told that he is wealthy and therefore it would appear that he can provide adequate accommodation for Fiona and Henry as benefits their circumstances. In determining what kind of order to make under s24 the court has considerable flexibility and its decisions will rest ultimately on practical consideration such as the size and value of the matrimonial home, the availability of sums to provide alternative accommodation and the shares in the property that the court determine for each party.

One possible order that could be made is that of a deferred trust as in *Mesher* v *Mesher* (1973) reported in 1980, which usually involves the property being held in the joint names of the parties upon trust until, for example, the youngest child reaches school-leaving age, whereafter the trust for sale is implemented and the parties receive their interests in the property upon sale, the division of the shares depending largely on the needs of the parties at the date of the realisation of the trust. The *Mesher* order has, however, received some criticism in recent years in view of the recognition that the party remaining in the house, usually the wife, to look after the children, is often at a disadvantage when the house has to be sold in that she may suffer difficulty in re-housing herself, particularly where the interests in the proceeds of sale are small.

In *Martin* v *Martin* (1978) the deferred trust was extended to allow the wife to remain in occupation of the matrimonial home during her lifetime or until her remarriage or voluntary removal from the property, whichever first occurred, provided that she paid the mortgage instalments. The house was held on trust, the proceeds of sale being divided equally between the parties. In the latter case of *Harvey* v *Harvey* (1982) the court in making an order similar to that in *Martin* provided that the wife should pay an occupational rent to her husband when the mortgage had been discharged to compensate him for the fact that he was being deprived of the use of the property for a long period.

As an alternative to the deferred trust, Fiona could seek a transfer of the cottage into her sole name on the basis, for example, that she takes over the mortgage instalments and foregoes her maintenance claims or agrees to accept a reduced maintenance order: *Hanlon* v *Hanlon* (1978). This method of dealing with the matrimonial home gives certainty to the parties in that the wife would not have to worry that she might be forced to sell the property to buy out her husband's interest, and has advantages for the husband in that he may be freed from maintenance commitments to his wife, or they may at least be reduced. However, Edward would not be liable to support Fiona indefinitely in any event, although she would require maintenance from him for some while she remains at home to look after Henry. If she has no other source of income he will have to continue to maintain her for the time being whatever order is made in respect of the house. Further, such an order would not be appropriate if the equity in the property is high as it would be considered unfair to Edward if he was in effect transferring a value in excess of what the court would normally order for Fiona taking into account her needs and contributions.

A more appropriate alternative measure might be an order transferring the house to Fiona with an immediate or deferred cash payment being made to Edward. As it seems unlikely that Fiona has any property out of which to compensate Edward at this time for his interest, unless she could take out an additional mortgage to raise the sum, which is unlikely, or there is matrimonial property in which she would be deemed to have an interest which she could agree to forego in consideration of the transfer of the house, it is probable that a deferred payment would be appropriate in these circumstances, that is the payment of cash being deferred until say the property is sold, in which case the court will usually give the party affected a charge over the property for a share in the proceeds of sale or more unusually a specified sum: *Hector* v *Hector* (1973).

Any mortgage commitment in respect of the property would rest with Fiona, but while she is unemployed she will obviously require assistance with this expense from Edward as part of her general needs. However, if a deferred charge is ordered there could be more flexibility as to payment to Edward in that when Fiona resumes her career and becomes more or totally financially independent of him, a second mortgage could be taken out by her to pay off his interest. The feasibility of such a solution would depend very much on the value of Edward's interest in the property.

On balance, in view of the age of Henry, Fiona's future prospects and the criticisms levelled at the *Mesher* type of order, it is unlikely that the court will make an order in such terms. On these facts, it is perhaps more appropriate to consider an outright transfer to Fiona at this time, but with a deferred charge in Edward's favour for a share in the proceeds of sale.

Such an order would be made on the condition that Fiona be responsible for the outgoings on the property, including the mortgage, and although it is anticipated that she would receive some assistance in this respect from Edward initially, such commitments are likely in due course to become her sole responsibility when she resumes her career.

Question 5

Judith and Michael married in 1984 and have twin girls who were born in 1986. The couple have lived separately since 1988. Judith, who works as a dentist, remains in the jointly owned matrimonial home with the girls and Michael rents a small flat. In December 1990, Michael, who is a teacher, began cohabiting with Stella who owns a large house and is extremely wealthy. He now wishes to divorce Judith and she has indicated that she will consent to the divorce.

Advise Michael, who wishes to know the likely financial orders which the divorce court may make.

University of London LLB Examination
(for External Students) Family Law June 1991 Q5

General comment

This is a straightforward question on financial provision and property adjustment on divorce. The only difficulty with it lies in the fact that candidates are given no detailed information as to the value of the property or the value of the parties' interests in that property, so the advice given on the property adjustment aspect of the question is necessarily rather general.

Skeleton solution

* Outline orders available under s23, 24 and 24A MCA 1973.

* Discuss in some detail the relevant factors in s25(2) referring first to the welfare condition in s25(1) MCA 1973.

* Discuss s25(2)(a), (b), (c), (d), (f), (g) and discount (h).

* Refer to s25(3) MCA 1973 in relation to the children.

* Discuss the clean break principle in s25A MCA1973.

* Discuss periodical payments for the children, discount such an order for a spouse. Discuss property adjustment orders - consider the options. Discuss in detail an outright transfer and *Mesher* order.

Suggested solution

The court has power to make various orders for financial provision for a party to the marriage and/or any children of the family pursuant to divorce proceedings under s23 Matrimonial Causes Act 1973 (hereinafter MCA 1973), namely periodical payments and lump sum payments for a spouse and/or the children. Further, under s24 MCA 1973 the court may make a property adjustment order, that is, it can, inter alia, order one party to transfer to the other party such property, or an interest in such property, as may be specified by the court, or to order the settlement of such property for the benefit of the other party and/or the children. It can also order the sale of property under s24A MCA 1973.

When deciding what, if any, orders to make the court will consider the matters set out in s25 MCA 1973 as substituted by s3 Matrimonial and Family Proceedings Act 1984. The court is under a duty to have regard to all the circumstances of the case and must give first consideration to the welfare of any minor children of the family (s25(1) MCA 1973). This means that the twins' welfare will be a first consideration for the court although it will not be paramount (*Suter* v *Suter & Jones* (1987)).

In addition the court will have regard to the matters set out in s25(2) MCA 1973 in respect of a spouse's claim and s25(3) in respect of the twins' claims.

Under s25(2)(a) MCA 1973 the court will consider the income, earning capacity, property and other financial resources which each of the parties has or is likely to have in the foreseeable future, including any increase in earning capacity which it is reasonable to expect a party to take steps to acquire. In this case we are given no details of the spouses' incomes but it is clear that both parties have secure jobs which

117

will earn them reasonable incomes. It is likely that Judith earns more than Michael, particularly if she is working full time. Michael is now cohabiting with Stella who is wealthy. The court has no power to make an order which would in effect provide for the children out of Stella's resources (*Macey* v *Macey* (1982)). However, the court may consider Stella's resources to the extent that they will release more of Michael's own income to discharge his obligations towards his family (*Slater* v *Slater* (1982), *Suter* v *Suter & Jones*).

The resources of the parties must be balanced against their financial needs and obligations both now and in the foreseeable future (s25(2)(b) MCA 1973). These needs include the everyday living expenses of the family such as food, clothing and accommodation costs. The children live with Judith and therefore their needs will be greater than those of Michael, who has only his own needs to cater for, particularly in relation to accommodation. The children's welfare requires that they be provided with adequate accommodation so far as practicable (*Harman* v *Glencross* (1986)). At the moment Judith and the children live in the former matrimonial home and, in the absence of evidence to the contrary, it is likely to be adequate accommodation and not excessive to their needs.

The standard of living enjoyed by the family before the breakdown of the marriage will be considered under s25(2)(c) MCA 1973, not so as to place the parties in the position they would have been in had the marriage not broken down, for this is seen as an impossible task, rather, to distribute any drop in living standards as evenly as possible so far as this is reasonable and fair. In this case Judith and Michael earn reasonable salaries so it is unlikely that there has been any appreciable drop in living standards since they separated in 1988. This factor in s25(2)(c) is likely to be considered more relevant in relation to the accommodation requirements, particularly of the children. The court will wish to ensure that they are provided with accommodation of the same standard as that enjoyed during the marriage, so far as this is practicable. Clearly this would be practicable and reasonable in this case.

The age of the parties is relevant when assessing the future earning capacities of the parties and their ability to be financially independent of one another. The duration of the marriage is relevant under s25(2)(d) also, and linked to this will be the consideration of the contribution made by each party to the marriage, including any future contribution likely to be made to the welfare of the family (s25(2)(f); *Wachtel* v *Wachtel* (1973)). It is probable that both Judith and Michael have made equal contributions during the marriage which effectively lasted four years. Judith will continue to make a contribution in the future in that she will be responsible for the care of their children.

Conduct, if it is considered inequitable to disregard it, will be taken into account under s25(2)(g) MCA 1973. Generally the court is unwilling to investigate the cause of the breakdown of the marriage particularly, as in a case such as this, where it is likely that both parties are responsible for the breakdown. We are given no reason why Judith and Michael separated in 1988. If, as seems likely, it occurred because of mutual incompatibility then the conduct issue is irrelevant in this case and will not affect the outcome of their financial proceedings.

Finally, it is unlikely that the court will have to consider losses of benefits under s25(2)(h) MCA 1973 in view of the parties' ages and financial independence.

In addition to the factors mentioned above the court must also consider those set out in s25(3) in relation to the children, namely in this case their financial needs, incomes and resources (if any) and the manner in which they are being and in which the parties expect them to be educated or trained.

The court is now also under a duty to consider the clean break provisions contained in s25A MCA 1973, that is to decide whether it is appropriate to terminate all further financial obligations of each party towards the other pursuant to orders made under ss23 and 24 MCA 1973, or in the case of a periodical payments order in favour of an applicant, to limit the period for which such payments are made. It is clear from caselaw (see *Suter* v *Suter & Jones*) that even if orders are made in favour of children, it is not inconsistent to impose a clean break as between the spouses themselves.

Turning now to the orders which the court is likely to consider appropriate in this case, it seems that a periodical payments order for the children is necessary. Both Judith and Michael will contribute towards their children's maintenance and in effect the periodical payments order will reflect Michael's contribution towards that maintenance. Judith will also contribute towards the children's welfare by looking after them so it is appropriate that Michael should make a financial contribution, particularly as he can afford to do so and the court will consider that in view of his cohabitation with Stella, who will be deemed to be making a contribution to their joint living expenses, more of his earnings are available to expend on the children's needs.

It is submitted that a periodical payments order in Judith's favour is inappropriate because she is financially independent and will continue to be so. Therefore a clean break under s25A MCA as between Judith and Michael is appropriate. There is no suggestion either that Michael should receive financial assistance from Judith even if she is earning more than him unless their earnings were very disparate.

With regard to the matrimonial home, it is jointly owned but we are given no information as to its value or any equity value therein. It is likely, unless it is excessive to the needs of Judith and the children, that the court will be minded to retain it to provide suitable accommodation for the children. Generally if it was of great value and provided accommodation in excess of the family's needs then it could be sold immediately and the proceeds divided between Judith and Michael, enabling them to obtain alternative, more appropriate accommodation for themselves. In such a case it would be likely that Judith would be granted a greater share than half in respect of the proceeds to reflect the fact that she would be seeking new accommodation for herself and the children.

It is more likely that the house provides no more than adequately for the family's accommodation needs. It may also be the case that the equity in the property would not be sufficient to enable Judith to easily acquire alternative accommodation with her share of the proceeds, even if that share was enlarged. Other options therefore should be considered. The court could order that Michael transfer his interest in the property outright to Judith so that the home becomes hers absolutely. This has the advantage of providing certainty as to the future in that the children have secure accommodation while they need it, and Judith's future accommodation requirements are adequately provided for as well. Michael is now living with Stella and certainly, if the relationship is a stable one, the court could take the view that he does not require his share of the equity in the house to secure alternative accommodation for himself. It is, however, difficult to be certain as to the relevance of such an order as we have no idea of the value of any interest we would be transferring to Judith if such an order was made. If the equity in the property was large and the value of the shares was great it may do an injustice to Michael to transfer his entire share to Judith.

A more appropriate option may be to retain the property in joint names and to suspend sale of it until the children reach school leaving age, that is for twelve or thirteen years. Thereafter the property could be sold and the proceeds divided between Judith and Michael in the shares deemed appropriate by the court at this time. If necessary the court could give Judith a greater share in those proceeds to reflect the fact of her continued contribution to the welfare of the children in her looking after them and also the fact that she will be using her share to finance the purchase of alternative accommodation (*Mesher* v *Mesher* (1980)). As Judith has a good income it is unlikely that she would suffer such hardship at the time when the house was sold as was envisaged in cases such as *Carson* v *Carson* (1983). However, the *Mesher* order does create a possible problem in that if Judith wished to move before the end of the period for which the sale is postponed, she would not be entitled to use Michael's share of the proceeds when purchasing alternative accommodation for herself and the children (*Thompson* v *Thompson* (1985)).

Another, perhaps more appropriate option, may be to transfer the house to Judith outright but to give to Michael a charge over the property in respect of his share in the proceeds of sale (see *Knibb* v *Knibb* (1987)). The charge could provide that the statutory power of sale would arise in certain circumstances such as Judith's remarriage or cohabitation with another man for a specified period, or when she voluntarily left the house.

As an alternative to that order the house could be transferred to Judith outright and she would make an immediate payment to Michael effectively in settlement of his interest. Such an order may be appropriate if Judith could raise the sums necessary to buy Michael out. In such circumstances it is unlikely that she would have to pay him the equivalent of a half share as the court may be minded to increase her share to take into account her continued contribution to the family in the case of the children, the needs of heself and the children for suitable accommodation and the fact that Michael is receiving his share immediately.

7 DOMESTIC VIOLENCE

7.1	Introduction
7.2	Key points
7.3	Recent cases
7.4	Analysis of questions
7.5	Questions

7.1 Introduction

In this chapter we are looking at the way the law attempts to deal with the social problem of domestic violence. The emphasis here is on wife abuse (which expression should be taken to include violence in the unmarried family) although, of course, child abuse is an equally common occurrence. Child abuse is dealt with under the chapters dealing with the law relating to children. It is most unlikely that an examiner would set one question dealing with both wife and child abuse. There are a variety of jurisdictions in which a matrimonial injunction can be sought and an examiner would expect a candidate to show knowledge not only of the criteria to be satisfied in order to obtain an injunction but also the proper jurisdiction to use on the particular facts of the case in question. NB: The expression wife abuse is used for convenience. Violence by wives against husbands is not unknown - and, of course, the law applies equally to men and women. In the text however it is assumed the applicant is female.

7.2 Key points

a) *The different jurisdictions*

You can seek an injunction either in the Magistrates' Court or the County Court.

  i) The Magistrates' Court

  The relevant Act is the Domestic Proceedings & Magistrates' Courts Act 1978 (DPMCA 1978) ss16-18 - the orders are known as Family Protection Orders.

  - Either a personal protection order and/or an exclusion order can be obtained.

  - The applicant must be married (cohabitees cannot use this Act).

  - An order can only be obtained by showing physical violence or a threat of physical violence (for the specific criteria see ss16(2) and 16(3)) and the order cannot protect the applicant from other than violence or a threat of violence. If, therefore, the complaint was of mental harassment it would be necessary to apply to the County Court.

ii) The County Court

In the County Court two types of injunction are available: non molestation and/or ouster and exclusion injunctions.

If all that is sought is a non-molestation injunction (and the applicant is married to the other party) then there is a choice:

- If the applicant has issued divorce proceedings then a non-molestation injunction can be granted ancillary to those divorce proceedings pursuant to the inherent jurisdiction of the court.

- If the applicant has not issued divorce proceedings then a non-molestation order can be granted but only under the provisions of the Domestic Violence and Matrimonial Proceedings Act 1976 (DVMPA 1976).

- If the applicant seeks an ouster or exclusion order (ouster throws someone out, exclusion prevents them from returning) then there is no inherent jurisdiction to grant such an injunction.

- If the applicant has issued divorce proceedings then in order to exclude or oust someone as part of those proceedings the application must be made under the Matrimonial Homes Act 1983 (MHA 1983). This is the effect of the House of Lords' decision in *Richards* v *Richards* [1984] AC 174.

- If the applicant has not issued divorce proceedings then the application to exclude or oust must be made under the DVMPA 1976.

b) *The criteria for obtaining an injunction - in the County Court*

i) Non-molestation injunctions

Any injunction is a serious matter and the courts do not grant them lightly. However with non-molestation injunctions the court is simply requiring someone to refrain from doing that which they ought not to do anyway. Accordingly, as long as the applicant can show that there has been molestation an injunction is likely to be granted.

The very wide meaning of 'molestation' should be noted; it is much wider than physical violence. It includes mental harassment, pestering, introducing a lover into the home - indeed anything that causes distress or harm.

For example, in *Johnson* v *Walton* [1990] 1 FLR 350 molestation was held to include the publication in a newspaper of an article about the applicant which included partially nude photographs.

ii) Ouster and exclusion injunctions

Since the applicant is seeking to oust someone from their home or prevent them returning thereto the courts are reluctant to make such orders.

Whether the application is under the DVMPA 1976 or the MHA 1983 ancillary to divorce proceedings the court must consider the criteria laid down in s1(3) of the MHA before granting an exclusion/ouster injunction.

You must, therefore, know the s1(3) criteria namely:

- the respective financial position of the parties
- the conduct of the parties
- the interests of the children
- all the circumstances of the case

How do the courts apply the s1(3) MHA 1983 criteria?

The function of the court is to make a just and reasonable order having regard to the above criteria.

The courts have repeatedly stated that the judge, when considering an application to oust or exclude, must balance the s1(3) factors (none of which carries more weight than the others) but to throw into that balancing exercise the facts that:

- to make such an order is a 'drastic' or 'draconian' thing to do: *Summers* v *Summers* [1986] 1 FLR 343;
- such orders should not be made as a 'routine stepping stone on the road to divorce': *Burke* v *Burke* [1987] 2 FLR 71;
- it is not enough to assess whose case is stronger on the s1(3) criteria. It must also be shown that the applicant's case is strong enough to justify ousting someone from their home: *Wiseman* v *Simpson* [1988] 1 All ER 245.

In summary, while it is possible to obtain an ouster/exclusion injunction in the County Court even though there has not been actual physical violence, it would only be in the most exceptional cases. That an ouster order is possible in the absence of physical violence was confirmed by the Court of Appeal in the case of *Scott* v *Scott* [1992] 1 FLR 529. In this case the husband would not accept that the marriage was at an end and had repeatedly asked his wife to reconcile. There was no violence. However his pestering of her about a possible reconciliation was in breach of an earlier undertaking given by him to the court not to molest or otherwise interfere with her. In these circumstances the Court of Appeal confirmed the granting of an order ousting the husband from the matrimonial home.

In *Brown* v *Brown* (1993) The Times 6 October the Court of Appeal extended the approach in *Scott* v *Scott* to exclude a husband who had been guilty of having a 'jealous, strict and unyielding nature' but who was not violent.

c) *The criteria for obtaining an injunction - in the Magistrates' Court*

As indicated above, in order to obtain a personal protection order the applicant must show physical violence or a threat thereof: s16(2) DPMCA 1978.

If an exclusion order is sought, a threat of violence is not sufficient - actual physical violence must be proved except where someone is in breach of an existing personal protection order: s16(3) DPMCA 1978.

d) *The position of cohabitees*

Cohabitees can obtain both non-molestation and ouster/exclusion orders but the only Act under which they can apply under is the DVMPA 1976.

To bring themselves under this Act they must show that their relationship is one of living with each other as husband and wife in the same household.

If they are no longer living together when the matter complained about occurs they can still use the DVMPA so long as the living together was 'shortly before' the incident relied upon: *Harrison* v *Lewis* [1988] 2 FLR 339. In practice this is taken to mean within three months of the separation.

If the incident occurs outside this three month period then the DVMPA cannot be used by the cohabitee - instead an action for damages based on, for example, the tort of assault would have to be commenced, and the injunction sought ancillary to those assault proceedings.

But suppose the plaintiff cannot show the existence of a tort (assault, trespass, nuisance)? For example, the ex-girlfriend living in her parents' home who is continually pestered (but not threatened) by the ex-boyfriend who is begging her to return to him. Such behaviour would not amount to one of the recognised torts; it is simple harassment/molestation. In *Patel* v *Patel* [1988] 2 FLR 179 the Court of Appeal refuses to accept the existence of a tort of harassment, but it appears to have changed its mind in the recent decision of *Khorasandjian* v *Bush* [1993] 3 All ER 669. This was just such a case of the pestered ex-girlfriend held to be entitled to an injunction. The Court of Appeal repeated concerns about the fact that there is not one all-embracing code applying to violence within family relationships generally; such a code has been the subject of a recent recommendation of the Law Commission (Law Commission Report No 207 (1992)).

e) *The duration of injunctions*

If parties are married the injunction is meant to offer short term relief and ordinarily will not last more than three months: *Practice Direction* [1978] 1 WLR 1123.

The reasoning behind this practice direction was that during the three month period the married applicant can decide whether to reconcile or end the marriage by starting divorce proceedings. The three month period provides a breathing space.

Note, however, if the married applicant is not able to start divorce proceedings because, for example, the only ground she can rely upon is five years separation (as in *Galan* v *Galan* [1985] FLR 905) then the injunction can be of indefinite duration.

If the parties are not married the injunction may last longer and, indeed, can be indefinite. This is because the unmarried applicant has no other remedy available to her - she cannot divorce her partner: *Spencer* v *Camacho* (1983) 4 FLR 662.

f) *Powers of arrest*

Whenever an injunction is granted, whether it be in the County Court or the Magistrates' Court and whether it be under the DVMPA 1976, the DPMCA 1978 or ancillary to divorce, the court can attach to the injunction a power of arrest. This enables the police to arrest without warrant anyone whom they have reasonable cause to believe is in breach of an injunction. It is, therefore, a very useful power offering, as it does, an immediate remedy for the applicant who finds she is being terrorised by someone against whom she has obtained an injunction - she can call the police.

But remember that the court may only attach a power of arrest where there has been actual bodily harm and there is a likelihood of repetition.

7.3 Recent cases

Johnson v *Walton* [1990] 1 FLR 350 emphasises the wide meaning of 'molestation'.

Brown v *Brown* (1993) The Times 6 October indicates the behaviour short of violence which will justify exclusion.

7.4 Analysis of questions

Usually this area is examined by way of a problem question; it is not unusual for it to be combined with another aspect of family law eg nullity or divorce. Essay questions are sometimes set - they tend to require the candidate to critically assess the existing law and comment on its adequacy or otherwise in dealing with domestic violence.

7.5 Questions

Question 1

'The major object which the domestic violence legislation sought to achieve was first aid but not intensive care for "battered wives".' (Lord Salmon, *Davis* v *Johnson* (1979)).

To what extent has the legislation, as it has been interpreted, gone further than the provision of 'first aid'?

University of London LLB Examination
(for External Students) Family Law June 1986 Q5

General comment

This essay question requires candidates to consider in detail the principle that ouster orders made in domestic violence situations are a short term relief only and will not provide long term protection relating to occupation of the home for an applicant. The topic centres mainly around the Domestic Violence and Matrimonial Proceedings Act 1976 and candidates will be required to consider case law on the issues raised. Consideration should also be given however to the other procedures available for ouster orders, namely the Matrimonial Homes Act 1983, because of the effect of *Richards* v *Richards* (1984), and the Domestic Proceedings and Magistrates' Courts Act 1978, both of which may be used in domestic violence situations.

Skeleton solution

* Section 1(1) DVMPA 1976: - orders that can be made.

    - persons protected; effect of *Davis* v *Johnson* (1979) regarding time limits in ouster orders; consider case law showing an inclination to make longer term orders in exceptional circumstances.

    - consider what those circumstances may be.

* Discuss other ouster procedures: - MHA 1983.

    - consider the effect of *Richards* v *Richards* (1984); DPMCA 1978.

    - orders that can be made under both jurisdictions.

Suggested solution

The Domestic Violence and Matrimonial Proceedings Act 1976 was the first piece of matrimonial legislation designed to improve the law with regard to domestic violence and be of material assistance to those faced with this problem. It provides a comprehensive system of relief in situations of domestic violence and molestation. The court has power to order the respondent to restrain from molesting the applicant and or any child living with the applicant. The term 'molesting' is wide and covers pestering and harassment as well as the threat or use of violence: *Vaughan* v *Vaughan* (1973); *Horner* v *Horner* (1982). Further the child who may be protected by this legislation need not be a 'child of the family' and so will include a foster child, or any child residing with the applicant at the time of the application.

The court can order that a party be excluded from the matrimonial home or a part of it, or a specified area in which it is situated and can make an order requiring a party to permit the applicant to enter and remain in the matrimonial home or a part of it. This final order will often be used in conjunction with an order excluding the other spouse from the home.

Prior to the 1976 Act a right to an injunction could only be ancillary and incidental to some pre-existing cause of action such as a divorce; and if no such proceedings were contemplated the court had no powers to grant injunction relief. The 1976 Act provides that a county court could grant injunctions in the terms specified above, without the institution of any other proceedings. Further the Act applies to unmarried couples as well as spouses, so long as they are living together in the same household as man and wife, although relief is still available to separated parties so long as they were living together as man and wife, before the incident which gives rise to the application: *Davis* v *Johnson* (1979); *O'Neill* v *Williams* (1984).

The Act was designed to protect a wide range of persons and to offer relief against violence and molestation by orders protecting the person, and ouster orders. The scope of the Act in relation to ouster orders was however severely restricted by the House of Lords' decision in *Richards* v *Richards* (1984) which provided that ouster applications made by a spouse during the marriage must be made under the Matrimonial Homes Act 1983. The 1976 Act will still apply so far as ouster applications are concerned, to two types of applicants, namely the unmarried couple, and, more rarely a married couple where the court has no power to grant an order under the Matrimonial Homes Act 1983 for example where neither spouse is entitled to occupy the matrimonial home by virtue of any estate, interest or enactment giving them the right to occupy, as in the case of licensees.

In applications under the Act it must be noted that the courts have generally followed the principle emphasised in *Davis* v *Johnson* that the Act seeks to afford personal protection only to a spouse, that is 'first aid but not intensive care'. Therefore where a spouse has no property rights in the matrimonial home, any ouster order against the other spouse will be of a temporary character and the aim of the courts is to allow the parties time to readjust themselves after the traumas attached to the marital breakdown and to deal with accommodation problems in safety and calm. The policy of the Act is not to adjust the owner's proprietory rights but to suspend them for a short period of time: *O'Neill* v *Williams* (1984). This policy has been reinforced by the *Practice Direction (injunction: domestic violence)* (1978) which provides that on making an ouster order the court shall consider whether the order should be limited in time, and usually a period of up to three months will suffice, at least at first instance, although either party may apply for its discharge or modification.

It must be noted however that the Practice Direction does not state a rule, but merely requires a judge to consider whether a time limit should be imposed on the ouster order and there have been cases where the courts have felt that it would be appropriate for a time limit not to be imposed, but to exclude one party 'until further order': *Spencer* v *Camacho* (1983). It is argued that such orders would be more appropriate to applications relating to unmarried couples where the courts have no powers to adjust property rights. However it has been used in cases of spouses. In *Galan* v *Galan* (1985) the parties had separated and the wife remained in the matrimonial home with the children. The wife commenced divorce proceedings, but they were eventually dismissed and the only option left to the wife was to wait to present a petition based on the parties' separation for five years. During the divorce proceedings there had been several injunctions granted against the husband. The husband had applied to revoke the exclusion orders so that he could visit his children at the home, although he later admitted he only wanted to gain contact with his wife and check the house. He had been committed to prison for breach of the previous orders but at the date of the hearing of his application, and his wife's cross application to continue the injunctions, there had been no recent incidents of violence. However as the court found the wife's case to be proved and the husband to be irrational and solely responsible for the current situation, it concluded that there was a present risk of violence and an exclusion order was made unlimited in time. On the husband's appeal the Court of Appeal considered the propriety of making an order unlimited in time. The court recognised that normally an order under the Act would be for a short period of time, but there was nothing in the Act which expressly limited the discretion of the court regarding the duration of the order, and that in exceptional circumstances an order could be expressed to continue 'until further order'. Referring to *Davis* v *Johnson* the Court of Appeal pointed out that the thinking behind short term orders was that there were other remedies available to the parties to resolve the problem of occupation. However in this case a stalemate had been reached in the divorce proceedings and no order regulating occupation could be made therefore under the divorce jurisdiction. In view of that fact and the risk of further incidents of violence it was appropriate to grant an injunction in the terms 'until further order'.

The court also pointed out that there was nothing in the wording of the Act to give an answer to the question how long should a party be excluded for, and answers given in previous authorities must have reference to securing the safety of the wife and children until some other protection is available to them.

It can be said therefore that in relation to the 1976 Act ouster orders will generally be restricted in time, but that in exceptional circumstances, usually arising where there is no other jurisdiction available to provide protection for the applicant, an order can be made in the terms 'until further order', thereby allowing a party to remain in the property until a further application is made in respect of the order.

It should be noted that in view of the decision in *Richards* v *Richards* (1984) it is more likely that orders dealing with occupation of the matrimonial home under the Matrimonial Homes Act 1983 will be sought by spouses facing a domestic violence situation. The Act provides in s1(2) that so long as one spouse has rights of occupation in the home, either of the spouses may apply to the court for an order:

a) declaring, enforcing, restricting or terminating those rights;

b) prohibiting, suspending or restricting the exercise by either spouse of the right to occupy the dwelling house, or

c) requiring either spouse to permit the exercise by the other of that right.

The wording of this provision does suggest more long term orders than those expected in the Domestic Violence and Matrimonial Proceedings Act 1976.

Similarly in the Magistrates' Court where under s16 Domestic Proceedings and Magistrates' Courts Act 1978 the magistrates have power to order that the respondent shall not use or threaten to use violence against the applicant or a child of the family; and on proof that the respondent has used violence against the applicant and/or child, or has threatened to use violence against the applicant and/or child and has used it against someone else, or where the respondent has contravened a personal protection order; and that the applicant and/or child is in danger of being physically injured, the court may order the respondent to leave the home, and/or prohibit the respondent from entering the home and there are no provisions in the Act limiting the period of time that the ouster order will remain in force and the matter will lie with the discretion of the magistrates.

Question 2

Harry and Jane are a married couple occupying a council flat rented by Harry from Dimchester Borough Council. Also living in the flat are their sixteen year old daughter, Karen, and her seventeen year old unemployed boyfriend, Len. In February 1987 Harry decided to buy a new video with the money set aside for the rent. Jane constantly nagged him about 'wasting rent money' and Dimchester threatened to evict the family. Jane rang up the housing department and offered to pay the arrears herself out of her savings, but an official replied that Harry had to pay since he was the tenant.

One evening in May 1987, after Jane had complained yet again about Harry's extravagance, Harry brandished a carving knife and threatened to 'do Jane in' if she kept on nagging. At this moment Len entered the room and said to Harry: 'Stop shouting, you nasty old git'. Harry immediately attacked Len with the carving knife, inflicting injuries which required hospital treatment.

Jane now considers that it is unsafe for the family to continue living in the council flat with Harry.

What procedures can Jane invoke to exclude Harry from the council flat? Do you think that an application to exclude Harry is likely to succeed?

Adapted from University of London LLB Examination
(for External Students) Family Law June 1987 Q5

General comment

This is a typical problem question requiring as it does a discussion of the various jurisdictions available to those who wish to obtain an injunction namely the DVMPA 1976, the DPMCA 1978 and the MHA 1983.

Skeleton solution

- Discount the inherent jurisdiction to grant injunction relief as no divorce proceedings are contemplated.

- Explain the reliefs available under the DVMPA 1976 and the MHA 1983, that is the scope of these jurisdictions and the orders available.

- Discuss and apply the principles of s1(3) MHA 1983.

• Discuss the DPMCA 1978 application in detail and comment on whether the conditions required to be satisfied under s16 DPMCA can be met on these facts.

Suggested solution

There are various jurisdictions available to Jane to exclude Harry from the council flat. The parties are married but there is as yet no talk of a divorce and so it is unlikely that Jane will be able to invoke the matrimonial court's inherent jurisdiction to grant injunction relief against molestation of the applicant or any child of the family, and an exclusion order within the terms of the Matrimonial Homes Act 1983 (hereinafter MHA 1983).

However there are three other procedures available to Jane on these facts.

Under the Domestic Violence and Matrimonial Proceedings Act 1976 (hereinafter DVMPA 1976) the county court has the power to grant an injunction against molestation of the applicant or any child living with the applicant. The child concerned need not be the applicant's or the other party's child, nor need he be a child of the family as defined in s52 Matrimonial Causes Act 1973 and so under s1(1)(b) DVMPA 1976 the court may make an order in respect of a child merely lodging with the applicant, and this would mean that Len, as well as Jane and Karen could be protected by an order.

The word 'molest' has a wide meaning and includes pestering the applicant (*Vaughan* v *Vaughan* (1973)), causing trouble, vexing, annoying, putting to inconvenience, and will also include physical interference and assault (see also *Horner* v *Horner* (1982)). Further the court may exclude a spouse from the matrimonial home, or part of it, or from an area in which it is situated (s1(1)(c)), and may make an order requiring a spouse to permit the applicant to enter and remain in the matrimonial home or part of it: s1(1)(d).

The jurisdiction of the DVMPA 1976 is available whether or not any other relief is sought in other proceedings.

It has been argued that the scope of the DVMPA 1976 to exclude a spouse from the matrimonial home has been reduced by the decision of the House of Lords in *Richards* v *Richards* (1984) which indicated that applications by spouses for ouster injunctions should be brought within the terms of the MHA 1983. However it seems that the decision should be restricted to the procedure to be adopted in the matrimonial court's inherent jurisdiction, and that the DVMPA 1976 is unaffected by the decision save that the principles to be applied are the same as under the MHA 1983, namely the factors set out in s1(3) MHA 1983 must be considered by the court, that is the conduct of the spouses in relation to each other and otherwise, their respective needs and financial resources, the needs of any children, and all the circumstances of the case (*Richards* v *Richards* (1983); *Lee* v *Lee* (1984)). No one factor will have priority over any of the others and the children's interests are no longer to be considered paramount as they once were.

The jurisdiction of the court under the provisions of the DVMPA 1976 will extend to rented property and so Jane will be entitled to make an application for an injunction restraining Harry from molesting herself and the two children, Karen and Len, and to exclude him from the matrimonial home or a part of it, or even an area in which it is situated if there is a fear that he will continue to harass the family from outside the home.

It should be noted that the remedies under the DVMPA 1976 in respect of occupation are intended to be short term (*Davis* v *Johnson* (1979)), and the Act does not confer any rights on the parties which are capable of binding third parties, such as the council. Where an applicant has no property rights the ouster order will be temporary as the object of the Act is to provide relief against violence and if necessary merely to interfere with a party's occupation of the home for a short period to allow the applicant time to make suitable alternative arrangements. To this end it is provided in *Practice Direction (injunction: domestic violence)* (1978) that where an ouster order has been made the court must consider imposing a time limit on the order and usually three months will be sufficient period to allow the necessary adjustments to be made. The DVMPA 1976 does not impose any restrictions on the court's discretion however, and orders have been made in the terms of 'until further order' in cases where no other reliefs may be available to the applicant: *Spencer* v *Camacho* (1983); *Galan* v *Galan* (1985).

Alternatively, Jane could invoke the jurisdiction of the MHA 1983 to exclude Harry. Section 1(1) MHA 1983 provides that a spouse will have rights of occupation under the Act 'where one spouse is entitled to occupy a dwellinghouse by virtue of any estate or interest or contract, or by virtue of any enactment giving him or her the right to remain in occupation and the other spouse is not so entitled'. In this case Harry is entitled to occupy the flat by virtue of his tenancy agreement, whereas Jane is not as she is not party to the agreement. Therefore Jane will have rights of occupation under the Act, which include the right not to be excluded from the home without court order: s1(1)(a).

So long as one party has rights of occupation under the Act, either spouse may apply to the court for an order enforcing, restricting or terminating those rights, or prohibiting, suspending or restricting the exercise by either spouse of the right to occupy the dwellinghouse, or requiring either spouse to permit the exercise by the other of that right: s1(2) MHA 1983. From the wording of this section it can be seen that potentially longer term orders could be made than under the DVMPA 1976. However, as with the DVMPA the MHA 1983 does not confer any proprietary rights on the parties.

In dealing with an application under s1(2) MHA 1983 the court must consider all the circumstances of the case, including the matters specifically referred to in s1(3) MHA 1983 and referred to above, to reach a reasonable and just decision.

On these facts Jane's prospects of excluding Harry from the flat under either the DVMPA 1976 or the MHA 1983 are good. In both cases the principles of s1(3) MHA will apply and so Harry's conduct will weigh heavily against him, that is his extravagance which has given rise to tension in the family, but particularly his threats of violence to Jane, and his actual violence towards Len. In view of this behaviour considering this and other factors in s1(3) it is appropriate that Harry should be the one to be excluded. His financial resources appear to be better than Jane's and therefore his opportunities for finding alternative accommodation will be greater. Jane has to accommodate herself and Karen (Len will not be taken into account in the MHA application, although he will be in the DVMPA application) and so their joint needs must be considered against Harry who is on his own and who will therefore experience less difficulty in finding suitable accommodation. In both jurisdictions the exclusion of a party from the home is seen as a drastic course of action which will be undertaken only if absolutely necessary. It appears that such as situation has arisen in this case and so Harry should be excluded to enable the parties to make long term arrangements for their future accommodation requirements without the fear of further incidents occurring.

Finally Jane could invoke the magistrates court procedure to exclude Harry. Under s16 Domestic Proceedings and Magistrates' Courts Act 1978 (hereinafter DPMCA 1978) the magistrates have the power to grant personal protection and exclusion orders against a spouse although their jurisdiction is not as extensive as that of the county court for, whereas in the higher court evidence of molestation is sufficient to obtain personal protection and is not essential though desirable for an exclusion order, in the magistrates court there must be evidence of violence or the threat of it to obtain any form of relief.

Under s16(2) DPMCA 1978, if satisfied that the respondent has used violence against the applicant or a child of the family or has threatened to use violence against them, and that, objectively viewed, it is necessary for the protection of the applicant or child that an order be made, the magistrates may order the respondent not to use or threaten to use violence against the applicant or child, and may also provide that the respondent do not incite or assist any other person in using violence or threatening to use violence against the applicant or child: s16(10).

In this case Harry has threatened to use violence against Jane, and in view of the tensions between the parties it seems that a personal protection order will be necessary (although as Len is not a child of the family it cannot extend to him).

The magistrates also have the power to exclude a spouse from the home or part thereof and prohibit his or her return thereto. They must be satisfied as to various conditions under s16(3), namely that the respondent has used violence against the applicant or child, or has threatened to use it against the applicant or child and has used it against someone else (in this case Len), or in contravention of an order made under s16(2) has threatened to use violence against the applicant or child, and that the applicant or child is in danger of being physically injured by the respondent, or would be if they were to enter the matrimonial home.

In view of Harry's threat of violence to Jane and his actual assault of Len it seems that the primary condition under s16(3) can be established. Further, it is submitted that there is a danger of physical injury for Jane if Harry should remain in the home in view of the tensions over his extravagance. There must be an objectively observable danger although it need not be immediate: *McCartney* v *McCartney* (1981). Therefore it seems that under the DPMCA 1978 also Jane has a good prospects as to excluding Harry from the flat.

Question 3

Antonia, who is seventeen and who has just left school, married Bertram, an eighty year old millionaire, in January 1985. Antonia's parents were unaware of the marriage until after it had taken place. Bertram was beginning to show signs of senility. He appeared at the time of the marriage ceremony to understand perfectly what was happening, but afterwards he was vague as to whether he had married Antonia or whether she was just a good friend. Sexual intercourse took place on one occasion two months after the marriage ceremony, but did not subsequently prove to be possible.

After the marriage the couple occupied Bertram's house, Tottering Towers. When Antonia's parents had been informed of the marriage they accepted an invitation to sell their home and take over the top floor of Tottering Towers.

In January 1988 Antonia became friendly with Bertram's butler, Cedric. Bertram is jealous of this friendship and wants to bring the marriage to an end. He has ordered Antonia and her parents out of the home.

Can Bertram evict Antonia and her parents from Tottering Towers?

Adapted from University of London LLB Examination
(for External Students) Family Law June 1988 Q1

General comment

A more limited question concentrating simply on the law applicable when one seeks an ouster injunction ancillary to divorce or nullity proceedings.

Skeleton solution

- In nullity or divorce proceedings - use of inherent jurisdiction.
- Effect of *Richards* decision and use of MHA 1983 to be explained.
- Consider in detail use of the MHA 1983 jurisdiction against Antonia, with reference to s1(1) and (2) MHA 1983, as well as s1(3) MHA and s1(11) MHA 1983.

Suggested solution

If Bertram institutes nullity or divorce proceedings the court has the inherent jurisdiction to grant an injunction ancillary to those proceedings if necessary (Supreme Court Act 1981). Such relief is available only ancillary to other proceedings and there must be a sufficient link between the relief sought by way of injunction and those other proceedings; and the injunction must be in support of a recognised legal or equitable right. In *Richards* v *Richards* (1984) the House of Lords restricted the scope of the court's inherent powers to grant ouster injunctions stating that such relief must be sought under the Matrimonial Homes Act 1983 (hereinafter the MHA 1983).

In practice this will mean, the High Court and County Court rules having been amended, that the application for ouster can be brought under the court's ancillary jurisdiction although the order must be within the terms and meaning of the MHA 1983 if it applies to the circumstances of the parties, that is, if they fall within the jurisdiction of the MHA 1983 itself. In this case they clearly do. Bertram is the legal owner of the home and is therefore entitled to occupy it by virtue of his interest. Antonia, however has no such entitlement because she has no legal interest in the house and therefore she will be deemed to have rights of occupation under the MHA 1983. Section 1(1) MHA 1983 provides:

'Where one spouse is entitled to occupy a dwelling house by virtue of a beneficial estate or interest ... and the other spouse is not so entitled, then subject to the provisions of this Act, the spouse not so entitled shall have the following rights;

a) if in occupation a right not be be evicted or excluded from the dwelling house or any part thereof by the other spouse except with the leave of the court given by an order under this section.

b) if not in occupation a right with the leave of the court so given to enter into and occupy the dwelling house.'

Even if Antonia had an equitable interest, then she would still have rights of occupation under the Act (s1(11)). Those rights exist during the subsistence of the marriage, that is until it is terminated by death or a decree of divorce or annulment.

Having established that the MHA 1983 applies in this case then Bertram must be advised that he will be unable to evict Antonia without a court order. However, s1(2) MHA 1983 provides that:

'so long as one spouse has rights of occupation, either of the spouses may apply to the court for an order –

a) declaring, enforcing, restricting or terminating those rights; or

b) prohibiting suspending or restricting the exercise by either spouse of the right to occupy the dwelling house; or

c) requiring either spouse to permit the exercise by the other of that at right.'

So Bertram could apply to the court for an order restricting or terminating Antonia's rights of occupation and/or prohibiting, suspending or restricting her occupation of the home.

In deciding what order, if any, to make the court must have regard to s1(3) MHA 1983 and in this case therefore must consider the conduct of the spouses in relation to each other and otherwise, their respective needs and financial resources, and all the circumstances of the case. No one factor is any more important than the other (*Richards* v *Richards* (1984)), and an exclusion order must be shown to be necessary: *Wiseman* v *Simpson* (1988). The fact that the relationship between Bertram and Antonia has deteriorated to the extent of Bertram wanting her to leave the home will not in itself be sufficient to merit an exclusion order. In *Wiseman* v *Simpson* (1988) the Court of Appeal held that although it was no longer practical for the parties to cohabit and there was no prospect of reconciliation, an exclusion order could be made only if on consideration of all the matters in s1(3) MHA 1983, the case of one party was stronger than the other, and was such to justify the making of an order. It is not clear on these facts whether there are grounds to justify an exclusion order at this time, particularly as Antonia may have nowhere else to live at the present time, nor the means to provide alternative accommodation for herself. Bertram's only complaint against her is her friendship with Cedric and without further information on this point it is difficult to see how Bertram's jealousy could justify an ouster order being made against Antonia. Of course an option available to the court is to restrict Antonia's occupation of the home and if Tottering Towers is large enough this could be achieved by forming two separate households thereby allowing each party to remain in and occupy a part of the house to the exclusion of the other.

There are other procedures available to regulate the occupation of the home such as the Domestic Violence and Matrimonial Proceedings Act 1976 which is a jurisdiction available to cohabitees as well as spouses and under which proof of violence is not necessary before an exclusion order can be made (*Wiseman* v *Simpson* (1988), but to which s1(3) MHA 1983 applies (*Richards* v *Richards* (1984); *Lee* v *Lee* (1984)) so the outcome of the proceedings would be the same as those under the MHA 1983 as discussed above. The other major jurisdiction, namely the Domestic Proceedings and Magistrates' Courts Act 1978, would not apply on these facts as there is no allegation of violence or the threat of it.

In the light of the advice given above it is likely that Bertram will seek to exclude Antonia by invoking the MHA jurisdiction ancillary to the divorce or more likely nullity proceedings, although his prospects of success appear doubtful on these facts. It must also be noted that the jurisdictions referred to above would apply only to Antonia and the courts would have no power on these facts to exclude her parents under them so Bertram would have to seek their eviction by other means. If, however, there was evidence that Antonia's parents were taking Antonia's side and, for example, were being abusive to Bertram then such abuse would come within the meaning of 'molestation'. Accordingly Bertram could seek a non molestation injunction against Antonia arguing that she was 'molesting' him through her servants or agents namely her parents.

Question 4

Robert and Nellie married in 1987. They have one child and Nellie is expecting another in September 1992. The matrimonial home, Rose Cottage, was purchased by Robert out of money he inherited from his grandparents and registered in his own name. Since the birth of their first child, Nellie has acted as a housewife and Robert has paid her a weekly allowance to run the household and purchase clothes for herself and the children. Nellie, who is good with money, saved some of this allowance, using it to buy shares and art deco china.

In 1992 Robert developed a mental illness, as a result of which he enjoys frightening Nellie and their child, sometimes by brandishing imitation weapons. Nellie has become extremely tense as a result of this behaviour.

In March this year Robert and Nellie had a violent quarrel in the course of which Robert threatened to throw her and the child out. The following day Nellie left Rose Cottage to stay with her brother Joseph and his wife. In April Robert met Joseph in the local post office and threatened to kill him if he did not return Nellie and the child to the home.

Advise Nellie who wishes to return, safely, to Rose Cottage and would like, further, to dispose of the shares and china.

University of London LLB Examination
(for External Students) Family Law June 1992 Q6

General comment

This question concerns occupation of the matrimonial home and the ways in which a party to the marriage may be excluded from the home. It also deals with ownership of marital property.

Skeleton solution

a) • Consider rights of occupation of non-owning spouse under the Matrimonial Homes Act 1983 s1(1) and s1(2) - by which either spouse may apply to the court to restrict, vary, enforce, declare rights - s1(3) factors.

   • The Domestic Proceedings and Magistrates' Court Act 1978 should also be considered.

   • The Domestic Violence and Matrimonial Proceedings Act 1976 s1.

b) • Regarding the shares and the china:

   - consider common law position; and

   - s1 Married Women's Property Act 1964.

Suggested solution

a) *'Rose Cottage'*

Nellie wishes to return to the matrimonial home, 'Rose Cottage'. Initially we must consider whether she has a right of occupation by virtue of ownership. Here the house was purchased by Robert out of his own money and registered in his sole name. Therefore Nellie does not have any such right.

Next we should consider s1(1) of the Matrimonial Homes Act (MHA) 1983 - this creates the statutory right of occupation in the matrimonial home for a non-owning spouse. Nellie falls within this section as Robert alone has the legal title. She can come under s1(1) even though she is not in occupation at the moment.

The right of occupation constitutes:

i) the right of a spouse in occupation not to be evicted or excluded from the dwellinghouse or any part thereof by the other spouse except with the leave of the court;

ii) the right of a spouse not in occupation to enter and occupy the dwellinghouse with the leave of the court.

Having established that the MHA applies to these facts, we must next consider s1(2) MHA which provides that 'so long as one spouse has rights of occupation, either of the spouses may apply to the court for an order:

a) declaring, enforcing, restricting or terminating those rights; or

b) prohibiting, suspending or restricting the exercise by either spouse of the right to occupy the dwellinghouse; or

c) requiring either spouse to permit the exercise by the other of that right.'

So here, Nellie should seek an order declaring her rights of occupation and, either prohibiting Robert exercising his rights to occupy the house or part of it or requiring him to allow her to return and reside there. It is not clear on the facts what Nellie wants to do in respect of Robert's occupation, we are only told that she wishes to return to Rose Cottage. However, on the assumption that the house is not large enough to accommodate two separate households, and in view of Robert's behaviour in the past it would seem that they cannot live together. It is therefore necessary that he be excluded from the house if she wishes to return to live there.

In deciding whether to make an order under the Matrimonial Houses Act the court must consider the factors set out in s1(3) of the Act:

i)   the conduct of the parties;

ii)   the needs and resources of the parties;

iii)   the interests of any children; and

iv)   all the circumstances of the case.

In *Lee* v *Lee* (1984) it was stated that no one element is more important than any other. Dunn LJ stated that it is for the judge to carry out a balancing exercise and to decide what emphasis should be placed on each factor including the need for the children to see the family unit re-established in the matrimonial home.

So, firstly we must look at the conduct of the parties to see whether this justifies the grant of an exclusion order.

Anderson v *Anderson* (1984) stated the court has to take all the circumstances of the case into account and assess the risks to the family. When considering the parties' conduct, the court will look at the reasonableness of the applicant in refusing to live with the respondent. Robert's behaviour in this has caused problems for Nellie and even though his behaviour is involuntary to the extent that it derives from his illness, it will be taken into account against him: *Wooton* v *Wooton* (1984).

Next the court will look at the needs and resources of the parties. Nellie has no job and therefore has no income of her own. It is not clear what Robert's financial position is because we are not told whether he is still working. Nellie has to provide for the children therefore her need appears to be greater. Also the housing needs of the parties will be considered, and this relates particularly to the ability of either party to find alternative accommodation and the court will further consider the availability of council housing: *Thurley* v *Smith* (1985). It may feel that Nellie and the children have a greater chance of being provided with local authority housing than Robert, as a single man. However, Nellie should be reassured by the fact that despite the availability of council accommodation in Thurley v Smith, the relief sought was granted when all the other criteria had been taken into account.

The next factor for the court to consider is the needs of the children. The court in the case of *Richards* v *Richards* (1984) stated that it is merely one factor to be taken into account. Notwithstanding, it should be stated that if all the other factors are evenly balanced, then it may be that the children's interests will become the deciding element.

Finally, the court is required to consider all the circumstances of the case and a relevant point could be that Robert has threatened to throw Nellie and his child out of the house. Therefore an order could be made to allow them to return to Rose Cottage to live there until he provides them with suitable alternative accommodation as in *Lee* v *Lee* (1952). This may be appropriate if he wants to continue to live there since it would encourage him to rehouse his family quickly.

Taking all these facts into account it would seem that only one spouse can remain in the house in view of the matrimonial difficulties stemming from Robert's behaviour. Thus Nellie has a good chance of succeeding in her application to exclude Robert and to allow her to re-enter and occupy the house with the child and the baby when born.

Nellie should be advised, however, that this statute may not be the solution to all her problems. The injunction is granted subject to the discretion of the court and there is no power for the court to attach a non-molestation order to one granted under the MHA 1973.

Therefore her alternatives should be pointed out to her (as outlined below):

Nellie may make an application under s16 Domestic Proceedings and Magistrates' Courts Act (DPMCA) 1978. The applicant and respondent must be married to make an application under this Act. Nellie satisfies this. One of the orders the court can grant is an exclusion order - that the respondent leave the matrimonial home or be prohibited from entering the matrimonial home: s16(3). It is necessary to show:

i) use of violence against applicant or child; or

ii) threat of violence against applicant or child and use of violence against some other person; or

iii) threat of violence against applicant or child in breach of personal protection order under s16(2);

and in any of above cases that the applicant or child is in danger of being physically injured by the respondent.

The principles here are very strict and on these facts it is not likely that Nellie would succeed. There has not been actual violence, although there has been a threat of violence, but that was not to Nellie but to Nellie's brother, Joseph.

The other order that can be made under s16 is a personal protection order ie that the respondent shall not use or threaten to use violence against the person of the applicant and/or child of the family. Here it is necessary to show use or threat of violence and a need for protection. Again on the facts of this case it does not seem that these criteria will be satisfied unless the violent argument Nellie and Robert had before she left did actually involve physical violence or the threat of physical violence against her and/or the child.

Therefore it appears that Nellie will not be able to rely on the provisions of this Act. She must instead rely on the MHA or the Domestic Violence and Matrimonial Proceedings Act (DVMPA) 1976 s1. She can apply for a non-molestation order - a provision restraining the other party to the marriage from molesting the applicant or any child living with the applicant. Molestation should exist before a remedy will be granted, but molest has a broad definition and as well as violence it includes pestering, annoying conduct and therefore Nellie is more likely to be able to rely upon it.

Nellie may also apply for an ouster order under this Act. An ouster order is a provision excluding the other party to the marriage from the matrimonial home or part thereof or a provision requiring the other party to permit the applicant to enter and remain in the house or part thereof. This is what Nellie wants. However, before the court makes an ouster order it will have regard to the criteria in s1(3) of the MHA 1973: *Richards* v *Richards*. These have been discussed above in the MHA provisions - the same principles apply here. The court seeks to make an order that is 'fair, just and reasonable'.

b) *The shares and the china*

Nellie saved some of the allowance paid to her by Robert to buy the shares and the china.

At common law if a husband provided an allowance out of his income to his wife to pay housekeeping expenses, any sums not spent for that purpose prima facie remained his and he would be entitled to any property purchased with such savings: *Blackwell* v *Blackwell* (1943).

This principle was altered by s1 Married Women's Property Act 1964 which provides that:

'Where any question arises as to the right of a husband or wife to money derived from any allowance made by the husband for the expenses of the matrimonial home or for similar purposes, or any property acquired out of such money the money or property shall, in the absence of any agreement between them to the contrary, be treated as belonging to the husband and wife in equal shares.'

Here the shares and the art deco china are bought with money from the housekeeping allowance therefore prima facie Robert and Nellie will have equal shares in them.

Robert and Nellie may be able to reach an agreement as to the ownership of the shares and china but if they cannot, an application may be made to the High Court or county court (probably county court here) under s17 Married Women's Property Act 1882. The court has the power to resolve disputes between the spouses as to their property, and the court may order a sale of the property in which case Robert and Nellie would each get a half share in the proceeds.

8   PARENTAL RESPONSIBILITY

8.1   Introduction

8.2   Key points

8.3   Recent cases

8.4   Analysis of questions

8.5   Question

8.1   Introduction

In disputes concerning children, whether between parents or between parents and the State, broadly speaking the issue to be decided by the courts was who shall exercise parental rights in respect of the child and where the child should live on a day to day basis. The Children Act 1989 redefines the term to one of parental responsibility reflecting more accurately the nature of the relationship. Furthermore parental responsibility will in future rarely be lost by a parent and even on the making of a care order responsibility will be notionally shared. Parental responsibility can also be acquired under the Act by for example the father of a non-marital child, a stepfather where a residence order is made in his favour (see Chapter 10) and of course guardians.

The subtleties of the parent-child relationship make any clear definition of parental responsibility difficult. Previous legislation, much of which is repealed under the Act (eg Children Act 1975 and Child Care Act 1980) makes reference to 'parental rights and duties' but it has been left to the courts to define the concept more closely.

8.2   Key points

a) *What is parental responsibility?*

Section 3(1) Children Act: 'all the rights, duties, powers, responsibilities and authority which by law a parent of a child has in relation to the child and his property.'

i)   The responsibility of care and control

Parental wishes give way to the exercise of choice by the child 'according to the child's age, maturity and understanding,': see *Hewer* v *Bryant* [1970] 1 QB 357 quoted with approval in *Gillick* v *West Norfolk and Wisbech Area Health Authority* [1985] 3 All ER 402 - 'parental rights to control a child do not exist for the benefit of the parent. They exist for the benefit of the child and they are justified only insofar as they enable the parent to perform his duties towards the child ...' per Lord Fraser of Tullybelton.

ii) Education of the child

Parental responsibility is largely circumscribed by statute. Children between the ages of 5 and 16 must receive a full time education: Education Act 1944.

iii) Parental consent to the marriage of a child between the ages of 16 and 18: see Marriage Act 1949.

iv) To determine a child's religion.

v) To determine the child's surname.

No-one can change the child's surname without the written consent of every person who has parental responsibility or with the leave of the court: s13(1) Children Act 1989. See too *W* v *A* (*child: surname*) [1981] 1 All ER 100.

vi) Medical treatment of the child

- A person over the age of 16 may validly consent to medical treatment s8(3) Family Law Reform Act 1969. Under that age the position is ambiguous. There are circumstances in which the court will override the wishes of the parent.

- If satisfied that an alternative course of action is in the child's best interest: *Re B (a minor) (wardship: medical treatment)* [1981] 1 WLR 1421; *Re D (a minor) (wardship: sterilisation)* [1976] 2 WLR 279; *Re P (a minor)* [1986] 1 FLR 272.

- A life threatening situation

- Where the child's age, maturity and understanding is such that he or she is able to give valid consent.

    In *Gillick* v *West Norfolk and Wisbech Area Health Authority* (above) the issue was whether girls under the age of 16 could be prescribed contraception without their parents' consent. The court ruled that each case should be decided on the basis of each individual child's welfare taken alongside the maturity and understanding of the child. Much will therefore depend on the discretion of the medical profession.

- In *Re R* it was suggested that a *Gillick* competent child has no right to refuse treatment if the parents consent. In *Re R (a minor) (wardship: medical treatment)* [1991] 4 All ER 177; [1992] 1 FLR 190 the child suffered a mental disability whose understanding fluctuated on a week to week basis.

vii) Discipline

Any form of correction must be reasonable. Ill-treatment will result in criminal liability and care proceedings.

viii) The responsibility to maintain the child. See chapters on maintenance.

b) *Who exercises parental responsibility?*

    i)   Section 2(1) confirms that where a child's parents were married to each other at the time of birth they share parental responsibility.

    ii)   Section 2(2) provides that where the child's parents were not married at the time of birth the mother shall have parental responsibility exclusively. A father must acquire parental responsibility by a court order or by a parental responsibility agreement: see s4. Note that a father of a non-marital child could acquire parental rights under the Family Law Reform Act 1987: see *Re H* (*illegitimate children: father: parental rights*) [1989] 2 FLR 215 and *D* v *Hereford and Worcester County Council* [1991] 2 All ER 177; [1991] 1 FLR 205.

    iii)   There is no independent scrutiny by the courts of a parental responsibility agreement. It must be in the prescribed form.

    iv)   A person in whose favour a residence order is made shall acquire parental responsibility: s12(2).

        •   The factors that the court will take into account in deciding whether to grant a non-marital child parental responsibility have been considered in *Re H (minors) (local authority parental rights) (No 3)* [1991] 2 All ER 185 and *Re C (minors)* [1992] 2 All ER 86. They are: a) the degree of commitment shown towards the child; b) the degree of attachment between him and the child; and c) the reason for the application.

        •   The fact that circumstances may not make it possible for the father to exercise parental responsibility does not of necessity mean the court will not grant the application. A parental responsibility order gives an unmarried father locus standi to make applications to the court for orders a married father is entitled to: *Re C* [1991] 1 FLR 223.

    v)   A person without parental responsibility caring for the child can do what is reasonable in all the circumstances to safeguard the child's welfare.

    vi)   A person does not cease to have parental responsibility because someone else acquires it ie step-parents or the Local Authority.

8.3   Recent cases and statutes

Re C (minors) [1992] 2 All ER 86

Re H (minors) (local authority parental rights) (No 3) [1991] 2 All ER 185

Re W (a minor) (medical treatment) [1992] 3 WLR 758

8.4   Analysis of questions

An essay type question specifically on parental rights is sometimes asked. It is often joined together with some consideration of the 'welfare principle' and students are asked to consider to what extent the 'welfare principle' has eroded the concept of parental rights. It is also an area that students should understand to better inform any consideration of disputes between parents, disputes between parents and the Local Authority, the position of the father of a non-marital child and the position of third parties. See chapter 10: *Section 8 orders* for other examples of questions covering parental responsibility.

Students can also expect an essay type question on the area when topical, as following the *Gillick* case. The question below is an example of this. Under the Children Act 1989 the concept of parental rights is replaced by the concept of parental responsibility.

8.5 Question

Does English law recognise the concept of children's rights? Should it?

University of London LLB Examination
(for External Students) Family Law June 1990 Q6

General comment

An example of a question testing the student's knowledge of the changes brought about by the Children Act 1989 as they affect Children's rights. The Act came into force in October 1991 and examiners may well ask this kind of question.

Skeleton solution

- The concept of parental responsibility - the impact of *Gillick* - the contrast with parental rights.

- The welfare principle: s1(3) Children Act 1989.

- Public law - the greater accountability of the local authority.

- Section 8 orders - application by the child.

Suggested solution

Children's rights, an issue which has been the subject of much discussion in recent years, particularly following the House of Lords decision in *Gillick* v *West Norfolk and Wisbech Area Health Authority & Another* (1986), include not merely a recognition of a child's claim to self determination, but also an element of protectionism. Much child law is based on principles which support the protectionism view, for example the law seeks to protect children from exploitation by adults and from their own, presumed, inability to make decisions regarding their own welfare. It extends to legislation designed to help them reach their full potential for example by providing for compulsory education, and to ensure that a child receives a basic standard of care and is not ill treated (Children Act 1989).

While a child lives with his parents however, the parents exercise considerable control over his life, for example, in making decisions on education, such as on which school he will attend, and on medical treatment, which decisions are rarely questioned unless specifically brought to the attention of a court either by the parents themselves or a third party.

In Victorian times the father had near absolute rights over his child and could exercise them without considering the child's welfare. However the concept of the child's welfare became increasingly important and nowadays, in for example disputes concerning the child's custody and upbringing, this welfare principle is a court's paramount consideration and will prevail over parents' wishes (s1 Children Act 1989; *J* v *C* (1970); *B* v *B* (1971)).

The exercise of the welfare principle reflects the role of protectionism in child law and has not necessarily facilitated the promotion of a child's claim to self determination. However it is argued (see the Children Act 1989; Andrew Bainham (1990) Fam Law 311) that the Children Act 1989 goes some way towards taking the concept of children's rights seriously and does not identify those rights exclusively with the welfare concept.

The modern concept of parental power as enunciated in the Children Act 1989 is now one of responsibilities rather than of rights. Section 3 Children Act 1989 defines such responsibilities in terms of 'rights, duties and powers' and recognises a point confirmed in the *Gillick* case that parental responsibility diminishes as the child matures. In *Hewer* v *Bryant* (1970) Lord Denning MR stated that such responsibility '... starts with a right to control and ends with little more than advice'. Therefore as a child grows older his ability to make his own decisions increases. This view was recognised and discussed further in *Gillick*. In that case the House of Lords made pronouncements on inter alia, two important issues. Firstly, with regard to the age of consent to medical treatment, the Lords accepted that a child who was capable of making a reasonable assessment of the advantages and disadvantages of the medical treatment under discussion, could give a valid consent to it.

Secondly, the Lords expressed opinions on the nature and extent of parental power and whether children could act independently. Lord Fraser stated that parental rights '... exist for the benefit of the child and are justified only in so far as they enable a parent to perform his duties toward the child.' Lord Scarman, agreeing with this view, added that the parental rights '... yield to the child's right to make his own decisions when he reaches sufficient understanding and intelligence to be capable of making up his own mind on the matter in question.'

Whether a child is of sufficient maturity and understanding to make his own decision is a question of fact and of course it is still possible for a person who disagrees with the child to conclude that his decision is incorrect due to immaturity. On the specific issue raised in *Gillick*, concerning medical treatment and consent to the same, the Lords gave differing guidelines about what a child would have to understand to establish he had capacity to make the decision. This illustrates the need for further clarification. In *Gillick*, the Lords did not consider fully the scope of parental powers although the case is recognised as having wide implications and is not to be confined to decisions on medical treatment alone.

Andrew Bainham in his article referred to above argues that the emphasis in the Children Act 1989 on parental responsibilities rather than rights recognises children as persons to whom duties are owned rather than as possessions. He argues that this

145

recognition requires a greater effort to be made to involve children in decisions affecting them. Section 1(3) Children Act 1989 now provides a statutory check-list to be considered by a court in applying the welfare principle and the first factor in this list is 'the ascertainable wishes and feelings of the child concerned (considered in the light of his age and understanding)'. Similar duties are placed on local authorities and voluntary organisations in relation to children in their care. The court, local authority etc must give 'due consideration' to the child's views in reaching a decision. However it is not clear what is meant by this term 'due consideration' and the weight to be attached to the child's view is uncertain, particularly where it conflicts with that of an interested adult such as a parent. As indicated earlier the child's views could be discounted as immature or lacking in understanding, or as being outweighed by other factors in the application of the welfare principle. As Professor Cretney points out in Principles of Family Law (Fifth Edition), where there is a dispute over a child's upbringing the court's decision will be made by applying the welfare principle and not on the basis of the child's rights and the child need not necessarily be a party in those proceedings.

Where the child is in local authority care or is the subject of child protection proceedings the Children Act 1989 recognises the child's right to decide to a greater extent, as under the Act a local authority is more accountable for decisions relating to children. When a local authority reviews the case of a child it may be required to seek the child's view and to inform the child of the outcome of the review. The child will be entitled to make representations or complaints about the discharge by a local authority of its functions and internal procedures will have to be established, with an independent element, to deal with these representations. Once again however it is difficult to say how much weight will be attached to the child's view particularly when it conflicts with those of the concerned adults. Bainham argues that the true significance of these provisions is that a local authority will no longer be able to look at a child as an object of welfare, but the child must be involved to some extent in the local authority's decisions even though ultimately the child's views are outweighed by other considerations.

To conclude on this point it is clear that under the Act the child is afforded some say in matters affecting him, but not the final say.

The Children Act 1989 contains provisions which appear to uphold the child's right to take independent action, for example the consent of a mature child will be required for medical or psychiatric examinations of the child even where such examinations have been ordered by a court (s44 and Schedule 3 para 4(4) Children Act 1989). This goes beyond the *Gillick* decision which in essence held that ultimately the decision on whether a girl should be given contraceptive treatment should be made by the medical practitioner who would need to be satisfied as to the girl's maturity and understanding and other matters. The *Gillick* decision supports a partial independence for the child, in this case a right to be involved in the decision making. However it seems that the intention of Parliament in the Children Act 1989 in relation to medical and psychiatric examinations is that the mature child should have an absolute right to refuse to undergo the examination. It must be noted however that the child has to satisfy the maturity test and of course a child who is unwilling to undergo such an examination may be viewed as immature.

Under the 1989 Act a child will be able to apply for one of the new s8 orders on his own volition with leave of the court which will be granted if the court is satisfied that he has sufficient understanding to make the application (s10(8) Children Act 1989). Further, he may also apply for, inter alia, discharge of a care order or for discharge or variation of a supervision order (s39(1) and (2) Children Act 1989).

Section 8 orders will cease to have effect after the child has attained the age of sixteen years, and the courts will have powers to make such orders or allow them to remain in force in respect of a child over that age only in exceptional circumstances (s9(6) and (7) Children Act 1989). Under the old law custody and access orders lasted and could be made up until the child attained the age of eighteen years. This change recognises that orders relating to children over sixteen years of age are unenforceable without the child's cooperation and that in practice these older children decide where and with whom they shall live and with whom they will have contact.

The age limits for care and supervision orders remain unchanged, that is no order may be made in respect of a child who has attained the age of seventeen years (or if married, sixteen years). However it must be noted that whereas under the previous law the wardship jurisdiction could be invoked to commit a child aged seventeen or over to care, the Children Act 1989 now precludes such an order being made (s100(2)(a)).

There remain some important aspects of a child's life where the Children Act 1989 has done nothing to improve his right to self determination. In the field of education there is no provision made for notice to be taken of a mature child's views on say the choice of school or religious education. The parent is recognised as entitled to make a decision on choice of school and to make representations to the relevant education authority, and the parent may withdraw a child from religious education provided by the school. Professor Cretney argues that the fact that parents are under a duty to ensure that their child is educated between the ages of five and sixteen, and to maintain them until they are sixteen, is not sufficient justification for giving parents such control over their child, to the exclusion of the child's views.

The Children Act 1989 goes some way to ensuring that courts, local authorities and other decision makers take proper account of the views of the child under consideration although the extent to which those views must be taken into account is difficult to assess. However it is the first legislation to recognise the child's claim to self determination as an aspect of children's rights and for that reason must be seen as an important milestone in the development of a recognition of children's rights.

9 THE PARAMOUNTCY OF THE CHILD'S WELFARE

9.1   Introduction

9.2   Key points

9.3   Recent cases and statutes

9.4   Analysis of questions

9.5   Question

9.1   Introduction

The dominant principle in child care law has been the welfare of the child. The Children Act 1989 promotes this principle - 'the indications are that the paramountcy of the child's welfare needs to be strengthened and supported rather than replaced' - Law Commission. The 'welfare principle' expressed in the Guardianship of Minors Act 1971 is repealed but replaced with an almost identical provision in the new Act. Three changes should be noted:

a) The Act introduces a statutory checklist that the court should have regard to in exercising its jurisdiction;

b) Delay in determining any matter in relation to the child is a specific consideration that the court should have regard to;

c) The 'welfare principle' applies both to private law disputes and to care proceedings.

9.2   Key points

a) Section 1 provides that where a court determines any question with respect to either the upbringing of a child or the administration of a child's property, the child's welfare shall be the paramount consideration. This is not a new concept but the factors the court shall have regard to are identified in a statutory checklist: s1(3). The factors identified are already considered in custody disputes but it is hoped that greater consistency will be achieved by ensuring that all relevant factors are taken into account.

    i)   The ascertainable wishes and feelings of the child concerned (considered in the light of his age and understanding)

        • Consider here the effect of what has been termed the epochal case of *Gillick* v *West Norfolk and Wisbech Area Health Authority* [1986] AC 112.

- Note that the court will nevertheless override the views of the child if that course of action is not considered to be in the child's best interests: *Re DW (a minor) (custody)* [1984] Fam Law 17: *Re P (minors) (wardship care and control)* [1992] 2 FCR 681.

- The court must take account of an older child's wishes where that child may 'vote with its feet': *Williamson v Williamson* [1986] 2 FLR 146.

ii) The physical, emotional and educational needs of the child.

- Physical needs may be relevant perhaps where medical treatment a child needs is better provided in a particular area. Otherwise the courts have powers to provide for maintenance etc.

- Emotional needs of young children have in the past been regarded as more effectively met by mothers: *Re W (a minor)* (1983) 4 FLR 492; *Re W (a minor) (residence order)* [1992] 2 FLR 333. However changes in the social order now make it more likely that fathers should be considered: *Re H (a minor)* (1990) The Times 20 June CA.

- Brothers and sisters should not be separated: *C v C (minors) (custody)* [1988] 2 FLR 291; *B v T* [1989] 2 FLR 31.

- The courts will place great emphasis on a child's educational needs: *May v May* [1986] FLR 325.

- In *Re P (a minor) (education)* [1992] 1 FLR 316 the court ordered that the child should attend the school he wanted to attend. Both the child's wishes - he was considered sufficiently mature to make the decision - and his education were both factors important to the decision.

iii) The likely effect on him of any change of circumstances.

- Referred to as the 'status quo'. The courts have always placed emphasis on the need for continuity in a child's life.

  '... continuity of care is a most important part of a child's sense of security and that disruption is to be avoided wherever possible': Ormrod LJ in *D v M (minor) (custody appeal)* [1983] Fam 33.

- On status quo v maternal preference: see *Allington v Allington*: [1985] FLR 586; *Re H (a minor) (custody)* [1990] 1 FLR 51.

- The status quo obviously favours the person with whom the child is actually living. But note the cases of *Allington v Allington*: (above) and *Edwards v Edwards* [1986] 1 FLR 187.

- Where there is an obvious risk to the child the 'status quo' will yield to the need to provide emotional stability: *Re G (minors)* (1992) The Times 9 October.

iv) His age, sex, background and any characteristic of his the court considers relevant.

- These considerations are virtually open ended. Many are reconsidered elsewhere in the checklist.

v) Any harm he has suffered or is at risk of suffering.

- Clearly the court would be unlikely to make an order in favour of a parent who has abused the child. The presence of a blood tie would be of little significance: *Re R (a minor) (child abuse: access)* [1988] 1 FLR 206.

vi) How capable each of his parents are and any other person the court considers relevant to meeting his needs.

- The capacity of the parents to form caring and supportive relationships will be relevant here. The lifestyle of a parent with a criminal record and a drink problem would not be suitable: see for example *Re R (minors) (custody)* [1986] 1 FLR 6.

- There is a statutory acknowledgement of the importance of other significant adults in the child's life - grandparents and other relatives for example who themselves will in future be able to apply for orders in respect of children (see Chapter 10).

vii) The range of powers available to the court under this Act in the proceedings in question.

- The range of orders is extensive. Furthermore the court could for example make a residence order in favour of a grandparent in proceedings brought by the local authority under s31 for a care order.

b) The paramountcy of the child's welfare applies in almost all proceedings involving children but note:

i) In adoption proceedings the child's welfare is the *first* consideration: s6 Adoption Act 1976. Other considerations are also relevant.

ii) In applications to exclude the parent from the matrimonial home the interests of the children are one of several factors: see *Richards* v *Richards* [1984] AC 174.

c) The court should not make an order under the Act unless it considers that to do so would be better for the child than making no order at all. This is termed the 'non interventionist approach' and will have particular implications in private law. In circumstances where the parents agree on issues of residence, contact and so on the court will make no order at all.

The court will make an order where it would be in the child's interests for there to be the stability that follows from an order: *B* v *B (grandparent: residence order)* [1992] 2 FLR 327.

9.3 Recent cases and statutes

Children Act 1989

Re H (a minor) (custody) [1990] 1 FLR 51

Re P (a minor) (education) [1992] 1 FLR 316

Re W (a minor) (residence order) [1992] 2 FLR 333

Re J (a minor) (wardship: medical treatment) [1992] 3 WLR 507

B v *B (grandparent: residence order)* [1992] 2 FLR 327

9.4   Analysis of questions

Questions in this area have traditionally focused on the application of the welfare principle to custody disputes. In future students should use the statutory checklist as a framework for their answers. Much of the case law that predates the Act will continue to be relevant. Students should also remember that s1 of the Act has a wider application than the welfare principle previously had in that it applies to proceedings initiated by the local authority. In the past questions have sometimes been linked to other topics and no doubt that practice will continue.

9.5   Questions

Question 1

Consider the extent to which the welfare principle embodied in the Children Act 1989 prevails over the concept of parental responsibility.

Written by the Editors

General comment

Examiners have in the past asked students to consider the extent to which the welfare principle prevailed over parental rights. The Children Act redefines parental rights in terms of parental responsibility and provides that parents should not lose parental responsibility despite divorce. There remains the issue of decision making in a context of dispute however.

Skeleton solution

- Explain concept of parental responsibility
- Define parental rights/responsibility
- Explain welfare principle and the factors that the court must take into account under s1
- Consider briefly s8 orders
- Care proceedings under s31.

Suggested solution

Section 1 of the Children Act (CA) 1989 is largely a restatement of the welfare principle contained in s1 of the Guardianship of Minors Act 1971 - where a court determines any question with respect to either the upbringing of a child or the administration of a child's property, the child's welfare shall be the paramount consideration. The Act breaks new ground in that factors are identified which the court should have specific regard to: s1(3). These factors are: 1) the ascertainable wishes and feelings of the child; 2) the physical emotional and educational needs of the child; 3) the likely effect on him of any change in circumstances; 4) his age, sex, background and any characteristic of his the court considers relevant; 5) any harm he has suffered or is at risk of suffering, and 6) how capable each of his parents are and any other person the court considers relevant in meeting his needs.

Parental responsibility is defined as 'all the rights, duties, powers, responsibilities and authority which by law a parent of a child has in relation to the child and his property': s3(1) CA 1989. Reliance will still have to be placed on the common law for future guidance. Parental rights have in the past included a right to physical possession of a child, the right to determine his education and religion, the right to consent to medical treatment and adoption, the duty to maintain and represent the child in legal proceedings. The Act provides that parental responsibility may not be surrendered or transferred. The effect is that parental responsibility will rarely be lost by a parent, other than on adoption, which is in contrast to the position under the previous legislation.

The objective of the Act is to minimise disputes between parents by ensuring that they continue to have responsibility for their children following divorce. The court will of course in certain circumstances have to decide with whom the child should live. Such decisions will be based on s1 considerations. Thus a parent who has abused the child (*Re R* (1988)) would be unlikely to be awarded custody. The effect on the child of disrupting the status quo will be important: see *Allington* v *Allington* (1985). A consideration of the abilities of parents to meet the child's needs (*Re R* (1986)) will be weighed and so on. On this basis the court will make a residence order under s8 which will settle the arrangements as to where the child should live but parental responsibility for the child will continue to be shared by both parents. The Act anticipates potential disputes given that neither parent has a pre-emptive right over the other to make decisions on the child's upbringing. Again under s8 of the Act either will be able to apply for a specific issue order or a prohibited steps order, both of which are intended to settle particular disputes between the parents on the exercise of parental responsibility. In reality however the parent with a residence order in their favour will continue to make day to day decisions and the Act provides that either may act independently.

Before leaving a consideration of the welfare principle in the context of private law disputes it is important to consider the factor of the child's own ascertainable wishes. The important case of *Gillick* v *West Norfolk and Wisbech Area Health Authority* (1986) established that a child under the age of 16 could be prescribed contraception without the parents' knowledge and consent. Clearly the welfare principle dominates here over parental responsibility but dependent on the child's understanding of the proposed treatment.

Parental responsibility will not in future cease despite a child being in care. If a local authority successfully brings care proceedings under s31 of the Act establishing that a child is suffering or is likely to suffer significant harm, persons with parental responsibililty will continue to enjoy certain rights in respect of the child, in particular the right to apply for access: s34 CA. However the sharing of parental responsibility will be somewhat notional because the major decisions will be taken by the local authority. It is important to note here that the court must consider, in addition to the provisions of s31 CA, the welfare principle embodied in s1.

There are, however, some proceedings relating to children where the welfare principle will not be applied, and although in most of these proceedings a child's interests will be a first and therefore important consideration, it will not necessarily prevail over the interests of others such as parents. In adoption proceedings for example, the court is required to consider all the facts of the case, the first consideration being given to the need to safeguard and promote the child's welfare throughout his childhood. In most adoption cases, those interests probably will be the most important factor that the court will consider, and it has been argued that adoption law has become increasingly child-centred over recent years: see *Re F (a minor) (adoption: parental consent)* (1982). This has been recognised by the courts - in *Re H(B) (an infant); Re W(N) (an infant)* (1983) a decision on unreasonable withholding of consent by a parent in adoption proceedings, it was stated that in these applications the courts had moved towards a greater emphasis on the welfare of the child. However, in that case the court also recognised that without further legislation on the point, or further consideration by the House of Lords, there must be a limit to the shift towards this emphasis and consequently more consideration should be given to the rights of other parties, such as parents and their views on the matter. The court recognised that although it may be accepted by professional advisers that an adoption order would be best for the child, it does not necessarily follow that such an order should be made where the natural parent disagreed and refused to give his consent. The test to be applied will be that of the hypothetical reasonable parent. In considering that test the court does of course take the view that such a parent would be primarily concerned in promoting the child's welfare and would give this precedence over his or her own wishes. However, in view of the nature of the adoption order and its effect which is to extinguish the parental links between the child and his or her natural parents and establish analogous links with his or her adopters, it is considered a very serious step which is not to be lightly undertaken unless there is evidence that the circumstances demand it, and where there is no alternative.

Generally the courts explain their attitude by reference to the welfare of the child requiring the preservation and promotion of his ties with his natural parent. However, it is also recognised that adoption concerns a parent/child relationship generally and that parties other than the children have rights in such relationships, and that those rights should be preserved unless the circumstances clearly demand otherwise. Thus in *Re W (a minor) (adoption)* (1984) there was held to be a material misdirection where the judge had held that the child's interests were paramount and that he was not concerned as to whether it was fair and just to the parents. It was decided that 'all the circumstances' to be considered included the interests and claims of all parties concerned. However, generally it can be said that in these proceedings a child's welfare will usually be a deciding factor in the court's consideration. While it is now recognised that an adoption order need not necessarily be made, even if it is shown that it would be in the interests of the child, where the natural parent refuses to give his or her consent, the hypothetical reasonable parent test to be applied in such circumstances when deciding which course of action to take is based essentially on the consideration of what is best for the child in the light of the natural parent's ability and willingness to care for the child while remaining in contact with him.

In wardship proceedings the interests of the child in question will once again be a most important factor and generally speaking will prevail unless they conflict with the rights of a third party whose rights are liable to be seriously infringed if protection is given to the ward. Therefore in *Re X* (1975) the court would rarely, if ever, permit the interests of the ward to prevail over the wider interests of the freedom of publication. However, wardship proceedings have been used to provide protection for a child against the action or decision of his parents although there are also instances where the jurisdiction is used by parents to protect their children and to maintain control over them. The procedure may be used by a person other than a parent who wishes to invoke the jurisdiction of the court on the grounds, for example, that the child's parents are not fit to have control. If a child is made a ward of court in such circumstances the responsibility for the child is vested in the court who will delegate some of those powers, such as day to day supervision of the child to some other person such as the parents, who will then exercise these powers subject to the supervision of the court. It is recognised that such a step should be taken only where the circumstances seem serious enough to warrant such action. An example of where such a power has been used is in cases involving medical treatment of a child. In *Re D* (1976) a third party successfully warded an 11-year-old child to prevent her from being sterilised even though the girl's mother had consented to the operation, and in *Re B (a minor)* (1981) a local authority, at the instigation of medical staff at a hospital, sought to make a child a ward of court with a view to obtaining the consent of the court to an operation. The child was suffering from Down's Syndrome and without the operation would have died within a few days. On appeal the Court of Appeal gave consent to the operation, although the parents had decided to withhold their consent to the operation, and it was accepted that they did so in the belief that this would be in the best interests of the child. The court overruled their decision holding that the parents could not legally deprive the child of a potentially life-saving operation and therefore it upheld the rights of the child, the rationale of the case being the supremacy of the child's interests. A similar inference can be drawn from the circumstances surrounding the criminal prosecution of Dr Arthur in 1981. This case also involved medical treatment for a baby suffering from Down's Syndrome, where the baby's parents had rejected him and where the medical staff had decided that the child would be given nursing care only. The decision to bring a criminal prosecution against the doctor involved infers that the natural parents do not have the right to decide whether the child should be allowed to live or die in these circumstances, and is a further illustration of where the independent interests of the child will prevail over parental rights. However, in such circumstances as these medical cases illustrate, where rational decision making is required, it has been argued that the parents are not capable of this in view of their emotional involvement and it is therefore necessary that an independent tribunal, such as a court exercising wardship jurisdiction, should be involved in such decisions to ensure that all relevant considerations are taken into account and a balance is struck between responsibilities and those of children.

Question 2

'The development of a true children's rights movement will always be hampered by the law's not unreasonable assumption that children have a right not to be required to decide important matters relating to their upbringing.'

Discuss.

University of London LLB Examination
(for External Students) Family Law June 1992 Q2

General comment

An essay question that requires consideration of the historical rights of parents and the changes that have taken place since the *Gillick* case, and the effect of the new Children Act 1989.

Skeleton solution

- State that children's rights amd parents' rights are linked and state historical position.
- Consider the effect of *Gillick* - ie the recognition of the rights of mature children to make their own decisions.
- Consider effect of *Re R (a minor)*.
- Consider effect of the Children Act 1989.

Suggested solution

The issue of children's rights is tied up with the issue of parental rights. The law relating to children is based on principles which support the view that children should be protected, and seeks to protect children from exploitation by adults and from their own, presumed inability to make decisions regarding their own welfare. It may be a valid point that these views are relevant to immature children but at what time is a child not a child any longer?

Children's rights is an issue that has been the subject of much discussion in recent years, especially after the decision in *Gillick* v *West Norfolk and Wisbech Area Health Authority and Another* (1986) where the House of Lords reversed the decision of the Court of Appeal which had declared that a doctor could not lawfully give contraceptive advice to a girl under the age of 16 without her parent's consent.

When a child lives with his parents the parents control all aspects of his life, they decide where he is to go to school, where he will holiday and what medical treatment he receives - and these parental decisions are not usually questioned unless brought to the court's attention specifically, as in the *Gillick* case.

155

In Victorian times the father had near absolute rights over his child and could exercise them without considering the child's welfare. However the concept of the child's welfare has become increasingly important and today, in for example disputes concerning the child's custody and upbringing, this welfare principle is a court's paramount consideration and will prevail over parents' wishes: s1 Guardianship of Minors Act; s1 Children Act 1989.

However, it can be said that the welfare principle reflects the role of protectionism in English child law and has not aided the child's claim to self determination.

The Children Act 1989 supposedly redresses the balance between parental rights and children's rights. The Act does not refer to parental rights as such but instead to the concept of parental responsibility - 'all the rights, duties, powers, responsibility and authority which by law a parent has in relation to the child and his property (s3) and recognises a point made in *Gillick* that parental responsibility diminishes as the child matures. In this case the House of Lords made two important statements:

1) regarding the age of consent to medical treatment - the Lords accepted that a child who was capable of making a reasonable assessment of the advantages of the medical treatment under discussion could give a valid consent on it; and

2) the Lords expressed opinions on the nature and extent of parental power and whether children could act independently. Lord Fraser stated that parental rights 'exist for the benefit of the child and are justified only in so far as they enable a parent to perform his duties toward the child. Lord Scarman agreeing with this view added that the parental rights 'yield to the child's rights to make his own decisions when he reaches sufficient understanding and intelligence to be capable of making up his own mind on the matter in question'.

On the specific issue raised in *Gillick* concerning medical treatment and consent to the same, the Lords did not give clear guidelines as to what a child would have to understand to establish he had capacity to make the decision. *Gillick* was seen as not just relating to medical treatment issues but to other areas where a child's wishes may be different to those of parents.

The issue of medical treatment for minors has been considered again recently - in the case of *Re R (a minor) (wardship: medical treatment)* (1991). In this case the Court of Appeal had to answer the question whether refusal to consent by a mature minor is effective to veto treatment. R in this case was disturbed and it was held by the court that she could not validly refuse treatment.

This is a confusing case with many different issues arising, but basically Lord Donaldson held that the parental power to consent to medical treatment on behalf of a child was not lost when the child acquired competence to give consent. It continued until the child reached 18 and could be used to authorise treatment which the child refused.

This case and its consequences are discussed in 'Adolescent Crisis and Parental Power' by Judith Masson ((1991) Family Law p28). She states 'that the paternalistic approach of the Court of Appeal allows adult views to dominate. It does not provide a legal framework for good practice which stresses involving children in decisions about themselves, respecting their views and helping them to take responsibility for themselves. The lack of clarity in the decision and the diverse reasoning means that this issue will need to come before the House of Lords again. It is hoped that the Law Lords will remember that children are people not objects for concern and that sometimes bringing children within the law relating to adults may enable their welfare to be safeguarded and their rights protected better than extending the legal disabilities of childhood'.

The provisions of the Children Act 1989 may still, even in the light of *Re R*, be seen to be helping the children's rights movement. Section 1(3) provides a statutory checklist to be considered by a court in applying the welfare principle and the first factor in this list is 'the ascertainable wishes and feelings of the child concerned (considered in the light of his age and understanding). Similar duties are placed on local authorities and voluntary organisations in relation to children in their care. The court, local authority etc must give 'due consideration' to the child's views in reaching a decision - but it is not certain what due consideration entails.

Andrew Bainham in 'The Children Act 1989 - Parenthood and Guardianship' ([1990] Fam Law 311), argues that the Children Act 1989 goes some way towards taking the concept of children's rights seriously and does not identify those rights exclusively with the welfare concept.

It is contended, however, that the weight to be attached to the child's view is uncertain, especially where it conflicts with that of an adult. The child's view could be discounted as immature or lacking in understanding or as being outweighed by other factors in the application of the welfare principle.

The Children Act 1989 recognises the child's right to decide to a greater extent where the child is in local authority care. The child will be entitled to make representations or complaints about the discharge by a local authority of its function and internal procedures will have to be established to deal with these.

Also under the Act a child will be able to apply for one of the new s8 orders on his own accord with leave of the court which will be granted if the court is satisfied he has sufficient understanding to make the application (s10(8) CA 1989). He may also apply for, inter alia, discharge of a care order or for discharge or variation of a supervision order: s39(1) and (2) CA 1989.

Section 8 orders only have effect up to the 16th birthday of a child - under the old law, orders lasted until the child reached 18. This change recognises that orders relating to children over 16 years of age are unenforceable without the child's cooperation and that in practice these older children decide where and with whom they shall live.

The Children Act has not had any effect on the choice of school that a child must attend or on the choice of religious education. The parent retains the rights to make decisions on choice of school etc.

However, as it is the first legislation to recognise the child's claims to self determination as an aspect of children's rights, it must be seen as an important milestone in the development of a recognition of children's rights. It is hoped that the law will continue in this mode and not regress as in *Re R*.

10 SECTION 8 ORDERS

10.1   Introduction

Part II of the Act introduces new orders known as the 'section 8 orders' to replace custody, care and control and access. There are two totally new orders, the specific issue order and the prohibited steps order, both of which are modelled on the wardship jurisdiction. The objective of the legislation is to provide a statutory framework within which all decisions can be made in respect of children, to clarify the law and to provide for a scheme of unified orders that do not differ according to the type of proceedings being brought. The following points should be noted.

a) The court can make a s8 order in any family proceeding. This will for example include proceedings under the Domestic Violence and Matrimonial Proceedings Act 1976, care proceedings under Part IV of the Act and proceedings for financial support.

b) Parental responsibility for the child will continue beyond divorce or separation as will the power of parents to act independently unless the court orders otherwise: s2(7).

c) The specific issue and prohibited steps orders will reduce the need to resort to the wardship jurisdiction to resolve specific problems that relate to some aspect of a child's upbringing. Grandparents and others who have been significant in the child's life will be able to apply for leave to apply for a s8 order.

10.2   Key points

a) *The orders*

   i)   Residence order

      This settles the arrangements to be made about where the child should live. The order is sufficiently flexible for the court to specify periods which the child should spend with each parent and will be appropriate where, for example, the child shares a week between the parents. Without the written consent of everyone with parental responsibility or a court order no person may cause the child to be known by a new surname. There are restrictions on removing the child from the jurisdiction.

On shared residence orders see *Re H (a minor) (shared residence)* [1993] Fam Law 463.

ii) Contact order

This replaces the access order. Note that these two orders replace the orders of custody, care and control and access. The ambiguity surrounding the exercise of parental rights (see *Dipper* v *Dipper* [1981] Fam 31) becomes irrelevant in view of the fact that parental responsibility will continue to be shared.

It seems to be an established presumption that the emotional needs of the child are best met by continued contact with both parents. Note however in *Re F (a minor) (access)* [1992] Fam Law 484 and *Re SM (a minor) (natural father access)* [1991] 2 FLR 333 contact was refused on the basis that disruption would result because of the difficult and fraught relationship between the parents.

iii) Specific issue order

This order will enable the court to give directions over how a feature of parental responsibility should be exercised, for example whether or not a child should be known by a particular surname, educated at a particular school and so on. The Lord Chancellor has indicated that this will include power to determine whether a child should undergo irreversible medical treatment such as sterilisation or abortion.

iii) Prohibited steps order

This order will direct that no steps should be taken in respect of a child without the consent of the court. This order too is modelled on the wardship jurisdiction and intended to 'include in the statutory jurisdiction the most valuable features of the wardship jurisdiction' (see Law Commission report No 172). The court will have to spell out those matters that must be referred back to it, thus being more specific than is the case under wardship jurisdiction. An example here would be the removal of the child from the jurisdiction where no residence order was in force.

b) *Power to give directions and impose conditions*

The court has power to give directions as to how an order is to be carried into effect (s11(7)(a)) and powers to impose conditions (s11(7)(b)), for example directions as to how a contact order should be phased in following a long period of no contact and a condition attached to a residence order as to which school a child should attend.

c) *Who can apply for a s8 order*

Applications may be made in the context of family proceedings or on a free-standing basis. A parent or guardian, a person in whose favour a residence order is in force or a person with custody under existing provisions can apply for any s8 order. In addition the following can apply for a residence and contact order:

i) a person who is a party to the marriage in respect of a child of the marriage as defined by s105(1) ie step-parents;

ii) a person with whom the child has lived for at least three years. This provision caters by and large for foster parents (note the custodianship provisions have been repealed);

iii) a person with the consent of the local authority in respect of a child in care;

iv) a person with the consent of those with parental responsibility;

v) leave to apply: the child can apply for leave to apply.

Other persons may also apply with the leave of the court ie grandparents but they must satisfy the court as to their relationship with the child and the court must have regard to any disruption that might result to the child from the proposed application: *JR* v *Merton LBC* [1992] 2 FCR 174; *Re A and others (minors) (residence orders)* [1992] 3 WLR 422.

d) *Wardship*

Wardship is an inherent jurisdiction of the High Court. Any child can be made a ward of court by the issue of a summons under s41 of the Supreme Court Act 1981. Once an application is made no important steps in respect of the child can be made without the leave of the court.

There are no preconditions and the jurisdiction is extremely flexible. Any person with a legitimate interest in the child can apply and this includes parents, step-parents, foster parents and the local authority. It has therefore been used by non parents who had no rights under legislation pre the Children Act 1989. In recent years the local authority has increasingly used the jurisdiction to supplement its statutory powers particularly in complex cases. For these reasons the number of applications has grown considerably but the provisions of the Children Act in public and private law - see in particular s8 orders (prohibited steps orders and specific issue orders) and s100 of the Act - seem likely to bring to an end the extensive use made of the wardship jurisdiction.

10.3 Recent cases and statutes

Children Act 1989

JR v *Merton LBC* [1992] 2 FCR 174

Re A and others (minors) (residence orders) [1992] 3 WLR 422

Re H (a minor) (shared residence) [1993] Fam Law 463

10.4 Analysis of questions

Questions on this area are fairly straightforward and require the student to apply the welfare principle. As elsewhere, the questions often also cover another topic, for example, in the suggested solution following it is adoption. Essay questions are often linked with parental rights. The consideration of s8 orders under the Children Act 1989 will undoubtedly be examined.

10.5 Questions

Question 1

Simon and Tania married in 1971 and have two children, Una, now aged eight and Vita, aged seven. The marriage ran into difficulties when Simon had a mental breakdown and in 1980 they separated. Tania went to live with William, taking the children with her. Shortly after the separation Simon and Tania had a fierce argument about how the children should be educated. Simon wanted to pay for the children to be privately educated, whereas Tania wanted them to attend the local state school in the small town in which they live.

Simon has now recovered from his mental breakdown and is living with Yvonne. They visited Una and Vita regularly and consider that they can provide a better home for them than Tania and William. Tania wants to divorce Simon, marry William, and to have the children adopted by her and William. Una and Vita want to stay with Tania and William.

a) Assuming that Simon and Tania do not obtain a divorce, what procedures must Simon and Yvonne invoke if they want to obtain a residence order in respect of the children? Is the application for custody likely to succeed?

b) Assuming that Simon and Tania do not obtain a divorce, how can the dispute about the education of the children be resolved?

c) If Tania divorces Simon and marries William, what steps must they take if they want to adopt the children? Is the adoption likely to succeed?

Adapted from University of London LLB Examination
(for External Students) Family Law June 1985 Q8

General comment

This is a wide-ranging question on residence disputes and adoption orders, but it is not difficult as the advice sought is obvious and relatively restricted by the form of questions.

Skeleton solution

a) Residence order applications under s8 Children Act 1989 with an assessment of the welfare principle and an application of that principle to the facts. Wardship should be discounted.

b) Applications to resolve a dispute relating to the upbringing of a child, under s8 Children Act 1989, with reference to the relevant factors to be considered by the court.

c) Conditions to be fulfilled for an adoption application by relatives and step-parents with advice on the attitude of the courts regarding such applications and the view

162

that the divorce court's jurisdiction to make custody orders is likely to be more appropriate to these circumstances.

Suggested solution

a) On the assumption that Simon and Tania do not divorce at this time there are two procedures which could be invoked to settle the custody dispute, namely an application in the High Court, County Court or Magistrates' Court under s8 of the Children Act 1989.

Section 10 of the Children Act 1989 provides that the parents of a child may apply as of right for any s8 order which includes a residence order. A residence order decides the arrangements to be made over where a child should live. Section 10 would not give Yvonne any rights to apply, indeed she would have to seek leave of the court but the court would have to be satisfied as to her relationship with the child and have regard to any disruption that might result to the child from the proposed application. In the circumstances it is unlikely that she be granted leave.

The decision of the court would be guided by the 'welfare principle' in s1 of the Act. The child's interests will be the paramount consideration. Section 1 includes a 'statutory checklist' to assist the court. The factors include:

i) the physical, emotional and educational needs of the children. It may be that the court will take the view that relatively young girls are best cared for by their mother although the cardinal rule seems to be that the capacity of the adults to form loving relationships. Certainly there is no longer a presumption that mother is best *Re H* (1990). The courts are unlikely to separate the girls: *C v C* (1988).

ii) The likely effect on the child of any change of circumstances The court will seek to maintain the status quo regarding continuity of care as important: see Ormrod LJ in *D v M* (1983). The status quo will of course favour William and Tania.

iii) How capable each of his parents are and any other person of meeting the child's needs. The lifestyle of the parents will be relevant here: see *Re R* (1986). The court will also see relevance in being reassured on the personalities of both William and Yvonne.

iv) The ascertainable wishes and feelings of the children. Both children are relatively young but their views will be relevant depending on their maturity and understanding. The question of the child's views has become of greater importance since the case of *Gillick* v *West Norfolk and Wisbech Area Health Authority* (1986). Una and Vita want to stay with William and Tania.

v) The range of powers available to the court under the Act - a wide range of provisions including for example the attaining of conditions to a residence order see s11. Such a condition could relate to the education issue.

In the circumstances therefore it would seem highly likely that the court will favour William and Tania, although in the absence of any major concerns relating to Simon a contact order will be granted to him.

b) Prior to the enactment of the Guardianship Act 1973 the mother of a legitimate child had during her husband's lifetime, and in the absence of a court order, no parental rights over the child and subject to certain exceptions, both the common law and equity recognised a father's absolute right to determine the form of his legitimate minor children's education and his wishes had to be respected even after his death. From the end of the nineteenth century, however, the courts began to pay more attention to the welfare of the child than to the father's wishes and since the Guardianship of Infants Act 1925 the court is obliged to put the welfare of the child first. Under the Children Act 1989 the natural parents of children share parental responsibility.

Today, therefore, the court must give effect to both parents' wishes unless they are displaced by considerations of the children's welfare. If there is a dispute between Simon and Tania regarding the children's education, the Act provides machinery whereby an application can be made by either party to the court for its direction on a particular issue and the court may make such order as it thinks proper. Again application is under s8 for a specific issue order.

It is difficult to advise on the likely outcome of this dispute as there is no information in the question to indicate which system of education will be better for these children. There is nothing to suggest that the school proposed by Simon would be any better than the school presently attended by the children. If Simon is proposing that the children be removed from their present school the court would have to consider the problems attendant upon such a move involving as it will the loss of established friends and the need to make new ones as well as to adapt to the methods of the new school. Further, although we are given no details on this point, if Simon's proposals would involve the children being sent away to school as boarders, this would be a very important consideration and it may be that it would be detrimental for the children to leave their established home environment at this time. Even if they are to attend the new school on a daily basis, the practical arrangements for doing so would have to be investigated.

The court will also consider the future education of the children and it may be that Simon's proposals would provide for a better education for the children at this level so that whereas the court may be hesitant to change the children's schooling at this time, when they reach secondary education level a change may be more feasible, particularly if they are to attend the new school on a daily basis. The decision will be made on a consideration of the welfare principle.

In conclusion, therefore, the court will be concerned to promote the welfare of the children and their education will be considered in this light. On the basis that Simon's proposals would involve uprooting the children from their present school at this time, it would seem that this would not be to the advantage of the children unless it could be shown for example that their present school is not catering for their needs adequately and that the facilities provided by the proposed school would be superior in this respect. However, as far as their secondary education is concerned, it is more than likely that when they reach secondary school age they will have to change schools in any event and at that stage the proposals made by Simon may be more attractive to the court.

c) An adoption order which extinguishes the parental links between the child and his natural parents and creates analogous links between the child and his adopters cannot be accomplished other than by a court order. Therefore Tania and William will have to apply to either the High Court or County Court or Magistrates' Court to adopt the children. An adoption order cannot be made upon the application of more than one person unless the applicants are married to one another as Tania and William are in this case, in which case they may apply for an order jointly. Both must be over 21 and one of them must be domiciled in the United Kingdom, Channel Islands or Isle of Man: s14 Adoption Act 1976.

Before a court can make an adoption order a number of preliminary conditions have to be satisfied. Under s13(1) Adoption Act 1976 it is provided, inter alia, that where the applicants or one of them is a parent, step-parent or relative of the child, as here, where Tania is the children's mother and William is their step-father, no order shall be made unless the child is at least 19 weeks old and at all times during the preceding 13 weeks has had his home with the applicants or with one of them. A child is to be regarded as having his home with a person who, disregarding the absence of the child at a hospital, boarding school and any other temporary absence, has actual custody of him. Here both conditions are satisfied as the children are eight and seven years old and have been living with Tania all their lives, and indeed with William for the last five years.

In principle, Tania and William may apply for an adoption order in respect of the children. In deciding whether to make an adoption order the court must have regard to all the circumstances of the case, the first consideration being given to the need to safeguard and promote the children's welfare throughout their childhood, and so far as it is practicable, to ascertain the children's wishes and feelings regarding the decision, having regard to their age and understanding. Unlike the wording of s1 Children Act 1989 which requires the courts to have regard to the welfare of the children as a first and paramount consideration, this merely requires that the children's welfare be considered of the first importance, but it is not given the pre-eminence that it enjoys by virtue of s1 Children Act 1989 in other proceedings relating to the upbringing of children. It seems that the children's welfare is to be given greater weight than other considerations but it need not prevail over those other considerations: *Re H(B) (an infant)*; *Re W(N) (an infant)* (1983); *Re W (a minor) (adoption)* (1984). In this case it may be that the children are too young to understand the nature of the adoption order and therefore it would not be practicable to question them as to their wishes on the matter.

Tania and William must be advised that generally the court will be reluctant to grant an adoption order to relatives unless there are special circumstances in the case making it desirable in the children's interest. It might be considered contrary to their interests to allow them to be adopted by their mother and step-father as this might be used to sever their relationship with Simon, their natural father, and it is provided in s14(3) and s15(3) Adoption Act 1976 that if an adoption application is made by a step-parent either alone or jointly with a natural parent, the court is required to dismiss the application if it considers the issue affecting the children's custody would be better dealt with under the Divorce Court's matrimonial jurisdiction. It was said in *Re S* (1977) that the court should only make an adoption order in these circumstances if adoption would safeguard and promote the welfare of the children better than the existing arrangements and better than any other arrangements that could be made under the divorce jurisdiction. It is not sufficient to show that the adoption will be beneficial to the children, but that it would be better than the other alternatives. It is generally thought desirable that the children retain contact with their natural parent unless such contact would be harmful to them. There is no evidence in this case to suggest that adoption would be a better alternative than the arrangements that could be made in the divorce jurisdiction where custody and care and control of the children would most likely be awarded to Tania, with access being allowed to Simon. In earlier decisions the courts have looked for exceptional circumstances necessitating an adoption order. So in *Re S (a minor)* (1974) an order was made where the step-parent had been the father figure in the child's life from an early age. In this case William has been living with Tania and the children it would seem for approximately five years and therefore since the children were three and two respectively. However, although he has had a long relationship with them from their early years, it is not clear how much contact they have had with their natural father, and certainly there is nothing about Simon's illness that has now been cured which would be serious enough to warrant a complete break with the children.

These principles regarding the adoption of children by step-parents are viewed very seriously by the courts and are reflected by the fact that all cases where they are relevant must be brought to the attention of the judge and application cannot proceed unless the judge gives directions as to its further conduct. So it may be that Tania and William's application is brought to an unsuccessful conclusion at a preliminary stage in the proceedings as it is unlikely that on these facts they will be able to show that an adoption order is necessary as it would appear that the children's interests can be protected by the Divorce Court quite adequately, which court would undoubtedly grant a residence order to Tania, but who would preserve the relationship between the children and Simon by allowing a contact order in favour of Simon. It would seem that the main reason for the adoption application would be to sever the relationship between the children and Simon, but on the facts this would not seem to be appropriate or necessary.

Question 2

Rick and Samantha, a married couple, have two children, Tara born in 1975, and Ursula, born in 1978. They separated in 1986 and agreed that Samantha, who was unemployed, could look after the children at her sister's home in London from Monday to Thursday and that Rick, a self-employed music teacher who lives in Wales, would have the care of the children from Friday to Sunday.

This arrangement continued until 1989 when a disagreement arose concerning Ursula's education. Rick wants her to attend a comprehensive school in Wales, while Samantha, a Roman Catholic, wants her to attend the convent school in London which Tara already attends. In January 1990 Rick refused to return the children to Samantha after a weekend stay and placed Ursula at the comprehensive school. Shortly afterwards, Tara became pregnant and, as she wanted her pregnancy terminated, Rick has made arrangements for her to have an abortion.

i) Assuming that Samantha and Rick do not obtain a divorce, advise Samantha as to the procedures she must invoke if she wants Ursula to attend the convent school and to prevent Tara from having an abortion. Are her applications likely to succeed?

ii) Assuming that Samantha obtains a divorce from Rick, advise Rick on whether he is likely to obtain a joint custody order. If joint custody is granted, what form is it likely to take?

University of London LLB Examination
(for External Students) Family Law June 1990 Q7

General comments

Students were invited to answer the 1990 paper on the basis of the then existing law or on the assumption the Children Act 1989 was in force. The latter assumption makes part (ii) of the question 'short and sweet'.

Skeleton solution

i) • Parental responsibility: s2 CA 1989

   • Application for s8 orders under the Children Act 1989 - specific issue orders, prohibited steps order.

   • The welfare principle: s1 CA.

ii) • Notion of joint custody no longer applicable under CA 1989. Parental responsibility continues beyond divorce.

   • Split residence.

   • Welfare principle.

Suggested solution

i) Under the Children Act 1989 married parents of children share parental responsibililty for their children. Parental responsibility is defined as 'all the rights, duties, powers, responsibilities and authority which by law a parent of a child has in relation to the child and his property'. Such responsibilities will include decisions in respect of education and medical treatment which would include abortion. The act provides that parental responsibility cannot be surrendered or transferred and will therefore continue beyond separation or divorce. Furthermore

167

each person with parental responsibility for a child may act alone and without the other in meeting that responsibility.

Parents of children resolve differences of opinion over children's upbringing but where they fail to do so - as is perhaps more likely in the event of separation and divorce - the law provides mechanisms for such resolution. Prior to the Children Act Samantha could have invoked the wardship jurisdiction. Wardship is an inherent jurisdiction of the High Court. On application the court becomes the child's guardian and all major decisions affecting the child are made by the court. Wardship has in the past been used by parents and others with an interest in the child in situations analagous to this. See *Re P (a minor)* (1986) when the court decided the pregnancy of a child aged 13 should be terminated despite her parents' objections on religious grounds.

The Children Act introduces two new orders - the specific issue order and the prohibited steps order which are intended to minimise the need to resort to wardship. They are 'intended to cover everything from disagreements about which school the child should attend to major decisions such as whether a child should undergo major and irreversible treatment such as an abortion or sterilisation.' Application for such 'section 8 orders' would include any parent or guardian of the child - s10 - so Samantha should make application for a specific issue order to resolve the dispute over both Ursula's education and whether Tara should have an abortion.

The decision of the court must be informed by the 'welfare' principle: s1. The court must have regard to the 'statutory checklist.' We can, on the facts, assume both parents enjoy a good relationship with the children and can equally meet their physical and emotional needs. The courts have tended to assume mothers can best meet the needs of younger children although they have recently stated there is no presumption in favour of the mother: see *Re H* (1990). In any event both Tara and Ursula are not young in that sense. In respect of Ursula's education then the question would be whether a Catholic religion would best meet her needs - this would raise wider questions of religious upbringing - and whether a change of circumstances would undermine Ursula's security. It is worth noting that Ursula has lived with her father for some months but the court may well regard the status quo as being with the mother in terms of her weekday commitments, friends and so on: see *Edwards* v *Edwards* (1986). Overlaying these factors would be Ursula's own view depending on her age, maturity and understanding: see *Gillick* v *West Norfolk and Wisbech Area Health Authority* (1986). The court will override the child's view if it is not deemed to be in the child's best interests. The fact that Ursula is now living in Wales suggesting a complete break from her friends and schooling in London may well pre-dispose the court to an order in favour of a return to the convent school in London. In respect of Tara the child's physical and emotional needs will be the major consideration alongside of her own views. She is 15 years old. In view of the dispute between the parents Tara's view may well be conclusive.

ii) Under the Children Act of 1989 the concept of joint custody will disappear. The implication of such an order was that the parents continued to share parental rights in respect of their children following divorce. Under the Act parental responsibility in respect of children continues beyond divorce. If Samantha and Jack cannot resolve the issue of where the two girls are to live application should be made for a residence order which will settle arrangements for where the children are to live. The Act foresees circumstances where a split residence order should be made. Such an order could specify the periods during which the child is to live in each of the households. If under s1 the welfare of the child favoured an order in the terms of the pre-January arrangements then a 'split' residence order may well be made.

Question 3

'Section 8 of the Children Act 1989, when implemented, will provide a coherent and rational scheme for reaching decisions about a child's future upbringing.' Discuss.

University of London LLB Examination
(for External Students) Family Law June 1991 Q6 ('or' option)

General comment

This 'or' option requires consideration of the reformed law relating to custody disputes under the Children Act 1989.

Skeleton solution

- Outline old law, discuss Law Commission's objects for reform.

- Examine law under Children Act 1989 - who may apply?; discuss new principles of retention by both parents of parental responsibility; explain s8 orders and principles to be applied in reaching decisions.

Suggested solution

The resolution of issues relating to a child's care and upbringing prior to the implementation of the Children Act 1989 was possible under a variety of jurisdictions. The basis of such applications varied considerably, for example, custody and related issues could be dealt with pursuant to a divorce, nullity or judicial separation petition under the Matrimonial Causes Act 1973, or pursuant to a claim for financial provision under either s27 Matrimonial Causes Act 1973 or s2 Domestic Proceedings and Magistrates' Courts Act 1978, or as an independent issue under the Guardianship of Minors Act 1971. Further, isolated issues relating to a child's upbringing could be dealt with in the wardship jurisdiction or under the Guardianship Act 1973. Third parties such as relatives or foster parents who had no right to institute proceedings under the statutory provisions referred to above were able to apply for a custodianship order under the Children Act 1975.

The principle which governed the determination of these proceedings was the same, namely the welfare principle as established in s1 Guardianship of Minors Act 1971, but the orders which could be made by the courts and their effects as well as the parties who could make these applications and the children to whom the order related, could

169

vary according to the jurisdiction adopted. This plethora of jurisdictions made the law relating to a child's upbringing complex and confusing. There seemed to be no real consistency as to the application of the principles to be applied, for example the attitude of the courts towards joint custody orders varied considerably. It was generally recognised that both parents should continue to play an active role in their children's lives after divorce or separation, but there seemed to be no agreement as to whether a joint custody order could achieve this aim.

In considering reform of the law relating to child care and upbringing the Law Commission set out to create a framework of law which would recognise and encourage the continued relationships between the child and his parents. Orders relating to children would continue to be available in three circumstances, namely an application in certain family proceedings (for example under the Matrimonial Causes Act 1973, the Domestic Proceedings and Magistrates Courts' Act 1978, the Adoption Act 1976, etc), at the court's initiative in those proceedings and as an independent application in the absence of other family proceedings. However, the orders available in any of these applications are now uniform. The parties entitled to apply for such orders and the children to whom they relate will also be the same whatever proceedings are implemented.

Under the Children Act 1989 the potential applicants for orders relating to children (to be known as s8 orders) are parents of the child (whether married or unmarried); a party to the marriage to whom the child is a child of the family; any person in whose favour a residence order is in force, and other third parties (s10(4) and (5) Children Act 1989).

A basic premise on which the new law operates is that both parents will retain parental responsibility for their children and may act independently of each other so long as this is not incompatible with a court order. The orders available under s8 Children Act 1989 are designed to provide practical solutions to problems which arise in relation to a child's upbringing and to encourage the parties to maintain their involvement in the children's lives. The law no longer emphasises the custodial or non-custodial status of a parent and the s8 orders replace the powers of the courts to make custody, legal custody or access orders which applied prior to the implementation of the 1989 Act.

Under s8 Children Act 1989 the available orders are as follows: a residence order which will settle the person with whom the child will live; a contact order will require the person with whom the child is living to allow the child to visit or stay with the person specified in the order, or for that person and the child to have contact with each other in some other way, for example telephone calls, letters etc; a prohibited steps order will provide that no step of the kind specified in the order which could be taken by a parent meeting his parental responsibility, shall be taken without the court's consent; and a specific issue order will give directions to determine a specific question which has arisen or may arise in connection with any aspect of parental responsibility, for example education.

Such orders may be made at any time until the child reaches the age of eighteen although generally they would not be made after the child's sixteenth birthday.

When deciding what order, if any, to make the court will apply the welfare principle, namely that the child's welfare is paramount, by adopting the statutory checklist contained in s1(3) Children Act 1989. The court will therefore consider similar issues as under the application of the welfare principle in the old law. However, the Act also provides that the court '... shall not make the order or any of the orders unless it considers that doing so would be better for the child than making no order at all.' Where the parties agree on the arrangements to be made for the child no order may be necessary. However, in some cases it may be desirable to obtain one to clarify the parties' roles and to safeguard their positions in relation to other proceedings (for example the fact there is no order would affect the right to remove the child from local authority accommodation).

Cretney and Masson in *Principles of Family Law* (fifth edition) argue that this non interventionist policy may create problems in that it may conflict with the welfare principle to a degree. It is accepted that generally children adjust best to marital breakdown if they maintain contact with both parents, but where parents agree arrangements as to the children's care and upbringing the issues of the child's wishes and welfare may not be properly addressed as the court may decide, applying the non interventionist policy, that there should be no further enquiry and therefore no order under s8 Children Act 1989. The policy accords primacy to the wishes of the adult parties who will usually be the child's parents. Given that the welfare principle states that the child's welfare is paramount there could be an apparent conflict between the two principles.

The Children Act 1989 goes a long way to dealing with the problems associated with the complex and confusing jurisdictions which applied prior to the implementation of the Act. The fact that there is now a uniform approach, whatever the proceedings, to the orders available, the applicants and the principles to be applied is generally welcomed and certainly the law will be simpler to understand and implement.

11 ADOPTION AND CUSTODIANSHIP

11.1   Introduction

11.2   Key points

11.3   Recent cases

11.4   Analysis of questions

11.5   Questions

11.1   Introduction

Adoption irrevocably transfers all the parental duties in a child from the birth parents and others who may at the time of the order have parental rights in the child eg the local authority and vests those rights and duties in the adopters. Legal adoption first became possible in 1926 with the passage of the Adoption Act. Adoption was a means whereby childless couples could fulfil their desire to have a family by providing a home for an illegitimate child. Adoption has since then changed significantly in character. The number of children, particularly babies, available for adoption has decreased and adoption has been increasingly seen as a solution for children in care.

The Children Act 1975 placed a ban on private adoption placements and entrusted the local authority with the duty of providing a comprehensive adoption service. While it is only the court that can make an adoption order, adoption agencies (ie the local authority or an adoption society approved by the DHSS) are charged with making arrangements for assessing children and prospective adopters and placing children for adoption. The agency establishes a 'panel' and before placing a child for adoption the agency must refer a prospective adoption to the panel.

It is now a criminal offence for anyone other than an adoption agency to place a child for adoption. There are of course still some adoptions, for example where foster parents or relatives apply to adopt, where no agency is involved and in those cases the local authority must be notified and will undertake the reporting function: s11(1) ie to present reports to the court on the child and the prospective adopters. It is also an offence under s57(1) to make payments to achieve the adoption of a child, but note that in *Adoption Application: Surrogacy* AA 212/86 [1987] 2 All ER 826 a payment made in respect of a surrogacy arrangement was held not to contravene s57.

In *Re GD (adoption application)* [1992] 1 FCR 176 payments were made in respect of a home study report and a lawyer in El Salvador. The court held that the child's welfare outweighed other considerations and an order was made.

In reaching a decision about the proposed adoption of a child a court or adoption agency shall have regard to all the circumstances of the case - 'first consideration being given to the need to safeguard and promote the welfare of the child throughout his childhood; and shall so far as is practicable ascertain the wishes and feelings of the child ...': s6 Children Act 1989. Note the tacit acknowledgment that there are other interests at issue as well as the child, for example the natural parents: see *R v Avon County Council, ex parte K and others* [1986] 1 FLR 443; *Re W (a minor) (adoption)* [1984] FLR 402.

In the 1970s the Houghton committee argued for a legal status short of adoption to protect long term carers of children such as foster parents and relatives (see Report of the Houghton Committee Cmnd 5107 1972). The concept of custodianship was introduced in the Children Act 1975, did not come into force until 1985 and has never really found favour with the courts. The Law Commission concluded that many features of custodianship are unsatisfactory (see Law Commission Report No 172 *Family Law - Review of Child Law - Guardianship and Custody (1988)*) and the Children Act 1989 abolished it in favour of extended rights to apply for s8 orders under the new Act. Such applications will be from foster-parents, relatives or other long-term carers.

11.2 Key points

a) *Applying for adoption*

   i) Applicants must be over 21, married and at least one of the applicants must be domiciled in the UK. Orders may be made in favour of a sole applicant but if married the court must be satisfied that the applicant's spouse cannot be found, or is incapable of making an application by reason of ill health or the spouses are permanently separated. If an adoption application is by the mother or father alone the court would need very good reason for excluding the other parent.

   ii) Step-parent applications

   The policy of the law is to facilitate the continuing relationship between the children and their natural parents. The policy of the court is flexible and following the case of *Re D (a minor) (adoption by step-parent)* (1981) 2 FLR 102 the question is whether adoption would provide a better solution than custody.

   The Children Act 1989 repeals the restriction on step-parent applications.

   iii) Relatives

   Section 37 of the Children Act 1975 stated that if an adoption application is made by a relative of the child the court will consider the application as a custodianship application if satisfied that the child's welfare would not be better safeguarded and promoted by the making of an adoption order. The courts have demonstrated their preference for adoption. This approach is justified on the grounds of the child's need for permanence and long term security: *Re S (a minor)* (1986) The Times 31 December. Where there is a real likelihood of the family being re-united in the future the court would favour custodianship but otherwise adoption was preferred.

The Children Act (CA) 1989 abolishes custodianship. Note that adoption proceedings are family proceedings s8(4) CA so the court can make a section 8 order ie residence or contact order either on application or, if the court feels such an order should be made, even if no application is made. Third parties could apply to intervene achieving far greater flexibility.

b) *Conditions for adoption*

   i)   The child must be at least 19 weeks old and must have lived with the prospective adopters for the preceding 13 weeks. If the child has not been placed by an adoption agency the child must have had his home with the prospective adopters for at least 12 months unless one of the applicants is a parent, step-parent or relative. Once an adoption application is pending there are restrictions on the removal of the child from the applicants without the leave of the court: ss27 and 28 Adoption Act 1976.

   ii)   Parental consent

Each parent or guardian must freely and unconditionally consent to the making of the order with full understanding of the implication: s16 Adoption Act.

An unmarried father is a parent whose consent is required if he has parental responsibility for the child by agreement or order under s4 or if he has a residence order (s8) in his favour.

   iii)   Dispensing with consent

Section 16(2) Adoption Act specifies six grounds on which the court can dispense with consent. The court has in recent years been increasingly asked to dispense with consent and this is partly attributable to parental challenge to the local authority whose long term plans for a child in care include the adoption of that child. The grounds are that the parent or guardian:

- cannot be found or is incapable of giving his consent.

- is withholding his consent unreasonably. This is the most common head and gives rise to two types of situation. The first is where the parent gives consent and then subsequently changes her mind, the child having been placed at birth. The second involves the child in care where the local authority has decided that rehabilitation with the natural parents is not in the child's long term interests but the parents object to adoption.

The leading case is *Re W (an infant)* [1971] 2 WLR 1011. The crucial question seems to be whether or not there is any likelihood of the rehabilitation of the parent-child relationship. In *Re W* the court considered this possibility as unrealistic but in *Re V (a minor) (adoption:*

consent) [1986] 1 All ER 752 the Court of Appeal took the alternative view and ordered that the foster parents should continue to have access. A similar decision was reached in *Re H(B) (an infant)*; *W(N) (an infant)* (1983) 4 FLR 614.

- has persistently failed without reasonable cause to discharge the parental duties in relation to the child. A parent who has 'washed his hands' of the child would fail to discharge his duties but not a parent who visited the child occasionally: *Re D (minors) (adoption by parent)* [1973] 3 WLR 595.

- has abandoned or neglected the child. Abandonment must be total.

- has persistently ill-treated the child.

- has seriously ill-treated the child.

iv) Freeing the child for adoption

Introduced by the Children Act 1975, this procedure enables the issue of parental consent to be dealt with prior to the adoption application. The application is by an adoption agency. If successful, parental rights are vested in the agency until the child is adopted and the uncertainty over the question of parental consent is thus resolved in advance. Note that if a parent objects to the application an agency can only make application if the child is in its care.

c) *The changing concept of adoption*

As mentioned above, adoption, while still providing a solution for childless couples, is now increasingly relevant in the context of children who are 'in care'. The issue for the court is the need to safeguard and promote the welfare of the child but this is overlaid with the decision of the local authority that rehabilitation is not in the child's interests (see above). This can, of course, change the emphasis from the establishment of a new family to one of substitute parenting and in such circumstances the court seems increasingly prepared to grant adoption orders with conditions attached. In *Re C (a minor) (adoption: conditions)* [1988] 1 All ER 705 a condition was made that a brother should see his 13 year old sister. Furthermore the court has even favoured adoption to custodianship where the application has been by grandparents (see below). Finally, adoption applications now sometimes confront sensitive social definitions of a child's best interest, for example in *Re P (a minor)* (1989) The Independent 1 September trans-racial adoption did not find favour.

d) *Reform*

Adoption is increasingly used for older children who have knowledge of their birth family, who have emotional problems or who come from ethnic minority groups. Adoption law has remained unchanged for 20 years. The Department of Health published 'A Review of Adoption Law' in 1992 and a government white paper is expected shortly. It is anticipated that the legal transfer of parental responsibility may in future take place with much more openness and there will be greater use of adoption with conditions achieving far greater flexibility. Residence orders may be considered a better alternative in certain situations.

11.3   Recent cases

Re N (a minor) (adoption) [1990] 1 FLR 58

Re P (a minor) (1989) The Independent 1 September

Re GD (adoption application) [1992] 1 FCR 176

11.4   Analysis of questions

Adoption is a popular examination topic in the University of London External LLB. Questions are invariably problem type. Occasionally the area is examined on its own but students may find that it is included with another topic, particularly children in local authority care. Questions are fairly straightforward and the focus is often the issue of parental consent and/or step-parent and relative adoptions.

11.5   Questions

Question 1

Lawrence and Maud were married in 1980. Throughout 1984 Lawrence, who is a successful business executive, worked in his company's Hong Kong office. While he was away Maud had an affair with the milkman, Neil, and had a child, Oscar, by him. She wrote to Lawrence confessing her adultery and Lawrence replied that he would consult his solicitor when he returned to England but that, meanwhile, he would make financial provision for Maud and Oscar.

He continued to send cheques regularly to Maud, and paid her extra money in respect of Oscar's needs. When he returned to England, however, he immediately divorced Maud on the ground of her adultery.

Shortly after the divorce Maud married Paul, who is unemployed. Maud and Paul want to adopt Oscar but this is strenuously opposed by Neil who believes that he will no longer be able to visit Oscar if the child is adopted.

a) Will Maud and Paul be permitted to adopt Oscar?

b) Assuming that Oscar is not adopted, can Maud obtain financial provision in respect of Oscar and, if so, from whom?

> Adapted from University of London LLB Examination
> (for External Students) Family Law June 1986 Q6

General comment

This question raises the regularly examined topic of adoption, although there is something of a twist in this case as the child to be adopted is illegitimate and candidates must consider therefore the meaning of 'parent' in these applications. Part (b) is a straightforward question on financial provision for a child.

Skeleton solution

a) Adoption proceedings - outline general requirements - ss13 & 14 Adoption Act 1976; general policy regarding applications by step-parents; meaning of 'parent' in such proceedings; comment on effect of child's illegitimacy on the outcome of the application.

b) Maintenance from Lawrence - divorce proceedings - s23 MCA 1973 - meaning of 'child of the family' - treatment as a child of the family - principles to be applied; discuss and apply s25(3) MCA 1973 and s25(4) MCA 1973.

Suggested solution

a) An adoption order extinguishes the parental links between the child and his natural parents and creates analogous links between the child and his adopters, and cannot be accomplished other than by court order. So Maud and Paul will have to apply either to the High Court, County Court or Magistrates' Court to adopt Oscar. As Paul and Maud are married they can make a joint application so long as they are both over 21 and one of them at least is domiciled in the UK, Channel Islands, or Isle of Man (s14 Adoption Act 1976).

The preliminary conditions relating to applications by, inter alia, a parent and/or a step parent under s13(1) Adoption Act 1976 are satisfied here, namely that Oscar is over 19 weeks old and has lived with either or both applicants during the preceding 13 weeks.

In principle therefore Maud and Paul may apply for an adoption order in respect of Oscar. In deciding whether to make the order, the court will have regard to all the circumstances of the case, the first consideration being given to the need to safeguard and promote the child's welfare throughout his childhood, and, so far as is practicable (which it would not be here as Oscar is only two years old), to ascertain the child's wishes and feelings: s6 Adoption Act 1976. It should be noted that unlike s1, the child's welfare is considered as of first importance, but it is not paramount, and although greater weight will be attached to the child's welfare than to other considerations, it need not prevail over those other considerations: *Re H(B) (an infant)*; *Re W(N) (an infant)* (1983); *Re W (a minor) (adoption)* (1984).

Generally the courts have been reluctant to grant an adoption order to relatives unless there are special circumstances in the case making it desirable in the child's interests. It might be considered contrary to a child's interest to allow him to be adopted by his mother and stepfather as this could be used to sever the relationship with the child's natural father, and in fact ss14(3) and 15(3) Adoption Act 1976 provided that if an adoption application is made by a step-parent alone or jointly with a natural parent, the court is required to dismiss the application if it considers the issue affecting the child's custody would be better dealt with under the Divorce Court's matrimonial jurisdiction. Case law on this matter does however suggest that the real question was whether a custody order would be better than an adoption order in all the circumstances of the case, and it must be borne in mind that first consideration is to be given to the child's welfare: *Re D (a minor) (adoption by*

177

step-parent) (1981). It may be therefore that adoption would be appropriate in cases where, for example, the step-parent has been the father figure in the child's life from an early age, particularly where the natural father has shown little or no interest in the child. Paul may be better advised to apply for a residence order under s8. See s10(5) CA 1989.

One particular point must be noted on these facts, namely that Oscar's natural father is Neil and Oscar is therefore illegitimate. It appears that the natural father of an illegitimate child is not a parent for the purposes of adoption proceedings. Therefore, unless he had already obtained a residence order under the CA 1989 or a parental responsibility order under s4 his consent would not be required. The father of an illegitimate child has no rights as such in respect of his child; they all vest in the mother.

It would appear, therefore, that in the absence of any action by Neil to obtain formal and legal recognition of his relationship with Oscar, there are no parents or guardians who can object to the adoption application by Maud and Paul. Therefore, if on considering all the facts of the case the court concludes that it is in Oscar's interest that he be adopted by Maud and Paul, an order will be duly made. Certainly it seems that Paul has been the father figure in Oscar's life from an early age and therefore it could be argued that an adoption order would be appropriate in the circumstances to enable him to assume irrevocably all the parental rights and obligations with Maud.

b) Oscar is the natural child of Maud and Neil, but he may be deemed to be a child of the family of Maud and Lawrence under s52 Matrimonial Causes Act 1973 (hereinafter the MCA 1973) as he is Maud's child, if it can be shown that he has been treated as a child of the family by both parties. Treatment as a child of the family is a question of fact, is viewed objectively and involves behaviour towards the child. We are told that although Lawrence reserved his position regarding divorce proceedings, he agreed to make financial provision for Maud and Oscar. This would amount to treatment of Oscar as a child of the family, and therefore, even though he divorced Maud immediately upon his return to England, this would not affect his past behaviour and the finding that he treated Oscar as a child of his family by maintaining him.

Therefore the divorce court is empowered to make financial provision for Oscar in the divorce proceedings under s23 MCA 1973 by means of periodical payments and/or a lump sum order, as well as a property adjustment order under s24 MCA 1973.

In deciding what if any order to make, the court will consider all the circumstances of the case, their first consideration being Oscar's welfare while a minor, and in this case will also take into account Oscar's financial needs, his income, property and other financial resources, if any, any mental or physical disability suffered by him, and the manner in which the parties expected him to be educated or trained: s25(3) MCA 1973. The court will also consider, inter alia, the parties' financial resources, their financial needs and obligations, the standard of living enjoyed by the family before the breakdown of the marriage, and the disabilities (if any) of either party: s25(3).

However there are further considerations to be taken into account in this case as Oscar is not Lawrence's natural child. So the court must also consider whether Lawrence had assumed any responsibility for Oscar's maintenance (which he did), and if so, the extent to which, and the basis on which he assumed that responsibility, and the length of time he discharged that responsibility. The court must also consider whether, in assuming and discharging that responsibility, he did so knowing that Oscar was not his own child, and the liability of any other person, in this case Neil, to maintain Oscar: s25(4) MCA 1973.

Here Lawrence had assumed financial responsibility towards Oscar, seemingly from his birth, although it is not clear whether he is still maintaining him. He knew that Oscar was not his own child when assuming the responsibility, although he reserved his position as to the consequences of Maud's confession with respect to their marriage. However Neil is also responsible for Oscar's maintenance, as his natural father, and can be ordered to make provision for him. It may be therefore that if Lawrence is ordered to pay anything towards Oscar's maintenance, the amount will be small, to take into account Neil's responsibility.

Maud could institute proceedings in the Magistrates' Court against Neil to claim maintenance for Oscar under the Children Act 1989. Under this jurisdiction, if Neil is adjudged to be the putative father of Oscar, he may be ordered to pay periodical payments for his maintenance and education, and/or a lump sum.

If it is shown that Neil is the putative father, and this can be done on the evidence of blood tests, birth registration etc, the court, when deciding whether to exercise its powers and if so, in what manner, will have regard to all the circumstances of the case. The factors that will be considered in this case therefore will be the income, earning capacity, property and other financial resources which Oscar's mother and his putative father have or are likely to have in the foreseeable future; their financial needs, obligations and responsibilities in the foreseeable future; the child's financial needs as well as any income, property or other resources he may have, and any physical or mental disability of the child.

Therefore Maud can, and should, apply for maintenance for Oscar from Neil as his natural father. She may also claim maintenance for him from Lawrence, although in view of Neil's liability in this respect, it is likely that at the very least Lawrence's responsibility will be reduced, perhaps considerably.

Question 2

John and Susan were married in 1979. In 1981 they had a son, Dominic. When he lost his job, John began drinking heavily and one night he battered Susan and Dominic. John voluntarily entered a mental hospital to seek help for his drinking problem.

Susan obtained a divorce and was granted custody of Dominic. In 1984 she married Tony Jones. Tony loves Dominic and is anxious to adopt him. John has recently left hospital, cured of his alcoholism. He has tried to see Dominic but Susan has refused on the grounds that she is anxious that she and Dominic should have 'a fresh start' with Tony.

a) What procedure must Susan and Tony follow if they wish to adopt Dominic?

b) Are the courts likely to allow the adoption application to go ahead?

c) Can an adoption order be made if John refuses to agree to the adoption?

d) In the event of the adoption order not being made, can Tony and Susan lawfully change Dominic's surname from Smith to Jones?

Adapted from University of London LLB Examination
(for External Students) Family Law June 1984 Q7

General comment

This is a wide-ranging question on parent and child issues involving consideration of adoption procedures, dispensing with parental consent to adoption and the prospects of success of an application made by a parent and step-parent, parental rights and custody and access in matrimonial proceedings. The issues raised in the question are straightforward and should pose no problem to the well-prepared student.

Skeleton solution

• A simple statement of procedure - including definition of adoption.

• A consideration of the issues relevant to adoption applications in the light of s3 Children Act 1975 and case law pertinent to the section.

• The grounds for dispensing with consent with emphasis on 'withholding consent unreasonably'.

• Case law on the changing of a child's surname and the circumstances when the court would sanction it based on the child's best interests.

• The 'welfare principle'.

Suggested solution

a) An adoption order which extinguishes the parental links between a child and his natural parents and creates analogous links between the child and his adopters cannot be accomplished other than by a court order. So Susan and Tony will have to apply to either the High Court, County Court or Magistrates' Court to adopt Dominic. An adoption order cannot be made upon the application of more than one person unless the applicants are married to one another, as Susan and Tony are in this case, in which case they may apply for an order jointly. Both must be over 21 and one of them must be domiciled in the United Kingdom, Channel Islands or Isle of Man: s14 Adoption Act 1976.

Before a court can make an adoption order, a number of preliminary conditions have to be satisfied. Under s13(1) Adoption Act 1976 it is provided, inter alia, that where the applicants or one of them is the parent, step-parent or relative of the child, as here, where Susan is Dominic's mother and Tony his step-father, no order shall be made unless the child is at least 19 weeks old and at all times during the preceding 13 weeks has had his home with the applicants or with one of them. A child is to be regarded as having his home with the person who, disregarding the absence of the child at a hospital, boarding school and any other temporary absence has actual custody of him. Here both conditions are satisfied as Dominic is now three years old and has been living with Susan all his life, and indeed Tony may have been living with them for the 13 week period, depending on when the marriage took place.

Normally it is necessary for them to give the local authority within whose area Dominic has his home three months' written notice of their intention to apply for the order, as Dominic is below the upper limit of compulsory school age. However, as Susan is Dominic's mother this provision will not apply.

b) In principle Susan and Tony may apply for an adoption order in respect of Dominic. Under s6 Children Act 1989, in deciding whether to make an adoption order the court must have regard to all the circumstances of the case, the first consideration being given to the need to safeguard and promote the child's welfare throughout his childhood, and so far as it is practicable to ascertain the child's wishes and feelings regarding the decision, having regard to his age and understanding. Unlike the wording of s1 Children Act 1989 which requires the courts to have regard to the welfare of the child as a first and paramount consideration, s3 merely requires that the child's welfare be considered of the first importance, but it is not given the pre-eminence that it enjoys by virtue of s1 Guardianship of Minors Act 1971 in other proceedings relating to the custody and upbringing of the child. It seems that the child's welfare is to be given greater weight than other considerations but it need not prevail over those other considerations: *Re H(B) (an infant); W(N) (an infant)* (1983); *Re W (a minor) (adoption)* (1984). In this case Dominic is too young to understand the nature of the adoption order and therefore it will not be practicable to question him as to his wishes on the matter.

Susan and Tony must be advised that generally the court was reluctant to grant an adoption order to relatives unless there are special circumstances in the case making it desirable in Dominic's interest. It might be considered contrary to his interests to allow him to be adopted by his mother and his step-father as this might be used to sever his relationship with John, his natural father, and it was provided in s14(3) and s15(3) Adoption Act 1976 that if an adoption application is made by a step-parent either alone or jointly with a natural parent, the court is required to dismiss the application if it considers the issue affecting the child's custody would be better dealt with under the Divorce Court's matrimonial jurisdiction. It was said in *Re S* (1977) that the court should only make an adoption order in these circumstances if adoption would safeguard and promote the welfare of the child better than the existing arrangements and better than any other arrangements that could be made under the divorce jurisdiction. It is not sufficient to show that the adoption will be beneficial to Dominic, but that it will be better than the other alternative. It is generally thought desirable that a child retains contact with his natural parent unless such contact would be harmful to the child. There is little evidence in this case to suggest that adoption would be a better alternative than the arrangements that have been made in the divorce jurisdiction where custody has been awarded to Susan, and access could be allowed to John. In earlier decisions courts have looked for exceptional circumstances necessitating an adoption order. So in *Re S (a minor)* (1974) an order was made where the step-parent had been the father figure in the child's life from an early age. We are not told in this question when John went into the mental hospital for treatment, and when Tony began his relationship with Susan, but he has been married to her for only a few months and it is submitted therefore that he would not be in the same circumstances as the step-father in that previous decision. Further, John's alcoholism has now been cured and therefore there seems to be no problem here serious enough to warrant a complete break with Dominic, and this therefore would appear to fall outside the rare type of case illustrated in *Re D* (1977) where such an exceptional step was deemed necessary in the interests of the child, as the father was homosexual. Under the Children Act 1989 restrictions on step-parent adoptions are repealed. If however John is considered to be a parent whose relationship with Dominic should be encouraged an adoption application may be unsuccessful.

Certainly the main reason for the adoption seems to be to sever the relationship between Dominic and John. On the facts this would not seem to be appropriate or necessary.

c) Prima facie the adoption could not proceed without John's consent because s6 Adoption Act 1976 provides that no adoption order shall be made unless a child is free for adoption or in the case of each parent or guardian of the child, that the court is satisfied that he freely and with full understanding of what is involved agrees unconditionally to the making of the order, or his agreement should be dispensed with on the grounds specified, that is:

 i) the parent or guardian cannot be found or is incapable of giving his agreement;

 ii) the parent is withholding his consent unreasonably;

 iii) the parent has persistently failed without reasonable cause to discharge the parental obligations towards a child. Those obligations include the natural and moral duty to show affection, care and interest towards the child as well as the legal duty to maintain him: *Re P* (1962);

 iv) the parent has abandoned or neglected the child and this involves neglect and persistent ill-treatment and connotes conduct which would render the parent or guardian liable to criminal proceedings under the Children and Young Persons Act 1933;

 v) the parent has persistently ill-treated the child. This cannot be made out here as there is evidence of ill-treatment on only one occasion;

 vi) the parent has seriously ill-treated the child and the rehabilitation of the child within his household is unlikely. Here it is unlikely that Dominic will live with John as the Divorce Court will probably grant custody, care and control of him to Susan. Further, in the absence of any evidence as to the extent of injuries inflicted by John when he battered Susan and Dominic on that one occasion, it is unsafe to allege this ground.

If any one of these grounds is made out the court may dispense with the need for parental consent to the adoption altogether, in which case the adoption will proceed without that parent's co-operation.

It is submitted that in this case the grounds specified in (i), (iv), (v) and (vi) cannot be applied here as there is no clear evidence from the facts to suggest any such conduct on John's part or an inability on his part to give consent. Further, it is unlikely that reliance can be placed on (iii), namely that he has persistently failed to discharge his obligations towards Dominic, as any such failure must be culpable and as stated in *Re D* (1973) must be '... of such gravity, so complete, so convincingly proved that there can be no advantage to the child in keeping continuous contact with the natural parent ...' In that case the court refused to dispense with the father's agreement, solely on the ground that he failed to provide for his child or see her for a year. Here it seems that John has not seen Dominic since he voluntarily went into hospital for treatment of his alcoholism, which has now been cured, although he has tried to see him without success since he was discharged. There is no evidence therefore of any culpable failure on John's part in this respect and although he has beaten Dominic once it is unlikely to be repeated as he has been cured of his alcoholism which seems to have been the reason for the assault. It is submitted therefore that the court would not rely on his previous behaviour, and dispense with his agreement on this basis.

The only ground that could be applied would be (ii) that is that John is unreasonably withholding his consent to the adoption. However, it must be noted that the mere fact that the order would be in Dominic's interest if this were the case, which it does not necessarily appear to be, would not in itself be sufficient to show that John is withholding his consent unreasonably although Dominic's welfare would be an important consideration: *Re P* (1977). The test is objective and all the circumstances which would weigh upon a reasonable parent should be considered, including the child's prospects and outlook if adopted as compared with those if not. Material and financial prospects are relevant as are education, stability and general happiness. However, in *Re H(B) (an infant)*; *Re W(N) (an infant)* (1983) the Court of Appeal held that there was room for the reasonable withholding of consent by the natural parent even though those responsible for the child's welfare, who are often professionals, held the acceptable view that the child's welfare demanded adoption. The courts had to look at the attitude of the natural parent as one of the potential relevant factors when assessing the attitude of the hypothetical reasonable parent, and where the natural parent presented himself or herself at the time of the hearing as someone capable of caring for the child, that was one factor that the reasonable parent should take into account. Where there was an inherent defect, which was likely to persist, in the natural parent, however, that would be an important factor. But where, as in this case, the unsuitability of the parent could only be related to

183

past history, unless the past history was likely to influence the future position, then it could carry little weight in the mind of the hypothetical reasonable parent. The chances of a successful reintroduction to, or continuation of, contact with the natural parent was also a critical factor in assessing the reaction of the reasonable parent: *Re F (a minor)* (1982).

Here, it is submitted, there is little likelihood of John being granted the care and control of Dominic in the future and thus he will remain with Susan in any event and so it seems that the purpose of the application is to cut John out of Dominic's life altogether. However, there is nothing on the facts to suggest that the relationship should be brought to an end and ordinarily the court would have no hesitation in allowing John access to Dominic. Further, in *Re D* (1975) it was said that it would rarely be in the interests of a child to sever links with his parent in this way. John's alcoholism has been cured and therefore would not pose any threat to Dominic's welfare in the future. As stated earlier, his welfare is an important factor but it need not prevail over other considerations such as John's wishes and rights: *Re W (a minor: adoption)* (1984). The issue is the parent/child relationship itself and in that relationship the parent as well as the child has rights. Further, although it is not necessary to show that there is a likelihood of lasting damage to Dominic if the adoption order is not made, there must be some really serious factor justifying the making of the order, involving as it does the complete extinction of the relationship between the child and his natural parent. It was said in *Re W* (1971) that the agreement may be dispensed with if the parent had ignored or disregarded some appreciable ill or risk or some substantial benefit likely to arise from the adoption. There is no evidence to suggest that this applies to John at all and therefore it would seem that if John refuses to give his consent to the adoption, it cannot proceed as the court will not dispense with his agreement.

d) In divorce proceedings, any order giving a parent a residence order provides that no steps shall be taken to change the child's name before the child attains 18 years, or if female, marries below that age, without the consent of the other parent or leave of the court. Here in the divorce proceedings between Susan and John, Susan did obtain a residence order and there will be a prohibition in the terms referred to above against changing Dominic's name. Therefore, unless John consents or the court so orders, Susan and Tony cannot lawfully change Dominic's name to Jones.

If John does not consent Susan could apply to the court to seek an order allowing her to change Dominic's name. As in all disputes involving the upbringing of a child the court must be guided by what is in Dominic's best interests: see s1 Children Act 1989. Most of the case law concerns situations as here, where a mother has been granted custody of the child in divorce proceedings and remarries and wishes the child to be known by her new surname. Early case law on this point such as *Re T* (1963) and *Y v Y* (1973) suggested that the change of a child's name was an important matter which should be permitted only when the child's welfare demanded such a step. Later cases suggested, however, that it was a relatively unimportant matter and that fathers were tending to lay too much emphasis on it when the purpose was to avoid embarrassment and there was no intention to destroy their links with their children: *R* v *R* (1978). Thus two opposing views have been taken in such a matter. However, more recently in *W* v *A* (1981) the Court of Appeal decisively took the former view when it upheld a decision prohibiting a mother from changing her son's name even though he was emigrating to Australia with her and his step-father. However, in *R* v *R* (1982) it was recognised that in some circumstances there is little a court could do to enforce an order that a child be known by his first surname. In that case a wife had remarried after divorcing the child's father and in order to integrate the child into the new family, the wife allowed the child to be known in the neighbourhood by her step-father's surname. The child knew who her real father was and what her real name was. When the father objected to the use of the new surname the wife applied for leave to change the child's name and it was held that it would not be in the child's interests to suppress the use of the step-father's name. On appeal the Court of Appeal held that it would not be in the child's interests and it would be totally unrealistic to attempt to forbid the use of the new surname by the child as it would be impossible to enforce the order. It was accepted that the matter of the child's surname was important, but more important was the child's knowledge of her own identity and her relations with her father. She had access to her father which worked well and her relationship with him was good and would not have been affected by the use of a new surname.

That case can be distinguished on the facts in this question because there the new surname had been in use for some time and it would have caused embarrassment to the child if the name had to be changed. However, we are dealing with a younger child in this case, whose name has not yet been changed, and the prevailing view is that it is an important matter and that the court will be seeking to preserve links between the father and the child, whereas a change of name may weaken those links. This would suggest that an application to change Dominic's name would be unsuccessful. All the circumstances of the case will be considered by the court on Susan's application. However, in the absence of any good reason why Dominic's name should be changed, for example if John were to disappear from their lives altogether, which seems unlikely, it would be deemed not to be in Dominic's best interests to change his name at this time.

Question 3

In June 1988, Mary who was aged 16 and unmarried, gave birth to Norman. Norman's father, a married man, made several payments to Mary to help her, although he made it clear to her that he did not want to see Norman, nor would he leave his wife.

Mary was unable to find a job which paid well enough to enable her to employ someone to look after Norman. She became depressed because of her financial position and the constant demands of the baby and in December 1988 decided that it would be best if the child was adopted. The Doogood Local Authority placed Norman with Mr and Mrs Price, a couple in their thirties who are financially comfortable and who have long wanted, but been unable, to have a child of their own.

Mary visited Norman occasionally, but concluded, in the summer of 1989, that she had made the wrong decision with respect to his future. She told the local authority that she had changed her mind about the adoption and she indicated that she was now working hard to save enough money to provide a home for the child. Mr and Mrs Price reluctantly allowed Mary to see Norman one afternoon a week and she did so until January 1990 when she met Robert.

Mary and Robert married in February 1990. Mary became pregnant and stopped visiting Norman, writing to Mr and Mrs Price in September 1990 telling them that it would be best if they adopted Norman after all.

In February 1991, Mary had a miscarriage and now wants Norman returned to her. Mr and Mrs Price, supported by the local authority, have applied to adopt the child, but Mary will not consent.

Advise Mary.

University of London LLB Examination
(for External Students) Family Law June 1991 Q7

General comment

This is a straightforward question on adoption which requires candidates to discuss in detail an issue tested regularly in previous examinations, namely the grounds for dispensing with parental agreement to the adoption. However, candidates should also consider the alternatives to an adoption order, namely a residence and/or contract order under s8 Children Act 1989.

Skeleton solution

• Explain the effect of an adoption order.

• Outline the basic requirements for such an order to be made.

• Consider whether Mary's consent will be dispensed with - in particular discuss in detail the grounds set out in s16(2)(b) and (c) Adoption Act 1976.

• Consider as an alternative to an adoption order a residence and/or contact order under s8 Children Act 1989.

Suggested solution

An adoption order extinguishes the parental links between a child and his natural parents and creates analogous links between the child and his adopters. It cannot be accomplished other than by a court order and the application may be made to the High Court, County Court or Magistrates Court. An adoption order cannot be made upon the application of more than one person unless the applicants are married to one another as the Prices are in this case. They must both be over 21 years of age (here they are both over 30) and must be domiciled in the United Kingdom, Channel Islands or Isle of Man (s14 Adoption Act 1976).

Only a local authority or an adoption agency may place a child for adoption with an applicant who is not a relative of the child, (s11(1) Adoption Act 1976). Here the

Doogood local authority (which is probably also an adoption agency) placed Norman with Mr and Mrs Price for adoption. Before an adoption order can be made Norman must have been in the Prices' care for at least three months. This requirement is clearly satisfied as Norman has been in their care since 1988/1989.

It is clear that the local authority did not apply to free Norman for adoption, nor could it do so at this time for the Children Act 1989 provides that where a freeing application is made without parental agreement, only local authorities which have obtained a care order can make such an application (s18(2) Adoption Act 1976 as amended by Children Act 1989). The agreement issue will be tested before the court therefore at the application by Mr and Mrs Price for the adoption order to be made.

Mary will be advised therefore that prima facie Mr and Mrs Price can apply to adopt Norman. However, the outcome of the application will depend on two major factors - the child's interests and the objections of Mary. In the meantime Mary has no automatic right to have Norman restored to her now that she has withdrawn her agreement (s27(1) Adoption Act 1976).

Section 6 Adoption Act 1976 provides that in deciding whether to make an adoption order the court must have regard to all the circumstances of the case, first consideration being given to the need to safeguard and promote the child's welfare throughout his childhood and, so far as is practicable, to ascertain the child's feelings and wishes on the matter. This means that Norman's welfare will not be the paramount consideration. It will be given greater weight than other considerations but it will not necessarily prevail over those other considerations, *(Re H(B) (an infant)*; *Re W(N) (an infant)* (1983); *Re W (a minor) (adoption)* (1984)). In a case such as will arise here, where Mary does not give her consent to the adoption, the principle set out in s6 will not apply to all aspects of the dispute. *In Re P (an infant) (adoption: parental consent)* (1977) the Court of Appeal held that s6 does not apply to the decision to dispense with parental agreement on the ground that he/she is withholding it unreasonably. The court should first consider whether adoption is in the child's best interests, and then decide whether parental agreement should be dispensed with. If the adoption is not deemed to be in the child's best interests then the application will fail and the question of parental agreement does not have to be considered. If the court decides that the adoption would on balance be in the child's interests, the order may still be refused if the court decides that parental agreement should not be dispensed with.

On the facts of this case there is an argument for saying that an adoption would be in Norman's best interests. He has lived with and been cared for by Mr and Mrs Price for practically all his life. He went to live with them when he was six or seven months old and he is now three. His contact with Mary has been somewhat intermittent in that she visited him only occasionally for the first few months of his placement with Mr and Mrs Price. Thereafter, for approximately six months, she saw him once a week for an afternoon and then for almost a year it seems she saw little if anything of him. It is not clear how much contact there has been with Norman since February this year.

If the court decides that on balance an adoption order would be in Norman's interest it must now consider the question of Mary's agreement.

Section 16(1) Adoption Act 1976 provides that no adoption order can be made unless Mary gives her consent to the adoption freely and with full understanding of what it involves, or her agreement is dispensed with on one of the grounds set out in s16(2) Adoption Act 1976. As Norman's natural father has no parental responsibility for Norman his consent is not required to the adoption. In theory therefore the adoption cannot proceed without Mary's agreement which obviously she will withhold. It must now be considered whether any of the grounds for dispensing with agreement under s16(2) can apply to Mary. If none do the adoption cannot proceed even if it is clear that it would be in Norman's best interests to make an adoption order.

There are two possible grounds to consider in this case. Under s16(2)(b) Adoption Act 1976 Mary's agreement could be dispensed with if she is deemed to be withholding her consent unreasonably. However, the mere fact that it would be in Norman's interest to be adopted, if that is the case, is not in itself sufficient to show that this ground is made out (Re P (an infant)), although his welfare is relevant to determine if the refusal is unreasonable (Re W (an infant) (1971); Re F (a minor) (1982)). The test is objective and all the circumstances of the case which would weigh with a reasonable parent should be considered including Norman's prospects and outlook if adopted as compared with those if not (Re H(B) (an infant); Re W(N) (an infant); Re L (1962)). Mary's decision not to agree to the adoption will not be viewed as unreasonable merely because the local authority have decided that adoption would be in Norman's best interests. However, where, as here, a parent initially agreed to an adoption and the baby has established a new relationship with the adoptive family, the court may be unwilling to accept that the parent's withholding of agreement is reasonable (Re H (infants) (adoption: parental consent) (1977)). Mary's agreement would be final only when the adoption order is made. However, a reasonable parent would be expected to favour the preservation of an existing relationship for the child. The importance of this issue depends on the level of contact Mary has had with Norman, which as indicated earlier, has been somewhat sporadic and in the last year may not have taken place at all.

The courts have held that where there is a realistic hope of maintaining or re-establishing a relationship between a parent and child the parent is reasonable when refusing to agree to the adoption (Re BA (1985); Re M (1986)). However, if there is no realistic hope of rehabilitation or contact, a refusal may be viewed as unreasonable. Here again the level of contact which Mary has had with Norman will be an important factor and it could be argued that if she has not visited him or seen him for over a year, which may be the case, then the prospects of him being returned to her are remote.

Under s16(2)(c) Adoption Act 1976 a persistent failure, without reasonable cause, to discharge parental duties in relation to the child would be another ground for dispensing with parental agreement. To make out this ground, however, it must be shown that the failure is persistent and that probably means that it has to be a permanent abrogation of responsibility (Re D (minors)) (1973)); and the failure must be without reasonable cause. Parental duties include a duty to show affection and an interest in the child as well as a duty to maintain him. Whether Mary's failure to visit Norman would be viewed as a permanent abrogation of her parental responsibilities may be debateable and will depend on whether there has been any contact with Norman since January 1990. It should be noted that if she had neglected Norman in the past to the extent required for s16(2)(c), but is now able to provide a satisfactory home, then the ground under s16(2)(b) cannot be made out unless the past neglect is likely to influence the future (*Re H(B)*; *Re W(N)*). This limitation does not apply to s16(2)(c).

In conclusion Mary will be advised that the adoption cannot proceed without her agreement unless the court is prepared to dispense with it. The most likely ground it would rely on would be s16(2)(b), that is that Mary is withholding her consent unreasonably taking into account her lack of contact with Norman for, apparently, over a year, his settled relationship with Mr and Mrs Price and the fact that Norman is unlikely to be returned to Mary, all factors which could weigh with a reasonable parent.

Mary should also be advised that if the court decides not to dispense with her agreement Mr and Mrs Price will be able to apply again to adopt Norman unless the court bars them (s91(14) Children Act 1989).

Further, even if the adoption application is not successful, Mr and Mrs Price could seek a residence order in respect of Norman and the court is empowered to make such an order on an adoption application even where agreement is not forthcoming and has not been dispensed with (ss8 and 10 Children Act 1989). Before making such an order the court must be satisfied that it is in Norman's best interests, and better than making no order under the 1989 Act. If such an order is granted in favour of Mr and Mrs Price it vests parental responsibility for Norman in them until he reaches the age of 16 or 18. Effectively they will have the same control over him as if they had adopted him save that they cannot change his name or remove him from the United Kingdom for more than one month. Further, a residence order can be varied or revoked. A residence order does not terminate Mary's parental responsibility in relation to Norman although naturally her exercise of it is curtailed. However, a contact order could be made in her favour although if she had not seen Norman for over a year, any such contact will be limited initially at least.

Question 4

Josephine and Vincent were married in 1986. Throughout 1990 Vincent, an international lawyer, worked in the offices of the United Nations in Geneva. While he was away, Josephine had an affair with one of his colleagues, Gerald, and in early 1991 had a child, Conrad, by him. She confessed her adultery to Vincent and he agreed to consider his long term position at the end of 1991, but said that he would, until then, continue to support Josephine, who remained in their jointly-owned London apartment, and Conrad.

Vincent remitted a monthly sum to Josephine's bank account, frequently augmenting this with presents for Conrad. However, in September 1991 he decided to divorce her on the grounds of her adultery.

Shortly after the divorce, Josephine met Max, a wealthy industrialist, whom she married. Josephine and Max wish to adopt Conrad, but this is opposed by Gerald who believes he will no longer be able to have contact with the child if they are successful. Gerald's father has just died leaving his substantial property to 'my grandchildren'.

Advise Gerald whether he can oppose Conrad's adoption, Josephine whether she is entitled to any financial provision for herself from Vincent, from whom she can seek financial provision for Conrad, and whether Conrad can claim a share in his grandfather's estate.

University of London LLB Examination
(for External Students) Family Law June 1992 Q7

General comment

This is a straightforward question concerning adoption by a parent and step-parent of the child – and financial provision for a non-marital child.

Skeleton solution

- Adoption proceedings:
    - outline general requirements
    - consider the relevant sections: ss13 and 14 Adoption Act 1976; s8 Children Act 1989.
- Maintenance from Vincent:
    - define child of the family;
    - treatment of Conrad; did it amount to him being a child of the family? Apply principles and discuss;
    - an application under s15 and Schedule 1 of CA 1989 for maintenance from Gerald.
- Deal in general outline with succession rights of a non-marital child and effects of Family Law Reform Act 1969.

Suggested solution

a) An adoption order ends the legal relationship between a child and his/her parents and creates a new and exclusive relationship between the child and the adopters. An adoption order gives parental responsibility for a child to the adopters.

An application must be made to the High Court, county court, or magistrates court. Josephine and Max must satisfy the requirements of the Adoption Act 1976 (as amended by schedule 10 – Children Act (CA) 1989).

If they wish to adopt Conrad Josephine must be at least 18 years of age and Max at least twenty-one.

The preliminary conditions relating to applications by, inter alia, a parent and stepparent under s13(1) Adoption Act (AA) 1976 are satisfied here, namely that Conrad is over 19 weeks old and has lived with either or both applicants during the preceding 13 weeks.

In principle therefore Josephine and Max may apply for an adoption order in respect of Conrad. Adoption proceedings are family proceedings within the meaning of s8 of the CA 1989 and so the court considering the adoption application may make a s8 order with respect to the child if any application has been made by a person entitled to apply for s8, or by a person who has obtained the leave of the court to make such an application, or the court considers that such an order should be made even though no application has been made. As a result the court could make, for example, residence and/or contact orders instead of an adoption order.

In deciding whether to make the order the court shall have regard to all the circumstances of the case, first consideration being given to the need to safeguard and promote the welfare of the child throughout his childhood; and shall so far as practicable (which is not possible here as Conrad is only 18 months) ascertain the wishes and feelings of the child regarding the decision and give due consideration to them, having regard to his age and understanding.

It should be noted that this is not the same test as that applied in s1 CA 1989, since the child's welfare is considered as of first importance but it is not paramount. While the child's welfare remains the single most important factor it does not necessarily outweigh all other circumstances: see *Re W (a minor)* (1984); *Re D (an infant)* (1977).

The court must also have regard to the general principle that any delay in determining the question of adoption is likely to prejudice the child's welfare: s1(2) CA 1989.

An adoption order cannot be made unless:

   i)   the child has been freed for adoption; or

   ii) in the case of each parent or guardian of the child the court is satisfied that the parent or guardian freely and with full understanding of what is involved agrees unconditionally to the making of an adoption or agreement of the parent or guardian can be dispensed with under a ground in s16(2) AA 1976.

On these facts, Conrad's natural father is Gerald, and Conrad is therefore non-marital. A parent for the above purposes does not include an unmarried father of a child unless he has obtained a custody order or an order under s4 Family Law Reform Act 1987 with respect to the child, whereupon he is treated as a guardian of the child or if he has parental responsibility for the child under s4 CA 1989 or has a residence order under s10 CA 1989. Unless Gerald has acquired any of these orders, his consent to the adoption will not be required. He may, however, as stated, apply for a s4 order – parental responsibility – and if successful he can then object to the adoption. Once a father has acquired parental responsibility he is in the same

191

position with regard to his legal rights in respect of the child as if he were married to the mother.

b) Josephine wants to know if she is entitled to any financial provision for Vincent.

Where a spouse has remarried she is not entitled to make a claim for lump sum or periodical payments or any other financial order. As Josephine is now married to Max she is not entitled to any financial provision from Vincent for herself.

Conrad is the natural child of Josephine and Gerald but he may be deemed to be a child of the family of Josephine and Vincent under s52 MCA 1973 as he is Josephine's child, if it can be shown that he has been treated as a child of the family by both parties: s105 MCA. Treatment as a child of the family is a question of fact, is viewed objectively and involves behaviour towards the child. We are told that although Vincent reserved his position regarding divorce proceedings, he agreed to make financial provision for Josephine and Conrad. He remitted a monthly sum to Josephine's bank account and frequently sent presents for Conrad. This would amount to treatment of Conrad as a child of the family and therefore even though he divorced Josephine in September 1991, this would not affect his past behaviour and the finding that he treated Conrad as a child of the family by maintaining him.

The Divorce Court is empowered to make financial provision for Conrad in the divorce proceedings under s23 MCA 1973 by means of periodical payments and/or a lump sum order as well as a property adjustment order under s24 MCA 1973.

In deciding what, if any, order to make the court's first consideration will be Conrad's welfare while a minor, and in this case the court will also take into account Conrad's financial needs, his income, property and other financial resources if any, any mental or physical disability suffered by him, and the manner in which the parties expected him to be educated or trained: s25(3) MCA. The court will also consider, inter alia, the parties' financial resources, their financial needs and obligations, the standard of living enjoyed by the family before the breakdown of the marriage, and the disabilities (if any) of either party: s25(3) MCA.

Here, as Conrad is not Vincent's natural child the court must also consider whether Vincent had assumed any responsibility for Oscar's maintenance (which he did), and if so the extent to which and the basis on which he assumed that responsibility, and the length of time he discharged that responsibility. The court must also consider whether in assuming and discharging that responsibility, he did so knowing that Conrad was not his own child, and the liability of any other person, in this case Gerald, to maintain Conrad: s25(4) MCA 1973.

Here Vincent had assumed financial responsibility towards Conrad seemingly from his birth, although it is not clear whether he is still maintaining him. He knew that Conrad was not his own child when assuming the responsibility, although he reserved his position as to the consequence of Josephine's confession with respect to their marriage. However, Gerald is also responsible for Conrad's maintenance, as his natural father.

Josephine may make an application under s15 and Schedule 1 of CA 1989 to the High Court, county court or magistrates' court. Under this section the court can order either parent to make to the other periodical payments and/or a lump sum payment for the benefit of the child. The courts can also make orders for secured periodical payments and property transfer on settlement.

Before the court will make any order against Gerald it must be proved that he is the father of Conrad and this can be done by producing evidence, such as results of blood tests and DNA tests.

Josephine's evidence does not have to be corroborated any longer, but this does not necessarily mean the courts will act on uncorroborated evidence and in the absence of an admission of paternity by Gerald, cogent evidence will have to be produced by Josephine.

In part (a) the fact that Gerald wishes to have contact with Conrad was discussed. This should mean that the question of paternity will not be in issue because Gerald will have admitted he is the father.

There are no longer any time limits to bringing proceedings for maintenance against the father of a non-marital child. Although if there has been any delay in bringing the action, the court may consider this delay as a relevant factor. This is not relevant here because Conrad was born in 1991 and now it is 1992, no real delay.

When deciding what order, if any, to make the court must consider all the circumstances of the case including in this case the income earning capacity and other financial resources which each parent has or is likely to have in the foreseeable future, as well as those of the child; and their financial needs and obligations: Schedule 1 para (4). It should be noted that the court is not specifically enjoined to have regard to the family's standard of living and no weighting of the child's welfare is specified.

Here Gerald is a colleague of Vincent's so presumably is also a lawyer and will have a good income and be able to provide for Conrad. However, we are not told if Gerald has any other financial obligations ie if he is married and has any children, in which case he may not have many resources available to provide maintenance for Conrad. Also, Josephine is married to Max, 'a wealthy industrialist' and this will also be taken into account.

In conclusion, Josephine can and should apply for maintenance for Conrad from Gerald, his natural father. She may also claim maintenance for him from Vincent, although in view of Gerald's liability in this respect it is likely that at the very least Vincent's responsibility will be reduced, perhaps considerably.

c) At common law a gift by will to a group of relations is construed prima facie as a gift to legitimate members of that group only. This presumption could be rebutted by evidence of contrary intention.

This common law rule of construction was reversed by the Family Law Reform Act 1969 which stated a gift by will to persons related in some manner to some other person is to be construed as including any illegitimate persons of that class. This rule applies unless a contrary intention appears.

This rule was changed slightly by the Family Law Reform Act 1987. The general principle of the Act is that references to any relationship between two persons are to be considered without regard to whether the father and mother of either of them, or the father and mother of any person through whom the relationship is deduced, were married to each other at any time. Again, this rule of construction applies 'unless the contrary intention appears'.

The above removed many of the succession disadvantages attached to illegitimacy. Therefore a non-marital child now has the same rights as a marital child to share on the intestacy of his parents, although not on the intestacy of more remote relatives.

With regard to Conrad taking under the will of Gerald's father, a gift 'to my grandchildren' now includes marital and non-marital children alike unless a contrary intention appears. We are not told of any such contrary intention therefore (unless there is one) Conrad will take under his grandfather's will.

12   THE FAMILY AND THE STATE

12.1   Introduction

During the last 30 years the State, through local authorities, has increasingly played a role in providing care for children in need. The powers of the local authority were largely derived from two statutory sources - the Child Care Act 1980 and the Children and Young Persons Act 1969. The first of these measures imposed duties on the local authority to provide care for children deprived of a normal home life and the local authority provides a wide range of resources to meet the needs of such children. The second, involving more formality and court proceedings, empowered the local authority to take parental rights in respect of children who had been abused and who were at risk.

In recent years there has been much criticism of the framework of child law. Many children in care are in care on a 'voluntary' basis and yet are never rehabilitated with their natural parents, and parents in need of social service support because of their emotional or environmental circumstances often regard local authority intervention with suspicion. Furthermore the legislation had been criticised for placing excessively wide powers with the local authority with little opportunity for the parent to challenge in court the exercise of local authority discretion.

Local authorities' powers and duties in this context are now contained in the Children Act 1989 which has made extensive changes seeking to define more clearly the powers of the local authority whilst ensuring the rights of parents and the child are safeguarded.

12.2   Key points

a) *Voluntary care*

   i)   Section 17 of the Children Act 1989 lays down the general duty of the local authority to safeguard and promote the welfare of children in need and to promote the upbringing of such children by their families. The Act anticipates a range and level of services appropriate to the needs of such children. 'Need' is defined in s17(10).

ii) Section 20 places a duty on the local authority to provide accommodation for children where either there is no person with parental responsibility for the child or that person is unable for whatever reason to look after him. The section anticipates circumstances such as homelessness, poverty, hospitalisation, inadequacy etc which resulted in the parent being unable to provide suitable care and is largely a rewording of s2 of the Child Care Act 1980. The local authority cannot provide care under this section if any person with parental responsibility objects and is prepared to provide accommodation. Furthermore a person with parental responsibility may remove a child from accommodation provided under s20 at any time.

iii) The previous provisions were controversial and unpopular. Reception into care under s2 should have had no direct effect on the parents' legal rights. Their position was however more tenuous.

- Under s13(2) Child Care Act 1980 a parent had to give the local authority 28 days notice of intended removal: see *Lewisham London Borough Council* v *Lewisham Juvenile Court Justices* [1980] AC 273.

  Under s20 Children Act 1989 any person with parental responsibility may remove a child from care at any time. There is no need for written notice. If the local authority have concerns for the safety of the child an application must be made for an emergency protection order and care order.

- The local authority could pass a parental rights resolution under s3 Child Care Act 1980. The procedure was essentially administrative and parents had no rights to attend the committee meeting: see *R* v *Harrow London Borough Council, ex parte D* [1990] 3 All ER 12. Certain conditions had to be satisfied and the resolution, once passed, had to be served on the parent within 14 days: see generally *Wheatley* v *Waltham Forest London Borough Council* [1980] AC 311 and *W* v *Nottinghamshire County Council* [1982] 1 All ER 1.

  Under the Children Act 1989 this procedure is discontinued.

iv) Uncertainty existed over the legal position of the parent whose child is in care. The de facto control that the authority exercised often precluded parents from decisions relating to foster parent placement and other matters relating to the child's care. Under s22 Children Act the local authority is under a duty to consult with the child, the parent, persons with parental responsibility and other relevant persons before making decisions in relation to the child. The local authority has a duty to rehabilitate the child and the family. The voluntary nature is thus emphasised.

v) There is a duty to encourage contact between the parent and the child. With the repeal of the Child Care Act 1980 s12A to 12G of that Act go: see generally *Re Y (minors) (wardship: access challenge)* [1988] 1 FLR 299 and *R* v *UK* (Case No 6/1986/104/152) [1988] 2 FLR 445.

b) *Compulsory care*

Care proceedings

i) Section 31 CA 1989 empowers the court to place a child in the care of the local authority or under the supervision of that authority. The court must be satisfied that:

- the child concerned is suffering or is likely to suffer significant harm and
- that the harm or likelihood of harm is attributable to
    - the care given to the child not being what it would be reasonable to expect a parent to give to him or
    - the child being beyond parental control.

The court can judge a child's health and development against what would reasonably be expected of a similar child. The terms harm, health, ill treatment are defined in s31(9).

In *Northamptonshire County Council* v *S* [1992] 3 WLR 1010 the court held that the words in s31(2)(a) referred to the point immediately before the process of protecting the child began. The care which other carers may give (in this case the grandparents) only became relevant once the section had been satisfied and the court had to decide what order to make. This is an interesting case involving an application for a residence order by the paternal grandmother, the maternal grandmother and the father, and an application for parental responsibility by the non-marital father.

ii) This section replaces s1(2) of the Children and Young Persons Act 1969. Under that section the court had to be satisfied that one of seven conditions were satisfied and that the child was in need of care and control. Anticipated harm was sufficient in two of the conditions, see s1(2)b and s1(2)(bb), but for the remainder future anticipated events could not be considered: see *Re D* [1987] 1 All ER 20 and *Essex County Council* v *TLR and KBR* (1978) 9 Fam Law 15. Note that the new provision accommodates anticipated harm.

The term 'similar' child was a focus in *Re O (a minor) (care order: education: procedure)* [1992] 1 WLR 912. It meant a child of equivalent intellectual and social development. Non-attendance at school in this case constituted significant harm.

iii) In addition to the provision of s31 the court must also have regard to the welfare of the child: see s1(1). The court cannot make an order unless it considers that doing so would be better for the child than making no order at all see s1(5).

iv) The orders the court can make now include in addition to care and supervision orders

- a residence order. Parties involved in the care proceedings can make application: see s10. This may be of particular relevance to foster parents.

- a contact order. Any person other than a parent can apply for leave.

Emergency Protection Order

i) Section 44 replaces the Place of Safety Order with the Emergency Protection Order. The court must be satisfied that the child is likely to suffer significant harm if he is not removed to accommodation provided by the applicant. The order also can prevent the child being removed from such accommodation where he was accommodated immediately before the application.

ii) The Cleveland Report highlighted the inadequacies of the existing law. Under s28 of the Children and Young Persons Act 1969 the local authority had powers to detain the child. Parents could not challenge the order during that period: see *Nottinghamshire County Council* v *Q* [1982] Fam 94. Further the legal position of parents was unclear over the question of contact with the child.

iii) The following provisions are important:

- The order lasts for eight days with the possibility of a seven day extension in exceptional circumstances,

- Parents have a right to challenge the order once 72 hours have elapsed.

- There is a presumption of reasonable contact by the parents and others: see s44(13) subject to the directions of the court

- The court may give directions in respect of the medical examination of the child. This includes that the child should not be medically examined.

Child Assessment Orders

i) The Child Assessment order - s43 - is a new order, intended to be used where the concern over a child does not warrant the more drastic step of an emergency protection. Its objective is to allow the local authority to make an assessment without taking the child away from the home.

ii) The court must be satisfied that there is reasonable cause to suspect that the child is suffering or is likely to suffer significant harm and an assessment is necessary to determine this. It is anticipated that it will be appropriate in cases where the parents are refusing to allow examination.

iii) The order must specify what examination is to be carried out and the person to whom the child is to be produced. The child can be kept away from home but this should be exceptional. The order can last for a maximum of seven days. A child may refuse to submit to an examination if of sufficient understanding: s43(8).

Police powers

A police officer has powers to remove a child to reasonable accommodation where he has reasonable cause to believe that a child would otherwise be likely to suffer harm: see s46(3).

Access to children in care

i)   Section 34 deals with parental contact with children in care. There is a statutory presumption of reasonable contact with a parent, guardian or any person in whose favour a residence order was in force immediately before the care order. The section represents an attempt to provide clear legal remedies to parents who disagree with the authority's decision to restrict contact with their children.

ii) The child or any person listed in s34(1) can make application to court for contact toe defined. This includes the parents. Grandparents will have to have the leave of the court.

iii) The local authority can refuse contact for up to 7 days if they feel this to be necessary in the interests of the child's welfare and the court can authorise the authority to refuse contact where the objective of the proceedings was to eliminate contact between the child and a particular person.

Local authorities' use of wardship

Prior to the Children Act the local authority used wardship in a variety of ways:

i)   To gain the authority of the High Court to confirm its decision. See *Re B (a minor) (wardship: sterilisation)* [1987] 2 FLR 400; *Re Baby J* [1990] 3 All ER 930.

ii) Where there were no grounds for care proceedings: *Re P (a minor) (child abuse: evidence)* [1987] 2 FLR 467.

iii) Where there were no grounds for a s3 resolution but the local authority wished to prevent the return of the child to the parent: *Re CB (a minor) (wardship: local authority)* [1981] 1 WLR 379.

Section 100 Children Act provides that the local authority must obtain leave of the court for a wardship application. That leave will not be granted if the order they wish to achieve could be achieved under the Act.

Challenging local authority decisions

i)   Parents' use of wardship

Parents and non parents have not been successful in using the jurisdiction to challenge local authority decisions in respect of their children see *A v Liverpool City Council* [1982] AC 363 and *Re W (a minor) (wardship: jurisdiction)* [1985] 2 WLR 892. The Act does not alter this position.

ii) Judicial review

This remedy is available where it can be established that the authority has acted irrationally, illegally or there has been procedural impropriety. Judicial review is of course only concerned with the procedure and not whether the decision is right or wrong.

iii) European Court of Human Rights

The European Convention of Human Rights formally guarantees certain basic rights and although it has not been ratified by the UK Parliament complaints to the European Court do lie. The court has held the UK to be in breach of article 6 which guarantees a fair hearing and article 8 which guarantees a right to family life: *O* v *United Kingdom* (1987) The Times 9 July.

12.3 Recent cases and statutes

Children Act 1989

Northamptonshire County Council v *S* [1992] 3 WLR 1010

Re O (a minor) (care order: education: procedure) [1992] 1 WLR 912

12.4 Analysis of questions

Questions on this area have traditionally been problem questions involving the legal rights of the local authority often with a consideration of the wardship jurisdiction and/or adoption law (see chapters 10 and 11). Again, as is so often the case in Family Law, students must be able to draw on more than one topic because of this interrelationship. With the advent of the Children Act 1989 similar questions may be asked but of course on the basis of the new law. Custodianship for example as a legal concept has gone although it will continue to be possible for long-term carers to seek to protect their legal position in respect of the child. An essay question on the changes would seem equally likely.

12.5 Questions

Question 1

Maurice and Nellie began living together in 1979 and had a child, Oliver, born a year later. Maurice left Nellie in 1981 when she was two months pregnant. Being unable to cope, she placed Oliver in the care of the local authority on the understanding that he would be returned to her after the birth of her baby.

When the baby, Pamela, was born later in 1981 Nellie suffered from post-natal depression and told the local authority that they should keep Oliver 'for the time being'. Oliver was placed by the authority in the care of Mr and Mrs Jones. Nellie visited Oliver regularly.

In 1984 Nellie began living with Robert. Shortly afterwards, one of the local authority's social workers discovered that Pamela was badly bruised. Nellie and Robert denied that they had battered the girl.

Outraged by the local authority's allegations, they paid an immediate visit to the social services department and demanded that Oliver be returned to them.

a) Can Nellie and Robert insist upon the immediate return of Oliver?

b) What steps can the local authority take if they do not want to return Oliver to Nellie and Robert?

c) What steps can Mr and Mrs Jones take to ensure that Oliver is not taken away from them?

d) What steps can the local authority take if they think that Pamela is being battered?

University of London LLB Examination
(for External Students) Family Law 1985 Q7

General comment

This question should pose no problems for the well prepared candidate given a thorough knowledge of those aspects of the Children Act 1989 that relate to voluntary care, compulsory care proceedings and the provisions of s10 of the Act - who can apply for a residence order?

Skeleton solution

a) Provision of voluntary care by the local authority. The rights of parents and those with parental responsibility.

b) Procedures for emergency protection order by local authority.

c) Application under s10 by foster parents for a residence order.

d) Section 31 compulsory care proceedings.

Suggested solution

a) Under s20 of the Children Act 1989 the local authority are under a duty to provide accommodation for children in need where the child has been abandoned, where there is no person with parental responsibility for the child or where the person who has been caring for the child is prevented from providing the child with suitable accommodation or care. The section is largely a rewording of s2 of the Child Care Act 1980 which is repealed. To emphasise the voluntary nature of the provision the section stipulates that the local authority may not provide care under the section if a person with parental responsibility for the child objects and is prepared to provide accommodation. Persons with parental responsibility include the natural parents of a child where the couple are married, and persons who have parental responsibility as a result of a residence order made in their favour. An unmarried father does not have parental responsibility for a child unless he acquires it in accordance with provisions in the Act - that is by a parental responsibility agreement or a shared parental responsibility order: s4.

The Children Act abolishes the old 's3 resolution' whereby a local authority could assume parental rights in respect of a child in voluntary care by passing a resolution based on one of the grounds in s3. Furthermore once a child had been in care for six months the parent had to give 28 days notice of intention remove the child. It was felt that these contentious provisions undermined the basis of voluntary care and resulted in mistrust. Consequently the position now is that under s20(8) of the Children Act 1989 a person who has parental responsibility for a child may remove the child from accommodation provided by the authority at any time.

Consequently Nellie could demand the return of Oliver although of course Maurice, the child's natural father, does not have parental responsibility as he and Nellie were unmarried, and Robert does not enjoy parental responsibility as there is no indication of a residence order in his favour. Such action could of course be potentially damaging to Oliver and the local authority would have to apply for an emergency protection order to acquire parental responsibility. In the event of Nellie turning up at the home of the foster parents unexpectedly it could be that s3(5) would authorise them to refuse Nellie. Section 3(5) provides that a person who does not have parental responsibility but has care of the child may do what is reasonable in all the circumstances of the case for the purpose of safeguarding or promoting the child's welfare. Such action would of course be very temporary.

b) The local authority must acquire parental responsibility in respect of Oliver. This they could do in a situation of crisis by applying to the court for an emergency protection order - s44. The court must be satisfied that the child is likely to suffer significant harm if either he is not removed to accommodation provided by the applicant or he does not remain in the place in which he is then being accommodated. The local authority acquires parental responsibility although this is notionally shared with the parent. The order lasts for eight days and can be extended for a further seven days. There is a presumption of reasonable contact with the parent and that person can challenge the order after 72 hours.

The section clearly anticipates circumstances similar to the facts of this case. Given that Oliver has been with foster parents for a substantial time immediate removal may be emotionally traumatic. Furthermore there remains the ambiguity surrounding Pamela.

c) The custodianship provisions of the Children Act 1975 under which Mr and Mrs Jones could have applied for a form of legal custody over Oliver has been repealed. It has been replaced by a provision in s8 of the Children Act 1989 under which Mr and Mrs Jones could apply for a residence order which would vest parental responsibility in them. Section 10 specifies who can apply for a section 8 order and Mr and Mrs Jones would qualify as of right in view of the fact that Oliver has lived with them for at least three years: s10(5)(b).

The decision of the court would be made on the basis of the 'welfare principle' in s1 of the Act - the child's welfare shall be the paramount consideration in any question with respect to the upbringing of the child. The court shall be guided by the factors listed in s1(3).

The relevant factors here would be a consideration of the child's physical, emotional and educational needs: see *Stephenson* v *Stephenson* (1985), the likely effect on Oliver of a change in circumstances - the status quo - which courts consistently attempt to retain, any harm he has suffered or is likely to suffer - there remains the question of Pamela's alleged abuse and Oliver's own ascertainable wishes. Oliver is only six but nevertheless the court would establish his view depending on his understanding: see generally *Gillick* v *West Norfolk and Wisbech Area Health Authority*. Despite taking into account the blood link it would seem likely that Mr and Mrs Jones could succeed in their application but much would depend on the relationship Nellie and Robert have with Oliver, the frequency of contact and so on. In the longer term and again dependent on the above factors Mr and Mrs Jones could apply to adopt and this would sever irrevocably Nellie's legal ties.

d) Regarding Pamela the local authority could in the first instance apply for an emergency protection order. The procedure would be as outlined above. An alternative would be a child assessment order under s43 of the Act which would authorise the local authority to assess Pamela and oblige Nellie to allow such an examination. The local authority would again have to satisfy the court that Pamela was 'likely to suffer significant harm'. The objective of such an order is to allow an assessment to be made without the need for the child's removal from home.

Ultimately the local authority could apply for a care order under s31 Children Act. The local authority would have to satisfy the court that Pamela was suffering significant harm or was likely to and that the harm was attributable to the child not receiving care that it would be reasonable to expect a parent to give. The grounds are wider than those previously contained in s1 of the Children and Young Persons Act which it replaces. Evidence would be necessary from child welfare professionals including medical evidence to establish whether the bruising was non-accidental.

During the currency of a care order there is a presumption of reasonable contact with persons with parental responsibility. Indeed the court must consider such arrangements. In addition to the above grounds the court must consider the welfare principle discussed above.

In circumstances such as those outlined wardship proceedings can be discounted in future. Under s100 of the Children Act the local authority cannot institute wardship proceedings without the leave of the court and leave will not be granted unless the objective to be achieved could not be achieved under the Act and the child is likely to suffer significant harm in the event of leave being refused.

Question 2

In 1985 Molly had a daughter, Nellie, by Oliver with whom she had lived for a month. Oliver left Molly soon after Nellie was born. A year later Molly started living with Quentin who is the high priest of a small religious group known as the Solitarists which discourages all forms of contact with people who do not belong to the group and which believes that all children should be brought up on a diet of bread and water. Molly became pregnant and is due to have a child by Quentin in August 1990.

Neighbours have recently reported Molly and Quentin to the local authority on the ground that Nellie looks undernourished and is not allowed to talk to other children. Quentin and Molly have refused to allow social workers into the house and say that Nellie is being brought up properly in accordance with the beliefs and practices of the Solitarist religion. Oliver has heard of Nellie's condition and now wishes to obtain custody of her, or at least to have a say in her moral and religious upbringing.

i) Advise the local authority as to what action, if any, it can take to ensure the good health and proper development of Nellie and Molly's expected child.

ii) Advise Oliver as to whether he can obtain custody of Nellie, or if he does not obtain custody, whether he is entitled to have his views taken into account in Nellie's moral and religious upbringing.

University of London LLB Examination
(for External Students) Family Law June 1990 Q8

Skeleton solution

i) • Local authority application for care order under s31 CA 1989.

   • Criteria of significant harm and the child's welfare under s1 CA 1989.

   • Section 31 includes anticipated harm which would include risk to Molly's expected child.

ii) • Section 8 orders under the CA 1989 - residence orders.

   • Position regarding parental responsibility.

   • Section 4 CA 1989 - Welfare principle relevant in court's decision.

Suggested solution

i) In the first instance the local authority could apply for either a child assessment order under s43 of the Children Act 1989 or an emergency protection order under s44. The former gives the local authority powers to make an assessment of the child and obliges the parent to co-operate in that assessment by producing the child. It is intended to be used in circumstances where it is not considered necessary to remove the child from the home. The latter empowers the local authority to remove the child for up to eight days to accommodation provided by them. The parent has rights of contact and a right to challenge the order after 72 hours. The court can give directions, for instance on medical examination.

It would seem likely in the circumstances that an emergency protection order would be appropriate in view of Nellie's health and the obstructiveness of Quentin and Molly.

The local authority could institute proceedings under s31 of the Children Act 1989. The Act came into force in October 1991. Section 31 replaces s1(2) of the Children and Young Persons Act 1969. That legislation necessitated the local authority satisfying the court that one of the grounds set down in s1(2) had been made out and that the child was in need of care and control. Section 31 Children Act provides that the grounds for a care order are that the child has suffered significant harm or is likely to and that the harm or likelihood of harm is attributable to

i) the standard of care given to the child being below that which it would be reasonable to expect of a parent of a similar child, or

ii) the child being beyond parental control.

The court must also be aware that in determining the application the child's welfare is the paramount consideration: s1(1), and an order must not be made unless making an order would be better for the child than making no order at all. The court must have regard to the 'statutory checklist' in s1(3). Harm is defined as the impairment of health or development or ill treatment.

In respect of Nellie the isolation imposed on her and the Spartan diet she endures could constitute evidence of significant harm. Her undernourished appearance could be objectively measured against children of a similar age. Furthermore it is accepted that the emotional and psychological development of children is partly dependent on social contact with peers. In *M* v *Westminster City Council* (1985) a care order was made in respect of children whose parents had a drink problem and left them alone in the house for periods. The parents showed a lack of reaction to the children in times of stress.

If the court decides that s31 is satisfied there are a number of orders which could be made. A supervision order would mean that Nellie would remain with Molly and Quentin but be under the supervision of the local authority. A care order would vest parental responsibility in the local authority although it would be notionally 'shared' with Molly. A residence order, establishing with whom the child is to live, could be applied for by Oliver, who is the natural parent. Care proceedings are family proceedings and such an application could therefore be made. Note however that Oliver does not as the unmarried father have parental responsibility as of right although if the court were to make a residence order in his favour he would be given parental responsibility.

With regard to the unborn child the local authority are in a stronger position under the Children Act than they were. With some exceptions, which would not apply here (unless Nellie had already been taken into care), care proceedings may have failed on the basis of predicted harm: see *M* v *Westminster City Council* (1985) and *Re D* (1987), a case concerning a child born with a drug dependency to a registered drug addict. Neither could the local authority institute wardship proceedings in respect of an unborn child: see *Re F* (1988). However, under the provisions of s31 it could well be the case that the court would make a care order in respect of the unborn child on birth on the facts given.

ii) As the unmarried father of Nellie, Oliver has no parental responsibility in respect of her: s2 CA 1989. The concept of parental responsibility is not defined in the Act other than in terms of all the rights, duties, powers, responsibilities and authority which by law a parent has in relation to the child and his property. This would include Oliver's entitlement to have his views taken into account in Nellie's moral and religious upbringing.

There are two courses of action open to Oliver on the question of 'custody'. Oliver could apply for a residence order: s8 CA 1989. A residence order settles the arrangements as to the person with whom the child is to live. As natural parent Oliver could apply as of right for a residence order: s10 CA 1989. In deciding such an application the court must have regard to the welfare principle (s1 CA) which provides that the child's welfare is the paramount consideration: See *J* v *C* (1970). Under the CA a statutory checklist is included and the court must have regard to those matters. They include: (1) the ascertainable wishes and feelings of the child concerned - see *Gillick* v *West Norfolk and Wisbech Area Health Authority* (1986) in which it was decided that a child's wishes should be taken into account according to the age, maturity and understanding of the child; (2) the physical, emotional and educational needs of the child; (3) the likely effect of any change of circumstances; (4) the age, sex and background of the child; (5) any harm the child has suffered or is at risk of suffering; and (6) how capable his parents are to meet his needs.

We are not told in the problem the extent, if any, of the contact between Oliver and Nellie. The court would be unlikely to make a residence order in Oliver's favour if there has been no opportunity to develop a relationship. On the other hand if they do enjoy a good relationship the court may consider an application favourably, particularly if the alternative would be care.

Oliver could also apply for a parental responsibility order: s4 CA. Again the court would decide such an application on the welfare principle.

Question 3

Clive and Denise have two children, Edward and Fiona, who are aged 7 and 5. Denise is expecting twins in July 1991. In January 1991, Clive, a stockbroker, lost his job and in order to pay off his debts, sold the family home and the Porsche. The family moved into a small flat. Clive and Denise had frequent arguments in front of the children and Clive suffered a nervous breakdown.

Denise, who has been unable to cope with Clive and the children in the small flat, has placed the children temporarily in the care of the Helpful Local Authority. Miss Friend, the Local Authority social worker, believes that Edward and Fiona have suffered psychological damage as a result of the family crisis and their father's illness. However, in May 1991, after Clive recovered and secured a job as a financial consultant, Denise demanded the return of her children.

The children were returned despite Miss Friend's misgivings. On Wednesday 5 June at 1pm, she visited Denise without prior arrangement. She found that the children were not at school and still in bed. Denise looked dirty and dishevelled and had a bruise on her arm which she said had occurred when she fell downstairs the night before. Miss Friend noticed a box of empty sherry bottles in the kitchen.

Miss Friend is not satisfied with the situation and is fearful for the well-being of Edward and Fiona and the twins who are due to be born in two weeks.

Advise her of the procedures she can invoke to protect the children.

University of London LLB Examination
(for External Students) Family Law June 1991 Q8

General comment

This is a question on children and local authorities and whereas under the existing law the advice sought is relatively straightforward, under the new law as represented by the 1989 Act the procedures to be discussed are less obvious, mainly due to a lack of detailed information as to what harm, if any, is being suffered by the existing children or is likely to be suffered by the twins when born.

Skeleton solution

- Care proceedings: s31 Children Act 1989. Discuss grounds to be established for such proceedings, explain the meaning of the term 'significant harm'.

- Explain orders available - care and supervision or s8 Children Act orders.

- Apply welfare principle - discuss the guidelines in the checklist contained in s1(3) Children Act 1989.

- Consider alternatives for care proceedings - education supervision order - grounds for such an order, and effect.

- Child assessment order - grounds and effect.

Suggested solution

Under the Children Act 1989 a local authority has a duty to investigate all cases where it has reasonable cause to suspect that a child is suffering, or is likely to suffer, significant harm. The local authority must make enquiries to determine whether it should exercise its powers, for example to bring proceedings to take a child into care or to provide services.

In this case therefore if Mrs Friend, being concerned for the welfare of Edward and Fiona, decides that legal action is necessary she should be advised that either a local authority or the NSPCC is empowered to institute care proceedings (s31 Children Act 1989) in either the High Court, County Court or Magistrates Court. It will then be for the court to decide firstly if any grounds for an order are established, and if so secondly which order, if any, should be made in respect of the children.

Section 31(2) Children Act 1989 provides that the court may make a care or supervision order only if it is satisfied that the children are suffering or are likely to suffer significant harm (s31(2)(a)) *and* inter alia that the harm or likelihood of it is attributable to the care given to the children or likely to be given to them if the order were not made, not being what it would be reasonable to expect a parent to give them (s31(2)(b) Children Act 1989).

207

Further , the court must then consider the children's welfare by applying the welfare test using the checklist set out in s1(3) Children Act 1989. The court may make an order only if it decides that to do so would be better than making no order at all (s1(5) Children Act 1989).

'Harm' means 'ill-treatment or impairment of health or development'. This would encompass physical and emotional abuse and neglect and development means physical, intellectual, emotional, social or behavioural development (s31(9) Children Act 1989). There seems to be no allegation of ill-treatment in this case, rather it is of neglect. In this context 'significant' entails comparing children with what could reasonably be expected of similar children (s31(10) Children Act 1989). The children's non attendance at school could produce significant harm for example if it means that the children are receiving no education at all.

It is not sufficient merely to show significant harm or its likelihood. Such harm must be attributable to the care given by the parents. In these circumstances parental care is judged objectively in relation to the particular children. Therefore a parent is expected to take account of any special needs of the children. In this case the psychological damage done to the children may entail them having special needs.

A care order is possible not only where significant harm is established but also where it is likely to occur. This may be of importance to Mrs Friend in relation to the unborn twins. Obviously an order in relation to them cannot be made at this time. However once they are born it may be necessary to obtain an order on the basis that they are likely to suffer significant harm if significant harm is established in relation to Edward and Fiona, for example in respect of their care. If the court is satisfied that significant harm is established it may make a care or supervision order. A care order gives the local authority parental responsibility for the child and lasts until the child is 18 unless discharged earlier (s91(12) Children Act 1989), but it does not remove the parents' parental responsibility. The local authority may decide the extent to which parents may exercise their responsibilities towards the children but it has no power to, inter alia, change the children's religion or agree to the children's adoptions. A supervision order lasts for one year although it may be extended for up to three years. It places the children under the supervision of a social worker who is under a duty to advise, assist and befriend the children (s35(1)(a) Children Act 1989). The supervisor is required to take such steps as are necessary to give effect to the order and in this case she may require Denise and Clive, with their consent, to take reasonable steps to ensure that the children comply with directions, for example as to school attendance. The children may also be required to submit to such medical or psychiatric examinations or treatment as the court thinks fit, but whether this will be necessary will depend on an assessment of the 'psychological damage' suffered by Edward and Fiona. A supervision order would not give Mrs Friend, or any other supervisor, the right to enter the home or to remove the children if they failed for example to attend a medical examination. However she would be able to apply for a variation and the court could impose penalties for non compliance with its orders. On an application for variation the court may grant a care order only if the significant harm test is re-established.

As an alternative to a care or supervision order the court may make a Section 8 Children Act 1989 order even though significant harm is not proved.

In deciding what order, if any, to make the court must give paramount consideration to the children's welfare, applying the checklist set out in s1(3) Children Act 1989. Therefore the court's decision must be that which must promote the children's welfare and is in their best interests (*J* v *C* (1970); s1(1) Children Act 1989).

The checklist provides a guideline to assist the court in applying the welfare principle but it is not exhaustive and the court may have to consider the relevance of other factors also. Under s1(3) the court must have regard to the ascertainable wishes and feelings of the children considered in the light of their age and understanding (s1(3)(a)). In this case it is submitted that Fiona may be deemed too young to express her wishes on this matter. However Edward's wishes may be considered relevant. In care proceedings the guardian ad litem will normally be the person who will make the children's wishes known.

Under s1(3)(b) the court must also have regard to the physical, emotional and educational needs of the children. In this case it seems the educational needs are an obvious concern, but the children's other needs must be considered, particularly as there may be evidence that they are not being met due to Denise's drinking habits.

The court must consider the likely effect on the children of any change in their circumstances (s1(3)(c)). This will be particularly relevant if a care order is being sought as the trauma to the children which will be involved in their removal from home must be recognised particularly as apparently they have already suffered psychological disturbance due to the family crises and their father's breakdown.

The age, sex, background and any characteristics of the children which the court considers relevant must be taken into account under s1(3)(d). The court must also consider the harm which the children have suffered or are at risk of suffering (s1(3)(e)) and in this case 'significant harm' should already have been established.

Under s1(3)(f) the court must consider how capable each parent is of meeting the children's needs and must also consider this question in relation to the local authority if a care order is sought. It seems that Clive has recovered from his breakdown and we are told that he has got a job. It appears therefore that he is returning to normality. The problem seems to centre around Denise who, it appears, is drinking heavily and as a result is unable to care for herself or the children.

Finally under s1(3)(g) the court must consider the range of powers available to it under the Act in these proceedings. The court may make a care or supervision order only where the grounds relating to significant harm as discussed above are made out. Alternatively it may decide that a s8 order is more appropriate. But before making any order the court must be satisfied that to do so is better for the children than making no order at all (s1(5) Children Act 1989) and in this connection the children's long term interests must be taken into account as well as their short term ones.

As an alternative to care proceedings, the necessity of which Mrs Friend may have difficulty in establishing unless the children's non attendance at school produces significant harm or there is clear evidence of other significant harm arising out of the lack of care of the children, Mrs Friend should be advised that an education supervision order may be appropriate on these facts although this would relate only to Edward and Fiona and would not deal with her concerns for the unborn twins. If a child is of compulsory school age and is not being properly educated the local education authority may apply in a family proceedings court for such an order (s36(1) and (3) Children Act 1989). This replaces applications for care orders made under the Children and Young Persons Act 1969 on the ground of non attendance at school. The children would be treated as being properly educated if they are receiving efficient full time education suitable to their age, ability and aptitude (s36(4)). They would be treated as not being educated if, inter alia, they are registered pupils at a school which they are not attending regularly unless it can be proved that they are being properly educated, for example at home. Obviously no alternative arrangements have been made for the children's education at home and so it is likely that Edward and Fiona would be treated as not being educated at this time.

An education supervision order places a duty on the supervisor to advise, assist and befriend and give directions to the supervised children and their parents in such a way as will ensure that the children are properly educated. Before giving such directions the supervisor must, so far as is reasonably practicable, ascertain the wishes and feelings of the children and the parents. The order lasts for one year although it may be extended for up to three years.

Mrs Friend should also be advised that before any proceedings are started an investigation of the children's circumstances can be undertaken by means of a child assessment order. This requires the children's parents to produce them, for example at a hospital, or to allow them to be visited at home, so that their health and development or the way in which they are being treated can be assessed. This would enable the local authority to decide whether the children are suffering, or are likely to suffer from significant harm before deciding whether to commence care proceedings. To obtain such an order the local authority must satisfy the court it has reasonable grounds to suspect that the children are suffering or are likely to suffer significant harm and an assessment of the state of the children's health or development, or the way in which they are being treated, is required to enable the local authority to determine if the children are suffering or are likely to suffer significant harm; and it is unlikely that such an assessment will be made, or be satisfactory, unless a child assessment order is made (s43(1) Children Act 1989).

The children's welfare will be paramount and the court must be satisfied that making an order would be better than making none. Therefore such an order may be particularly relevant if the parents unreasonably refused to allow the children to be assessed. It should be noted however that the order lasts for a maximum of seven days.

Finally, Mrs Friend should be advised that another alternative to a care or supervision order would be a family assistance order which would require a social worker to advise, assist and befriend any person named in the order, namely Clive and Denise and the children. However, such an order, which lasts for up to six months, is possible only if Clive and Denise consent to it.

It seems that an emergency protection order which, for example, could authorise the local authority to remove the children from home, may not be appropriate here as it is not clear from the facts whether the children are likely to suffer significant harm.

Question 4

Maria and Toby, who already had one child, married in January 1990 when they were both 16. Neither had much education, but Toby has been employed as a painter and decorator since their marriage, while Maria has had occasional cleaning jobs. In December 1991, their second child, Roxanne, was born.

Roxanne has been a difficult baby, constantly crying and refusing to settle for more than ten minutes at a time. Midwives and health visitors from the Eatenswill Local Authority paid special attention to Maria and Roxanne, visiting the council flat where the family lived until Roxanne was two months old. In March 1991, the social worker from the local authority decided to pay Maria an unexpected visit, but although Maria was at home and she could hear the baby and the older child crying she could not gain access to the flat. Neighbours told the social worker that Toby had not been seen for some time, that the children were frequently crying and that Maria looked worn and tense.

The Eatenswill Local Authority is now extremely concerned about the welfare of the children and seeks your advice as to the action it may take.

University of London LLB Examination
(for External Students) Family Law June 1992 Q8

General comment

This question will be answered on the basis of the Children Act 1989. The Child Care Act 1980 and the relevant provisions of the Children and Young Persons Act 1969 are repealed by this Act.

Skeleton solution

• Discuss s31 Children Act 1989, including the criteria in s31(2).

• Discuss ss1(1), 1(5) and 13(3) CA 1989.

• Consider the different options available to court:

  - care order;

  - supervision order;

  - family assistance order.

• Consider the need for a child assessment order.

Suggested solution

The local authority can apply for a care order under s31(1)(a) Children Act (CA) 1989

211

or a supervision order under s31(1)(b) CA 1989. The application may be made with a minimum of three days' notice. Care proceedings must be started in the local magistrates' court, called the Family Proceedings Court for these purposes (rule 3(1) Children (Allocation of Proceedings) Order 1991). Cases may be heard by the higher courts if they involve a novel point of view, or will be long and complex, eg perhaps involving sexual abuse. The respondents to the application are the parents, so here it will be Maria and Toby who both have parental responsibility.

There is only one ground on which the local authority may make an application - 'the threshold criteria' in s31(2):

'A court can only make a care order or supervision order if it is satisfied:

a) that the child is suffering significant harm or is likely to suffer significant harm; and

b) the harm or likelihood of harm is attributable to –

   i)   the care given to the child being not what is (would be) reasonable to expect a parent to give to his/her child (or the care likely to be given to the child falls below that standard; or

   ii) the child being beyond parental control.'

On these facts there is no concrete evidence that the children are suffering significant harm but it appears that Toby may have deserted the family and Maria is having difficulty coping with the children on her own; she is only 18 (approximately) years of age and the responsibility of looking after two children is very great. Also it is stated that Roxanne is a difficult baby and that both children seem to be crying most of the time. It should be noted that the threshold criteria can involve future harm, namely harm which has not yet occurred but which is likely to happen. This may be relevant here because it is likely that in the present circumstances if this state of affairs continues the children will come to harm. Harm is given a wide meaning in this section; it includes ill treatment or impairment of health or development. There is a risk here of emotional abuse and perhaps even physical abuse and the local authority can base its application on this.

In making its decision the child's welfare shall be the court's paramount consideration: s1(1) CA 1989. The court cannot make an order unless it considers that doing so would be better for the child than making no order at all: s1(5) CA 1989. So the court must be satisfied that its intervention will improve things for the child - an entirely new consideration for the court.

In particular the court must have regard to the 'checklist' in s1(3) CA 1989:

a) the ascertainable wishes and feelings of the child, taking into consideration the age and understanding of the child. Here Roxanne is only six months old and we are not told how old the other child is but it can be presumed that it is only about three, so they will not be very helpful in this case as they are too young;

b) the child's physical, emotional and educational needs;

c) the likely effect on the child of any change in the child's circumstances;

d) the child's sex, age, background and any characteristics of the child which the court considers to be relevant - the fact that Roxanne is a 'difficult' baby could be relevant here;

e) any harm which the child has suffered or is at risk of suffering;

f) how capable each of the child's parents and any other person in relation to whom the court considers the question to be relevant is of meeting the child's needs. This could be particularly relevant here, because of the age of Maria, the pressure she is obviously under and the lack of support from Toby;

g) the range of powers open to the court under the CA 1989.

If the threshold criteria are satisfied and the court has considered the above checklist then it may decide what order to make. It may make a care order, a supervision order or a family assistance order in this case. A care order gives parental responsibility of the child to the local authority - parents also retain parental responsibility for their child (s2(5), (6)) and theoretically hold their responsibility jointly with the local authority. The local authority must consult the parents about its plans for the child and must give the parents' views due consideration: s22(4). The local authority may, however, limit what a parent may do to meet his or her parental responsibility if it is necessary to do so in order to safeguard and promote the child's welfare: s33(4). It should be noted here that before a care order is made the court will require to know the arrangements the local authority has made for the parents to have contact with the child. The local authority is required under s34 to allow such contact.

A supervision order may be made. Here the supervisor will have a duty to advise, assist and befriend the supervised child(ren): s35(1). A supervision order lasts for one year unless extended: Schedule 3, para 6(3).

A family assistance order may also be an alternative - the threshold criteria need not be satisfied for this order to be made. The court must be satisfied that the circumstances of the case are exceptional and that every person named in the order, other than the child, has consented to it: s16(3). This order requires a social worker (or probation officer) to advise, assist and befriend any person named in the order. This might be useful in these circumstances because Maria could probably benefit under such an order - it must be noted that she would have to agree to this order.

All the above illustrate the different actions that the local authority may take in this case. However, before the local authority applied for any of these orders it may want a child assessment order made. Under such an order the child's parents, in this case Maria and Toby, if he is around, will be required to produce the children or allow them to be visited at home so that the child's health or development or the way in which the child has been treated can be assessed. This enables the local authority to decide whether the child is suffering, or is likely to suffer, from significant harm before deciding whether to commence care proceedings: s43(1)(b), (2) and (6).

This would appear to be a good idea in this case, because no-one from the local authority has actually seen the children and it would allow them to determine if the children have suffered harm or are likely to suffer harm.

Notice of the application will have to be given to Maria and Toby: s46(11).

The local authority must satisfy the court that:

1. it has reasonable cause to suspect the children are suffering or are likely to suffer harm; and

2. the assessment of the state of the child's health or development, of the way in which the child has been treated, is required to enable the applicant to determine whether or not the child is suffering, or is likely to suffer, significant harm; and

3. it is unlikely that such an assessment will be made, or be satisfactory, in the absence of a child assessment order: s43(1).

In this case it is very likely that Eatenswill local authority will be able to satisfy the court of the above because on the facts, the social worker was not able to gain access to make any sort of assessment about the children. She did, however, hear them crying and she was further told by neighbours that this was a regular occurrence, all pointing to there being a chance that the children are suffering harm or likely to suffer harm.

The court will have regard to the principle that the child's welfare is paramount (s1(1)) and may feel that in this case it is necessary for the children's welfare that they are assessed and that such an assessment is likely to improve things for the child and thus make an order. The order will specify what kind of assessment is to be carried out, when it is to be carried out, the duration of it, and where it is to be carried out.

Eatenswill should be advised to obtain an assessment order first and then depending on the findings proceed with the other applications if necessary.

It should also be noted that wardship is no longer available to local authorities: s100 CA 1989.

13 THE LAW'S RESPONSE TO THE UNMARRIED FAMILY

13.1 Introduction

The umbrella term the family has come to include various relationships outside marriage and there is no longer the stigma attached to heterosexual cohabitation that there once was. Such relationships may be transitory and always intended as such, others may be entered into as a prelude to marriage, others may be for much longer periods and mirror the marriage relationship. Such relationships, lacking formal status, do not attract the same clear definition of rights and duties that marriage brings and this in turn can cause difficulties if the relationship breaks down.

Statistical studies indicate that the incidence of cohabitation outside marriage is increasing as is the number of children born to cohabiting couples. Traditionally our legal system has only acknowledged rights as existing within marriage, but this becomes more problematic, particularly for example in respect of parental rights over children and the status of those children. To accord rights to cohabitees analogous to a married couple is seen as undermining the ideological values associated with marriage and the response of the law to date has been to attach legal consequences to cohabiting relationships for specific purposes only. This often leaves the unmarried 'wife' in a much worse position on breakdown of the relationship than would be the case if the parties were legally married. The classic example of this is the case of *Burns* v *Burns* [1984] Ch 317 in which a woman who had given over twenty years of her life to her partner and the three children of the relationship received nothing on the breakdown of the relationship. Had she been married it is probable that she would have been granted a sufficiently large lump sum to enable her at least to purchase suitable alternative accommodation for herself.

Of course one cannot simply look at the position of the unmarried cohabitee; the rights and responsibilities relating to children of that relationship have also to be considered. Until the passing of the Family Law Reform Act 1987 (see now the Children Act 1989) the children of unmarried partners were treated much less favourably than marital children. Many of the differences have since 1987 been abolished. To that extent many of the rights and obligations in relation to the non-marital child are dealt with in the chapters relating to the Children Act 1989. However some differences remain and they are dealt with in the latter part of this chapter.

Accordingly we deal with the unmarried family in two parts; firstly we look at the position of the unmarried cohabitee as against her partner; secondly we look at the position of children of such unmarried relationships.

A   THE POSITION OF THE UNMARRIED COHABITEE

13.2   Key points

a) *Property disputes*

Under s24 of the Matrimonial Causes Act 1973 the court has a discretion to adjust property rights between spouses. Home ownership between unmarried couples is decided in accordance with the general principles of property law. 'The law gives no rights to a mistress by reason of her relationship with her lover, but neither does she lost any rights she would have had in law or equity': Purchas J in *Dennis* v *MacDonald* [1981] 1 WLR 810.

   i)   Joint ownership

   • A conveyance of land which declares in whom the legal title and the beneficial interest is to vest is conclusive evidence as to ownership: *Goodman* v *Gallant* [1986] Fam 106; *Turton* v *Turton* [1987] 2 All ER 641.

   • It is important to have an express declaration about the holding of beneficial interests. An ambiguous clause will not be sufficient: *Huntingford* v *Hobbs* [1992] Fam Law 437.

   • If a conveyance of land declares in whom the legal title is vested but is silent on the question of beneficial ownership, the parties can argue that they intended the beneficial ownership to be in unequal shares. The respective interests will be ascertained according to the general law of trusts: *Walker* v *Hall* [1984] FLR 126.

   Note if the legal title to the property is in the joint names of the parties there will be a presumption that the beneficial interests are owned equally. However this presumption is rebuttable. For example in *Young* v *Young* [1984] FLR 375 although the legal title of the family property had been put in the joint names of the unmarried parties the evidence was that the woman had paid all bar £500 of the monies to purchase the property. The Court of Appeal held that in such circumstances the man was entitled to nothing of the beneficial interest.

• Apportioning the equity in these circumstances can be complex and uncertainty surrounds the determination of the beneficial interest. What is clear is that 'equity is not equality' - in other words just because a party shows that he/she has a beneficial interest does not mean that he/she is entitled to an equal division of the equity. The guiding principle remains the size of the respective parties' contributions. Generally speaking a party will receive a share of the equity proportionate to the amount of money put into the property (see *Bernard* v *Josephs* [1982] Ch 391). A common intention as to the extent of the beneficial interest must be communicated: *Springette* v *Defoe* [1992] 2 FLR 388.

ii) Sole ownership

Section 53 of the Law of Property Act stipulates that no interest in land can be created or disposed of except by signed written document. However s53(2) provides that the above rules do not affect the creation or operation of resulting, implied or constructive trusts. In *Gissing* v *Gissing* [1971] AC 886 the house was in the husband's sole name. On separation he said 'Don't worry about the house - it's yours. I will pay the mortgage and other outgoings.' The wife had no claim on the basis of that statement.

Note that the establishment of a beneficial interest in property by cohabitees is very similar in principle to a spouse establishing an interest under the Married Women's Property Act.

The objective of these equitable doctrines is to prevent the legal owner standing on his strict legal rights when it would be unconscionable to allow it. The courts however require substantial evidence to establish the existence of a trust and therefore of a beneficial interest. In *Gissing* v *Gissing* (above) and *Pettitt* v *Pettitt* [1970] 2 WLR 966 some improvements to the home gave rise to no property rights and in *Burns* v *Burns* [1984] Ch 317 living together for 19 years and raising the couple's two children was held to be an insufficient contribution.

It has always been clear law that contributions to the initial deposit required to purchase the property and/or contributions towards the mortgage re-payments will (in the absence of evidence of intention to make a gift or a loan as, for example, in *Richards* v *Dove* [1974] 1 All ER 888) go a long way towards proving the existence of an implied/resulting trust in the contributor's favour. The courts readily infer that a sum of money may constitute a beneficial interest. In *Risch* v *McFee* [1991] 1 FLR 105 what was initially a loan was construed as a beneficial interest in the light of the subsequent co-habitation. It suggested that exceptionally later and more indirect contributions (eg paying for the installation of a major household item such as central heating at a time when the relationship was 'on the rocks') might operate as evidence of such a trust. (See, for example, *Cowcher* v *Cowcher* [1972] 1 All ER 943.)

However the possibility of such later contributions being of value in proving an implied/resulting trust has been severely doubted by the House of Lords in *Lloyds Bank* v *Rosset* [1990] 1 All ER 1111.

It is not easy to distinguish between implied/resulting trusts on the one hand and constructive trusts on the other; indeed the courts frequently do not distinguish between them. The courts attempt to establish the parties' intention from their conduct and the following general principles apply.

- If there is evidence of contribution to the purchase price this will normally be sufficient to prove that the parties intended a trust - ie the court will find an implied/resulting trust.

- In the absence of such direct contributions then the court will only find the existence of a trust (ie a constructive trust) if the non-legal owner can show (1) that such was the common intention of the parties and (2) he/she has acted to his/her detriment in reliance on such common intention: *Grant* v *Edwards* [1986] 3 WLR 114. See too *Springette* v *Defoe* [1992] 2 FLR 388.

A beneficial interest has been established in the following circumstances.

- Direct contributions to the purchase price: *Re Rogers Question* [1948] 1 All ER 328.

- Regular contributions to the mortgage repayments or contributions to the household expenses which enable the other to meet the mortgage repayments: *Fribrance* v *Fribrance* [1957] 1 All ER 357; *Grant* v *Edwards* [1986] 3 WLR 114. In *Grant* v *Edwards*, the man whose salary was £1200 per annum could not have supported a mortgage of £600 per annum without the salary of the cohabitee and she was therefore entitled to a half share.

- A direct contribution by labour towards the home: *Eves* v *Eves* [1975] 1 WLR 1338; *Cooke* v *Head* [1972] 1 WLR 518.

In *Cooke* v *Head* Miss Cooke had done substantial manual work in helping to build a bungalow. Denning LJ: '... Whenever two parties by their joint effort acquire property to be used for their joint benefit, the courts may impose or impute a constructive or resulting trust. The legal owner is bound to hold the property on trust for them both ... It applies to husband and wife, to engaged couples and to man and mistress, and maybe to other relationships too.'

(NB These two cases were decided ten years prior to *Grant* v *Edwards* at a time when the Court of Appeal took a much more flexible view of the requirements necessary to prove the existence of a constructive trust. On the approach in these cases the woman in *Burns* v *Burns* would have received a share in the value of the family home. Accordingly the question has to be raised as to whether *Cooke* v *Head* or *Eves* v *Eves* would be decided the same way today ie although the detriment may be shown could the common intention be proved?)

In *Ungarian* v *Lesnoff* [1990] 2 FLR 299 sufficient common intention and detriment to establish a constructive trust were found in a case where a woman gave up her university studies abroad to join her cohabitee in England.

The courts have not accepted the following to be sufficient.

- Being an unmarried housewife and looking after the other partner and their children: *Burns* v *Burns* [1984] Ch 317.

  In *Burns* the parties had lived together as husband and wife for 19 years and towards the end of the relationship she had put her earnings into the housekeeping. The Court of Appeal held that she did not have a share in the beneficial interest in the house which was in the man's sole name.

- Being a man's mistress for 13 years and living with him for five years: *Layton* v *Martin and others* [1986] 2 FLR 227.

  Here the judge made the point that the services she was expected to provide were to all intents and purposes those of a wife but her contribution was held to be insufficient.

  There must be evidence of a common intention that whereas one party has the legal estate in the property the other has a beneficial interest in it and that other party has acted to their detriment.

iii) Quantifying the beneficial interest

- In the event of the contributions of the parties being direct and quantifiable the courts will usually establish the beneficial interest in accordance with those shares.

- In other circumstances the courts will take into account all the relevant factors. In *Cooke* v *Head* (above) the court acknowledged the relevance of the following: '... the background of the parties with their earnings and contributions; the statements made to third parties ...; the method by which they saved, such as the money put in the money box; the method of repaying the mortgage instalments; the amount of the direct cash contribution of each; the amount of the work each had done on the property; the part each had taken in planning and designing the house ...' Miss Cooke obtained one third. In *Eves* v *Eves* however the claimant received one quarter. There is no set formula and decisions tend to be arbitrary.

• The other issue is at what time the resulting trust comes to an end. In *Hall* v *Hall* [1982] 3 FLR 379 Denning LJ, after establishing that the respective shares of the parties depended on all the circumstances (in this case the plaintiff was entitled to one fifth), argued that the trust should come to an end when the relationship comes to an end and accordingly the parties' interest should be valued at that time. More recently however in *Walker* v *Hall* [1984] FLR 126 and *Turton* v *Turton* [1987] 2 All ER 641 the Court of Appeal has stated that the shares should be valued at realisation.

b) *Occupation rights*

   i) Joint ownership

       • If spouses or unmarried couples hold property on a trust for sale as beneficial owners and the relationship breaks down, application can be made to the court under s30 of the Law of Property Act for an order of sale on the basis that one of the legal owners is unreasonably refusing his/her consent to a sale. The court can make an order that it thinks fit in the circumstances and will look to the original purpose of the trust. The court will ask itself the question: has the purpose behind purchasing the property together come to an end? Clearly if the relationship has ended then the purpose would have come to an end but not, necessarily, if there are children of the relationship.

       In *Re Evers' Trust* [1980] 1 WLR 1327 the court refused to order a sale as the house was still required to provide a home for the woman and the children. The court held that the house should not be sold until the youngest child reached 18.

       • Where an order for sale is not made the court will consider compensating the one party by for example requiring the party in occupation to pay the mortgage or an occupation rent.

       In *Dennis* v *McDonald* [1982] Fam 63 the applicant had left her cohabitee. The court did not make an order for sale but ordered the man to pay an occupation rent.

       Note that the right to remain in occupation for the sake of the children is subject to the rights of creditors should the other joint owner become bankrupt. In *Re Citro (a bankrupt)* [1990] 3 All ER 952 the Court of Appeal held that in such circumstances the cohabitee will be required to sell within a reasonably short period (ie 12 months) to allow the creditors to receive some of the monies due to them from the sale proceeds of the debtor's share in the house. (See also s336 of the Insolvency Act 1986.)

ii) Sole ownership

The unmarried cohabitee unlike the married partner does not enjoy the protection of her occupation rights given by the Matrimonial Homes Act 1983. However the cohabitee may gain a right of occupation in a number of ways:

- if she has a beneficial interest then she cannot be ejected by her partner and, furthermore, if she is also in actual occupation at the time of sale to a third party she may not be able to be evicted by the third party purchaser or mortgagee. She may well be able to rely on the principles enunciated in *City of London Building Society* v *Flegg* [1988] AC 54 (see chapter 5).

- Contractual licence

  A contract protected a woman in *Tanner* v *Tanner* [1975] 1 WLR 1346. She had given up the security of a flat to live in the house bought for her and her daughters by the male partner. She had a contractual licence to remain until the children had finished their schooling or until her circumstances changed.

  In *Layton* v *Martin and others* (see above) however, the courts refused to find that there had been any intention to create a legally enforceable contract.

  Note that in *Hardwick* v *Johnson* [1978] 2 All ER 935 Lord Denning, faced with this difficulty of showing an intention to create legal relations in order to prove a contract, reverted instead to the concept of an equitable licence. This concept has now been absorbed in the principle of proprietary estoppel.

- Proprietary estoppel

  In *Pascoe* v *Turner* [1979] 1 WLR 431 the plaintiff made improvements to a property, spending most of her savings, after being told following the breakdown of her relationship that the house and contents were hers. The plaintiff had relied on this statement and acted to her detriment on it. Furthermore the estoppel could only be satisfied in these particular circumstances by the transfer of the legal estate to her.

  Note that in *Re Basham* [1986] 1 WLR 1498 it was stated that there was no difference between the ingredients of proprietary estoppel and those required to prove a constructive trust.

13.3 Recent cases and statutes

Family Law Reform Act 1987

Children Act 1989

Springette v *Defoe* [1992] 2 FLR 388

Risch v *McFee* [1991] 1 FLR 105

Huntingford v *Hobbs* [1992] Fam Law 437

13.4 Analysis of questions

The University of London external examinations have not frequently included questions specifically on cohabitation. The rights of cohabitees vis-à-vis one another is, however, an increasingly important issue as the number of couples who choose to cohabit rather than marry increases. What should happen to the home they have shared particularly if it is in the sole name of one and even more particularly if there are dependant children is problematic. Some examiners regularly ask questions on cohabitation and students should be aware of this.

13.5 Questions

Question 1

'The settlement of cohabitants' disputes by existing legal principles of contract and trust is fair and workable. The creation of special laws for cohabitants or the extension of marital laws to them retards the emancipation of women, degrades the relationship and is too expensive for society in general and men in particular.' (Deech). Do you agree?

University of London LLB Examination
(for External Students) Family Law June 1985 Q4

General comment

This question involves a discussion on the law relating to cohabitees. Candidates are expected to comment on the present law and the view that it is adequate despite current criticisms of it, and calls for reform.

Skeleton solution

- Give a resume of the law at present and compare it briefly with the law relating to property disputes between spouses with reference to case law.

- Thereafter give an appraisal of the recommendations for changes in the law.

Suggested solution

The rights of unmarried partners in respect of property are governed by orthodox principles of property law and there are no special rules to be applied in the case of cohabitees although the courts have developed principles for drawing inferences from the relationship of the parties in such the same way as they do for a husband and a wife. The number of cases involving proprietary disputes between cohabitees coming before the courts has increased in recent years due to the fact that such relationships are now more common and no longer attract the social stigma they once did. However, although the law to be applied by the courts is the same as for disputes between a husband and wife which are to be 'decided by the principles of law applicable to the settlement of claims between those not so related, while making full allowance in view of that relationship' (*Pettitt* v *Pettitt* (1970)), the courts have experienced difficulty in resolving these disputes between cohabitees and the results may often be different from those seen in the case of disputes between husbands and wives (see *Burns* v *Burns* (1984)).

The law recognises and imposes obligations between a husband and wife, for example the husband's duty to maintain and to provide suitable accommodation for his wife, and accordingly principles have been developed regarding the division of matrimonial assets whereby inferences are drawn regarding the intention of the parties that such property should be jointly owned as the commitment they have undertaken in married life of a permanent relationship and a sharing of its burdens and advantages, suggests a similar form of sharing in relation to the matrimonial assets. Therefore in applications such as under s17 Married Women's Property Act 1882 where a court is empowered merely to declare rights deemed already to have been in existence, where there is evidence of contributions made by the parties to the acquisition or improvement of property, the courts often infer their intention as being that the property should be held in joint names.

In the case of unmarried partners, however, no such obligations apply or are recognised and it is difficult to draw inferences of proprietary intentions from the mere existence of a sexual relationship. There may be many reasons for the couple not marrying, ranging from the situation where, although they would wish to marry, they cannot do so, for example, because of the existence of an earlier marriage; to a situation where the parties do not wish to commit themselves to such a relationship and thereby to protect their independence. Therefore, the courts will have to consider the nature of the relationship between the cohabitees and decide what inferences, if any, may be drawn from the same with regard to proprietary interests. However, even where it is clear the parties are or have been living together as husband and wife in the full sense of that phrase, in view of the lack of recognised obligations emanating from such a relationship, the courts have so far displayed a reluctance to draw the same inferences as to ownership of property as would be drawn in a case of a husband and wife.

One of the most obvious examples of this attitude is the recent case of *Burns* v *Burns* (1984) where the parties had cohabited for nineteen years during which time the woman had given up her job, had two children by the man, and had looked after the family in a way that any wife would have done. However she was deemed to have no interest in the home as she had made no contribution to the acquisition of the same, and whilst expressing sympathy for the woman, the court felt that it could not depart from the inference, as evidenced by the legal title to the property, that the man was the sole legal and equitable owner. If the parties had been married and the property dispute had been the subject of a property adjustment claim under s24 Matrimonial Causes Act 1973 it is clear that the woman would have been deemed to have earned at least half a share in the property although it must be said that even a wife claiming an interest in s17 Married Women's Property Act, proceedings would have difficulty in establishing the same on these facts.

In resolving property disputes between cohabitees the court will therefore apply ordinary principles of property law. So if there is an express contract between the parties the court will give effect to its terms. In the absence of express terms the court may infer terms if there can be shown to have been a meeting of minds between the parties, an intention to create a legal relationship, sufficiently clear terms and considerations. As an example of these principles the cases of *Tanner* v *Tanner* (1975) and *Horrocks* v *Forray* (1976) should be compared. In the earlier case the male partner purchased a house for the defendant and their daughters, and the defendant moved out of her rent-controlled flat to live there. When the relationship broke down and the plaintiff claimed possession of the house on the basis that the defendant had a bare licence which had been revoked, the Court of Appeal held that a contractual licence could be inferred, the consideration for which had been the defendant's release of her rent-controlled accommodation on the terms that she would look after the children in the house. Therefore she was entitled to remain in the house until the children were of school age. However, in *Horrocks* v *Forray* the court refused to infer a contractual licence where the defendant had been the plaintiff's mistress for 17 years and had had accommodation and financial support provided for her by him, for although there was evidence that he had provided the accommodation for the mistress and the child of the relationship for their security, the court's view was that he was motivated more out of generosity than out of a fulfilment of any legally binding obligation.

Once a contractual licence is established, however, a court will give effect to its terms strictly as illustrated in *Chandler* v *Kerley* (1978) where the plaintiff purchased the defendant's home after her divorce at a considerably reduced price. The plaintiff informed the defendant that he would never put her out of the house even if their relationship broke down, but when the relationship did the court refused to imply into the defendant's licence to live in the house a term guaranteeing her continued occupation after the relationship ended in the absence of any express promise to that effect.

The courts often use the concepts of trusts to establish the proprietary interests in disputes between cohabitees in the same way as they do in the case of a husband and wife, where it would be wrong to rely on the absence of all formalities where an agreement can be inferred from the behaviour of the parties. Therefore if a mistress has contributed in money or money's worth to the acquisition or improvement of property, she will be deemed to have an interest in the same, just as a wife would have an interest, although case law on this point indicates that the courts are cautious in their assessment of the shares to be taken in such circumstances by a mistress, and awards have often fallen below what would be expected for a wife who would benefit from the inferences to be drawn from the nature of her relationship with her husband. Thus in *Cooke* v *Head* (1972) and *Eves* v *Eves* (1975) where houses were purchased for the parties who intended to marry when free to do so, and in the former case when the mistress made indirect financial contributions to the acquisition of the property, and in both cases where she carried out substantial works on the property which were recognised as probably much more than would have been done by a wife in similar circumstances, she was awarded a third and a quarter interest respectively. It might be argued that had the parties been married in these cases the awards would have been larger for the reason that it is easier to justify an inference of equal sharing in such a case, particularly at this time when the trend is for equal interests in matrimonial property in view of the wider recognition given to the role of a wife and her contribution to the family, including in non-economic terms.

The difficulties faced by the courts in proprietary disputes between cohabitees are great in view of the wide range of relationships which fall within this category, but the legal principles presently applied do not appear to make the task any easier, for as discussed above a court has to consider the nature of that relationship and then decide what inferences as to ownership of property can be drawn from it. However, as illustrated in the *Burns* case, a great deal of injustice may be felt by a party who has made a substantial contribution to a relationship in non-economic terms, but who would come out of that relationship with nothing because as the law stands no recognition can be given for anything other than financial contributions. Although in the field of disputes between husband and wives under s17 Married Women's Property Act 1882 Lord Denning had attempted to extend the law to take into account contributions made by a spouse to the welfare of a family and thereby in effect to create interests for that spouse in much the same way as is done in the Matrimonial Causes Act 1973 jurisdiction, this trend was criticised and stopped by the House of Lords in *Pettitt* v *Pettitt* and *Gissing* v *Gissing*. Nevertheless writers such as Stephen Cretney in *Principles of Family Law* point out that the law relating to married couples under s17 has been left a long way behind the developments under the Matrimonial Causes Act 1973 and this disparity cannot really be countenanced in these times. To the same extent this can be said about the law relating to cohabitees. As the relationship is more common, and as recognition of it in social terms is wider, the law should recognise the roles that are taken on by the parties concerned and to cater for the different types of relationship that can arise within cohabitation. Not all parties in such relationships consider that their independence from each other is paramount and in fact they enter into the relationship, and may live together as husband and wife in exactly the same way as parties who go through the marriage ceremony. These cohabitees may make a commitment to each other and conduct themselves in accordance with that commitment in much the same way as the woman in the *Burns* case, and yet presently there is no facility for recognising that commitment and the conduct consequent upon it. This surely must represent a gap in the law which in the interests of justice should be filled and which probably can be done without any undue increase in the amount of work to be done by the court as they already have to make a detailed investigation into the nature of the relationship between the cohabitees. Further, a recognition of the fact that rights can be acquired by non-economic contributions to a relationship may make the parties consider more carefully their position and their wishes before embarking on such a relationship. It is difficult to see, however, how such a development could be said to retard women's emancipation or degrade that relationship. Emancipation could be said to be served and not hampered by a proper recognition of the role undertaken by a woman in such a relationship, to the extent that she could be viewed as the man's equal and this recognition of equality could hardly be said to degrade her relationship. It may be true that the men concerned in these relationships would find such a change in attitude and the law expensive in that their partners may be given a share in property acquired by them during the relationship. However, this is not to say that the men would suffer unfairly as a result of any change. In the interests of justice such a change may be warranted.

Question 2

When Ivan and Jane became engaged in 1980 they exchanged rings. Ivan presented Jane with a ring worn by his late grandmother during her fifty year marriage: Jane gave Ivan a gold signet ring that she had bought for him. Ivan purchased a small bungalow in his name. He paid the deposit, and the mortgage instalments were paid from his earnings as a merchant banker. Jane rewired the house and repaired the roof.

They married in June 1983 shortly after Jane had become pregnant. She gave up her career and was paid an allowance by Ivan which was used to pay for food, clothes and to pay off the fuel bills. Jane was able to save enough from the allowance to buy a second-hand car and a number of expensive dresses and coats. She gave birth to Karen in February 1984.

In January 1988 Jane confessed to Ivan that he was not Karen's father and that the plumber, Len, was the true father. Ivan immediately left her.

Jane does not want a divorce and hopes that she and Ivan may eventually become reconciled.

Advise Jane who wishes to know:

a) who is entitled to the rings they exchanged at the time of their engagement;

b) whether she has a property interest in the bungalow purchased by Ivan;

c) whether the car, dresses and coats bought from savings made from her allowance belong to her.

Adapted from University of London LLB Examination
(for External Students) Family Law June 1988 Q4

General comment

This is a fairly typical though wide ranging question in property and maintenance rights in a non-divorce situation. The question is relatively straightforward, but it is long and candidates will have to pay close attention to time to ensure that all parts of the question are answered adequately. Not all parts of the question will necessarily carry equal marks. On the whole this is not a difficult question for the well prepared candidate. Note that the issues raised in (b) are the same as those relevant in a property dispute between cohabitees. Section 20(1) Law Reform (Miscellaneous Provisions) Act 1970 is a relevant consideration in the case of cohabiting couples of course if the dispute arises before marriage - see *Bernard* v *Josephs* (1982).

Skeleton solution

a) • Discuss application of Law Reform (Miscellaneous Provisions) Act 1970 to the dispute over the rings, and explain the principle to be applied distinguishing between engagement rings and other gifts which may still be of some assistance in determining the intentions of the parties.

- Consider whether the grandmother's ring is an heirloom, as evidence of whether it was a conditional gift. With regard to the signet ring consider whether it is an absolute or conditional gift. Consider also whether it is an engagement ring.

- Refer to an application under s17 MWPA 1882 to resolve the dispute.

b)
- Explain the use of a s17 MWPA application to resolve the dispute over the bungalow.

- Explain the general principles of equity and property law to be applied to establish the existence of a trust - direct/indirect contributions to the purchase price should be considered but may not apply on the facts.

- Consider MPPA 1970 which applies also to improvements made during an engagement (s20(1) Law Reform (Miscellaneous Provisions) Act 1970), in detail, with particular reference to the distinction to be made between works of maintenance and works of improvement.

c)
- Consider s1 MWPA 1964 - savings made from a housekeeping allowance and items purchased therefrom - with regard to the clothes, consider whether an agreement can be implied that they belong to the wife absolutely in view of the personal nature of those items.

- Consider also the presumption of advancement in relation to the clothes in view of the intended use of the allowance monies.

Suggested solution

a) As Jane does not wish to divorce Ivan and therefore will not be in a position to invoke the Matrimonial Causes Act 1973 to resolve her property interests, the ownership of the items in dispute will be determined in accordance with the general principles of property law. In the particular case of the rings exchanged at the time of the engagement, however, reference must also be made to the provision of the Law Reform (Miscellaneous Provisions) Act 1970 which deals specifically with engagement rings.

Jane will be able to make an application under s17 Married Womens' Property Act 1882 (hereinafter s17 MWPA 1882) for a declaration as to the ownership of all the property in dispute, including the rings. Section 17 provides that in any question between a husband and wife as to the title to or possession of property, either party may apply to any judge and the judge may make such order with respect to the property as he thinks fit. In deciding the question of the ownership of the rings the principles of the Law Reform (Miscellaneous Provisions) Act 1970 will be of some assistance to the court although its provisions were intended to be applied in cases of engagements which had been terminated, that is to resolve property disputes between formerly engaged couples. Here, Ivan and Jane did marry and so normally the ordinary principles of property law would be applied in any application under s17 MWPA 1882 to resolve their disputes. In the case of the rings however references to the 1970 Act will be of assistance to determine the intentions of the parties.

The 1970 Act makes a distinction between engagement rings and other gifts made between engaged couples. In the case of an engagement ring there is a rebuttable presumption that is was an absolute gift and therefore that it may be retained by the donee. The presumption can be rebutted by evidence that the ring was given subject to a condition, express or implied, that the ring should be returned if the marriage did not take place: s3(2) Law Reform (Miscellaneous Provision) Act 1970.

There is no doubt that the ring, given by Ivan to Jane would fall under the classification of an engagement ring. However it is questionable whether the ring given by Jane to Ivan will fall into the same category. If it does not, then, as with other gifts, the general law must be referred to in order to decide if the gift is conditional or absolute.

With regard to the ring given by Ivan to Jane we can assume that it was an absolute gift even though it did belong to his grandmother, and may therefore have taken on something of the character of an heirloom. The presumption that it was an absolute gift should apply here because even if Ivan was interested in retaining it in his family, the condition referred to in s3(2) of the 1970 Act which may rebut the presumption of an absolute gift, has been complied with, that is Ivan and Jane did marry. So we would have to look for further evidence of an intention that the ring was given to her as Ivan's spouse only if the return of the ring to Ivan is to be considered.

This same principle will apply to the ring given by Jane to Ivan. Normally, property intended to become part of the matrimonial home or assets will be deemed to be conditional. The test is, was the gift made to the donee as an individual or solely as the donor's spouse. If the gift is given to the donee as the donor's spouse then the gift is conditional; if however it is given to the donee as an individual, it will be deemed to be absolute and will be recoverable only in the circumstances any other gift would be recoverable, that is, for example where fraud or undue influence can be shown.

In the case of these two rings, particularly because any condition (as to the marriage taking place) that could be implied has been fulfilled, it is suggested that they will be deemed to be absolute gifts. There is no evidence of any intentions of the parties that they should be returned to the donors in the event of a marital breakdown. This is clearly the case in respect of the signet ring by Jane to Ivan, and perhaps also applies in respect of Ivan's grandmother's ring. However if Ivan can show an intention that that ring be retained in his family, to be worn only by female members of it, then he may be able to recover it in any s17 MWPA 1882 proceedings.

b) The s17 MWPA 1882 application referred to in part (a) above will also include Jane's claim to an interest in the bungalow purchased by Ivan.

We are told that Ivan purchased the bungalow following his engagement to Jane and that he paid the deposit and the mortgage instalments. We can assume that the legal estate is vested in his sole name. Prima facie therefore he owns the legal estate absolutely and Jane has no interest in it. However, a proprietary interest may also exist in equity and the court may look behind the title deeds and may establish the existence of a trust in which case Ivan would be deemed to hold the property on trust for himself and Jane in the shares declared by the court. Under s17 MWPA 1882 the court cannot create an interest for Jane merely because it thinks it just to do so in view of her contribution to the marriage (*Burns* v *Burns* (1984)), it may only declare existing interests: *Pettitt* v *Pettitt* (1970).

The legal estate can be displaced where there is evidence of a contrary intention on the part of the spouses. If there is evidence of an intention of the parties at the date of the acquisition of the property, the court will give effect to it by imposing a trust in relation to the proceeds of sale in the shares agreed upon. The court may draw inferences which a reasonable person would draw from the parties' conduct at the date of acquisition and subsequently. In *Gissing* v *Gissing* (1971) it was accepted that the parties may have agreed to hold property jointly without having used express words to communicate that intention to each other.

It can be inferred that the parties intended both to have an interest in the property conveyed to one of them if both contributed towards the acquisition of the property, either directly or indirectly (*Cowcher* v *Cowcher* (1972)). In this case seemingly only Ivan has contributed directly to the acquisition of the property in that he paid the deposit, and the mortgage instalments were paid from his earnings. However, if Jane could show that she made an indirect contribution towards the acquisition of the property then she will take an interest in the property. In *Cowcher* v *Cowcher* it was stated that an indirect contribution would suffice to establish an interest if either the husband and wife have consistently applied a system of meeting all the expenses, including those of the house purchase out of a common fund formed by pooling their resources, or if those contributions are directly referrable to the acquisition costs. Until her marriage and pregnancy, Jane worked although no information is given as to how she expended her income after the purchase of the bungalow. There is no evidence of a common fund. Further it is not clear from the facts whether, after their engagement they cohabited at all prior to the marriage and Jane giving up her career. If they did cohabit and Jane used her income to pay household expenses she might be able to claim an indirect contribution to the acquisition costs if she could show that her contribution freed Ivan's own earnings and enabled him to pay the mortgage instalments (*Gordon* v *Douce* (1983)). However such a contribution must be substantial (*Gissing* v *Gissing* (1971)).

On these facts therefore it is uncertain whether Jane can claim any interest in the property by virtue of any indirect contribution to the mortgage instalments. However she may acquire, or increase an interest in the property by virtue of her work on the property in rewiring the house and repairing the roof. Section 37 Matrimonial Proceedings and Property Act 1970 (hereinafter MPPA 1970) provides that where a husband or wife contributes in money or monies worth to the improvement of real or personal property in which, or in the proceeds of sale which either or both of them has a beneficial interest, the husband or wife so contributing shall, if the contribution is of substantial nature, and subject to any agreement between them to the contrary, be treated as having acquired by virtue of his or her contribution, a share or an enlarged share, as the case may be, in that beneficial interest of such an extent as may then have been agreed, or in the absence of such agreement, as may seem just in all the circumstances of the case.

The contribution must be in money or monies worth. It is not clear whether Jane paid for the work to be done, or did it herself. However either form of contribution will suffice. The contribution must be of a substantial nature (*Re Nicholson* (1974)) and it must effect an improvement to the property as distinguished from merely maintaining it (*Pettitt* v *Pettitt* (1970)).

It is probable that the costs of rewiring the property and the roof repairs would be substantial. However it is not clear whether these works would be viewed as improvements rather than as maintenance. In *Re Nicholson* it was suggested that a 'replacement' may not consititute an improvement although Professor Cretney suggests that this must be a question of degree. However he also states in his book *Principles of Family Law* that it is unlikely that work such as rewiring the house or carrying out extensive roof repairs would be considered as anything other than maintenance work even though the value of the work may be substantial. Certainly such a view would seem to apply in this case with regard to the roof repairs which can be seen as maintenance work only. However it is submitted that the rewiring of the house should be viewed as an improvement although it is not certain that it will be so viewed.

It may be the case therefore that unless Jane can show that she made an indirect contribution to the mortgage repayments she will have no interest in the bungalow at all because it is perhaps doubtful whether the work she carried out on the property, or paid to be carried out, will be viewed as improvements.

It should be noted that although the possible contributions discussed above were made before the marriage, the same principles will be applied in assessing interests in property of cohabitees (*Bernard* v *Josephs* (1982)) although the nature of the relationship between the parties will be an important factor when deciding what inferences can be drawn from their conduct. Further, s20(1) Law Reform (Miscellaneous Provisions) Act 1970 provides that s37 MPPA 1970 shall apply to contributions made by a party to an engagement in the same way as it applies to spouses.

c) At common law if a husband provided an allowance out of his income to his wife to pay housekeeping expenses, any sums not spent for that purpose, prima facie remained his and he would be entitled to any property purchased with any such savings (*Blackwell* v *Blackwell* (1943)). This principle was altered by s1 Married Women's Property Act 1964 (hereinafter MWPA 1964) which provides that where 'any question arises as to the right of a husband or wife to money derived from any allowance made by the husband for the expenses of the matrimonial home or for similar purposes, or any property acquired out of such money, the money or property shall, in the absence of any agreement between them to the contrary, be treated as belonging to the husband and wife in equal shares'.

Expenses of the matrimonial home will involve money spent in running the home and so the fact that Ivan paid the allowance to Jane to purchase food and pay the fuel bills will mean that it falls within the category of matrimonial home expenses even if it may be debatable whether the purchase of clothes would do so.

It seems therefore that any savings made by Jane out of the housekeeping allowance, or property purchased out of them will on an application of s1 MWPA 1964, belong to Jane and Ivan equally unless there is evidence of any agreement to the contrary between them. On the facts there is no evidence of any express agreement to the contrary unless it could be argued, in respect of the clothes that as Ivan paid the allowance specifically to include the purchase of clothes the presumption of advancement in respect of the clothes would apply and so they would be deemed to be a gift from Ivan to Jane and she would be entitled to them absolutely. If this is not the case it would seem that the car and the clothes belong to the parties equally. It is not clear whether the courts would be prepared to infer an implied agreement between the parties to the contrary where the circumstances would seem to demand it as for example in this case with regard to the dresses and coats which Jane bought. One can see the logic of deciding that Ivan should have an equal interest in the second hand car, but the clothes are such personal items which presumably Ivan would not be particularly interested in in any event, unless they are particularly valuable. It is suggested in Bromley's *Family Law* that in such circumstances it might be argued that there would be a tacit agreement that the whole should belong to the wife. If however the items of clothing are valuable, for example they include fur coats, then it would be difficult to argue such a tacit agreement and Ivan would be deemed to have a half interest in the clothes and Jane would have to account to him for half their value, or depending on the relative values of the car and clothes, agree to a distribution of these items on the lines that Ivan takes the car and she keeps the clothes.

Question 3

Imogen and Bruce were married in 1984. They have one child, Deborah, who was born in 1986 and Imogen is expecting a baby in August 1991. The matrimonial home, 'Misrule', which was purchased by Imogen out of funds provided by her parents, is registered in her name alone. Bruce, who is a builder, has been unemployed since December 1987, and since that time he has taken care of Deborah and carried out various improvements to the house which include the installation of central heating and an ornamental gas fire. In return, Imogen, who works as a doctor, has paid him a weekly allowance, some of which he has invested in a deposit account.

Unknown to Bruce, in 1988 Imogen borrowed £25,000 from the bank using the house as security, but she has been unable to keep up the repayments. The bank would like 'Misrule' to be sold so that it can recover the money. Further, Imogen and Bruce have been unhappy since January 1991, often arguing in front of Deborah. Imogen, who is concerned about Deborah and the effect the situation is having on the unborn child, has asked Bruce to leave 'Misrule'.

University of London LLB Examination
(for External Students) Family Law June 1991 Q4

General comment

Note that the establishment of a beneficial interest in property by cohabitees is very similar in principle to a spouse establishing an interest under the Married Women's Property Act.

This question requires a long and detailed answer on ownership of the matrimonial home, applying the principles under s17 Married Women's Property Act 1882, and on protecting rights of occupation against the bank and the other spouse. The question raises issues which have been tested regularly in the past, so it should pose no real problems for the well prepared student.

Skeleton solution

• Discuss ownership of the matrimonial home - s17 MWPA 1882. Have direct or indirect contributions towards the acquisition of the property been made?

• Consider s37 Matrimonial Proceedings and Property Act 1970; discount s1 MWPA 1964 in relation to the deposit account.

• Consider whether Bruce can resist the bank's claim - discuss the effect of the decision in *Williams and Glyn's Bank Ltd* v *Boland* - establish whether the conditions applicable under that case can be made out.

• In the event Bruce cannot establish an equitable interest, discuss s30 Law of Property Act 1925 application for sale - principles to be applied.

• Consider dispute over occupation with Imogen - s1 Matrimonial Homes Act 1983 - right of occupation - application under s1(2) MHA 1983 - application of principles in s1(3).

Suggested solution

Bruce requires advice as to his general position with regard to the property 'Misrule' in respect of ownership and his continued occupation of the same. The ownership of the deposit account must also be considered.

On the assumption that divorce proceedings are not contemplated at this time and therefore that the provisions of the Matrimonial Causes Act 1973 cannot be invoked to settle the dispute over the ownership of the property, the issue could be resolved by reference to s17 Married Women's Property Act 1882 (hereinafter MWPA 1882). Under s17 an application may be made by either a husband or wife to settle any question between them as to the title to or possession of property.

Under s17 MWPA 1882 the matter will be resolved by the application of general principles of property law. The legal estate in 'Misrule' is vested in Imogen's name and therefore, prima facie, the legal title is vested in her absolutely and Bruce has no interest in the property. However, a proprietary interest may exist in equity and the court may look behind the title deeds and may establish the existence of a trust, that is that Imogen holds the property on trust for herself and Bruce. Under s17 the court may not create an interest in the property because it considers it fair to do so; it may declare existing interests only (*Pettitt* v *Pettitt* (1970)).

The legal estate may be displaced where there is evidence of a contrary intention on the part of the spouses. If there is evidence of a contrary intention at the date of acquisition of the property the court will give effect to it by imposing a trust in the shares agreed upon. The court may draw inferences which a reasonable person would draw from the parties' conduct at the date of acquisition and subsequently and in *Gissing* v *Gissing* (1971) it was recognised that the parties may have agreed to hold property jointly without having used express words to communicate that intention to each other.

In this case, 'Misrule' was purchased by Imogen out of funds provided by her parents. It is not clear when the property was purchased, that is, before or after the marriage, or whether the funds provided were a gift from Imogen's parents to her and intended to be used for the purchase of the house. If so the next question must be whether the gift of the money was intended for Imogen alone or for both herself and Bruce. If the funds were provided to Imogen to purchase a home for herself and Bruce then it is likely that Bruce would be deemed to have a joint interest in the property on that basis alone. However if the funds were provided for Imogen alone then Bruce will have to rely on agreements or conduct which took place subsequent to the acquisition of the property to establish the existence of a trust.

It can be inferred that the parties intended both to have an interest in the property conveyed to one of them if both contributed towards the acquisition of the property either directly (through payment of the deposit or mortgage repayments) or possibly indirectly (for example by meeting household expenses which the owner could not otherwise afford to make: *Cowcher* v *Cowcher* (1972) although in *Lloyds Bank plc* v *Rosset* (1990) the House of Lords doubted the possibility of establishing a trust by indirect contributions.

There is no evidence of direct or indirect contributions of the nature referred to above having been made by Bruce. However he would acquire an interest in 'Misrule' by virtue of his works of improvement carried out at the property. Section 37 Matrimonial Proceedings and Property Act 1970 (hereinafter MPPA 1970), provides that where a husband or wife contributes in money or money's worth to the improvement of real or personal property in which, or in the proceeds of sale of which, either or both of them has or have a beneficial interest, the husband or wife so contributing shall, if the contribution is of a substantial nature, and subject to any agreement between them to the contrary, be treated as having acquired, by virtue of his or her contribution, a share or an enlarged share in that beneficial interest, of such an extent as may then have been agreed, or in the absence of such agreement, as may, in all the circumstances, seem just.

The contribution must be substantial and in money or money's worth. In this case Bruce carried out the work himself. Certainly the installation of the central heating will be considered a substantial improvement within the terms of s37 (*Re Nicholson* (1974)), but the installation of the ornamental gas fire will not be considered substantial enough. It is not clear what other improvements were carried out by Bruce. To come within the terms of s37 the contribution must effect an improvement to the property as distinguished from merely maintaining it (*Pettitt* v *Pettitt*), and so, depending on the nature and extent of those other improvements, Bruce may be deemed to have an interest in 'Misrule' by virtue of them as well as the installation of the central heating.

The next question to consider is whether there was any agreement between Imogen and Bruce as to an interest, if any, he was to have in the property by virtue of these improvements. We are told that 'in return' for the works carried out by Bruce, Imogen paid him a weekly allowance. Such an allowance would not come within the terms of s1 Married Women's Property Act 1964, which, in the absence of contrary agreement, establishes that where a husband pays a housekeeping allowance to a wife, it shall be treated as belonging to them equally. This payment by Imogen to Bruce may not be a housekeeping allowance and in any event the Act only covers payments made by a husband to a wife. Prima facie therefore monies paid by a wife to a husband as an allowance would remain the property of the wife unless a contrary intention could be established and so prima facie the deposit account would belong to Imogen.

If Imogen made the allowance to Bruce in payment for the works carried out at 'Misrule' and the intention was that he was not to take any interest in the property by virtue of these improvements, then the deposit account belongs to Bruce. However if the allowance was not intended for that purpose then Bruce will take an interest in the property but the deposit account is likely to be deemed to belong to Imogen. When deciding the extent of Bruce's interest, if any, in 'Misrule' the court will consider the increase in value attributable to the improvements and calculate Bruce's share accordingly.

The next problem to consider is whether the sale of the property, desired by the bank, can be prevented. It is not clear what Imogen's position with regard to such a sale would be. In the event of a dispute between Bruce and the bank as to whether the sale should take place, Bruce may be able to protect his occupation of 'Misrule' on the strength of his beneficial interest, if he has one.

It is clear that Bruce has a right of occupation in 'Misrule' by virtue of s1 Matrimonial Homes Act 1983 (hereinafter MHA 1983). This is a right '... if in occupation ... not to be evicted or excluded from the dwelling house or any part thereof by the other spouse except with the leave of the court given by an order under this section' (s1(1)(a) MHA 1983), and '... if not in occupation, a right with leave of the court so given to enter into and occupy the dwelling house' (s1(1)(b) MHA 1983). If Bruce has no equitable interest in 'Misrule' then his right of occupation derives from s1(1) MHA 1983. If he has an equitable interest then the right derives from s1(11) MHA 1983.

This is a personal right which is capable of registration as a notice if the land is registered or as a Class F charge in the case of unregistered land. If registered the right binds all subsequent purchasers. It is unlikely that Bruce registered his right of occupation. However even if this is the case there is a possibility that Bruce could resist the bank's claim in any event. In *Williams and Glyn's Bank Ltd* v *Boland* (1981) the House of Lords decided that a wife who was in occupation of the property and who was admittedly an equitable tenant in common was deemed to have an overriding interest under s70(1)(g) Land Registration Act 1925 by virtue of her occupation of the premises and her right to exclude all others without a similar right. Therefore she was able to defeat the claim of the bank who had granted a mortgage on the property. The House of Lords suggested that these principles would extend to unregistered land also on the basis of constructive notice if the purchaser made no enquiry about the spouse's interest. The existence, or not, of such an overriding interest has to be determined in relation to the date of execution of the mortgage (*Lloyds Bank plc* v *Rosset*). It is clear that in 1988, when the mortgage came into effect, Bruce was in occupation, as he still is. However whether he had an equitable interest in the property at that time, depends on the matters referred to previously such as the intention of Imogen's parents when they supplied the funds to purchase the home, and whether Bruce's works of improvement give rise to an interest or whether Imogen's payment of an allowance 'in return' suggests otherwise. If he can establish an equitable interest then the decision in *Williams and Glyn's Bank Ltd* v *Boland* will mean that he will be able to resist the bank's claim for it is clear that he had no knowledge of Imogen's borrowing and mortgage arrangements (see *Abbey National Building Society* v *Cann* (1990); *Bristol and West Building Society* v *Henning* (1985); *Winkworth* v *Edward Baron Development Co Ltd* (1987)). However if he has no equitable interest in 'Misrule' he cannot have an overriding interest and therefore may be unable to resist the bank's claim (*Midland Bank plc* v *Dobson* (1986)). In this event, if the bank obtained judgment against Imogen and then obtained a charging order on her interest in the property it could then apply for the house to be sold under s30 Law of Property Act 1925. In deciding whether to order sale the court will consider all the circumstances of the case and '... whose voice in equity ought to prevail' (*Re Turner* (1975)). Generally the creditor's claim will prevail although the court may postpone sale to prevent hardship to the family (see also *Re Bailey* (1977); *Re Lowrie* (1981); *Re Holliday* (1981)).

Even if Bruce does establish an equitable interest in the property and is therefore able to resist the bank's claim, we must now consider whether he may have to leave 'Misrule' in any event in view of Imogen's request that he leave because of their matrimonial difficulties.

As indicated above Bruce has a right of occupation in 'Misrule' under s1 MHA 1983. So long as one spouse has a right of occupation under the MHA 1983, either spouse may apply to the court for an order under s1(2) MHA 1983 declaring, enforcing, restricting or terminating the right of occupation (s1(2)(a)), or prohibiting, suspending, or restricting the exercise by either spouse of the right to occupy the house (s1(2)(b)), or requiring either spouse to permit the exercise by the other of that right (s1(2)(c)).

Therefore Imogen could seek an order to restrict or terminate Bruce's right of occupation, that is to exclude him from the home, or Bruce could apply to have his right of occupation declared and enforced, although it is unlikely for reasons discussed below that he will be able to exclude Imogen from the home.

When deciding what order, if any, to make the court must consider s1(3) MHA 1983. The court must consider therefore the conduct of the parties in relation to one another and otherwise, their needs and financial resources and those of Deborah and the expected baby, and any other circumstances which the court thinks relevant. The children's needs are not considered to be paramount (*Richards* v *Richards* (1984)), although they are important and if all other considerations are evenly balanced between Imogen and Bruce, they could tip the balance in favour of the parent with whom they will live.

If Imogen sought to exclude Bruce, the first question must be, is an exclusion order necessary? On the facts the relationship between Imogen and Bruce has deteriorated and we are told that Imogen is concerned about the effects on Deborah and the unborn baby. However the court will view exclusion as a draconian measure and will not grant such an order merely because it is convenient to do so in view of the breakdown of the relationship (*Kadeer* v *Kadeer* (1987)). Proof of violence or conduct adverse to the applicant or child is not a necessary requirement to the making of an exclusion order, but the court must recognise its draconian nature and only make it if it is reasonable and necessary to do so (*Wiseman* v *Simpson* (1988)). In this case the only factor which might suggest that ouster may be necessary is the possibly adverse effect the arguments and deterioration of the relationship between Imogen and Bruce might be having on Deborah. It is submitted that the effects on the unborn child, being unknown, cannot be taken into account. However, as there is no concrete evidence of any adverse effect suffered by Deborah, it would be doubtful that an exclusion order could be made. Certainly the deterioration of the relationship between the spouses will not merit such an order.

If the court decides that one party must leave the home, the needs and resources of the parties will be considered. The court is likely to favour the spouse with whom Deborah will live, presumably Imogen, and in view of the impending birth it is likely the court will not be minded to uproot Imogen at this time. She would experience more difficulty in finding alternative accommodation for herself and the children than Bruce would do so for himself alone (*Lee* v *Lee* (1984)). Deborah's need for suitable accommodation will be another factor that will be relevant and will add weight to Imogen's case. However as indicated above, on the evidence before us, there is no obvious case for suggesting that it is necessary or reasonable to make an exclusion order.

B   THE NON-MARITAL CHILD

13.6   Key points

The number of children born outside of marriage has steadily risen since 1960. Recent statistics indicate that 19 per cent of all births are to women who are not married. The majority of these children are not, however, the result of casual relationships but of stable unions. The continued discrimination against 'illegitimate' children has been accepted as unsupportable and in 1987 the Family Law Reform Act removed almost all remaining legal disadvantages for such children. However, parents of non-marital children do not automatically share parental rights in respect of their children. These are exclusively the mother's unless the father makes a successful application for shared parental rights under the Children Act 1989.

a) *The presumption of legitimacy*

   i)   A child born to a married woman is presumed to be the child of the woman's husband.

   ii) A child may be legitimated by the subsequent marriage of its parents: Legitimacy Act 1976.

   iii) In the case of void marriages a child is treated as legitimate if at the time of the act of intercourse or of the celebration of the marriage both or either of the parties reasonably believed the marriage to be valid.

        Note that under s26 of the Family Law Reform Act 1969 the presumption can be rebutted 'by evidence which shows that it is more probable that the person is legitimate or illegitimate as the case may be'. The courts seem to take the view that the evidence will vary according to the consequences: *W* v *K* [1988] 1 FLR 86.

b) *Family Law Reform Act 1987*

   Section 1 of the Family Law Reform Act 1987 (FLRA 1987) lays down the general principle that the question as to whether a person's mother and father were married to each other is legally irrelevant. Since the legal distinction between children whose parents are unmarried and those whose parents are married has now all but gone these rules are of most significance in determining the status of the parents rather than the child. The effect of the act can be summarised as follows:

   i)   Section 18 of the FLRA 1987 extends the right of intestate succession to all relationships and thus extends the position under the Family Law Reform Act 1969 which gave illegitimate children the same rights on intestacy of their parents as the children of married parents.

   ii) Affiliation proceedings were abolished and maintenance could be sought under the Guardianship of Minors Act 1971 as for a child of married parents. The powers of the court have been extended to include the transfer or settlement of property on the child. There is no longer a time limit on application and there is no longer any need for the mother to satisfy the definition of a single woman. Parents whether single or married could apply under the section. These provisions are now contained in the Children Act 1989.

   iii) Section 15 FLRA 1987 allowed for application to the court for the variation of any maintenance agreement entered into for the benefit of the child - now see Children Act 1989.

FAMILY LAW

c) *Continuing discrimination*

In some respects there continue to be discrimination:

   i)   An illegitimate child cannot acquire British citizenship through his father.

   ii) An illegitimate child cannot succeed to a title of honour.

   iii) Parental rights vest jointly in the father and mother of a legitimate child. The father of a child born outside marriage continues to have no parental responsibililty unless successful application is made under s4 Children Act 1989. He may also apply for a residence order under the Children Act 1989. The decision of the court will be based on the 'welfare principle'.

d) *Parentage*

   i)   Cohabitation does not give rise to a presumption of parentage.

   ii) Blood test evidence has been of central importance in establishing paternity: see Family Law Reform Act 1969. The Family Law Reform Act 1987 gives the courts a general power to direct the use of scientific tests and this will include DNA fingerprinting which can establish conclusive biological links. A refusal to be tested allows the court to draw what inferences it thinks fit.

   iii) Registration of a child's name under the Births and Deaths Registration Act 1953 is prima facie evidence of paternity. The registration itself gives rise to no legal rights.

   iv) Section 27 of the Act provides that a child born to a married woman as a result of artificial insemination shall be treated as a child of the marriage unless it can be shown that the husband did not consent. A woman's cohabiting partner is not treated as the father under this section.

13.7   Recent statutes

Children Act 1989

13.8   Analysis of questions

The rights of cohabitees and their children is an increasingly important issue but it is not a topic on which the University of London external examiners have often examined specifically. However, some examiners regularly ask questions on cohabitation so students should check their own syllabus. In any event, a knowledge of the material is essential because questions on the position of children whose parents are unmarried can appear in the context of another topic, for example nullity. The question below demands an understanding of custody, wardship, surrogacy and financial support for non-marital children.

13.9   Questions

Question 1

Osbert, a university law lecturer, and Nellie have been married for ten years. Knowing that his father, Peter, had left all his property 'to my grandchildren', Osbert was anxious to father a child who could take a share of Peter's estate but Nellie was unable to have children. They agreed that Osbert should commit adultery with Mandy, one of his students, with a view to Mandy bearing a child who would be handed over to Osbert and Nellie. Mandy, who adored Osbert, agreed to commit adultery with him although Osbert told her that he would 'make sure that she incurred no financial loss' as a result of this arrangement.

Mandy became pregnant by Osbert but, before the child was born, Nellie changed her mind about the agreement and had a violent argument with Osbert about the ethics of surrogacy. She left Osbert and went to live with Vic, the Vice-Chancellor of Osbert's University. Mandy gave birth to a boy, Quentin, in March 1987 and handed him over to Osbert who intends to bring up the child himself. Peter died two days after Quentin's birth.

a) Both Nellie and Mandy would now like custody of Quentin. What procedures must they invoke to obtain a residence order? How do you think that the court will resolve the custody issues that have arisen between Osbert, Nellie and Mandy?

b) If Mandy obtains custody of Quentin, can she obtain:

  i)   financial compensation from Osbert for the year of her legal studies she has missed; and

  ii) continuing financial support for Quentin?

c) Would Quentin be entitled to a share of the property that Peter has left to his grandchildren?

Adapted from University of London LLB Examination
(for External Students) Family Law June 1987 Q7

General comment

This is the first time that the topical issue of surrogacy has been raised in this examination although candidates must not be unduly distracted by it as the answers to the problems raised in part (a) and (b)(ii) are to be found in the standard 'Section 8' applications and in financial proceedings. The issue raised in (b)(i) is more complex, involving as it does the doubts expressed as to enforceability of surrogacy agreements. This part of the question is awkward because the law on this point is uncertain. However the rest of the question touches upon issues regularly examined in the past and therefore should hold no surprises for the well prepared candidate.

Skeleton solution

a)   • Establish Quentin's status as non-marital; explain in whom parental responsibility vest and the legal position of all three parties.

- Discuss the applications available to Mandy under the Children Act 1989.
- Explain and apply the welfare principle under s1.
- Discuss Nellie's application and comment on her prospects of success.

b) i) Consider the legality of a surrogacy agreement; distinguish a commercial arrangement from a private one; consider case law involving surrogacy agreements in eg adoption proceedings.

    ii) Discuss in detail an application under the Children Act 1989 - conditions to be fulfilled, orders to be made, and principles to be applied.

c) • Consider the effect of illegitimacy on succession rights at common law.

    • Describe the major change wrought by the Family Law Reform Act 1987.

Suggested solution

As Quentin was born to Mandy who was not and is not married to Osbert his status is non-marital. As the mother of a non-marital child, therefore, Mandy has the legal right to his custody unless and until those rights are displaced by a court order, for during her lifetime the parental responsibility in respect of Quentin vests exclusively in Mandy. Osbert can acquire parental responsibility either by a successful application under s4 for a shared parental responsibility order, by agreement again under s4 or by a successful application for a residence order under s8.

Nellie has no rights to the custody of Quentin at all as she bears no relationship to him. She too would have to make application for a residence order. Section 10 Children Act (CA) 1989 provides who can apply for s8 orders (which includes a residence order). She has no rights to apply so she would have to apply for leave. The court would have specific regard to: a) the nature of the proposed application; b) the applicant's connection with the child; and c) the risk that the proposed application would disrupt the child's life to such an extent that the child would be harmed by it. It may be that leave would be refused.

In all considerations in relation to a child's upbringing the court will have regard to the welfare of the child as the paramount consideration - s1 CA 1989. Under the section the court must consider several factors in respect of the child - 'the statutory checklist'. The relevant points to consider here would be firstly the child's physical, emotional and educational needs. The courts have in the past indicated that the best person to have care of a young child is the mother: see *Re W* (1983). However it was emphasised in that case that a major consideration is the capacity of the adults to form loving relationships.

In *Re W* (1990) the court stated that there was an assumption that as between an 18 year old mother and a 47 year old father a child aged eight months was prima facie better with the mother although this was an assumption that could be displaced. Material advantages will not outweigh emotional consideration.

The second point for consideration would be the likely effect on the child of any change in circumstances. The child is of course presently with Osbert. However the period of

240

time has been relatively short and the court may well feel that other factors should outweigh this point: see *Allington* v *Allington* (1985). Given that on the facts there is no reason to suppose that the conduct of the parties will give rise to concerns about their treatment of the child the final factor that the court would consider is the orders available under the Act. The CA 1989 provides much greater flexibility and a wider range of orders - for example in addition to the section 8 orders, the power to give directions.

In conclusion we can say that the court would be faced with a difficult choice. Mandy's claims are strong as his natural mother. Nellie has left Osbert. It could well be that the court would grant a residence order in favour of Mandy and in the circumstances a shared parental responsibility order in favour of Osbert with regular contact.

b)   i)   Private, as opposed to commercial surrogacy agreements are not illegal under the Surrogacy Arrangements Act 1985. It has been argued that surrogacy arrangements should be publicly controlled in the same way that adoption arrangements are controlled.

In *Adoption Application: Surrogacy AA 212/86* (1987) the applicants applied to adopt a child who had been born as a result of a surrogacy agreement between the applicants and the child's mother. A fee had been agreed between the parties but the court found that the mother had not entered into the agreement for commercial purposes. The fee was to compensate her for losses and expenses incurred by reason of the pregnancy. The court had to consider whether there had been a payment or reward made in contravention of s50 Adoption Act 1958. It found that there had not been such a payment, but that even if there had been, there was no absolute prohibition against adoption regardless of the adverse effects on the child and its family. Section 50(3) Adoption Act 1958 provides that the prohibition would not apply to a payment or reward which had been authorised by the court, which authority could be given retrospectively or retroactively. In this case the court approved the payment and the adoption order was made.

The question of enforceability of the surrogacy arrangements has yet to be settled and therefore Mandy's position is somewhat unclear. If she obtains custody of the child her personal position is not altered or the situation made much clearer. As she is not married to Osbert she has no right to claim maintenance from him for herself and therefore it would appear that the only way she could try to recover compensation for her lost year would be through contract.

She can however make a claim under the Children Act 1989 for the support of Quentin. Under the Act a single woman, which term includes an unmarried woman, who is pregnant or who has had a non-marital child, may apply to the magistrates court for a summons to be served on the man she alleges to be the father of the child, and if he is adjudged to be the putative father, it may make an order that he shall pay maintenance in respect of the child.

ii) As indicated in (i) above, Mandy may make an application for financial support for Quentin.

If the defendant is adjudged to be the putative father, as Osbert will be in this case, the court may order him to make periodical payments for the child's maintenance and education, and/or lump sum provision and a property adjustment order in the child's favour. In assessing what order to make the court must consider the income, earning capacity, property and other financial resources of the parties and the child, their financial needs and obligations and any mental or physical disability suffered by the child.

Unless otherwise ordered the order must not run in the first instance beyond the date of the child's birthday next following his attaining the upper limit of the compulsory school age, but it may be extended and continue after his eighteenth birthday so long as he is receiving instruction at an educational establishment or undergoing training for a trade, profession or vocation, or in any event, if there are special circumstances justifying this.

Mandy will be able to obtain support for Quentin in these proceedings and not for herself as such although her requirements must be considered when assessing Quentin's needs.

c) At common law a non-marital child had no right to participate in the intestacy of either his parents or grandparents or brothers or sisters. It was possible for a testator to make provision by will for his non-marital child although such a gift could be defeated by the application of certain rules such as the rule of construction, under which words in a will denoting family relationships were construed as referring to legitimate relationships only (*Sydall* v *Castings* (1967)), or the rule of public policy under which an non-marital child conceived after a disposition was made could not take under the will no matter how clear it was from the wording of the will that it was intended that such a child should take.

The Family Law Reform Act 1987 effected major changes in these laws and it removed many, though not all, of the succession disadvantages attached to 'illegitimacy'. Therefore a non-marital child now has the same rights as a marital child to share on the intestacy of his parents, although not on the intestacy of more remote relatives.

Section 1 of the Family Law Reform Act 1987 establishes a general principle that there should be equality for all children at law irrespective of the fact that they are 'legitimate' or 'illegitimate'. Section 1 states 'in this act and enactments passed and instruments made after the coming into force of this section references ... to any relationship between two persons shall ... be construed without regard to whether or not the father and mother of either of them or the father and mother of any person through whom the relationship is deduced have or have not been married to each other at any time'.

It seems therefore that Quentin will be entitled to take under his grandfather's will alongside any legitimate grandchildren unless a contrary intention can be shown from other terms in the will and the surrounding circumstances.

Question 2

'The growth in unmarried cohabitation and, more especially, in births outside marriage has already shifted the focus of the legal regulation of relationships towards parenthood, as the state has sought to define and enforce financial obligations between family members irrespective of marriage in an attempt to reduce calls on the public purse.' (Dewar)

Discuss.

University of London LLB Examination
(for External Students) Family Law June 1992 Q1

General comment

An essay question concerning the shift in focus of the legal regulation of relationships towards parenthood rather than marriage.

Skeleton solution

- State modern view of marriage and consider issue of marriage versus parenthood - Clive, Hoggett.
- Consider legal definition of parent.
- The Children Act 1989 and responsibilities described therein.
- The child of the family formula.

Suggested solution

Marriage is no longer the institution it once was. In today's society couples are just as likely, if not more, to live together, ie cohabit, rather than get married. The stigma that was once attached to cohabitation and especially to having children outside marriage seems to be disappearing. The law it seems is becoming just as 'modern' by recognising non-marital relationships as being akin to marital ones, especially when financial provision is in question. Dewar states that this is an attempt by the state to reduce calls on the public purse.

It has been suggested that marriage could be dispensed with altogether as the necessary mediating legal concept in ascribing rights and remedies to family members (Clive EM (1980) 'Marriage: An Unnecessary Legal Concept?' in J Eekelaar & S Katz (eds) *Marriage & Cohabitation in Contemporary Societies*) and that the objectives implicit in modern family law, of economic and physical protection of weaker family members, could be more satisfactorily achieved by the development of alternative mediating legal concepts such as parenthood: Hoggett B (1980) 'Ends and Means: The Utility of Marriage as a Legal Institution' in J Eekelaar & S Katz (eds) *ibid*.

If marriage is to be superseded by parenthood as the central determinant of the legal rights and responsibilities of family members, it has to be established what is meant in a legal sense by 'parent' - who in law is regarded as a parent and what is the legal significance of being one? Where mother and father are married at the child's birth they will both as parents have parental responsibility under the Children Act (CA) 1989. 'Parental responsibility' means 'all the rights, duties, powers, responsibilities and authority which by law a parent of a child had in relation to the child and his property'.

Mothers and fathers have equal parental responsibility: s2(1) CA 1989.

The important point under the Children Act regarding parents is that an unmarried father with commitment to a child can take steps to acquire parental responsibility either by agreement with the mother or by court order.

Parents and parental responsibility may be taken separately - the latter is only concerned with bringing the child up, caring for him and making decisions about him, but does not affect the relationship of parents and child for other purposes (Department of Health (1991) The Children Act 1989 Guidance and Regulations: para 2.2). Thus the question of liability to maintain a child or of succession rights is determined independently of the question of whether the parent in question has parental responsibility for a child: s3(4) Children Act 1989. The Children Act at various points uses the term 'parent' as distinct from person with parental responsibility. The term parent will include both parents of the child whether they are married to each other or not, and irrespective of whether both parents have parental responsibility under the Act. Thus the concept of parental responsibility only partially determines the legal position of parents. Also it is suggested that the concept of parental responsibility is itself ambiguous. Eekelaar has noted that it is capable of becoming two different meanings: first that parents are responsible to their children and second that it is parents rather than the state who should care for children ie it is parents (rather than anyone else) who are responsible for children. Eekelaar argues that the Act embodies the second rather than the first meaning and that this 'sharply reflects the identifiable political position' ie that the state is not willing to have responsibility.

Another point that can be made is regarding the 'child of the family' formula - the effect of this is to construct a link between a spouse and any children who are not the biological offspring of that spouse but who have been treated by the spouse in the required way. Once the link is established the courts can make orders for maintenance and property adjustment for the children.

The right attaching to marriage which is generally considered the most significant is the right of spouses to claim private maintenance from each during marriage or following a divorce. This right is not available to cohabitees; however, the practical significance of the exclusivity of this right may be overestimated because:

a) private inter spousal maintenance, if claimed, only rarely forms a significant element of the recipient's overall claim. More significant are earnings from employment and welfare benefits provided by the state;

b) an increasingly important factor influencing the availability of such support is the presence of children in the relationship, regardless of the marital status of the parents. For example, the rights of an unmarried parent to seek maintenance from the other parent on behalf of the child have been greatly improved by the provisions concerning child maintenance contained in the Children Act 1989, while the rights of spouses to claim maintenance following divorce are increasingly defined in terms of the needs of any children for which that spouse is caring: s8 CA 1989.

This shows the increasing child-centredness of the law and supports the argument that parenthood is increasingly becoming the most significant determinant of the rights and responsibilities of family members, superseding marriage in significance.

14 UNIVERSITY OF LONDON LLB (EXTERNAL) 1993 QUESTIONS AND SUGGESTED SOLUTIONS

UNIVERSITY OF LONDON
LLB EXAMINATIONS 1993
for External Students
PARTS I AND II EXAMINATIONS (Scheme A) and
THIRD AND FOURTH YEAR EXAMINATIONS (Scheme B)

FAMILY LAW

Monday, 14 June: 10.00am to 1.00pm

Answer *FOUR* of the following EIGHT questions

1 'The Child Support Act 1991 is a substantial step forward in protecting the interests of children.'

Discuss.

2 Antonia married Benjamin in 1975. Their marriage was an extremely happy one until early 1988 when Benjamin started having an affair with Clarissa, the owner of a local health club. Benjamin chose not to leave the matrimonial home, but moved out of the bedroom he shared with Antonia and into the spare room in June 1988. Antonia continued to do Benjamin's laundry for him and he ate at least four meals a week with her. In late 1991, however, Benjamin decided to move in with Clarissa.

Benjamin now wishes to divorce Antonia and marry Clarissa. Antonia does not want to be divorced as she believes that she and her husband can be reconciled. She is, further, very worried about her position with respect to the private pension plan that Benjamin has been investing in since their marriage.

Advise Antonia.

3 In 1990, Deborah, who was then 30, married Edward, a successful barrister, who was then 50 years old. Deborah, whose first husband, Frederick, an accountant, had died in a car accident in 1988, originally trained as an actress, but has not been employed outside the home since the birth of her twins in 1987.

After her marriage to Edward, Deborah and the twins moved into Edward's Chelsea home, which he had inherited from his mother and is valued at £500,000. As his current income is approximately £70,000 per annum she and the twins enjoyed a comfortable lifestyle. Indeed, Edward employed a full time nanny so Deborah was able to secure a small part in a film.

246

In 1992 Deborah discovered that Edward was incapable of being faithful and she has filed a petition for divorce.

Advise Deborah of the likely financial provision, if any, she can obtain for herself and the twins.

4   In January 1990, on Francesca's 30th birthday, Francesca and Graham announced their engagement. Graham gave Francesca an emerald and diamond ring, now valued at £20,000, and a matching bracelet, valued at £10,000. They moved into a flat which was a birthday present from Francesca's grandmother. The flat, which was registered in Francesca's name alone, was dilapidated and required structural improvements and decoration.

Although Graham is a tax consultant, he is a competent builder and he devoted each weekend of 1990 to improving the flat. He installed central heating, rewired the flat and decorated it and in 1991 he completely replaced the bathroom with units that he and Francesca bought together out of a joint bank account. According to Francesca's brother, a property surveyor, the improvements effected by Graham doubled the value of the flat.

Francesca has now decided that she no longer wishes to marry Graham and has asked him to leave the flat.

Advise Graham who is curious to know if he has any interest in the flat and who would like the jewellery he gave to Francesca returned to him together with his share of the bank account.

5   'Both the cases of *Re R* (1991) and *Re W* (1992) strike at the very core of the *Gillick* principle of respect for the decision-making of "mature minors".'

Discuss.

6   Henrietta and Josh began living together in 1982. In 1983 they had a son, Kevin. In 1990, after fertility treatment at a clinic, licensed under the Human Fertilisation and Embryology Act 1990, Henrietta gave birth to a girl, Lyn, who was registered as Josh's child.

In December 1992, Henrietta left Josh, taking Lyn and Kevin with her and went to live with Mark, with whom she had been having an affair since 1989. Henrietta has refused to allow Josh to see the children. She has told him that Lyn is Mark's child and that she will swear to this in any legal proceedings. She has also revealed that she intends to change the children's surname to that of Mark and to start a new life where Josh will be unable to find them.

Advise Josh.

7   Nora and Oswald, who are 35 and 40 respectively, are married and unable to have children. In January 1992 Oswald, who works as a social worker, met Pippa, who was 15 and pregnant.

Conscious that he and Nora were possibly too old to be considered appropriate to adopt a baby, and aware that Nora's chronic asthma might also affect their chances

247

of success as applicants, he, Nora and Pippa agreed that as soon as Pippa's baby was born, she would hand it over to the couple, so that they could apply to adopt it. Oswald and Nora also agreed to pay her £700 per month during her pregnancy, any medical and hospital bills and £3,000 when the baby was delivered, which they described as an 'adjustment allowance'.

The baby, called Quentin, was born in June 1992. Pippa immediately handed him over to Nora and Oswald. However, she began to regret giving up the baby and repeatedly, but unsuccessfully, demanded his return. In May 1993 Nora and Oswald made a formal application to adopt Quentin.

Advise Pippa.

8   Rosemary and Simon, who are unmarried, have two children, Tim aged 14 and Ursula aged four. In January 1993 Rosemary, a television presenter, who was then three months pregnant, lost her job. Since that time, the family have found it increasingly difficult to live on Simon's salary and the couple have often argued, sometimes in front of the children. Simon began to drink heavily and has assaulted Rosemary.

In May 1993 Rosemary, who has become increasingly worried about the tension in the household and particularly concerned about the welfare of her unborn child, sought the assistance of the Helpful Local Authority social worker, Miss Vane.

Miss Vane, who visits regularly, has become aware that Tim rarely attends school, although his parents do insist that he does so, and that Ursula is withdrawn and tense. She has noted that Ursula appears particularly upset during the frequent visits of her 16 year old cousin, Wilfred.

Advise Miss Vane of the procedures she can invoke to address the problems of Tim, Ursula and the unborn child.

Question 1

'The Child Support Act 1991 is a substantial step forward in protecting the interests of children.'

Discuss.

University of London LLB Examination
(for External Students) Family Law June 1993 Q1

General comment

This question invites discussion of why the Child Support Act 1991 was enacted, what its provisions are and how they are likely to work. The discussion should concentrate on how the provisions are likely to affect the children of families in receipt of child support and of families where the parent has to pay child support. Though the Act is largely designed to have financial consequences it is likely to have emotional consequences (eg in affecting the degree of contact between absent parents and their children). These consequences should also be discussed. The conclusion should answer the question as to whether the provisions of the Act represent a substantial step forward in protecting the interests of such children.

Skeleton solution

- Why the former court-based system of child maintenance was perceived as not working.

- An outline of the formula-based system for child support and why it is considered an improvement on the court-based system.

- An outline of the collection and enforcement procedures of the Child Support Agency.

- The likely consequences for parents with care and their children of child support both financial and emotional.

- The likely consequences for absent parents and children living with them of child support, both financial and emotional.

- A summary of the likely advantages and disadvantages of the child support system for such children.

- A conclusion on whether the Child Support Act 1991 can be described as a substantial step forward in protecting the interest of children.

Suggested solution

On 5 April 1993 the major provisions of the Child Support Act 1991 came into force. From that date the jurisdiction of courts to provide for child maintenance largely ceased. The court-based system which relied on the use of discretion within broad guidelines was replaced by an administrative and bureaucratic body, the Child Support Agency, which calculates the amount of money to be paid by an absent parent for his or her child (called child support) using a rigid and complicated mathematical formula.

249

Before outlining how the child support system works and how it is designed to operate, the question as to why such a change was needed should be addressed, particularly in relation to the interests of children of separated parents. Various reasons have been given for this radical change. Firstly the record of the courts in assessing and collecting maintenance from absent parents and paying it to the parents with the children (often in single parent households) was poor. Only three in ten absent parents paid regular maintenance payments for their children. There could be lengthy delays before maintenance orders were made. When orders were made they were often in low amounts which did not reflect the true costs of bringing up children. There was little consistency in the way courts approached the levels of maintenance and therefore little consistency in the amounts courts ordered to be paid. There was no automatic uprating of the orders for inflation or to reflect the fact that children were older. Enforcing maintenance was seen as weak and ineffective with most absent parents either paying nothing or paying irregularly. This was said to cause hardship to children since the parent they lived with could not rely on regular maintenance and so often had to fall back on state benefits. The quality of life for such children then suffered. Another powerful reason for change was the enormous cost to the state of parents with children (again usually one parent families) claiming income support and family credit because absent parents did not meet their financial responsibilities. By forcing all separated parents to meet their financial responsibilities towards their children it is hoped to provide a better life for the children and reduce the burden on the state of family breakdown.

The Child Support Act 1991 is aimed at tackling these problems by ensuring that absent parents meet their financial obligations towards their children. A parent with children living with him or her (called the parent with care) is able to apply to the Child Support Agency (CSA) for a maintenance assessment. Parents with care in receipt of income support, family credit and/or disability working allowance will have to apply to the agency for a maintenance assessment. If a parent with care (or other person with care) in receipt of such welfare benefits fails to cooperate with the CSA by not providing information about the absent parent(s) (unless harm or undue distress would result) then the adult personal allowance part of their benefit will be reduced by 20 per cent for the first six months and by 10 per cent for a further 12 months after that. This element of compulsion may well not work in the interests of the children. A parent with care may have reasons why he or she prefers not to reveal information about the absent parent. The absent parent may have been violent to the parent with care or to the children. The absent parent's conduct towards the children may mean that it is best that any link between them remains severed. Whether such reasons not to give information about absent parents will amount to harm or undue distress remains to be seen. This element of compulsion appears more to protect the interests of the state in reducing the cost of welfare benefits than to protect the interests of the children.

Those parents with care not in receipt of such welfare benefits need not use the CSA but may choose to do so. They will have to pay a fee to make an application for a maintenance assessment (as well as a fee to enforce payment). Such fees will be less than those charged by solicitors but may mean that those who might otherwise have been entitled to free legal aid for applications to court for child maintenance will have to pay for the services of the CSA. The CSA will take some years before it can take on its full workload. It has started with new applications made by parents whether on benefits or otherwise. It will then take over all existing maintenance orders where the parent with care is in receipt of income support, family credit and/or disability working allowance. Thereafter it will phase in its workload up to 1997 replacing all existing child maintenance orders with newly assessed amounts. For some children there will be a substantial delay before any benefits of the child support system are felt.

From 5 April 1993 the courts retain only a limited jurisdiction for child maintenance. Wealthy families can still use the courts if the amount of child maintenance exceeds the ceiling set for child support. Disputes about property and capital will still be resolved through the courts. Applications to maintain step-children will still be dealt with through the courts. This may lead to a fragmented approach if, on a family breakdown, application has to be made to the county court for property and capital orders and spousal maintenance but application has to be made to the CSA for child support. This may make agreements between separating parents more difficult which may not be in the interests of the children.

Once child support is calculated it will be reviewed every year to take into account inflation, the ages of the children and the financial circumstances of both parents. This will be a distinct improvement on the court-based system where variations could only be ordered on the application of either party.

The formula used to calculate child support will in most cases considerably increase the amounts of money paid by absent parents for their children. The formula is made up of a number of calculations:

a) the maintenance requirement (which represents the day to day expenses of looking after children) and is based on the income support rates not only for the children but for the adult looking after them;

b) exempt income (which calculates each parent's 'spare income' by taking their separate incomes) and taking away various allowances representing their essential living expenses);

c) assessable income (this is the take home income minus the exempt income for each parent);

d) the deduction rate (which is one half of assessable income up to the amount of the maintenance requirement - there are special provisions to allow for extra money to be paid);

e) protected income (which prevents the liable parent's income being pushed down to income support levels).

The maintenance requirements for two children aged 12 and five living with their mother amounts to £75 at April 1992 rates. Though the amount of child support the children's absent father would have to pay may be less than this figure, given the other calculations, he is likely to pay more than would have been the case under the court-based system of child maintenance. One notable feature of the child support formula is that only a limited allowance is made for any new family an absent parent may have. Under the court-based system an absent parent could argue that he or she had to maintain a new family and that there was little left for the first family who were left to rely on state benefits (see *Barnes* v *Barnes* (1972); *Stockford* v *Stockford* (1982)). Under the child support system the situation is almost reversed - the emphasis is on paying child support for the children of the first family. This may cause hardship for children or step-children of a second family. It should be said that the formula is very complicated and tries to take into account the many variables of families which have broken apart. This complexity is likely to lead to teething troubles as CSA staff get used to the difficult calculations involved.

The first £15 of income from child support will be ignored in calculating a lone parent's entitlement to such benefits as family credit but this is not the case with income support. In cases of single parents with children receiving income support the payment of child support will make no difference unless the single parent is able to go back to work and receive family credit plus the first £15 a week of child support. For such single parents with an income the CSA promises more effective enforcement of payments. Considerable powers and resources have been given to the CSA to trace absent parents and to investigate their financial circumstances (eg access to DSS and Inland Revenue records). It remains to be seen if this leads to more regular payments.

If an absent parent has his or her child to stay for 104 nights or more in a year then the amount of child support he or she has to pay is proportionately reduced. This may persuade absent parents to ask for greater contact with their children and seek contact orders from the courts where there is disagreement. In most cases this will be of benefit to the children but there may be cases where contact is pursued by the absent parent not for the welfare of the child but to reduce the amount of child support which has to be paid.

In conclusion it is difficult to describe the Child Support Act 1991 as a substantial step forward in protecting the interests of children. Its probable effect will be to oblige more absent parents to meet their financial responsibilities to their children and to pay more in the process. This will reduce the burden on the state of many one parent families. This does not mean that the children will necessarily be better off. Families on income support may see no change in their circumstances. Those on family credit will only see a limited gain. Forcing some mothers to reveal the identity of fathers may not be in the children's best interests. The children or step-children of some absent parents may be left in a worse financial situation because of the amount of child support the absent parent is obliged to pay. The Child Support Act 1991 is very much in its infancy so perhaps the safest answer to the question is 'only time will tell'.

Question 2

Antonia married Benjamin in 1975. Their marriage was an extremely happy one until early 1988 when Benjamin started having an affair with Clarissa, the owner of a local health club. Benjamin chose not to leave the matrimonial home, but moved out of the bedroom he shared with Antonia and into the spare room in June 1988. Antonia continued to do Benjamin's laundry for him and he ate at least four meals a week with her. In late 1991, however, Benjamin decided to move in with Clarissa.

Benjamin now wishes to divorce Antonia and marry Clarissa. Antonia does not want to be divorced as she believes that she and her husband can be reconciled. She is, further, very worried about her position with respect to the private pension plan that Benjamin has been investing in since their marriage.

Advise Antonia.

University of London LLB Examination
(for External Students) Family Law June 1993 Q2

General comment

This question invites discussion as to whether Benjamin can satisfy one or more of the facts which establish irretrievable breakdown and so enable him to petition successfully for divorce. Particular attention has to be paid to the living apart facts, particularly the fact of five years living apart. Advice has to be given as to whether such a fact can be satisfied and, if it can, the special defences open to Antonia in ss5 and 10 Matrimonial Causes Act 1973 and how they might safeguard the position as regards her widow's pension.

Skeleton solution

- The ground of irretrievable breakdown for divorce.

- Which of the five facts in s1(2) MCA 1973 could Benjamin seek to satisfy?

- The fact of living apart for five years - in particular 'living apart' in the same household.

- The defence in s5 MCA 1973 of grave financial hardship and unjust to grant a divorce, with reference to Antonia and the widow's pension.

- The safeguard in s10 MCA 1973 with regard to the widow's pension.

Suggested solution

Antonia should be advised that there is only one ground for divorce, namely that the marriage has 'broken down irretrievably' (s1(1) Matrimonial Causes Act (MCA) 1973). Benjamin would have to satisfy the court that this was the case and also establish one or more of five facts before he could successfully petition for divorce (s1(2) MCA 1973, *Buffery* v *Buffery* (1988)). Before discussing whether Benjamin could establish one or more of those facts Antonia should be advised that if Benjamin does petition for divorce any solicitor acting for him has to discuss the possibility of a reconciliation with him (see s6(1) MCA 1973). It is assumed that Benjamin does not wish to be reconciled with Antonia notwithstanding her wish to be reconciled with him.

Benjamin cannot petition on the fact of his own adultery (see s1(2)(a) MCA 1973). There is no indication of adultery on Antonia's part. There is no indication that Antonia has behaved in such a way that Benjamin cannot reasonably be expected to live with her as is required to satisfy the second fact (see s1(2)(b) MCA 1973). There is no indication that Antonia has deserted Benjamin or has so behaved as to drive him out in a manner amounting to constructive desertion (see the fact in s1(2)(c) MCA 1973). Antonia has made it clear that she does not want a divorce so she would not give consent as is required to satisfy the fourth fact, that of living apart for two years and the respondent consenting to the decree (see s1(2)(d) MCA 1973).

This leaves one remaining fact upon which Benjamin might seek to rely, that of living apart for five years (see s1(2)(e) MCA 1973). The facts in this case suggest that in June 1988 Benjamin moved out of the matrimonial bedroom and moved into the spare room. However, he did not move out of the matrimonial home until late 1991. If Benjamin wishes to petition for divorce immediately using the fact of living apart for five years he must show that he and Antonia were living apart within the same household from June 1988 to the time he actually left the household. It will not be easy for Benjamin to satisfy a court in this respect. Firstly a court will look to the statutory interpretation of 'living apart' whereby a husband and wife shall be treated as living apart 'unless they are living with each other in the same household' (see s2(6) MCA 1973). Benjamin may seek to argue that he and Antonia were no longer 'living with each other' from June 1988 even though he remained in the same house. He may also seek to argue that there was no 'household' from June 1988. It is important to note that Antonia continued to do Benjamin's laundry and that he continued to share at least four meals a week with her. This suggests that there was still a common household even though they did not share the same bedroom. In *Mouncer* v *Mouncer* (1972) there were similar facts. The husband and wife slept in separate bedrooms but ate their meals together and with the children. The wife prepared the meals. They shared the cleaning though the wife in that case did not do the husband's laundry. It was held that the spouses had not been living apart. They still shared the same household. The rejection of the normal physical relationship between husband and wife and the absence of normal affection was not sufficient to constitute living apart. On the basis of that authority it would appear that Benjamin would be unsuccessful in petitioning on the basis of five years living apart.

There is another authority, *Fuller* v *Fuller* (1973), where spouses living in the same house were held to be living apart. That case had special facts and involved a gravely ill husband going to live in the house where the wife lived with another man. The wife prepared the husband's meals which he ate with the rest of the household. She did his laundry. However both spouses clearly regarded the marriage as at an end since the wife lived with another man. The husband was no different to a lodger. That case can be distinguished from that of Antonia. Antonia did not regard the marriage as at an end during the relevant period. She and Benjamin continue to share the matrimonial household and apparently carry on as a household in terms of meals and laundry. In such circumstances it is unlikely that Benjamin could successfully petition on the basis of five years living apart at this moment in time.

Antonia should be advised that 'living apart' only requires one party to recognise that the marriage is at an end. This need not be communicated to the other party at the time the 'living apart' is said to commence though the court must be able to identify some occurrence confirming the petitioner's recognition that the marriage was at an end (see *Santos* v *Santos* (1972)). In the unlikely event that Benjamin is able to establish living apart he can show the court that this began at the moment he started his affair with Clarissa even if Antonia was not aware of that at the time.

With regard to Antonia's pension position it is assumed that if there is no divorce her position will remain unaltered. If there is a divorce she could lose her right to a share in that pension after Benjamin has retired and, after his death, her right to the widow's pension. In this respect she could defend a petition brought under s1(2)(e) if she could show that the dissolution of the marriage would result in grave financial or other hardship and that it would in all the circumstances be wrong to dissolve the marriage (see s5 MCA 1973). The court would consider all the circumstances including the conduct of the parties. Hardship includes the chance of acquiring pension rights (including a widow's pension) (see s5(3) MCA 1973). A private pension plan, when compared with a state pension, is likely to be a substantial benefit to Antonia. Therefore the loss of the chance of acquiring such a pension could amount to 'grave financial hardship'. If Antonia is relatively young and able to go out to work and re-establish herself and the prospect of the pension is remote because Benjamin is also relatively young, then the loss of the pension rights may be too remote and so not grave (see *Mathias* v *Mathias* (1972)). If Antonia is older, has not worked during the marriage and so has little prospect of financial independence and the prospect of enjoying the pension rights is in the foreseeable future then the loss of those rights is more likely to be grave (see *Dorrell* v *Dorrell* (1972)). This could be the case given that Antonia has been married to Benjamin for some 18 years. If Antonia is able to satisfy the court that she would suffer grave financial hardship she must also satisfy the court that it would be wrong to dissolve the marriage. If Antonia has been blameless and is of such an age and situation as to have little financial independence (having depended on Benjamin financially) then the court may conclude that it is unjust to allow Benjamin to divorce her. Benjamin may argue that it would be just to dissolve the marriage so that he can marry Clarissa but such an argument is likely to fail if the court considers that he has treated Antonia badly. Benjamin can also seek to compensate Antonia for any loss that she would suffer if there was a divorce (see *Parker* v *Parker* (1972); *Le Marchant* v *Le Marchant* (1977)). Caselaw suggests that such compensation would have to be generous in order to safeguard Antonia's position (see *Parker* and *Julian* v *Julian* (1972)).

Antonia should also be advised that should Benjamin obtain a decree nisi of divorce under s1(2)(e) she could prevent the decree from being made absolute until Benjamin satisfies the court that he need make no financial provision for Antonia or that he has made reasonable financial provision for her or has put forward firm proposals for such provision (see s10 MCA 1973). This is likely to force Benjamin to provide for Antonia to make up for any loss in his private pension.

In conclusion Antonia can be advised that Benjamin is unlikely to be successful in petitioning for divorce at this point in time. The only fact upon which he could seek to rely is that of living apart for five years and that fact would be difficult to establish given that he remained in the same household as Antonia for most of the five years period. Even if he were successful Antonia's financial position would be safeguarded by firstly s5 and then by s10 of the Matrimonial Causes Act 1973. Benjamin will be able to bring a petition based on five years living apart in late 1996 but again Antonia's financial position is likely to be protected by ss5 and 10.

Question 3

In 1990, Deborah, who was then 30, married Edward, a successful barrister, who was then 50 years old. Deborah, whose first husband, Frederick, an accountant, had died in a car accident in 1988, originally trained as an actress, but has not been employed outside the home since the birth of her twins in 1987.

After her marriage to Edward, Deborah and the twins moved into Edward's Chelsea home, which he had inherited from his mother and is valued at £500,000. As his current income is approximately £70,000 per annum she and the twins enjoyed a comfortable lifestyle. Indeed, Edward employed a full time nanny so Deborah was able to secure a small part in a film.

In 1992 Deborah discovered that Edward was incapable of being faithful and she has filed a petition for divorce.

Advise Deborah of the likely financial provision, if any, she can obtain for herself and the twins.

University of London LLB Examination
(for External Students) Family Law June 1993 Q3

General comment

This question deals with one of the few areas of child maintenance where courts continue to exercise jurisdiction, the maintenance of step-children or 'children of the family'. The term 'child of the family' needs to be explained as well as the considerations in ss25 and 25A of the Matrimonial Causes Act 1973 which a court will take into account in deciding whether to exercise its wide powers of financial provision in ss23, 24 and 24A of the 1973 Act. The likelihood of a clean break order for Deborah and the particular considerations in s25(3) as far as the twins are concerned need discussion in advising on what kind of orders could be made against Edward.

Skeleton solution

- The jurisdiction of the court to deal with financial provision for step-children in light of the Child Support Act 1991.
- Definition of 'child of the family' and whether the twins are children of Edward and Deborah's family.
- The considerations in ss25 and 25A MCA 1973.
- The likely order for Deborah in light of the clean break provisions.
- Section 25(3) MCA 1973 and the likely orders for the twins.

Suggested solution

Advice is requested concerning the likely financial provision, if any, Deborah can obtain from Edward for herself and the twins. Since Deborah has filed for divorce she can seek orders for financial provision under ss23, 24 and 24A of the Matrimonial Causes Act (MCA) 1973. These sections give the court wide powers to make financial provision on divorce including orders transferring, settling or selling property, lump sum orders and maintenance orders.

Two matters need to be considered as far as financial provision for the twins is concerned. Firstly courts have largely lost the jurisdiction to make maintenance orders for children since the Child Support Act 1991 came into force on 5 April 1993 and a government agency (the Child Support Agency) took over the assessment and collection of financial support for children. Deborah can be advised that the Child Support Act 1991 only applies to the natural or adopted children of the absent parent (see s8 Child Support Act 1991). Since the twins are the step-children of Edward the court would retain the jurisdiction to make financial provision for them. Secondly the court could only order Edward to make financial provision for the twins if they were each a 'child of the family' ie they had been treated by both parties as children of the family (see s52 MCA 1973). The test is an objective test which looks at how Edward treated the twins. In this case it appears that Edward did treat the twins as children of his family by having them live with him and Deborah, employing a nanny to look after them and giving them a comfortable lifestyle over the two years of the marriage.

In deciding whether and, if so, how to exercise its wide powers to order financial provision, the court will have particular regard to certain considerations. The court will give first consideration to the welfare of the twins (se s25(1) MCA 1973). This does not mean that their welfare will outweigh all other considerations but will be of first importance in deciding what financial provision is just (see *Suter* v *Suter and Jones* (1987)). The need for the twins to be properly housed and maintained will be of first importance. The court will have regard to the income, property and other financial resources of Edward and of Deborah. It will take Edward's relative wealth and his inheritance into account. The court will consider both his and Deborah's earning capacity both now and in the foreseeable future including any increase in that capacity which it would be reasonable, in the court's opinion, for a party to take steps to acquire (see 25(2)(a) MCA 1973). The twins are now six years old and presumably attending primary school. Deborah has trained as an actress and has recently started to make use of her earning capacity in this respect. She should be prepared to make the most of her earning capacity in these circumstances.

The court will consider the financial needs, obligations and responsibilities of both Edward and Deborah as they are now and will be in the foreseeable future (see s25(2)(b) MCA 1973). Deborah's obligations will include the need to house the children and provide for them. Such needs will be particularly important since the welfare of the children is the first consideration. The court will consider the standard of living enjoyed by each party before the breakdown of the marriage (see s25(2)(c) MCA 1973). The court will have regard to the comfortable lifestyle Deborah and the children had while living with Edward for the two years of the marriage and may make orders reflecting that lifestyle (see *Foley* v *Foley* (1981)). The court will have regard to the age of the parties and the duration of the marriage (see s25(2)(d) MCA 1973). Deborah is of an age where she could reasonably be expected to have an earning capacity and enough time to establish some independence, though her obligations to her children limit her in this respect. The marriage was relatively short. This may persuade the court to limit Edward's duty to provide financially for Deborah though his duty towards the twins is likely to be more long term. The court will have regard to the contributions made by both Edward and Deborah to the welfare of the family, including looking after the home and caring for the children (see s25(2)(f) MCA 1973). Credit will be given to Deborah's contribution in looking after the twins though her contribution may not be counted as great as a full time mother given that a nanny was employed to look after the children. Edward will also be given credit for providing the family with a comfortable lifestyle and providing the nanny. If Edward neglected his responsibilities to Deborah and the twins this could be considered as a lack of contribution (see *West* v *West* (1977)) but there is no specific information on this point. Deborah should be advised that the court will only consider the conduct of the parties if it is such that, in the opinion of the court, it would be inequitable to disregard it (see s25(2)(g) MCA 1973). The court is unlikely to have regard to Edward's conduct since the ordering of financial provision is usually a mathematical exercise rather than a moral one (see *Duxbury* v *Duxbury* (1987)). A court would not be likely to increase any order for financial provision in order to punish Edward for his infidelities. If Deborah attempted to use the court in this way it would probably lengthen the proceedings with no likelihood of gain to her. Conduct has been considered relevant in some instances but these have been exceptional (eg where a spouse has unilaterally and unreasonably abandoned the other spouse who has been blameless - see *Cuzner* v *Underdown* (1974) and *Robinson* v *Robinson* (1983)). The court will also consider the value of any benefit Deborah would lose as a result of the divorce (eg a pension right) (see s25(2)(h) MCA 1973) but there is no information on this point.

Deborah should be advised that in considering financial provision for her the court will consider whether it would be appropriate to exercise its powers so that the financial obligations of each party towards the other will be terminated as soon after the divorce as the court thinks just and reasonable (see s25A(1) MCA 1973). If the court decides to make a maintenance order for her it must consider whether it is appropriate to require the payments under such an order to be made for only such term as would be sufficient to enable her to adjust without undue hardship to the termination of her financial dependence on Edward (see s25A(2) MCA 1973). The court will consider Deborah's age, her present work and how secure it is and her future job security in light of her need to care for the twins. If the court concludes that Deborah has little job security particularly in light of her responsibilities to the twins it may consider that a clean break is not appropriate (see *Day* v *Day* (1988)). If the court considers that she has job security even with her responsibilities for the children and the uncertain nature of the acting profession it may make no maintenance order for her or limit the period of any maintenance order it makes.

In considering financial provision for the children the court will take into account their financial needs and the way they are being educated, including what plans Deborah and Edward had for their education (see s25(3)(a) to (d) MCA 1973). Since the twins are not Edward's natural children the court will consider the extent to which he assumed responsibility for their maintenance over the two years of the marriage and on what basis (see s25(4) MCA 1973). He appears to have assumed full responsibility for them and is likely to be obliged to provide for them financially (see *Day* v *Day*).

In all the circumstances the court is likely to order that Edward make some financial provision for Deborah. The marriage was short, Deborah is relatively young and in work, albeit not very secure work. She enjoyed a comfortable lifestyle with Edward. The court is likely to make a clean break order by obliging Edward to pay a lump sum for her and/or provide her with a property for her and the twins to live in. The court may also make a limited period maintenance order. Such orders would provide her and the children with secure accommodation and Deborah with sufficient to enable her to adjust to the end of the marriage and maintain something of the lifestyle she has become used to. Edward appears to have the financial resources to comply with such orders. The court is unlikely to oblige Edward to maintain Deborah until her death or remarriage given the shortness of the marriage and the clean break provisions. Edward is likely to be obliged to maintain the twins until they finish full time education. Providing for their accommodation and enabling them to have a reasonable lifestyle will be the court's first consideration. The court may also take into account the twins' need to be looked after while Deborah is at work (though they will now be attending school). This could increase any maintenance order made for the children.

Question 4

In January 1990, on Francesca's 30th birthday, Francesca and Graham announced their engagement. Graham gave Francesca an emerald and diamond ring, now valued at £20,000, and a matching bracelet, valued at £10,000. They moved into a flat which was a birthday present from Francesca's grandmother. The flat, which was registered in Francesca's name alone, was dilapidated and required structural improvements and decoration.

Although Graham is a tax consultant, he is a competent builder and he devoted each weekend of 1990 to improving the flat. He installed central heating, rewired the flat and decorated it and in 1991 he completely replaced the bathroom with units that he and Francesca bought together out of a joint bank account. According to Francesca's brother, a property surveyor, the improvements effected by Graham doubled the value of the flat.

Francesca has now decided that she no longer wishes to marry Graham and has asked him to leave the flat.

Advise Graham who is curious to know if he has any interest in the flat and who would like the jewellery he gave to Francesca returned to him together with his share of the bank account.

University of London LLB Examination
(for External Students) Family Law June 1993 Q4

General comment

This is a straightforward question about property disputes between an engaged couple. The provisions of the Law Reform (Miscellaneous Provisions) Act 1970 have to be discussed in relation to the engagement ring, the bracelet and the bank account. The property dispute requires discussion of s37 Matrimonial Proceedings and Property Act 1970 (which appears to provide the most direct answer to the consequences of the work Graham has done on the flat). Given s37 of the 1970 Act there appears to be no need to explore the uncertain world of resulting and constructive trusts.

Skeleton solution

- Engagement ring is presumed to be an absolute gift (s3(2) LR(MP)A 1970).

- Bracelet may be an absolute gift or conditional on getting married.

- What was the intention of the parties in relation to the money in the joint bank account? Bank account may be held in equal shares but property bought with money from account may belong to individual. ·

- Application of s37 Matrimonial Proceedings and Property Act 1970 in terms of substantial improvements made to the flat.

- Application for declaration under s17 Married Women's Property Act 1882.

Suggested solution

Graham asks for advice as to whether he has any interest in the flat. He also asks whether he is entitled to have the engagement ring and bracelet returned to him. He also wants the return of his share of the bank account.

In relation to the emerald and diamond ring it is assumed that this was an engagement ring. The engagement ring is presumed to be an absolute gift by Graham to Francesca (see s3(2) Law Reform (Miscellaneous Provisions) Act (LR(MP)A) 1970). Graham could seek to rebut that presumption by proof that the ring was given with a condition that it be returned should the engagement be broken off. For example if the ring was a family heirloom Graham might persuade a court that the ring was meant to be kept in his family and that on the breaking of the engagement it should be returned. There is no evidence suggesting that this is the case. In the absence of such evidence it would appear that Francesca is entitled to keep the ring.

Whether Francesca can keep the bracelet will depend on the circumstances of Graham giving it to her. If he intended it as an absolute gift Francesca may keep it. If he intended it as a gift conditional on the parties marrying then it should be returned to him. Since the bracelet matches the ring the fate of the ring is likely to determine that of the bracelet. Therefore it appears that Francesca is entitled to keep the bracelet.

Ownership of the money in the joint bank account will depend on the intention of Graham and Francesca. If the bank account was intended to be held equally and used as a common purse (as opposed to being held in the shares each contributed to it) then a court is likely to order that Francesca and Graham receive the money in the bank account in equal shares (even if Graham put in more money than Francesca or vice versa) (see *Jones* v *Maynard* (1951)). However, property bought by one party for his or her own benefit using money from the joint account may be held to belong to that party since a joint bank account not only allows one party to spend money for the mutual benefit of both parties, but also to spend money for the sole benefit of one party (see *Re Bishop* (1965)).

Graham can be advised that the work he has done in the flat is likely to have given him an interest in it. He has contributed in money and money's worth to the improvement of the flat by the work he has done for many weekends over 1990 to improve the flat. His contribution appears to be substantial. The installation of central heating has been held to be a substantial contribution in this context (see *Re Nicholson* (1974)). Rewiring the flat is also likely to have been a substantial contribution as was the replacement of the bathroom. The redecorating in itself may not amount to a substantial contribution since that may be likened to normal DIY work (see *Button* v *Button* (1968)) but taken in the context of the other work may become 'substantial'. The substantial nature of the work is underlined by the effect that the work has had on the value of the flat Unless there was an express or implied agreement between Graham and Francesca otherwise, Graham will be treated as having acquired a share in the beneficial interest of such an extent as seems just in all the circumstances (in default of any agreement between the parties as to the quantification of shares) (see s37 Matrimonial Proceedings and Property Act 1970). Since Graham's contribution appears to have doubled the value of the flat he is likely to be entitled to a one half beneficial interest in it. Graham can be advised that the work he has done to the flat may give rise to an interest under a resulting or constructive trust. However the law covering resulting or constructive trusts is not easy to apply and is not always clear. Unless there is clear evidence of a common intention between Francesca and Graham that Graham have a beneficial interest in the flat and that Graham acted to his detriment based on that common intention it is likely to be difficult for Graham to establish a beneficial interest in the property (see *Lloyds Bank* v *Rosset* (1990)). He has not made any financial contribution to its purchase which might give rise to a resulting trust. In a case concerning an unmarried couple one party did substantial work to improve a house. It was held that he had no beneficial interest in the property in the absence of an express agreement or common intention. Since the man did the work without a clear understanding as to the financial basis on which the work was done he did so at his own risk (see *Thomas* v *Fuller-Brown* (1982)). As Graham's position by virtue of the engagement appears to be covered by clear statutory provision there appears to be no need to advise him further with respect to this difficult area of trust law.

Graham can be advised that he may apply to the court under s17 Married Women's Property Act 1882 for a declaration as to his interests in the jewellery, the bank account and the flat, provided that he makes the application within three years of the termination of the engagement (see s2(2) LR(MP)A 1970).

Question 5

'Both the cases of *Re R* (1991) and *Re W* (1992) strike at the very core of the *Gillick* principle of respect for the decision–making of "mature minors".'

Discuss.

University of London LLB Examination
(for External Students) Family Law June 1993 Q5

General comment

The question invites discussion of the House of Lords decision in *Gillick* and how it affected the rights of older children to consent to their own medical treatment. The *Gillick* decision was heralded by some as establishing the right of children to make decisions about themselves. A number of cases have considered the rights of 'mature' children and appear to have taken a narrower approach to the principles in *Gillick*. Such cases include *Re R (a minor)* (1991) and *Re W* (1992). These two cases appear to have restricted such rights but may be confined to their particular facts. The answer to this question involves outlining the facts and the basis of the decisions in each case (in particular in relation to s8 Family Law Reform Act 1969) and concluding as to the current situation as it has developed from *Gillick* and the extent to which *Gillick* competent children retain the right to make decisions about themselves.

Skeleton solution

- The position of parents and children in relation to the medical treatment of children and the required consent for such treatment - in particular s8 Family Law Reform Act 1969.

- The facts and decision in *Gillick* v *West Norfolk and Wisbech Area Health Authority*.

- The facts and decision in *Re R (a minor) (wardship: medical treatment)*.

- The facts and decision in *Re W(a minor) (medical treatment)*.

- Other relevant cases after *Gillick* and the impact of the Children Act 1989.

- Conclusion as to how the principles of *Gillick* have been affected by these subsequent cases and the position of mature children in relation to medical treatment.

Suggested solution

This question asks about the responsibilities and rights of parents and any child of such parents when that child requires medical treatment and consent has to be given for that treatment. Section 8(3) of the Family Law Reform Act 1969 provides that a child who has attained the age of 16 years can effectively consent to medical treatment. Such a child could consent to medical treatment even though a parent or other person with

LLB YEAR 2/3 E:
JUN

SUBJECT	DATE	
LAND LAW	17.6.94	
TORT	20.6.94	
FAMILY LAW	15.6.94	
INTERNATIONAL TRADE LAW	17.6.94	
INTRODUCTION TO E C LAW	16.6.94	
COMPANY LAW	15.6.94	
PUBLIC LAW 2	14.6.94	
AGENCY LAW	16.6.94	
EQUITY & TRUSTS	13.6.94	
LAW OF PERSONAL TAXATION	17.6.94	
EVIDENCE	21.6.94	

AM TIMETABLE
1994

ME	VENUE	DURATION
- 12.30	PS 136	3 HOURS
- 12.30	PS 529	3 HOURS
- 5.00	PS 136	3 HOURS
- 12.45	PS 235A/B	3 HOURS & 15 MINUTES
- 4.15	AWD 4	2 HOURS
- 12.30	PS 235	3 HOURS
4.00	PS 235A	2 HOURS
- 11.45	AWD 3	2 HOURS
- 5.00	PS 136	3 HOURS
- 5.15	AWD 6	3 HOURS
- 12.45	AWD 3	3 HOURS

parental responsibility did not consent. The position with regard to children under the age of 16 years is less clear but important guidance was given in the case of *Gillick* v *West Norfolk and Wisbech Area Health Authority* (1985).

The case of *Gillick* concerned written advice given to doctors through the defendant health authority stating that they could, in certain circumstances, give contraceptive advice to a child below the age of 16 years without the knowledge or consent of the child's parents. A mother of children below the age of 16 challenged the legality of the document. The House of Lords upheld the document's legality and in the process gave guidance on the medical treatment of children. Lord Fraser said that parental rights to control a child existed for the benefit of the child and not of the parents. In most cases parents relaxed their control as the child became older and more mature, though this varied with the particular child's understanding and intelligence. There could not be rigid parental rights over a child at any particular age - the situation depended on the judgment on what was best for the child. In most cases the best judges of a child's welfare were the child's parents and normally important medical treatment could only be carried out with parental consent. However there might be circumstances in which a doctor was a better judge than the parents of medical advice and treatment conducive to a child's welfare. Lord Fraser could find no provision compelling him to hold that a child under 16 lacked the legal capacity to give a valid consent provided the child had sufficient understanding and intelligence to know what was involved. Lord Scarman agreed and said that though statute held that a child over 16 could give a valid consent to treatment no statute or case ruled on the extent of parental rights in relation to children under that age. Unless Parliament intervened the courts could establish flexible principles to do justice in the particular circumstances of each case. The decision in *Gillick* was heralded as establishing the principle that a 'mature' child could make decisions about him or herself. The right of a parent to take decisions for the child lasted only as long as the child needed protection. Once the child was sufficiently mature such parental rights ended. However *Gillick* was only concerned with the giving of consent. The corollary of that is the right to refuse to give consent and the wider right to determine what medical treatment should be given. It was left to later cases to deal with situations where such issues were raised and to decide how far reaching the *Gillick* decision was.

The decision in *Gillick* was considered in *Re R (a minor) (wardship: medical treatment)* (1991) where a 15 year old girl had a history of disturbed behaviour. She suffered from a psychotic state which required medication. She was sometimes rational when she could refuse medication and then became irrational when medication would be given. She was made a ward of court so that medication could be given whether or not she consented. It was held that for a child to have a *Gillick* capacity to refuse medication there had to be a full understanding on a lasting basis of the consequences of the treatment and its withdrawal. Since the girl did not have a lasting capacity the court could authorise treatment against her will. The Court of Appeal also held that wardship involved powers wider than those of parents The court could override a ward's decision to refuse treatment (even where the child was *Gillick* competent) where this was in the child's interests. Lord Donaldson MR considered that a *Gillick* competent child had the power to consent to medical treatment but that power was concurrent with that of a parent. Only failure to consent or refusal of consent by both parent and child could create a veto. The consent of either parent or child enabled treatment to be lawfully administered. Lord Donaldson's view was that a *Gillick* competent child did not have the right to determine medical treatment. He went further than the other two judges of the court in suggesting that a parent could authorise treatment against the wishes of a *Gillick* competent child. It was clearly the majority view that the High Court via wardship could override the wishes of a *Gillick* competent child.

The position of a 16 year old was considered in *Re W (a minor) (medical treatment)* (1992). The girl was in local authority care. She suffered from severe anorexia nervosa and was admitted to a specialist residential unit. The local authority wished to move her to a hospital when her situation deteriorated but the girl wanted to stay in the unit and cure herself. The local authority asked the court to direct that she be moved to the hospital and be given medical treatment without her consent. The application was granted and the girl appealed. Her condition then deteriorated to such an extent that she had to be moved to the hospital as an emergency measure. It was held that the court could override the wishes of a child in the child's best interests where such refusal could lead to death or serious injury even where the child had sufficient understanding and intelligence to make an informed decision about refusing medical treatment. The court approached its decision by strongly favouring the child's wishes. Section 8 of the 1969 Act enabled a child of 16 years or older to give consent to medical treatment which would otherwise be a trespass on the child's person but it did not give that child the absolute right of veto to refuse medical treatment. This decision confirms the narrow interpretation of *Gillick* in limiting the right of a mature child to determine his or her own medical treatment.

In *Re E (a minor) (wardship: medical treatment)* (1993) the High Court overruled the wishes of a 15 year old boy and his parents in their refusal (for religious reasons) to allow him to be treated for leukaemia. The child's veto was not considered to be binding on the court. Great weight was given to his religious beliefs but his welfare was paramount. Without the treatment he would die. A similar conclusion was reached in *Devon County Council* v *S* (1993). It is accepted law that a doctor may treat a child in an emergency without the consent of the child or the parents.

In conclusion it is probably not accurate to say that *Re R* and *Re W* strike at the very core of the *Gillick* principle. The two decisions have taken a narrower view of *Gillick* than some may have wished. *Gillick* was concerned with the right of a child to consent to medical treatment. *Re R* and *Re W* were concerned with the right of a mature child to veto treatment or determine what medical treatment should be given. Advocates of children's rights would argue that in dealing with these situations the two cases have taken a restrictive view of the rights of mature children, particularly with the judgment of Lord Donaldson in *Re R*. What is clear is that a child's right to determine his or her own medical treatment is limited where that decision would lead to harm to the child. The court will either assume that the child is not *Gillick* competent or will use the wardship jurisdiction to override the child's wishes.

Question 6

Henrietta and Josh began living together in 1982. In 1983 they had a son, Kevin. In 1990, after fertility treatment at a clinic, licensed under the Human Fertilisation and Embryology Act 1990, Henrietta gave birth to a girl, Lyn, who was registered as Josh's child.

In December 1992, Henrietta left Josh, taking Lyn and Kevin with her and went to live with Mark, with whom she had been having an affair since 1989. Henrietta has refused to allow Josh to see the children. She has told him that Lyn is Mark's child and that she will swear to this in any legal proceedings. She has also revealed that she intends to change the children's surname to that of Mark and to start a new life where Josh will be unable to find them.

Advise Josh.

University of London LLB Examination
(for External Students) Family Law June 1993 Q6

General comment

This question deals with the legal status of an unmarried father in relation to his natural child and in relation to a child conceived after fertility treatment. The provisions of the Children Act 1989 in conferring 'parental responsibility' must be outlined as well as how an unmarried father can acquire parental responsibility. The status of a child born after artificial treatment needs to be clarified. Since paternity is in dispute the procedures for dealing with this must be discussed. Contact orders, prohibited steps orders and specific issue orders under the Children Act 1989 also require discussion in relation to changing the names of the children and taking them away from their father.

Skeleton solution

- Henrietta has parental responsibility for Kevin but not Josh under Children Act 1989.

- Legal status of Lyn under Human Fertilisation and Embryology Act 1990.

- Disputed paternity and procedures for determining paternity.

- How Josh can acquire parental responsibility for the children.

- Application by Josh for contact with the children and the principles under the Children Act 1989 which must be applied.

- Application by Josh for prohibited steps order preventing any change to the children's surnames and principles to be applied.

- Prohibited steps order in relation to removing the children away from Josh and principles to be applied.

Suggested solution

Josh firstly needs advice on his legal status in relation to Kevin and Lyn. In relation to Lyn she has been conceived after fertilisation treatment. Where the treatment is such that both Henrietta and Josh are the genetic parents of Lyn then both Henrietta and Josh are the legal parents of Lyn. If Lyn was born as a result of sperm donated by a stranger, since Henrietta was treated at a licensed clinic Josh would be treated as her legal father provided the treatment was provided for both Henrietta and Josh (see s28(3) Human Fertilisation and Embryology Act (HFEA) 1990). This is assumed to be the case since Lyn is registered as Josh's child. Any donor of sperm for licensed treatment is likely to have consented to the use of his sperm in accordance with the 1990 Act and would not be treated as Lyn's legal father (see s28(6) HFEA 1990). Henrietta has now stated that Lyn's father is Mark. It is difficult to see how Henrietta can sustain this assertion. If Josh's sperm was used for the fertility treatment then he is Lyn's genetic father. If Henrietta is stating that Mark donated the sperm then, as indicated by s28(6), he could not be treated as Lyn's father if the clinic followed the proper procedures. She may be stating that the fertility treatment was in fact not successful and that she only conceived as a result of her affair with Mark. If that is the case she would have the burden of overcoming s28(3). She could ask the court to direct blood tests to establish paternity through DNA analysis (see s20(1) Family Law Reform Act (FLRA) 1969). This would involve blood samples being taken from Henrietta and Lyn and from Mark and Josh then comparing them to ascertain the genetic parents of Lyn. Josh can be advised that there is no compulsion to comply with such tests but if a person fails to take any step required for the purposes of the tests the court may draw such inferences as appear proper in the circumstances (eg the person is afraid of the result - see s23(1) FLRA 1969; *McVeigh* v *Beattie* (1988). If Josh is the genetic parent of Lyn DNA tests would establish this and exclude Mark. However, a court may take some persuasion that Henrietta's assertion that Mark is Lyn's father (made some two years after her birth) has any credibility and so may consider that there is no need for tests and treat Josh as Lyn's legal father on the basis of the existing evidence (see *B* v *B and E* (1969)).

Josh should be advised that as an unmarried father he does not have parental responsibility for either Kevin or Lyn and that parental responsibility resides solely with Henrietta (see s2(2)(a) Children Act (CA) 1989). 'Parental responsibility' is defined as 'all the rights, duties, powers, responsibilities and authority which by law a parent of a child had in relation to the child and his property' (see s3(1) CA 1989). Josh should therefore seek to acquire parental responsibility for the children which he can share with Henrietta (see s2(5) CA 1989). He can acquire parental responsibility for the children by agreement with Henrietta (see s4(1)(b) CA 1989). This does not seem possible given Henrietta's views. He can apply for a residence order so that the children live with him whereupon a court would have to grant him parental responsibility (see s12(1) CA 1989). Josh does not appear to want the children to live with him so this does not seem appropriate. He can apply to the court for a parental responsibility order granting him parental responsibility for the children (see s4(1)(a) CA 1989). In order to persuade a court that he should have parental responsibility he would have to show that he has demonstrated commitment to each child and that each child is attached to him and state clearly the reasons why he wants parental responsibility and why it will benefit each child (see *Re C (minors)* (1992)).

Josh would have to apply for a contact order if Henrietta refuses to allow him to see the children. A contact order is an order requiring the person with whom a child lives to allow the child to visit or stay with the person named in the order or for that person and the child otherwise to have contact with each other (see s8 CA 1989). He could also apply for a prohibited steps order to prevent Henrietta from changing the children's surname. He could also ask for a prohibited steps order to prevent her from moving without informing Josh of the children's whereabouts including preventing her from going abroad with them if that is her intention. A prohibited steps order is an order that no steps which could be taken by a parent in meeting his or her responsibility for a child and which is of a kind specified in the order shall be taken by any person without the consent of the court (see s8 CA 1989). As a parent of Lyn and Kevin he has the right to make such an application (see s10(4) CA 1989 and *Re C (minors) (adoption: residence)* (1992)).

In considering whether to grant such orders the court will treat the welfare of Lyn and Kevin as paramount (see s191) CA 1989). All other considerations will be relevant only in so far as they shed light on what is in the best interests of each child (see *J v C* (1969)). The court will assume that any delay in deciding upon the applications is likely to prejudice the children's welfare (see s1(2) CA 1989). It will set down a timetable for the applications and ensure that the parties stick to it (see s11 CA 1989). The court must also be satisfied that to make an order would be better than making no order at all (see s1(5) CA 1989). Since Henrietta appears to have adopted an unreasonable and uncompromising attitude in trying to cut Josh out of the children's lives orders are clearly needed if it is in the children's best interests to maintain a relationship with their father. The court must also have regard to particular considerations in deciding whether to make any s8 order which is opposed (see s1(3), (4) CA 1989). The court will consider the wishes and feelings of each child considered in the light of their age and understanding (see s1(3)(a) CA 1989). Lyn is only aged three so she is too young to be able to express clear wishes and feelings. Kevin is aged ten. If he is a mature boy for his age then his views will be very important in deciding what is in his best interests (see *M v M (a minor: custody appeal)* (1987) and *M v M* (1992) where the views of eleven and ten year old children were decisive). The court will probably ask a welfare officer to prepare a welfare report. The wishes of the children will appear in that report so that neither child need come to court (though Kevin is of age where he could come to court to give his views).

The court will also consider each child's physical, emotional and educational needs (see s1(3)(b) CA 1989). If Henrietta wishes to uproot the children and take them to a strange place to live with Mark whom they may not know this may be very damaging emotionally (eg in the loss of contact with Josh and with friends of their own age) and educationally (eg in terms of Kevin's schooling). This will also be considered in terms of the likely effects on each child of any change in their circumstances (see s1(3)(c) CA 1989). The children may be very upset about not being allowed to see Josh with whom both Kevin and Lyn have had a relationship for almost all of their lives. The court will consider each child's age, sex, background and any particular relevant characteristics (see s1(3)(d) CA 1989). Any harm the children have suffered or are at risk of suffering will also be considered (see s1(3)(e) CA 1989). They may well suffer emotional harm if Henrietta is allowed to do what she proposes. The court will look at how capable Henrietta and Josh are in each meeting the children's needs and possibly how capable Mark is in this respect (see s1(3)(f) CA 1989). The court will also consider its range of powers in deciding how best to serve the children's interests (see s1(3)(g) CA 1989).

In all the circumstances Josh is likely to be successful in obtaining a contact order so that he can visit and be visited by the children who know him as their father. He is also likely to be successful in obtaining an order prohibiting Henrietta from moving abroad or from moving without notifying Josh and so frustrating any contact order. He is also likely to be successful in obtaining an order prohibiting Henrietta from changing the children's surnames. Both children have presumably had Josh (or Henrietta's) surname since birth. Kevin will be used to that surname and be known at school and by his friends by that surname. Changing the children's surname to that of Mark is unlikely to be in their best interests particularly if they have no firm relationship with Mark and treat Josh as their father (see *W v A (child: surname)* (1981)). If Josh has had an important role to play in the children's lives the court will seek to preserve their relationship despite Henrietta's wishes.

Question 7

Nora and Oswald, who are 35 and 40 respectively, are married and unable to have children. In January 1992 Oswald, who works as a social worker, met Pippa, who was 15 and pregnant.

Conscious that he and Nora were possibly too old to be considered appropriate to adopt a baby, and aware that Nora's chronic asthma might also affect their chances of success as applicants, he, Nora and Pippa agreed that as soon as Pippa's baby was born, she would hand it over to the couple, so that they could apply to adopt it. Oswald and Nora also agreed to pay her £700 per month during her pregnancy, any medical and hospital bills and £3,000 when the baby was delivered, which they described as an 'adjustment allowance'.

The baby, called Quentin, was born in June 1992. Pippa immediately handed him over to Nora and Oswald. However, she began to regret giving up the baby and repeatedly, but unsuccessfully, demanded his return. In May 1993 Nora and Oswald made a formal application to adopt Quentin.

Advise Pippa.

University of London LLB Examination
(for External Students) Family Law June 1993 Q7

General comment

This question deals with an adoption application made by a couple who have privately arranged to have the child placed with them and have made payments to the surrogate mother in consideration of the adoption. The legality of such a private placement and of such payments needs to be considered. The mother requires advice on her legal status and the likelihood of an adoption being granted. This will require discussion of the principles behind adoption and in particular the need for parental consent. Finally the mother will need to be advised as to how she can secure the return of the child using a residence order under the Children Act 1989.

Skeleton solution

- Prohibition on private placements for adoption (s11(1) Adoption Act 1976).

- Prohibition of payments in consideration of adoption and possible exceptions (s57 Adoption Act 1976).

- Requirements as to the making of an adoption order - in particular the need for parental consent.

- The likelihood of an adoption order being made.

- Obtaining a residence to gain the return of the baby (applying the principles of the Children Act 1969).

Suggested solution

Pippa needs advice on how she can oppose the adoption application made by Nora and Oswald and how she can obtain the return of Quentin.

Firstly Pippa should be advised that there is a legal prohibition on private placements for adoption unless the proposed adopter is a relative of the child or the placement is pursuant to a high Court order (see s11(1) Adoption Act (AA) 1976). It appears that Nora and Oswald have committed an offence punishable with imprisonment and/or a fine by arranging for Pippa to hand her baby over so that they could apply to adopt it (see ss11(3) and 72(3) AA 1976). Pippa would also be guilty of such an offence by being party to the agreement. However, given her age and the probable 'undue influence' of Oswald (who may possibly have been her social worker and in some other position of trust with her) and Nora it is unlikely that Pippa would be prosecuted or, if prosecuted, punished in any substantial way for her part in the agreement which she now regrets ever having made.

Pippa should also be advised that it is not lawful to give any person any payment or reward for or in consideration of an adoption or to gain a parent's agreement or in order to persuade a person to hand over a child with a view to adoption or to make any arrangements for adoption (see s57(1) AA 1976). It appears that Nora and Oswald have committed an offence, again punishable by a fine and imprisonment, by paying Pippa during her pregnancy, plus her medical bills and the £3,000 adjustment allowance (see s57(3) AA 1976). Pippa may also have committed an offence by receiving the money but she is unlikely to be prosecuted or substantially punished for the reasons already outlined. Nora and Oswald may try to argue that the payments to Pippa involved no profit or reward to her. If such financial arrangements are sincere and there is no profit motive then a court may either treat the payments as lawful or retrospectively authorise them (see s57(3) and *Re Adoption Application (surrogacy)* (1987)). This could be the position in Pippa's case if, for example, the £700 a month represented lost wages and the £3,000 lost employment opportunities. Given Pippa's age this does not seem probable and the payments are likely to be held to be unlawful. Given these breaches of the law Nora and Oswald's adoption application is so tinged with illegality as to have little prospect of success.

Pippa should also be advised as the requirements Nora and Oswald have to meet in making an adoption application. As a married couple of sufficient age Nora and Oswald can apply for adoption (see s14 AA 1976). Since neither are related to the baby and the placement has not been arranged through an adoption agency or by order of the High Court the baby must be at least 12 months old and have lived with them for at least a year preceding the making of the application (see s13(2) AA 1976). This latter condition is likely to invalidate Nora and Oswald's application since they have only had Quentin since June, 1992 yet have made the application in May, 1993, some 11 months afterwards.

In reaching a decision about whether the baby should be adopted the court must have regard to all the circumstances giving first consideration to the need to safeguard and promote the welfare of the child throughout his childhood and to ascertain the child's wishes and feelings and give due consideration to them (see s6 AA 1976). This means that the child's welfare is not paramount and does not outweigh all other considerations but is of the first importance (see *Re D (an infant) (adoption: parent's consent)* (1977)). Pippa must give her unconditional consent to the adoption with full understanding of what is involved or have her consent dispensed with by the court (see s16 AA 1976). Since Pippa clearly does not want Quentin adopted Nora and Oswald would have to persuade the court to dispense with her consent. They could argue that Pippa is withholding her consent unreasonably, or has persistently failed without reasonable excuse to discharge her parental responsibilities for her baby or that she had abandoned Quentin (see s16(2)(b), (c) and (d) AA 1976). It is difficult to see how a court could be satisfied as to any of these grounds. Pippa cannot be said to have 'abandoned' Quentin because she left the baby with people she presumably trusted would provide for him and has asked for his return (see *Watson* v *Nickolaisen* (1955)). She could not be said to have persistently failed to discharge her parental responsibilities for Quentin since she has not actually had the opportunity to look after him and has repeatedly asked for his return. Whether Pippa could be held to be withholding consent unreasonably is an objective test judged at the date of the hearing of the application. The court would ask itself what a reasonable parent would do taking into account the welfare of the child (see *Re W (an infant)* (1971)). In a similar case to Pippa's, a mother handed a child over to a couple for adoption under pressure and when she never wanted the child adopted. It was held that she withheld agreement reasonably in the circumstances since she reasonably hoped to provide a secure home for the child in the future. The upset of moving the child in that case (who had only lived with the applicants for a year) would be temporary. It was held that the child would benefit from the care of her natural mother (see *Re PA (an infant)* (1971)). If Pippa's circumstances are such that she could not reasonably expect to provide for Quentin while Norma and Oswald could provide a warm and secure home then her consent might be dispensed with (see *Re P (an infant) (adoption: parental consent)*

(1976)). The prospects of Pippa caring for Quentin properly would be crucial to how the court regarded her withholding of consent.

Since the adoption application would be opposed by Pippa the court would appoint a guardian ad litem (an independent social worker) to investigate the case on Quentin's behalf. Both the guardian and the local authority would prepare reports for the court. One matter which would be investigated is the health of the applicants. Norma and Oswald would have to provide medical reports about their health. Nora's chronic asthma would be revealed to the court and is likely to be an important factor in determining Quentin's long term future.

In all the circumstances of the apparent illegality of the arrangements for the adoption and the payments made and in all the other circumstances outlined above a court is likely to refuse the adoption application made by Nora and Oswald. Pippa should be made aware that she has sole parental responsibility for Quentin as an unmarried mother (see s2(2)(a) Children Act (CA) 1989 - assuming that she has not subsequently married the father). Norma and Oswald have no parental responsibility for Quentin unless they obtain a court order giving them that responsibility (which an adoption order would to the exclusion of Pippa). Pippa is entitled to the return of Quentin. If Norma and Oswald refuse to return him Pippa would be advised to make her own application for a residence order whereby the court orders that Quentin reside with her (see ss8 and 10 CA 1989) though the court has the power to make such an order of its own motion when dealing with the adoption application. When determining with whom Quentin should reside his welfare is the paramount consideration outweighing all others (see s1(1) CA 1989). The court will consider particular matters including the child's wishes and feelings (though Quentin is too young to be able to express these), his physical, emotional and educational needs, the likely effect on him of changing his residence from Nora and Oswald, and how capable Pippa is of meeting his needs as well as Nora and Oswald's capabilities in this respect (see s1(3), (4) CA 1989). The courts have assumed that a young child, especially a baby, is best brought up by his mother (see *Re W (a minor) (residence order)* (1992)). The courts have also assumed that a child is best brought up by his natural parents rather than by third parties (see *Re KD (a minor) (ward: termination of access)* (1988)). Quentin is unlikely to be upset at being moved to live with his mother having regard to his age. His mother is able to provide him with all the advantages of a young natural mother whereas Norma and Oswald have the disadvantage of being a lot older, having no genetic ties with Quentin and, in the case of Norma, health problems. Given Quentin's long term interests and the fact that his welfare is paramount it is likely that a residence order would be made in Pippa's favour (unless she is clearly incapable of providing for him).

Question 8

Rosemary and Simon, who are unmarried, have two children, Tim aged 14 and Ursula aged four. In January 1993 Rosemary, a television presenter, who was then three months pregnant, lost her job. Since that time, the family have found it increasingly difficult to live on Simon's salary and the couple have often argued, sometimes in front of the children. Simon began to drink heavily and has assaulted Rosemary.

In May 1993 Rosemary, who has become increasingly worried about the tension in the household and particularly concerned about the welfare of her unborn child, sought the assistance of the Helpful Local Authority social worker, Miss Vane.

Miss Vane, who visits regularly, has become aware that Tim rarely attends school, although his parents do insist that he does so, and that Ursula is withdrawn and tense. She has noted that Ursula appears particularly upset during the frequent visits of her 16 year old cousin, Wilfred.

Advise Miss Vane of the procedures she can invoke to address the problems of Tim, Ursula and the unborn child.

University of London LLB Examination
(for External Students) Family Law June 1993 Q8

General comment

The Children Act 1989 provides the framework for social work intervention where children are experiencing problems in families. The difficulties in this family centre around a truanting teenager and possible abuse of a four year old child. In the case of truanting application may be made for an education supervision order or, if the circumstances are sufficiently serious, for a care order. In the case of the younger child more information is needed before decisions can be taken about future action. An application for a child assessment order appears to be the appropriate course. If that reveals 'significant harm' then an emergency protection order application followed by care proceedings may be required. Finally advice has to be given about safeguarding the unborn child eg by an application for an emergency protection order as soon as the child is born.

Skeleton solution

- Application for education supervision order with respect to truanting child (s36 Children Act 1989).

- Application for care order if circumstances sufficiently grave to show 'significant harm' (s31 CA 1989).

- Application for child assessment order in relation to younger child (s43 CA 1989) and subsequent application for emergency protection order (s44 CA 1989) and care proceedings if 'significant harm' revealed.

- Protection for unborn child only after child's birth (eg via emergency protection order).

Suggested solution

Miss Vane asks for advice on the procedures she can invoke to address the problems of Tim, Ursula and the unborn child.

In relation to Tim the problem appears to be one of truanting from school. The clearest procedure to follow in this case would be the making of an application to the local family proceedings court for an education supervision order. The application must be made by the local education authority so Miss Vane should ask them to consider taking proceedings. Application for such an order may be made on the ground that Tim is of compulsory school age and is not being properly educated (ie he is not receiving efficient full time education suitable to his age, ability and aptitude) (see s36 Children Act (CA) 1989). This is assumed to be the case if he is a registered pupil at a school which he is not attending regularly. If an education supervision order is granted then a duty is placed on a supervisor to advise, assist and befriend Tim and give him and his parents directions in order to secure his proper education, after consulting Tim and his parents' wishes (see Sched 3, Part III CA 1989). The supervision may help to resolve the problems caused to Tim by the tension in the household. Such an order would only last one year though it could be extended for up to three years. There is an alternative or additional procedure via the criminal courts which the local education authority can proceed with. They can take Tim's parents before the local magistrates' court for the offence of failing to secure Tim's attendance at school (see s39 Education Act (EA) 1944). If found guilty the parents could be fined and the court could direct that the local education authority apply for an education supervision order (see s40 EA 1944). This procedure is perhaps least helpful if Miss Vane wishes to retain the parents' co-operation.

If, after considering the option of an education supervision order, Miss Vane considers that numerous attempts have already been made by the local education authority to advise, assist and befriend Tim in order to get him to school and that Tim's problems are now too serious to be dealt with in this way, then she can recommend that application be made for Tim to be taken into care. This might be the only option if the parents refuse to recognise Tim's problems and refuse to co-operate with any offers of assistance whether on a voluntary basis or under an education supervision order. A court could only make a care order if it is satisfied that Tim is suffering significant harm or is likely to suffer significant harm and that harm or likelihood of harm is attributable to the care given to him not being what would be expected of a reasonable parent or the child being beyond parental control. Harm is given a wide meaning to include impairment of intellectual, emotional, social and behavioural development (see s31 CA 1989). The court can judge Tim's development against what would be reasonably expected of a similar child of Tim's age and capabilities who had been attending school (see s31(10) CA 1989 and Re O (a minor) (care order: education: procedure) (1992)). If, as a result of his truanting and the tensions in the family, Tim cannot cope with boundaries and the difficulties of adult life and has a lack of commitment then a care order could be made (see Re O). This procedure is a drastic one and Miss Vane should consider what more work could be done with the parents before application is made to take Tim into care.

Miss Vane does not seem to know why Ursula is withdrawn and tense. She has noticed Ursula's reaction when Wilfred visits. This may indicate possible abuse on Wilfred's part, whether physical, emotional or sexual. Miss Vane should seek the parents' co-operation in having Ursula assessed by an expert in order to discover if she is being abused. Rosemary seems willing to co-operate. She can act independently of Simon in allowing Ursula to be assessed (see s2(7) CA 1989). If both parents will not co-operate in such an assessment Miss Vane may then apply to the local family proceedings court for a child assessment order. This is an order requiring Ursula's parents to produce the child for assessment or allow her to be visited at home for assessment so that the local authority can decide if she is suffering from significant harm (see s43 CA 1989). At least seven days' notice of such an application must be given to the parents (see s43(11) CA 1989 and r4 and Sched 1 Family Proceedings Courts (Children Act 1989) Rules 1991). The court must be satisfied that the applicant has reasonable cause to suspect that Ursula is suffering, or is likely to suffer, from significant harm and an assessment is required to enable the applicant to determine whether or not the child is suffering, or is likely to suffer, significant harm and it is unlikely that such an assessment will be made, or be satisfactory, in the absence of the order (see s43(1) CA 1989). In determining the application the court will treat Ursula's welfare as the paramount consideration and can only make an order if it is satisfied that it would be better than making no order at all (see s1(1) and (5) CA 1989). Miss Vane must be able to show that the parents are unreasonably refusing to allow Ursula to be assessed and that such an assessment will improve things for her. A child assessment order will take effect for a maximum of seven days. Once Ursula has been assessed then, if significant harm is revealed, consideration can be given to applying for a care order or supervision order using the grounds already discussed.

If Ursula's situation constitutes an emergency or the parents refuse to comply with the child assessment order the application can be made for an emergency protection order (see s44 CA 1989). Such an application may be made with one day's notice or, with the leave of the justices' clerk of the family proceedings court, ex parte (see r4 1991 Rules). She would have to satisfy a single magistrate or a family proceedings court either that there is reasonable cause to believe that Ursula is likely to suffer significant harm if she is not removed to local authority care or that the local authority reasonably suspects that Ursula is suffering or is likely to suffer significant harm but its enquiries are being frustrated by access to her being unreasonably refused and access to her is required as a matter of urgency. If an emergency protection order is granted it will only last a maximum of eight days during which application can be made for a care or supervision order (which requires at least three days' notice - r4 and Sched 1 1991 Rules).

In relation to the unborn child Miss Vane can be advised that no application can be made with respect to the child until it is born (see *Re F* (1988)). As soon as the child is born an application can be made for an emergency protection order (if the grounds as outlined above apply) and/or for a care or supervision order on the basis of the likelihood of future harm. If Miss Vane is able to work with Rosemary and the threat to the unborn child is the violence of Simon against Rosemary then Miss Vane may be able to persuade Rosemary to seek a non-molestation injunction and exclusion order against him. If the source of the violence is removed this may ameliorate the danger to the unborn child and the tension caused to Ursula and Tim.